THE SHAPE OF AMERICAN EDUCATION

THE SHAPE OF AMERICAN EDUCATION

GERALDINE JONÇICH CLIFFORD
University of California at Berkeley

Prentice-Hall, Inc., *Englewood Cliffs, New Jersey*

Library of Congress Cataloging in Publication Data

CLIFFORD, GERALDINE JONÇICH.
  The shape of American education.

  Includes bibliographical references and index.
  1. Education—United States. I. Title.
LA217.C52   301.5′6′0973   74-26534
ISBN 0-13-807891-2

© *1975 by Prentice-Hall, Inc., Englewood Cliffs, N.J.*

Printed in the United States of America

10 9 8 7 6 5 4 3 2 1

Prentice-Hall International, Inc., *London*
Prentice-Hall of Australia, Pty. Ltd., *Sydney*
Prentice-Hall of Canada, Ltd., *Toronto*
Prentice-Hall of India Private Limited, *New Delhi*
Prentice-Hall of Japan, Inc., *Tokyo*

To my parents, for whose confidence in schools
I am grateful.

And to Bill, whose lack of confidence in them
I understand.

CONTENTS

It is a fact of modernized societies that they devote much of their resources and public concern to elaborating specialized agencies of formal education; young nation-states, anxious to industrialize and modernize, imitate them as much as possible. This preoccupation of advanced nation-states with schools and colleges is somewhat paradoxical. For one thing, *alternative* means of achieving socialization and cohesion, and of exercising social control, do exist. In the United States, the more obvious of these are systems of mass communication and rapid transport, a national economy of standard goods and services, and the concentration of most political activity in just two parties. Another anomaly is that education—in the sense of formal instruction and transmission of information—is actually less essential in preserving a literate society than it is in a simpler one where, if a single generation fails to learn its lessons of irretrievable knowledge and lore, the culture suffers a permanent "loss of memory." Nonetheless, Americans are school-conscious and school-dependent, believing so deeply in schools and colleges that their confidence is vastly disproportionate to the actual role that formal education has historically played in our national life. But, as Lewis Mumford has written of the power of ideas:

> The "belief" that the world was flat was once upon a time more important than the "fact" that it was round; and that belief kept the sailors of the medieval world from wandering out of sight of land as effectively as would a string of gunboats or floating mines. An idea is a solid fact, a theory is a solid fact, a superstition is a solid fact as long as people continue to regulate their actions in terms of the idea, theory, or superstition; and it is none the less solid because it is conveyed as an image or a breath of sound.[1]

Thus, the story of any society's educational system is more than the recounting of enrollment statistics, subjects of the curriculum, school buildings, faculty competence, and university budgets; it is also the story of the ideas,

[1]Lewis Mumford, *The Story of Utopias* (New York: Viking Press, Inc., 1962), p. 14.

the theories, and the superstitions that wind about the educational enterprise more insistently and importantly than does the ivy that clings to college walls. And the most important of these for the American story is the credence given to schooling.

EDUCATION: THE AMERICAN RELIGION

The average American coming into legal adulthood in the 1970s has spent only 2 percent of his probable lifespan in school.[2] This figure does not begin to correspond to public or private faith in the indispensability of formal education. Education has been most valued as an *instrumentality,* and not as an end in itself. As Henry Steele Commager observes of the American, "Education was his religion, and to it he paid the tribute both of his money and his affection; yet, as he expected his religion to be practical and pay dividends, he expected education to prepare for life—by which he meant, increasingly, jobs and professions."[3]

Formal education now extends well into the productive adult years. By the middle 1960s, six of every ten persons in the age group 5–34 were enrolled in schools or colleges; this did not include those hundreds of thousands receiving instruction in ten thousand business colleges and other types of proprietary schools, in correspondence or extension courses, on-the-job training, or in the military. Each level of the educational structure has faced both growth and adjustment in its relationship to every other level. In 1900, for example, of the 17 million students enrolled, 94 percent were in six- or eight-year elementary schools. By 1965 that proportion had dropped to 65 percent, as the high school received an ever-larger share. The upward reach of schooling has changed the role of the college and university in American life. Before 1910, only 1 in 60 Americans in the 20–35 age group was a college graduate; now it is 1 in 8. Between 1960 and 1970, the percentage of 14- to 17-year-olds *in school* increased from 90 percent to 94 percent, of 18- and 19-year-olds from 38 percent to 50 percent, and of 20- to 24-year-olds from 13 percent to 23 percent.

New concepts of what constitutes regularity of educational progress are being developed. Numerous studies of high school and college students show that the high school graduate who immediately goes to college and graduates four years later—who "gets in, gets done, and gets out"—is now the atypical

[2]This figure is based on a life expectancy of 70 years, and the completion (on the average) of 12 years of schooling, each school year being typically 180 days long and each school day typically of 6 hours: Patricia Cayo Sexton, ed., *Readings on the School in Society* (Englewood Cliffs, N. J.: Prentice-Hall, Inc., 1967), p. 40.

[3]Henry Steele Commager, *The American Mind* (New Haven, Conn.: Yale University Press, 1950), pp. 10, 213. See also the provocative essay by Robert H. Wiebe, "The Social Functions of Public Education," *American Quarterly,* 21 (Summer 1969):147–64.

individual.[4] Delayed enrollments, changes of field, transfers between institutions, marriage, work, a temporary "dropping out"— all of these will increase in frequency as college-going reaches farther and farther into segments of the American population that have heretofore been strangers to higher education, and as many young people revise their conceptions of the meaning of formal studies for their own personal development, as well as for career.

The United States built its vast educational enterprise without coordinated state planning and educational design. To return to the analogy of education with religion, educational decisions in America tend toward *populism* (they bear the stamp of the people), *individualism* and *toleration* (they emphasize and sometimes encourage choice making), *emotionalism* (they respond to feeling as well as to reason), and *inventiveness* (virtually anything goes).

EDUCATION: THE STUDY OF A SOCIAL INSTITUTION

As education has grown in importance to individuals and to the society, the nation's need to *know* about schools has grown also. This need has not been fully met. Data about the effectiveness of teaching-learning are manifestly inadequate. Moreover, of the vast literature on schools, only a small part does justice to the interconnectedness of individual purposes, human functions, and social institutions. Instead, schools and colleges—their economics, history, philosophies, politics, as well as their curricula, instructional methods, and staffs—have often been treated as if educational organizations existed in a vacuum. Until very lately, a subject of such wide general importance as education has lacked scholars and social scientists who could meaningfully expand the one-sided and technical perspective of most educational analysis.

Now a socially richer and broader literature on education exists. In part it represents an intensification of *public* interest in such social policy areas as education, health, welfare, and crime; the nursing, medical, welfare, and legal professions have experienced a similar rise in external research of themselves. Sometimes that research is affected by a general skepticism of social organizations, including government, which is part of the climate of our times —a cynicism evident even before Watergate. Another factor operating is the gravitation of the interests of the several social sciences toward subjects that have more potential for casting light on such social agencies as schools.

Social historians are interested in the forces of social change, traditional values, and the mechanisms for maintaining social solidarity. Social psycholo-

[4]One study of an original population of 4,000 college-bound youth found that only 28 percent received the bachelor's degree within four years: James W. Trent and Leland L. Medsker, *Beyond High School* (San Francisco: Jossey-Bass, Inc. 1968), pp. 4–5. John Gardner, for one, suggests a thorough reexamination of the college calendar and the conception of a four-year college, in *Campus 1980,* ed. Alvin C. Eurich (New York: Delacorte Press, 1968). The Carnegie Commission on Higher Education has made similar recommendations.

gists are curious about communication, especially about how attitudes are formed and under what conditions they can be changed. There is a high probability that people have had most of their strongest opinions about education formed by the schools they personally know, images of the teaching profession formed by their own teachers, beliefs about the "high politics" of educational systems formed by the "facts" received first-hand from a school janitor or the principal's clerk.

Sociologists and anthropologists are concerned with the mechanisms of "socialization." This is the process whereby a society's various norms, values, and roles are learned and accepted by its new members. The ever-increasing centralization of teaching and training functions in systems called "educational" has led some researchers to shift their focus from the family and other socializing agencies to schools and colleges as the locus of socialization.

Economic analysis also helps to make education more fully understandable. Economists are now indicating that increases in actual job skill requirements do not themselves justify the great rises in Americans seeking advanced schooling; powerful other factors, principally noneconomic, are working— even in this ostensibly materialistic society.

THE APPROACH OF THIS BOOK

As there is now far more provocative and insightful research about education and society than ever before, so also is there more reason to provoke and enlighten the readership of all books on education. Leaving aside those who ponder educational decisions as students, parents, citizens, voters, and taxpayers, consider the questions which prospective teachers face today. Heretofore, most of them have been preoccupied with the matters of teaching strategies, of classroom management and discipline, of "how to survive when I'm on my own as a teacher." Such important and natural questions certainly remain, and will grip anew every new generation of those who choose to teach. But there are prior questions, issues now more insistent and relevant than they have previously appeared to be. These are such questions as "Do I really want to teach?" "Do I know what I mean by 'teaching'?" "Why do I think that *I* can be effective?" "What does 'effective' mean?" "Do I believe or know that teaching and learning can go on in places called schools and colleges?" "Of what kinds?" "Under what circumstances?" "For whom?" "For whose benefit?" "Am I willing to be held accountable?" While such questions have always been there for the asking—and have always been important—they have long been overshadowed by various social and cultural facts: by heavy demands for additional public school teachers, by the habit of considering teaching a natural career choice for a woman college graduate, by the image of schools as essentially pleasant places in which to work, and by a minimally questioning public faith in education.

All of these habits of mind and behavior are now severely challenged. New levels of intention and commitment are being demanded, and few prospective teachers can escape them altogether. Those who have habitually considered teacher training as an "insurance policy" must now consider that they may never be able to cash in that policy; whether or not there is a real teacher surplus, the marketplace will continue to behave as if there is one, and those who aspire to teach much sell themselves—first to teacher-training institutions that are under pressure to reduce the supply, and then to employing schools and school districts. Given intense competition for places as teachers and the demands of women's liberation upon the whole culture, decisions to teach are becoming less automatic for women students—as are decisions of employed women teachers to quit for family reasons. The image of teaching as an easy and pleasant occupation, never an entirely true picture, is now bankrupt. A quarter-century of varying exposés—of failures to learn, of apathetic or recalcitrant or hostile students, of violence and vandalism, of inept or culturally intolerant teachers, of repressive rules or intolerable permissiveness—have all undermined public confidence. If the criticism and the realities of schools-in-trouble are not unprecedented in our educational history (and I do not think they are unprecedented), they are nonetheless intense—and must provoke individual questions of one's will and competence to do the job.

Most clients and patrons of American education would admit ignorance of the origins and development of their schools and colleges, of how and probably even of why they came to be as they are. Yet people do believe that they know what American education is—and even how it might be improved. After all, have they not personally experienced it as they passed through the schools? Our confidence in our knowledge and understanding of education, as a result of personal experience, is probably misplaced. Our individual perceptions are circumscribed and distorted by numerous factors: the imperfections of memory, the limiting of first-hand contact to a tiny portion of the educational possibilities, the very diversity of American schools and colleges, the immature perceptions of students and the socially untrained observations of many teachers, the concentration of people within the schools upon other sorts of lessons. This seems true even of the professional educator enrolled in graduate courses in the social foundations of education, who is commonly surprised at how limited is his knowledge of what American education is like and what makes it tick. This book aims to be useful in amplifying and clarifying the reader's own impressions, formed both as student of the schools and student of education. For the educator, it aims to act as a guard against the tendency of the practitioner to particularize his private experiences onto an ever-smaller stage, to have his vistas progressively limited by the insular world of the classroom and the lesson plan and by the technical demands of his craft. *The Shape of American Education* is concerned, therefore, with venturing a panoramic description of the educational enterprise as housed in the schools, colleges, and universities of the United States.

The study of the history of formal education makes clear that education is all-of-a-piece, that no level of schooling is immune from what happens at any other. Colleges and universities, in various ways, have placed their stamp upon the operations and functions of the lower schools; they do so still, with the involvement of scholars and scientists in curriculum making being only one obvious recent example. In turn, the democratization of the lower schools, the academic improvements of the high school, even the student-centeredness of progressive education have forced accommodations upon higher education. Once aware of this interdependence, most prospective teachers appreciate a greater acquaintance with the various levels of schooling; grade-level emphasis, specialization of subject matter, and the prevalent divisions along elementary-secondary-higher education lines will all too soon segment their perspectives.

The Shape of American Education attempts to explain and to account for the predominant and determining characteristics of schools and colleges in this society. I have sought research and explanatory concepts in the disciplines of history and the social sciences. The emphasis is always, however, on *education*—not on the *history* of education, or the *philosophy* of education, or the *economics* of education; thus the title of this book is meant to be taken literally. International comparisons of educational systems are made where they seem useful in understanding the universals and the particulars of educational enterprises; *the story of American education is, after all, partly one of uniqueness, of departures from Western tradition, of new commitments, of widened purposes, of altered structures.*

Like every book, *The Shape of American Education* embodies choices made. It covers much ground, but not all the ground. It offers numerous facts and generalizations, but leaves out many others. It addresses challenging issues but ignores or moves lightly over some of potentially equal importance. As partial compensation for its necessary selectivity, the author offers instructions, in the footnotes, to a varied and rich literature on American education and the society which nourishes and suffers with it. While trying to avoid unnecessary repetitiveness, the deliberate decision was made at several places to introduce topics which are treated subsequently in different contexts and at deeper levels of analysis—a pedagogical principle that the French call *approfondissement.*

ACKNOWLEDGMENTS

It was historian Lawrence A. Cremin of Teachers College, Columbia University, whom I first heard describe American education by reference to the four traits of publicness, diversity, universality, and breadth. (He employed a fifth, comprehensiveness, which I have otherwise accommodated.) Trying them out first as interesting "intellectual handles" on the complex and unwieldy subject of American education, I found them to be powerful concepts around which to construct a synthesis. I thank Professor Cremin for these and for so many other favors—including helpful and supportive advice following his reading of an earlier draft of the manuscript.

The primary test of the ideas and the organization that came to be this book was their offering to students. For the candor and earnestness of their reactions I am indebted to many former students.

Jim Clark, then of Prentice-Hall, Inc., urged this book into being; I thank him and all those who assisted in the editorial process and made this a published work. Wendie Bremner and Bernice Nece typed most of the several versions of the manuscript and have my appreciation. Deep thanks to Bobbie Figy and Joyce Horowitz, who cleared so many other obstacles before the path of this book.

No one book should, I think, dominate a course nor eschew challenges to its synthesis. The footnotes mention many other works that may amplify, clarify, and even contradict my interpretations. Many have contributed formatively to this book; a large number I have taught from or urged upon students. To their authors I am indebted. I thank also the following publishers and individuals for permission to quote from their works or reproduce their illustrations: American Association of Colleges for Teacher Education, for "Realignments for Teacher Education"; Basic Books, Inc., for *Education in the Age of Science* (published for the American Academy of Arts and Sciences); Center for Research and Development in Higher Education, University of California, for *Research Reporter;* the *Chronicle of Higher Education;* Doubleday & Company, Inc., for *The Academic Revolution;* Harper & Row, Publishers, for *The Airtight Cage;* Lewis Mumford, for *The Story of Utopias* (Viking Press, Inc.); Saturday Review, Inc., for "September Song" and various illustrations; The University of Chicago Press, for *School Review;* The National Education Association, for *NEA Research Bulletin;* John Wiley & Sons, Inc., for *Who Runs Our Schools?;* Unesco; Bureau of Social Science Research, Inc.; Institut Pédagogique National; Baltimore *Sun;* Jossey-Bass, Inc., for *Beyond High School;* the President and Fellows of Harvard College, for *Harvard Educational Review;* United Press Syndicate; United Feature Syndicate, Inc.; Publishers-Hall Syndicate; *Time,* The Weekly Newsmagazine; and the United States Government Printing Office.

LIST OF TABLES

LIST OF FIGURES

PART

THE DETERMINING CHARACTERISTICS
OF AMERICAN EDUCATION

The dimensions of publicness, diversity, universality, and breadth make education in the United States unique among the world's systems. *Publicness,* one of its distinguishing characteristics, is the subject of chapter 1. All modern nations have public schooling in the sense that certain schools receive governmental support and are required to accept the public (or some designated segment of it) as their clientele. No other society, however, structures its apparatus of control so that its educational institutions are formally operated by laymen. Nor, elsewhere, is the desirability of having schools "open" to public attention and influence so much a part of the professional ideology as in this nation.

Diversity refers to a lack of formally decreed provisions for uniformity. There is a great range of opportunities for innovation and experimentation in the American educational enterprise, and chapter 2 explores the origins of diversity, how this freedom for variety has been utilized, and how it is compromised by various forces of standardization.

Universality refers to the fact that American education gears its curricula, methods, and standards to the proposition that public schools must reach "all of the children of all of the people," that public colleges should accept all who have the eagerness and (perhaps) the aptitude for college-level work. This universality is the subject of chapter 3.

Breadth refers to what the schools do—to what they attempt to teach and support as appropriate goals. American society has an exceptionally generous conception of the function and content of formal schooling, and the concluding chapter of this section analyzes the unfolding and implications of this characteristic of breadth.

American education does share certain specific traits with other nations. Switzerland and Canada, for example, also have decentralized control of public education. Other nations have experienced pressures for a greater breadth of curricula in their schools. Despite sharing selected features with other societies, however, education in the United States combines its features in a configuration that is like no other society's. An educational system is unique when its various components are formed into a distinctive totality.

PUBLICNESS

The "particulars" of publicness in American education may be better understood by a brief comparative world tour, examining various systems of control and suggesting the sociohistorical factors that can influence educational operations.

IN CONTRAST: FOREIGN PATTERNS OF EDUCATIONAL CONTROL

In the nations that experienced industrial development early—England, Germany, Belgium, the United States—formal schooling played a minor role in stimulating industrialization; the major factors were such basic production elements as the presence of capital, unskilled labor, and available land. Today's pre-industrial nations, however, consider education indispensable to economic development—as well as to the purpose of building national self-consciousness. Therefore, virtually all nations have a system of public schools and universities under varying degrees of governmental control and patronage.

In developed societies, education's announced objective for national planners is to maintain economic growth and to prepare the society for social change. Schools and universities also exist to conserve social class privileges and perpetuate political tradition. A case in point is the historic dependence of the English government upon preparation in a few selective secondary schools (called "public schools") and upon the personal contacts made at Oxford and Cambridge universities. Public school rituals, especially in chapel, pave the way for the ceremonials of political life.[1] The following national examples illustrate how different interactions of historical tradition and contemporary politico-economic forces affect education.

Japan and the Far East

Schools have been an instrument of nationalism and a concern of the Japanese state since the Meiji era (1868–1912). Within a century Japan

[1] Ian Weinberg, *The English Public Schools* (New York: Atherton Press, 1967), p. 11.

2

reached 99 percent effective compulsory schooling for nine school years. Over 55 percent of the students continue into the upper secondary schools, and some 20 percent of the eligible age group attend universities. Lacking extensive natural resources, Japan has highly developed her human resources. Contrasting Japan with other Asian countries that endured colonial governments until 1945 illustrates the retarding effects of colonialism and political instability upon education. In the formerly colonial nation-states, the supply of indigenous teachers and school administrators was very small and could not rise fast enough to supply the expansive plans of governmental leaders. Moreover, these same leaders, who frequently received their own schooling in "foreign" schools, may be ambivalent about shaping distinctly different national schools. The British sixth form, the French *explication de texte,* and the American dislike for centralized planning tend to hang on among Japan's neighbors, whereas Japan had but a brief postwar period of external political imposition.

Japan has the additional advantage of having only one language. In the Philippines there are eight major languages and many dialects, and the use of English and Tagalog as the instructional languages means that most students attend classes conducted in a foreign language. India (with 15 *major* languages) and Malaysia dissipate some of their energies in language wars and must spend valuable time translating central directives into local tongues. (Canada has a similar but less aggravated problem.)

The Japanese also benefit from being a homogeneous race. In Malaysia intense ethnic awareness suffuses all issues.[2] Ethnic diversity exists also in Burma, Indonesia, and India. This places great strains upon a national educational system, since the various ethnic groups consider governmental schooling a threat to their ethnic identity—just as Catholic and German immigrants distrusted public schools in the United States in the nineteenth century.

Distance and communication problems also hinder educational development. In every Asian country a centralized system faces the tremendous problem of implementing governmental policies in vast, sometimes inaccessible, regions. Japan, on the other hand, has excellent transportation and

[2]When Malaysia obtained independence from Britain in 1957, its new constitution explicitly favored the Malay ethnic group. The government has consistently used the school system to attempt to bring the Malays into economic and social parity with the large Chinese population (over 30 percent) of the country. Means used include establishing Malay-language secondary schools, automatic promotion into secondary schools, and special financial aid to Malay students. Allegations of tampering with university entrance examinations are widely believed by non-Malays, and some Malay militants are asking that admission into certain academic disciplines be based on an ethnic quota, rather than on examination scores: John C. Bock and Yoshimitsu Takei, *Education and Nation-Building: A Case Study of Malaysia* (Princeton, N.J.: Princeton University Press, forthcoming). See also Robert O. Tilman, ed., *Man, State, and Society in Contemporary Southeast Asia* (New York: Praeger Publishers, Inc., 1969). A sociological report that suggests considerable success in effecting pro-Malay educational change is Murad Bin Mohd. Noor, *Report to the Minister of Education,* Kuala Lumpur, Malaysia, February 1973.

communication networks. Over 95 percent of the country is reached by a full weekly program of school broadcasts.

India

Unlike Japan and the other Asian nations mentioned, which have centralized, national systems of educational control, India has a fragmented, decentralized, mixed (secular and religious) system, in which the states have major responsibility for pre-university education. The central government has emphasized raising the standards of higher education and coordinating national planning of resources. Although its role is largely advisory, the government operates with more official responsibility than does the American federal government. The example of India should clarify the fact that patterns of control are far less important than are the basic features of a nation's economic, political, social, and cultural life.

India began its national existence in 1947 with a multitude of problems including widespread poverty in a population of over 350 million, an overall illiteracy rate of 84 percent, an inefficient agricultural economy of extremely low production, a largely rural population (83 percent of all Indians lived in a half-million mostly isolated villages), manning a decadent village industrial system where the division of labor was along caste lines, and a rigidly stratified social structure in which caste pervaded all human relationships.

Five years of schooling are considered the minimum needed to establish literacy, but India has been unable to achieve even universal primary schooling with its present resources. Mass education is expensive, and in an underdeveloped nation education must compete with health, welfare, transportation, and communication needs for scarce resources. A large-scale educational system depends upon a favorable ratio of self-supporting adults to dependent individuals—the young, the aged, and the unemployable. This ratio was 496 dependent persons per 1,000 supporting adults in Great Britain in 1960. The comparable ratio in the United States was 702 per 1,000, but India in the same year had a higher proportion of dependents—1,317—than supporting adults, requiring a disproportionate allocation of resources for the simple maintenance of life.[3]

The Soviet Union

The Soviet Union, like all countries, requires a viable economy to provide adequate support for public services. So far, much of Soviet educational planning has been unrealized because of competing demands upon the output of

---

[3]Carl C. Taylor et al., *India's Roots of Democracy: A Sociological Analysis of Rural India's Experience in Planned Development Since Independence* (New York: Praeger Publishers, Inc., 1965).

state enterprises. Not surprisingly, urban areas come closer to the planned model than do rural areas, and the western republics surpass the eastern ones in level of general educational development.

Superficially, the Soviet system resembles the American decentralized pattern of control. Each republic is responsible for basic elementary, secondary, and higher education within its boundaries.[4] (A central Ministry of Education coordinates specialized education at both secondary and higher levels.) In practice, however, the Ministry of Education of the Russian Republic (RSFSR) and its Academy of Pedagogical Sciences coordinate the elementary and secondary schooling of all sixteen republics. The result is a standardized and centralized administrative structure. The Soviet Union resembles most developing nations by including education in state planning. Moscow's planning, which allocates substantial resources to education, including the informal educational programs of the mass media, recreation, libraries, as well as schools, supersedes each republic's separate budgeting and other formal powers. Admissions to technical schools and universities also depend upon central planning. In 1963, for example, the Communist Party Central Committee decreed that the chemical industry be expanded. Consequently, student stipends for this field were increased, laboratory and classroom facilities were added or converted from other uses, and faculty policies favored chemistry. In earlier years such means and others, including selective dormitory assignments, scholarships, and raising female medical school enrollments, were used to enhance the status of engineering studies and to lower the appeal of the medical profession.

A third influence upon the politics of Soviet education, one not appearing on organizational charts, is the Communist Party. The primary party unit, the smallest unit of party apparatus, exists in all schools, institutes, and universities—as in all institutions of Soviet society. Unlike their American counterparts, Soviet youth organizations—the Octobrists (ages 7–9), Young Pioneers (ages 10–15), and Komsomol (ages 16–28)—are firmly entrenched in the schools.[5] Members of the Komsomol (Young Communist League) that have acceptable grades and the recommendation of Komsomol leaders enjoy an edge in competing for admission to higher education. While it is not unusual in American education to find the local school board or the state's educational apparatus dominated by members of a single political party, there is no political counterpart of Communist Party influence in the American scheme of things.

[4]Herbert C. Rudman, *The School and the State in the USSR* (New York: Macmillan, 1969).

[5]William M. Cave, "The Young Pioneers," in *Political Youth, Traditional Schools*, ed. Byron G. Massialas (Englewood Cliffs, N.J.: Prentice-Hall, Inc., 1972), pp. 227–42; Urie Bronfenbrenner, *Two Worlds of Childhood: U.S. and U.S.S.R.* (New York: Simon & Schuster, 1972).

France

France is often considered the prototype of a highly centralized, professionally bureaucratized structure of national education—although a French school inspector once remarked, "In France, every teacher is supposed to be doing the same thing at the same time but nobody is, and in England, where everyone is supposed to be going his own way, nobody is."[6]

France is divided into 23 educational regions, called *académies,* each with its own university, whose *recteur* is responsible for all educational matters in his region, from the *école maternelle* through to the highest university degrees. In Paris the Ministry of National Education supposedly insures standardization through the issuance of directives and syllabic detailing of the curriculum, textbook selection, and the examination, appointment, transfer, and payment of teachers. Inspectors General report their school observations to the ministry. Theoretically, all local variation is virtually denied and every regional university is Paris's equal. In fact, the character of the schools is affected by local factors, and the University of Paris enjoys the highest prestige.

What is especially interesting about the political science of French education is the intense political self-awareness of teachers, their unprecedentedly high level of organized political activity, and their long-time identification with the working class and the trade union movement. The important teacher organization, FEN (National Education Federation), enjoys considerable influence in the professionally staffed Ministry of National Education. While traditional teacher organizations in the United States still rely heavily upon public relations tactics, the FEN first appeals to politicians and party structures, then turns to alliances with like-minded groups, and finally conducts brief work stoppages.[7]

As in most other European nations, moreover, French teachers reject the principle that education policy and school practices should be open to public scrutiny or lay decision making.

AMERICA: THE GRASS-ROOTS TRADITION

Publicness in American education is historically tied to local control of public schools. Although it is unlikely that such schools have had as much autonomy as is popularly believed, localism in the United States is basic to the "grassroots" theory of democratic government.[8] The United States Constitution

[6]James D. Koerner, *Reform in Education: England and the United States* (New York: Delacorte Press, 1968), p. 52.

[7]James M. Clark, *Teachers and Politics in France: A Pressure Group Study of the Fédération de l'Education Nationale* (Syracuse, N.Y.: Syracuse University Press, 1967).

[8]Roscoe C. Martin, *Grass Roots: Rural Democracy in America* (New York: Harper & Row, Publishers, 1965). See also Morton White and Lucia White, *The Intellectual Versus the City* (New York: New American Library, Inc., 1964); Robert H. Wiebe, "The Social Functions of Public Education," *American Quarterly,* 21 (Summer 1969):

gives to the separate states all functions not specifically reserved to the federal government. Moreover, tradition has encouraged the states to delegate much of their authority to local government. Tradition and literature assert that personal and civic virtues abound on the farms and in the small towns, while the cities breed most rebellion, disaffection, and poor adjustment. Until the Supreme Court mandated legislative reapportionment, urban dwellers were underrepresented. School-aid formulas still favor small-town and suburban districts. Like our other institutions, education has been marked by this grass-roots ideology.

A citizen in James West's *Plainville, U.S.A.* remarks, "If it weren't for the churches and the schools, land here wouldn't be worth ten cents an acre." In the simpler, inward-looking society of nineteenth-century rural America, the church and the schoolhouse were highly visible institutions. According to the direct-democracy, small-government principles of grass-roots politics, religion and education were acceptable alternatives to other public institutions in assuring civic good health. "Build a school and end pauperism," or "Open a church and close a prison" went the slogans. In addition to their functions of character-building and citizenship-training, these two institutions provided community entertainment. Church suppers and spelling bees were important social events. It is not surprising that, as their populations dropped, America's thousands of "Plainvilles" resisted closing their schoolhouses or losing a measure of control by merging adjacent school districts. Small wonder, too, that the state universities, "democracy's colleges," have held so tenacious a grip on the emotions of the still-rural Midwest and West. Although their scientific agriculture was geared to mass-production farming, these institutions conjured up the agrarian past and the independent yeoman of Jefferson's dreams.

In 1900 there were probably some two hundred thousand independent public school districts in the United States, each with state-conferred power to build and operate schools, enforce attendance, hire teachers, tax the residents. Yet, by the time the United States Office of Education began keeping records of the nation's school districts ("administrative units"), the inexorable march of social change was causing districts to reorganize, reducing their total number from 125,000 in 1932 to 85,000 in 1950; by the 1970 school year, the total was 17,662.

The great majority (87 percent) of today's districts are, as in the past, small—enrolling under 3,000 pupils; of the grand total, some 40 percent had 300 pupils or fewer.

Unification is the name given to the merger, in a given community or region, of once-separate elementary and secondary school districts. By 1970

147–64. On legal structures of authority see William R. Hazard, *Education and the Law: Cases and Materials on Public Schools* (New York: The Free Press, 1971), Chapter 1; Chester A. Bowers et al., eds., *Education and Social Policy: Local Control of Education* (New York: Random House, Inc., 1970). .

62 percent of all school districts were unified (or union) districts, administering schools that extended from kindergarten or first grade through grade 12. Aside from reducing the crazy quilt of numerous overlapping geographic and functional units, unification enhances coordination between elementary and secondary school programs and distributes the higher costs of secondary education more evenly over a geographic area's unevenly located tax resources. The principal opposition to unification comes from the fact that it reduces the number of independent school boards—seeming to threaten the principle of decentralization. Much the same sentiment prevails against district reorganization by *consolidation,* in which two or more separate (and usually small) school districts combine.[9]

Despite school district reorganization, grass-roots sentiment dies hard. Even when state legislatures encourage unification and consolidation by allocating extra funds to cooperating districts, local residents often vote down reorganization of their own districts. Aside from the emotional hold of tradition, several other factors sometimes combine to help explain the tenaciousness of localism: political activism, economic self-interest, and racial tensions.

Political Activism

To citizens with school-age children, public education and school board politics seem a natural target of attention. Enlarging school district size removes educational control from the community to that central government toward which they feel some estrangement and powerlessness. Other local concerns, such as property taxes, property values, and public order, also mesh with educational politics. During this century there has been a higher incidence of marriage and a lowering of the average age at marriage than in the past. More recently veterans' loans and affluence have established the pattern of early home-ownership. These factors and rising educational levels have probably intensified interest in local government and community welfare. It is frequently remarked, moreover, that public involvement in decisions affecting local public education represents the "last chance" for citizen participation in the affairs of government, in crucial matters of public policy and public administration. Movements to divide educational administration in large cities into small subdistricts and to decentralize a city-wide board into neighborhood "community boards" are the urban counterparts of "moving to the suburbs" to gain greater control of the schools. This movement represents a legitimate political and psychological objective, although its supporters argue for it on the disputable grounds that it will help increase student achievement.

---

[9]In *The American High School Today* (New York: McGraw-Hill Book Co., 1959), James B. Conant contended that a high school *graduating class* must number at least 100 for the school to offer an adequate program of courses, each taught by a qualified teacher, with sufficient books, facilities, and other resources necessary to preparation for college or employment.

Economic Self-Interest

In Springdale, the anonymous community in upstate New York described in *Small Town in Mass Society,* public education was the town's largest industry. The local board of education controlled more jobs, commanded a bigger payroll, and exercised greater purchasing power than any individual or firm.[10] The situation of Springdale is not unique, and the post–World War II movement toward suburbia has reproduced in many communities this economic centrality of schools and colleges. Because education seems especially expensive in such new communities—with high proportions of children, no existing school facilities to occupy, a dearth of other necessary public services, and little industrial or commercial property to tax—at the very least, local residents want to influence the spending of those school funds. District consolidation dilutes such influence and arouses resistance.

Racial Tensions

In 1869 the Massachusetts legislature authorized the spending of public funds to carry children to and from schools. By the time that motorized buses were available to replace horse-drawn vehicles, all the states had enacted similar legislation. In subsequent years operators of nonpublic schools, most notably the Catholic church, have pressured local and state governments and have gone to court to try to extend the privileges of tax-supported busing to their students. In 1953 the Department of Rural Education of the National Education Association lyricized the educational experiences to be gained on the school bus.[11] Yet the use of a small fraction of the nation's school buses for busing students to achieve school desegregation provoked shootings, burnings, and other destruction of buses. It suddenly became crucial that children walk to school, and the exhausting and traumatizing experience of a bus ride became a new article of faith and a flammable political issue.

Enforcement of the provisions of the 1964 federal Civil Rights Act, NAACP suits to end de facto segregation in northern cities, voter registration drives in the ghettos, and the failure of many "moderate" integration schemes have together radicalized America's racial minorities and have stirred fear and reawakened prejudice in the white world.[12] One consequence is the reassertion of decentralization and local control of public schools and the tightening of

[10]Arthur Vidich and Joseph Bensman, *Small Town in Mass Society* (Garden City, N.Y.: Doubleday & Co., 1960).

[11]Nicholaus Mills, "Busing: Who's Being Taken for a Ride?" *Perspectives on Education* (New York: Teachers College, Columbia University) 5:3 (Summer 1972):13–21; Howard Ozmon and Sam Craver, *Busing: A Moral Issue* (Bloomington, Ind.: Phi Delta Kappa Educational Foundation,1972).

[12]George R. La Noue and Bruce Smith, *The Politics of School Decentralization* (Lexington, Mass.: D. C. Heath & Co., 1973); Jay D. Scribner and David O'Shea, "Political Developments in Urban School Districts," *73rd Yearbook of the National Society for the Study of Education* (Chicago: University of Chicago Press, 1974).

trustee authority in the colleges and universities. Predominantly white suburbs have resisted educational "annexation" to communities having a sizable black citizenry, just as some rural communities once resisted consolidated districts to "protect" their children. White (and many black) residents of small cities having a stable middle-class black population oppose plans for regional "educational parks" that would mix their children with the "unknowns" of adjoining multiracial communities. In the cities—long the bastions of unified districting, centralized administration, and professionalism—black groups more successfully demand decentralized, neighborhood control over teacher hiring and curriculum. Many white citizens support them in order to lessen integration pressures. Despite the uncertain educational results of decentralized and populist school control, these political claims and social forces will probably triumph—at least in the short run.[13]

THE FORMAL-LEGAL OPERATION OF PUBLIC CONTROL

The structure of governmental responsibility for education in the United States emerged in the nineteenth century. The past intrudes upon the present in two interconnected ways. First, the structure of formal power has remained essentially unchanged since the nineteenth century. There are many consequences to such rigidity. Local districts wishing to experiment with teachers who lack orthodox credentials and recognized training must first seek state dispensation. There is longstanding fiscal inequality among school districts, guaranteed by rooting the base of local public school finance in local property taxes. Reform-minded students and faculty must still contend with lay school board members and trustees if they would introduce change.

Second, modern needs are met in a context suffused with traditionalized ideals. For instance, the ideal of small government and decentralized control shapes the conditions under which federal aid will be given, creates suspicion of efforts even to assess the educational state-of-the-nation, and challenges widespread attempts at school reform.

The Federal Government: The Reluctant and Uncertain Giant

After many decades of minimal attention to formal education, the federal government has emerged as a major influence upon the schools and colleges administered by state and local governments and by private bodies, although

---

[13]What one sees, it is argued, is the tension created by a bifurcated political legacy: the Athenian ideal of direct *citizen* participation (in the ideal of the town meeting) and *representative* government in the hands of elected officials (in the English tradition); Robert E. Agger and Marshall N. Goldstein, *Who Will Rule?* (Belmont, Calif.: Wadsworth Publishing Co., 1971). For a survey of research on community and client participation, see Carol Lopate et al., "Decentralization and Community Participation in Public Education," *Review of Educational Research,* 40 (February 1970):135–50.

there is virtually unanimous agreement that a federal system ("federal control") of education, which would undermine the principle of local control, must not be allowed. Despite this rhetoric, the inadequacies and inequities of local resources and the spreading awareness of the national character of many dimensions of educational functioning have drawn the federal government into an active role in educational policy making. We will provide illustrations of congressional action in education in chapter 2; here let us consider the force of the executive and judicial branches of the government of the United States.

Examples abound of the potential of the presidency for inaugurating and lobbying for legislative enactments, for influencing the various agencies of government, and for creating public opinion or articulating elements of the popular will. Consider the request of President Richard Nixon for a moratorium on court-ordered busing of students to achieve school desegregation; believing that the president, in an election year, was speaking for the majority of public opinion, the Congress complied by attaching a rider to an unrelated bill, the Higher Education Act (1972). An even better illustration of presidential command of significant events was the determination of Lyndon Johnson to be remembered as the "education president." Himself a graduate of a teachers' college and once a rural schoolteacher, President Johnson saw the federal government as filling a void in American education, especially in securing better schooling for disadvantaged children. The executive branch consequently sponsored a varied program of federal legislation, actively lobbied Congress, and sent staff from the Executive Office and the cabinet departments to Congress as expert witnesses. The White House created an environment for federal court activism in school civil rights cases, prosecuted federal enforcement of existing laws,[14] escalated the budget and staff of the United States Office of Education, and generally encouraged a public mentality favoring quickened educational expansion.[15]

The dramas of educational policy making increasingly play themselves out on the stage of the federal court system—a forum grossly underestimated and ill-understood by professional educators and public opinion alike.[16] In theory, the federal judiciary is a three-stage funnel. Federal district courts are the first stage. They process litigation in areas of federal jurisdiction—an expanding area because of the now-frequent use of the "due process" and "equal protection" clauses of the Fourteenth Amendment of the United States

[14]On the problems of enforcing antidiscrimination legislation, see Gary Orfield, *The Reconstruction of Southern Education: The Schools and the 1964 Civil Rights Act* (New York: John Wiley & Sons, Inc., 1970).

[15]See the discussion of the executive branch in Roald F. Campbell and Donald H. Layton, *Policy Making for American Education* (Chicago: Midwest Administration Center, University of Chicago, 1969).

[16]A brief introduction to important federal court action in matters of race, religion, and academic freedom is David Fellman, ed., *The Supreme Court and Education* (New York: Teachers College Press, 1960). More specialized and somewhat less dated is Albert P. Blaustein and Clarence C. Ferguson, *Desegregation and the Law* (New York: Vintage Books, 1962). The comprehensive survey is Hazard, *Education and the Law.*

Constitution to judge matters such as education that were once believed the sole discretion of state governments. Federal appeals courts, also arranged by districts (circuits), and the United States Supreme Court, a "court of last resort," make up the succeeding stages. In fact, appeal to the Supreme Court is taken for granted at the outset of much litigation, and its influence upon education grows commensurately.

Court decisions may concern matters that have indirect but critical implications for schools, students, and teachers. An example is the Supreme Court's decision in *Reynolds* v. *Sims* (1964). Its principle of "one man, one vote" has been applied in court tests of restrictions on the franchise in school board elections and the requirement of having more than a simple majority in school-bond elections.

The best-known federal court action specific to schools is the Supreme Court decision in *Brown* v. *Topeka Board of Education* (1954), which declared schools segregated by race to be inherently unequal, thereby depriving their students of the equal protection of the laws guaranteed by the federal Constitution. Voluntary and court-ordered plans to make schools racially nondiscriminatory subsequently have provoked numerous landmark decisions.

Cartoon by Donald Reilly. Copyright 1968 by Saturday Review, Inc.

"I'm so proud of you—imagine having your hair defended by the American Civil Liberties Union!"

The federal courts have also acted on a broad front of issues relating to civil liberties and Constitutional guarantees. Nonpublic schools are protected under *Pierce* v. *Society of Sisters* (1925), which overturned an Oregon law that had limited compliance with the state's compulsory school-attendance statutes to public school enrollment. The right of schoolchildren not to salute the flag on grounds of religious conscience was established in *West Virginia State Board of Education* v. *Barnette* (1943), and mitigation of Wisconsin's compulsory attendance laws was ordered under freedom-of-religion guarantees in *Wisconsin* v. *Yoder* (1971). Use of tax funds to provide textbooks *(Cochran* v. *Louisiana State Board of Education* [1930]) and bus transportation *(Everson* v. *Board of Education* [1947]) to parochial school students was declared not unconstitutional, but other church-state entanglements have been proscribed by such decisions as *Engle* v. *Vitale* (1962), which overturned a New York State-composed school prayer, and *School District of Abington Township* v. *Schempp* (1963), which concerned reciting the Lord's Prayer in public schools. The federal courts will certainly contribute decisively to the future history of American education.

The State: The Sovereign Unit

Under the Constitution of the United States, the separate states reserve to themselves all powers not specifically ascribed to the federal government. Education not being an area specified as a federal responsibility, the states' power in education is complete. State actions can be rescinded only when courts find that federally protected rights have been violated—as in the above-mentioned example of the Supreme Court decision of 1954 that countermanded school segregation practices.

The state structure for the governance of public education was established by men who had no expectation of federal action, but who rejected dependence upon purely community initiative and local resources. They were unafraid of the centralization of authority. Horace Mann was distressed by the laissez faire localism of his own Massachusetts and described the pattern of fiscally independent, nearly autonomous school districts as an educational tragedy. James G. Carter envisioned close state supervision of local public education via state normal schools to train the teachers and exercise leadership. Henry Barnard—a leader in state developments and the first United States Commissioner of Education—wanted an educational role for the federal government that would go far beyond the innocuous information-gathering duties ascribed to his office by Congress.

While the state may choose to delegate some of its powers (including those respecting schools) to county or other local units, it remains sovereign in law. Those powers that the state gives, it may subsequently take back. There are many examples of such shifts in delegated authority, relating to teacher licensing, textbook selection, curriculum regulations, and changes in the proportion of state-contributed school funds. Nevertheless, the average

American citizen is probably unaware of the state's ultimate sovereignty and is easily moved to complain about "state control." From time to time, as in Iowa, the state legislature has investigated the means whereby local "prerogatives" have been "endangered." Because localism in education is more visible, it is assumed that sovereignty belongs at the local level. What is easily forgotten is that local districts operate schools for the state, and that local school board members (whether elected or appointed) are state officials.

A state's educational powers apply to both public and private institutions within its boundaries. While the states have so far exercised little of their potential authority, they nonetheless do possess rights of reasonable regulation and supervision of nonpublic schools and colleges. Under the pressure of nationalist, ethnic, racial, or religious emotions, there have been instances of state movements into the ordinarily unregulated operations of nonpublic institutions. The future may well see more such state attention, especially if the use of federal or state funds makes private schools or colleges quasi-public instrumentalities. It is quite conceivable that the states may ultimately require that teachers in such state-aided private schools possess the standard state teaching credential, for example.[17] A sizable growth of the nonpublic schools—alternative schools, community schools, proprietary nursery schools, schools supported by a voucher system—would certainly provoke attempts at increased state regulation of parts of their operations. The trend to state-wide coordinating boards for higher education sometimes extends their membership and purview to private institutions and raises the possibility of limiting institutional autonomy. Future campus disturbances could open private colleges to closer state scrutiny—as has happened at many state institutions.

All three branches of state government exercise control over education. The governor submits an education budget, proposes legislation, has the veto power, appoints commissions, calls conferences, and otherwise acts to form public opinion. In many states he also appoints members to state educational boards or other offices. The state legislature establishes a financing system and appropriates funds, passes laws respecting education, holds hearings, creates investigations, and also molds public opinion. The courts review laws and judge their constitutionality. Illustrations of the range of state court action include the Michigan Supreme Court's landmark decision in *Stuart* v. *School District No. 1 of the Village of Kalamazoo* (1874), which upheld a school board's right to collect taxes for a high school; the West Virginia Supreme Court of Appeals decision in *Lance* v. *Board of Education of County of Roane*

---

[17]The implications of extending court-decided principles from tax-supported public schools to tax-aided nonpublic schools are intriguing. Would sectarian schools be proscribed from teaching religion and offering prayers, all private schools be proscribed from discriminating on the basis of race or social class, military schools be proscribed from thwarting expressions of personal freedom? See the discussion of voucher plans in George R. La Noue, "The Politics of Education," *Teachers College Record,* 73 (December 1971):304–19.

(1969), which overturned a state law and constitutional provision requiring more than a simple majority in passing increases in tax levies and bond issues; and the Louisiana State Supreme Court's decision in *Seegers* v. *Parker* (1970), against action that would have expanded public grants to church-operated schools. The courts may also supervise hearings on contested teacher dismissals or other disputes. In some states courts appoint educational officials.

State financing of public education   Members of state boards of education, like other Americans, usually prefer local control and distrust centralized decision making. Nevertheless, many state governments are being pressed to assume a larger share of the financial burden of public schools and colleges. In 1972 a presidential commission recommended that the states contribute most of the cost of running local public schools, assisted by augmented federal funds. Almost all public colleges once under municipal sponsorship have become state colleges because of the local community's inability to underwrite their costs. (In the case of the University of Cincinnati, now "municipally sponsored and state affiliated," the reconstituted governing board now has appointees of both the mayor and the governor.)

TABLE 1   Public elementary and secondary school receipts, by source, 1890–1970

School Year Ending	Total Receipts[a]	Sources of Revenue, by Percent		
		Federal	State	Local[b]
1970	42,379,987,000[c]	6.9	41.1	52.0
1960	17,362,325,000[c]	3.8	39.8	56.4
1950	5,437,004,000	2.9	39.8	57.3
1940	2,260,527,000	1.8	30.3	68.0
1920	970,120,000	0.3	16.5	83.2
1910	433,064,000		28.0	72.0
1900	219,766,000		32.0	68.0
1890	143,195,000		32.2	67.8

[a]Numbers rounded.
[b]Includes county and other intermediate sources of income.
[c]Includes Hawaii and Alaska.
Sources: Adapted from compilations reported in U.S. Bureau of Census, *Historical Statistics of the United States* (Washington, D.C.: U.S. Government Printing Office, 1960, 1965), pp. 208, 31; "Facts on American Education," *NEA Research Bulletin, 49* (May 1971): 53.

Table 1 summarizes the proportional shifts in the states' share of public school funding relative to local and federal sources; they are not great. The table conceals, however, the astonishing variation among the states in their dependence upon state support for elementary and secondary school operations. In 1964 (when the United States average of state-paid school costs was 37.2 percent) the range extended from Nebraska (where the state paid 5.2 percent of the public school bill) to New Mexico (88.1 percent). Table 2 shows the range of governmental support by region. Careful study of such variation in sources of school financing explains other characteristics of edu-

TABLE 2 Ranges of support, by source, of public elementary and secondary school, by lowest and highest region, 1963-64

Source of Support	Lowest Region, in Percent of Support		Highest Region, in Percent of Support	
State government	Plains states	26	Southeast	59
Local government	Southeast	36	Plains states	71
Federal government	Mid-Atlantic states	2.5	Southwest	4.9

Source: Drawn from data in "School Statistics, 1963-64," *NEA Research Bulletin*, 42 (February 1964): 6.

cational development within the United States. Local school boards in the southeastern states, for example, have found it difficult to desegregate their schools at a faster rate or by a different method than the one espoused in the state capital. That some state departments of education annually review local school budgets increases state authority. Hence, fiscal dependence limits local discretion in policy making. By contrast, the considerable fiscal independence of local districts in the Plains states helps to account for that region's minimal state-set standards governing such matters as teacher training and credentialing, and for its rather low level of total spending per pupil for schools. In any case, it is not strictly educational considerations that determine the specific relationship of local to state governments but rather the broader social and political forces that form a given area's historical development.

In the typical state's annual budget the largest spending item is for education. State financing of public elementary and secondary schools has several categories. *Basic state aid* (sometimes called "foundation" aid) is a sum guaranteed to each student in the public schools, subject to adjustment by the legislature. (In California, for example, the 1967 figure was $125 per pupil in elementary school districts; it was higher for unified and high school districts.) The manner in which basic aid is administered significantly affects schools.   A state that apportions basic aid on the basis of the number of teachers in a given district (rather than on the number of students) encourages local districts to reduce class size. Another means of limiting class size is to impose a financial penalty upon a school district, in the form of reduced aid, if class size in given grades—e.g., the primary grades—is larger than specified.

Equalization funds recognize the great disparities of ability among local communities to raise money for education. In New Jersey the range of possible taxable wealth (the assessed valuation of property) per school child varied, in a recent year, from $10,000 to over $1 million (in a school district possessing an airport to tax and only three pupils to educate). The range in the larger, more populous states can be greater still. The fact that Baldwin Park, California, was able, in 1968, to spend only $578 per pupil (on a tax rate of $5.48 per $100 of assessed valuation) while nearby Beverly Hills spent $1,232 (raised on the much lower tax rate of $2.38) led the California Supreme Court to challenge the constitutionality of school funding based on community ability to pay for schools; the decision in *Serrano* v. *Priest* (1971) stimulated court tests of school financing methods in many other states, including Minnesota, New Jersey, Arizona, and Texas. The United States Supreme Court agreed in 1972 to review a federal district court ruling in a Texas school case (*Rodriguez* v. *San Antonio*), thereby bringing the principal basis of school finance under the scrutiny of the nation's highest court. (See footnote 14, chapter 2.)

The state's equalization contribution compensates poorer districts more than richer ones. It does not equalize educational expenditures, however, because the richer districts easily can assess themselves more for schools than the state's minimum required rate; richer districts can also raise funds by increasing property taxes or by selling school bonds.

Many states provide aid by means of incentive bonuses. Consolidated and unified districts often earn extra state funds by providing community (junior) college programs. Closely related to incentive bonuses are special program funds, which go to districts that provide whatever special programs the state currently thinks worthwhile: special classes for the handicapped, gifted, or foreign-language child; extra compensatory education for minority, ghetto, or migrant-worker youth; or voluntary instruction in sex education, mental health, or computer programming. Recently, some of this aid has come from federal funds apportioned by the states. In 1970 70 percent of state aid to schools in New York state came through a general aid formula (including an equalization provision) and 30 percent came through "categorical aid"— i.e., funds for transportation, special urban programs, school construction, and bonuses for reorganized districts.

Legislating for education   California is an example of a state where education is the principal arena of legislative action; in each session legislators submit more bills concerning schools and colleges than any other issue. Since the mid-nineteenth century, when the Northeastern states began to require the teaching of American history and geography, most state legislatures have extended their educational activities—so much so as to encounter occasional executive opposition (as when a New York governor vetoed a corporal punishment bill) or constitutional challenge (as when the New Hampshire Supreme Court voided the legislature's granting of lottery funds to nonpublic schools). State constitutions have specified the language of instruction (as in Oklahoma, New Mexico, and Arizona), have required the teaching of "truth, temperance, purity, public spirit, and respect for honest labor" (North Dakota), have provided for statewide textbook selection (as in New Mexico and North Carolina), and have authorized teaching the metric system (Utah).

Much legislation, including constitutional amendments, originated in interest-group pressure. In the 1890s the many patriotic and ancestral societies forced flag ceremonies and the newly written Pledge of Allegiance into the schools. In the 1930s the American Legion passed resolutions to allow hiring only of teachers "of unquestioned patriotism" and pressed for the enactment of loyalty oath laws. The 1960s saw half the state legislatures debate or pass laws or resolutions concerning sex-education courses. Whether alcoholism-prevention instruction and wildlife appreciation courses are compulsory at a given time often depends upon the shifting political fortunes of temperance groups and humane societies. Having a stake in a matter and acting in self-interest are facts that politicians understand and appreciate. This is why elected officials ordinarily give teacher organizations a deferential hearing—one out of proportion to their political clout; the professional group is not only "expert," it also manifests the clearest self-interest in educational affairs.[18]

State administration of education   The typical state's main administrative unit for education is the state department of education (or public instruction). Public higher education may have its own administrative unit. In this case there may be one state agency for all public higher education (as in New York, where a single board controls sixty-seven institutions), or a division of responsibility according to type of institution (as in California), or a board for each institution (as in Washington state). Until 1966 New Jersey located control of its public higher education in the same governing body that administered its elementary and secondary schools.

The state's administrative unit generally has several divisions responsible for such concerns as budget, curriculum, special education, buildings and facilities, vocational courses, and other relevant matters. There is generally little field supervision of local teaching practices. In place of an inspectorate, the state in America usually accepts the local chief administrator's assurance that state directives are being followed.

Within the state department, division chiefs (perhaps titled assistant or deputy state superintendent) are typically appointed by the state superintendent (himself elected or appointed to office). The remaining personnel are generally civil service employees with reasonable job security. Their tenure and the bureaucratic nature of the administrative structure make it possible for unpopular, unwelcomed, and alien political appointees to be encapsulated and rendered impotent—without having to wait for a change in state administration following the next election.

New federal programs are another source of possibly unwelcome outside influences. In one carefully studied case a state department of education was able to "domesticate" federal programs assigned to its administration, to "socialize" new personnel hired under the federal program, and to carry on without disrupting its own policies and traditions. The principal means used were these: whenever possible, department personnel were promoted to fill the new positions; the department assisted in writing the state civil service

---

[18]Nicholas Masters et al., *State Politics and the Public Schools* (New York: Alfred A. Knopf, Inc., 1964), pp. 262–80; Thomas J. Gustafson, "Variables Which Affect the Success of Educational Pressure Groups" (paper read at the annual meetings of the American Educational Research Association, Minneapolis, March 1970).

examination by which new employees were selected; the existing organizational structure channeled policy decisions through itself; and the department gained control over promotion policies and salary scales covering the new federal programs.[19]

County Government: The Uncertain Link

In America's past, county government was important in the administration of justice, policing, taxation, land recording, welfare, and other functions. In the nineteenth century the county acted as the state's agent for examining and licensing teachers, devising courses of study, collecting and distributing the school fund, and many other educational services. Some states still require that teachers place their state licenses on file with the appropriate county superintendent, and the county may still function as the state's agent in enforcing certain state school policies. Where school districts are extremely small and do not employ a local superintendent, the county superintendent also may have specified powers.

County importance is greatest today in the South, where counties are usually smaller than elsewhere and have long been the basic unit of local government; there the local school district is usually countywide (sometimes excepting a large city whose schools are independent of most county administration). Elsewhere, the county unit has declined in importance. Many of its political and governmental functions have passed into local or state hands. New functions—such as air and water pollution control, rapid transit, conservation, irrigation, and flood abatement—have been given to new and specialized, single-purpose districts formed for each function.

As the county's administrative role diminishes, its educational offices come under attack as being useless intermediate units between local and state jurisdiction. To justify their continued life, many county boards have intensified their energies on behalf of the smaller local districts within their boundaries, administering such auxiliary services as the school bus transportation system, the lending of audiovisual materials, and health and lunch programs. New federal programs have allowed interested counties new functions. Under the National Defense Education Act, counties may write proposals for projects covering several small districts. Since the Elementary and Secondary Education Act allows local districts to petition directly for federal aid, wihout state mediation, county offices can assist in preparing such requests. And there is some evidence that the states have met their new educational responsibilities with county aid, e.g., using the county superintendent's staff to identify chil-

---

[19]Myron Milstein, "Functions of the California State Department of Education as They Relate to Two Federally Funded Educational Programs" (Ph.D. diss., University of California, Berkeley, 1967), esp. p. 230. See also Jerome T. Murphy, "Title I of ESEA: The Politics of Implementing Federal Education Reform," *Harvard Educational Review,* 41 (February 1971):35–63; and Laurence Iannaccone, *Politics in Education* (New York: Center for Applied Research in Education, Inc., 1967).

dren eligible to receive federal aid by collecting welfare statistics, distributing state and federal information on new programs, and arranging regional conferences.[20] County government is not yet moribund in education, and the American propensity for creating new governmental units without repealing the old augurs well for its continuance.

Local School Districts: The Granary of the Grass Roots

It is not uncommon today for one to live within the boundaries of six or seven overlapping governmental jurisdictions: municipal government plus assorted special districts, one of which is the public school or community college district. The authority of school boards derives from three sources: the power that comes from being a governmental unit, although this power must be exercised in the pursuit of the function of "educating"—not that of "governing"; the power delegated to local boards by state government; and the power exercised under common law to act "in loco parentis."

Over 80 percent of all school children in the United States go to school in fiscally independent school districts. (Fiscally dependent districts are concentrated in New England, the upper South [Maryland, Virginia, and North Carolina], and in some of the very large cities.) This means that while the district must depend upon local resources for most of its revenues, its budget and taxing powers are not subject to review by ordinary municipal government. One consequence of fiscally autonomous school districts is competition: various public services compete with education for public interest and voter approval in tax-rate and bond elections. Another consequence is fragmentation: the authority responsible for coordinating health, housing, streets and transportation, libraries, justice, and other municipal needs lacks legal responsibility for integrating these with school development. Moreover, there is the sheer multiplication of governmental units. In 1952 there were 116,743 such units in the United States; 58 percent of them were school districts. Yet one must not overemphasize the isolation of the school district from other local government. To the informal interaction of the past has been added new involvement by mayors and city council members in educational projects contained in Model Cities programs and other federal operations that require municipal coordination.

In the local school district the principal official participants in American-style publicness are the professional staff of administrators (headed by an appointed superintendent) and the laymen of the usually elected school board (variously called the "school committee" or "school trustees"); such board members constitute the largest category of elected officials in the United States.

Unlike the Soviet Union—where centralized planning limits the school (and university) administrator to implementing plans, supervising regulations,

[20]Milstein, "Functions of the California State Department of Education," p. 158.

and distributing funds—the American administrator may initiate plans, which he proposes to the board as new policy. He also plays a public relations role, mediating among partisans, trying to gain public confidence in proposed changes, and generally working to "sell the schools" to a community whose political interests may be segmented into various mobilized factions and an inactive majority.

Common observation and a few available empirical investigations suggest that administrators vary considerably in their effective power over the boards that hire them. Some are undoubtedly simple "mouthpieces" of the board, although many a superintendent may appear to be that while actually being a subtle manipulator of board members' thinking. Some are undoubtedly autocrats, dominating a cowed or lazy board; but probably many a shrewd board member, anxious to keep the political heat off himself, allows the superintendent to appear more influential than he actually is.[21] School functionaries who wish to avoid the full weight of the competing, privately communicated cross-pressures that are the burden of public officials wisely try to make all educational policy making appear to be the result of complex and convoluted group-think—and to leave their chance-taking to election day. As a consequence, middle-level administrators—department heads, supervisors, deputy superintendents—have often garnered much power.

There were 103,000 school board members in the United States in 1970, serving some 18,000 districts. Their powers include those of building, acquiring, and maintaining school facilities; hiring, promoting, and firing personnel; operating schools and compelling attendance; collecting and spending public funds (98 percent of all revenues raised by local boards—some $30 billion in 1968—are taxes on local real property); and submitting bond proposals to the voters (the National Education Association estimated the total *interest* on the nation's school indebtedness at over $800 million for 1965). While it is impossible to say anything both simple and definitive about so many individuals, the general characteristics of school board members as a group are apparently unchanged since George Counts wrote *The Social Composition of Boards of Education* in 1927. City and suburban boards are still dominated by business proprietors, professional men, corporation executives, and the wives of such men. Prosperous farmers run most rural boards. Although women are 51.2 percent of the population, they are 20 percent of school

---

[21]Neal Gross, *Who Runs Our Schools?* (New York: John Wiley & Sons, Inc., 1958), found that such factors in the superintendent's background as his age, years of administrative experience, tenure in his present post, and the level of his community activity and involvement were not related to the amount of pressure he reported receiving. This suggests that pressure is largely beyond the control of the individual administrator, that the elements are primarily political and sociological, not personalistic.

See also Edward B. Shils and C. Taylor Whittier, "The Superintendent, the School Board, and Collective Negotiations," *Teachers College Record*, 69 (October 1967):43–61; and the self-censored views of Chicago's former superintendent of schools, Benjamin C. Willis, *Social Problems in Public School Administration* (Pittsburgh: University of Pittsburgh Press, 1967).

board membership. As in their economic and social-class characteristics, school board members (whether elected or appointed) are also atypical of the average American in their educational levels: a much higher proportion (more than 40 percent) are college graduates than is true of the population at large. In 1970 almost two-thirds were registered as Republicans, compared to 37 percent of all American voters. Governing boards of nonpublic schools, colleges, and universities are similarly unrepresentative in their socioeconomic characteristics. A national study conducted by the Educational Testing Service in 1968 of the boards of trustees of public and private colleges and universities showed that membership on educational boards draws predominantly from the same pool: well-educated, politically and economically conservative, white Protestant, upper-middle or upper class, middle-aged and elderly men (90 percent of all college board members).[22]

While studies of community power politics have seldom treated schools, Harold Webb's analysis of three small Wyoming towns supports the propositions advanced in Floyd Hunter's much-discussed study of Atlanta that the "power brokers" are largely unknown to the typical citizen (even to top school administrators), and that they either hold seats on city boards or largely decide who will.[23]

To point out that the laymen who serve on governing boards in education are not statistically representative of Americans in general is not to say that this unrepresentativeness is necessarily bad. In education, as in other areas of public administration, atypical qualities and leadership skills may be of higher service to the public interest than would be the selection of more persons closer to the norm. There are, however, some reasons to work for greater heterogeneity in board membership. One is the average citizen's inability to identify with, or his actual estrangement from, the political processes by which issues are resolved locally. It is generally admitted that school matters are to the electorate the most broadly interesting of local issues, and it is often claimed that public participation in the governance of education is the average citizen's last chance to see his political sovereignty manifested. Yet interest groups have trouble recruiting members to try to influence school policy, and even "community control" spokesmen have complained of community apathy.[24] The purported average turnout at school elections is

---

[22]It appears from G. William Domhoff's *Who Rules America?* (Englewood Cliffs, N.J.: Prentice-Hall, Inc., 1967) that the upper class is more likely to dominate the governance of colleges and universities and the foundations that incidentally influence education, than to control state or local governments, including public education bodies. See also Otto F. Kraushaar, *American Nonpublic Schools* (Baltimore: The Johns Hopkins University Press, 1972), p. 111.

[23]Floyd Hunter, *Community Power Structure* (Chapel Hill: University of North Carolina Press, 1953); Harold V. Webb, *Community Power Structure Related to School Administration* (Laramie: College of Education, University of Wyoming, 1956).

[24]Suggestions for overcoming citizen reluctance in schools committed to parental participation in policy making appear in Steve Arons et al., *Doing Your Own School: A Practical Guide to Starting and Operating a Community School* (Boston: Beacon Press, 1972).

under 12 percent of registered voters. Intense pre-electoral discussion of the issues does *not* appear to raise consistently the percentage of voter turnout. Even in highly educated, prosperous suburban populations, where the schools are the pivot of communal politics, voter apathy is marked. The average school board election in New Trier, Illinois, draws 2 percent of the voters, a percentage lowered, no doubt, by the fact that no candidacy has ever been contested; the record turnout was in 1962, when 50 percent balloted in a school-bond referendum.[25] Nonelectoral participation is even less widespread, especially concerning broad policy questions. What little participation there is tends to be episodic, specific, and often negative—defeating a tax-override measure; challenging relaxed school dress codes; registering opposition to a sex-education course, a too-liberal board member, or a too-permissive administrator.[26]

A second reason to make board membership more "open" is the widely held conviction that such elites are unable to serve the interests of any but their own limited class. Many elected boards have become exclusive preserves. Incumbents who are never involuntarily removed by the electoral process screen all new members. The prestigious school board of Newton, Massachusetts, is an example. Protests against public school boards by spokesmen for blacks and other minorities echo past complaints made by labor, Catholic, Jewish, German, and other ethnic interests and by women's organizations. These protests are supported today by those middle-class campus protestors who satirize college trustees, picket their meetings, and write scathing denunciations of the bigotry, corruption, and war-mongering that they see (or assume to be present) on their governing boards, and who urge new procedures in selecting such boards—whether the institution be public or private. In recent years some parochial school systems have attempted to form school boards of laymen to share setting school policy with the episcopal authority.

Although 80 percent of the nation's school boards are filled by election, those in some of our largest cities are appointed. In New York City and Chicago, for example, an elected mayor appoints from a list submitted by a "blue-ribbon" civic committee, itself representative of the professions, universities, corporations, and unions.[27] Because such civic associations are

[25]Louis H. Masotti, *Education and Politics in Suburbia: The New Trier Experience* (Cleveland: Western Reserve University Press, 1967), p. 10.

[26]Frederick M. Wirt and Michael W. Kirst, *The Political Web of American Schools* (Boston: Little, Brown, 1972), esp. p. 76.

[27]Virtually no research exists on the relationship of educational politics to municipal government. See Bernard Mackler and Nancy Bord, "The Role of the Urban Mayor in Education," *Teachers College Record,* 69 (March 1968):531–39; and the community case studies in Peter Schrag, *Voices in the Classroom: Public Schools and Public Attitudes* (Boston: Beacon Press, 1965); David Rogers, *110 Livingston Street: Politics and Bureaucracy in the New York City School System* (New York: Random House, Inc., 1968); the twelve-year civic history of Teaneck, New Jersey, in Reginald Damerell, *Triumph in a White Suburb* (New York: William Morrow and Co., Inc., 1968); Robert L. Crain et al., *The Politics of School Desegregation* (Chicago: Aldine Publishing Co., 1968);

themselves "unrepresentative," so too usually are their nominees. On the other hand, appointed boards of education sometimes perform as superior public servants because their members are not mere aspirants to higher elective offices. This judgment stems from the fairly common belief that election to a school board is a steppingstone to a fuller political career. In Boston biennial school committee elections have drawn 18 to 20 candidates in the hope that the visibility of office-seeking will contribute to ultimate political success. The tough, costly, and often brutal campaigns prevent many outstanding persons from competing, however, and most successful office-seekers did not develop via educational politics.[28]

The lesson seems to be that too little (or too meaningless) a contest drives away the electorate while too much electoral competitiveness drives away from school board membership many able persons. This talent factor is important both for the conduct of the school or college and because individual board members today must take an ever more public and explicit stand on such matters as school integration, teacher strikes, campus morals, local-state relations, student power, and political "interference." Policy makers, like administrators, must deal with competing, determined power blocs. Hence it seems imperative that representativeness and ability be married in those governing bodies.

POWER AND INFLUENCE: THE INFORMAL AND EXTRALEGAL SYSTEM

Because the school is the only institution created exclusively for socializing the nation's youth, other institutions have a stake in school operations. They demonstrate their interest by their scrutiny of educational procedures and by their frequent attempts to interfere with school policies.

Power is a difficult concept to define in the abstract, although we usually believe that we know it when we see it operate. The power of authority inheres in certain positions in political and economic structures, but various holders of the same office may shrink or swell their power by subtle differences in their personal prestige or individual temperaments. *Influence* is even more subtle and perplexing, because it is informal, unofficial, and often unacknowledged power. But there is another reason why influence has been too little

---

the comparative study of two Oregon communities in Agger and Goldstein, *Who Will Rule the Schools?;* Henry M. Levin, ed., *Community Control of Schools* (Washington, D.C.: Brookings Institution, 1970); Marilyn Gittell, *Participants and Participation: A Study of School Policy in New York City* (New York: Praeger Publishers, Inc., 1967), p. 4. For an autobiographical account of a former Chicago school board member, see Jack Witkowsky, "Education of a School Board Member," *Saturday Review* (November 20, 1971):90–92.

[28]Peter Schrag, *Village School Downtown*, p. 10. An example of a school committee-woman who briefly attained a congressional seat through her school board activities is Louise Day Hicks.

studied and too much overlooked in the analysis of governance. This reason may be summarized in the slogan that "ours is a government of laws, not of men."

The American nation was established by men who held a mechanistic, Newtonian political philosophy. They believed that the universe is a perfectly contrived machine, that human institutions need only be brought into harmonious agreement with its inexorable laws. The Founding Fathers—being not only men of the Enlightenment, but also classicists—had the further assurance of Plato's *Republic* that "if once a republic is set a-going, it proceeds happily, increasing as a circle." The political theory of the eighteenth century made no place for political pluralism and compromise, the inertia of law, the spoils system, emotionality in public affairs, and voter irresponsibility or apathy.

Education has not been in step with the "invisible government" of functioning politics. Three explanations suggest themselves: the insulation theory, an obsolete civics teaching, and the preponderance of women in teaching.

The belief is widespread that education is, or can be, apolitical, that schools and colleges should be insulated from politics. Educators have not acknowledged Aristotle's contention that man is a "political animal," that he is enmeshed in political systems. Only recently converted to the view that the school functions as a social system, most educators do not yet admit that it is also a political system, that each school has a political structure because it is a persisting pattern of human relationships involving power, rule, authority, influence, and coercion. Relationships of authority and influence exist even among persons having no desire to wield them; hence, an "authoritarian" principal, a "power-hungry" dean, or a "political-scheming regent" is not required for an educational institution or school system to function as a political system. School affairs need not be entangled in "party politics" in order to become intensely partisan, because partisanship is an inevitable outcome of operating schools in a democratic and pluralistic society. As Iversen has pointed out, schools impose a body of doctrine upon their students by the curriculum and the very atmosphere of the school: "A democratic society that demands authoritarian imposition . . . compensates for this procedural contradiction by surveillance over what is being imposed and who is doing the imposing."[29]

Many highly publicized examples of "playing politics with the schools and colleges"—manipulating what is an elaborate system of controls and restraints, checks, and balances—have made unmistakable the fact of a politics of education. Nevertheless, many still define this political functioning too narrowly, e.g., as the governor paying off campaign debts with state university trusteeships, or as radical black students seeking to apply a political

[29]Robert W. Iversen, *The Communists and the Schools* (New York: Harcourt Brace Jovanovich, 1959), p. 5.

test in staffing a new black studies department. They ignore the fact that school officials have historically played politics by refraining from actions that would offend *any* important group's interests. Most persons continue to believe that the politicizing of education is a recent, a regrettable, and a remediable development.

American schools (and colleges, to a lesser extent) offer a curriculum of history and government courses and instruction in civics and public affairs that emphasizes a formal, legalistic, constitutional, and benevolent view of power and politics that most scholars find grossly inadequate. All levels of schooling teach that voting is the vehicle of citizen influence upon government and normally exclude other political behavior from analysis. As one educator has complained, "A patriotic acceptance and admiration of American institutions minimizes persistent, divisive value conflicts and problems of social injustice. . . . The effects of administrative bureaucracies, big business, labor, the mass media, the church, popular protest movements, or pressure groups . . . are largely ignored [as is] the significance of personal ambitions, motives, and passions in the formation of public policy. . . ."[30] Whether or not such a tradition of civics instruction has indeed fostered the "massive public apathy" of which so many complain, it appears bound to have affected those who teach it, since teachers will often internalize what they continually reiterate.

Over 70 percent of teachers below the level of higher education are women, but women are underrepresented in government. Women teachers, like other women, have found it difficult to identify with or to relate readily to formal government. A more important fact is that women are generally more disapproving of or passive toward the political realities, especially toward the processes by which conflicts are generated or exposed, debated, and resolved, than are men. Although differences do exist among the social classes in level of political awareness and involvement in nonvoting political activities, men take a more active stance than women at each level.

Women teachers are more likely to join professional associations than teacher unions. They are less likely than men to press for higher wages and basic changes in working conditions and are less likely than men to approve campaign contributions and political endorsements, sanctions, and strikes against school boards.[31] Whatever the root causes of these sexual differences, as long as the preponderance of school employees are women, the

[30]Fred W. Newmann, "Political Socialization in the Schools: A Discussion," *Harvard Educational Review,* 38 (Summer 1968):536–45.

[31]Harmon Zeigler, *The Political Life of American Teachers* (Englewood Cliffs, N.J.: Prentice-Hall, Inc., 1967). The style of educational politics tends to conform to a community's general cultural style, according to Alan Rosenthal, *Pedagogues and Power: Teacher Groups in School Politics* (Syracuse, N.Y.: Syracuse University Press, 1969); variations in response are portrayed in Marilyn Gittell and T. Edward Hollander, *Six Urban School Districts: A Comparative Study of Institutional Response* (New York: Praeger Publishers, Inc., 1968).

profession will interpret the extralegal system for resolving conflicting interests as being the immoral (if not the illegal) operation of politics.

Interest Groups

The often rowdy and sometimes violent town meetings of colonial New England have been called the epitome of democracy in action. Outward aspects of their form remain in the "open" portions of school board or trustees' meetings, in the public hearings of city councils or regulatory agencies, and in the annual stockholders' meetings of corporations. Although town government was not "democratic" in a modern sense—because there was, for example, no tolerance of other religious creeds or of disparate political ideologies—colonial town government was democratic in practice because its meetings brought together members of a broadly homogeneous economic and social class.[32] Time and immigration destroyed that homogeneity, and society now requires a conception of democracy that functions through a consensus arrived at after compromises between conflicting interests and differing values.

One unit that represents distinct interest groups in cities is the neighborhood. Residential areas define large racial, economic, ethnic and cultural, age, or religious clusters of people. School boards in the last century represented particular areas of the city. While such school boards were unwieldy in size—in 1905 Philadelphia's had 115 members—and became tainted by corruption, the ward system does have certain merits. Under it, ghetto residents and ethnic minorities can have some representation. A second, and related, virtue of representation by wards is that it costs less to campaign for office; even in a city of under 500,000 inhabitants, the great expenses of at-large or city-wide campaigns preclude effective campaigning by candidates from those groups presently underrepresented in the governance of education: the poor, the blue-collar worker, the black, the Mexican-American, and the young.

Many educational decisions must transcend the limited perspective and the characteristic needs of the neighborhood. Future employment and educational opportunities are city-wide and even national. New departures in curriculum and teaching methods seldom come from neighborhood thinking. State and federal operations more often provide the sources of financing. The problems and needs of students and teachers are transient. But it still remains evident that central boards are often out of touch with many of their constituents. If the formal-legal structure does not accommodate special interests adequately, the extralegal system will—through the formation of various pressure groups. Pressure groups transmit desires from citizens to officials. But these "transfer

[32]Page Smith, *As a City Upon a Hill: The Town in American History* (New York: Alfred A. Knopf, Inc., 1966), p. 110.

agents" often reformulate citizen demands, acting instead as "transformation agents."[33]

There are five noteworthy categories of organizations that attempt regularly to influence policy making in schools and colleges. These are school-oriented groups, patriotic organizations, minority-group organizations, taxpayer associations, and civic associations. The list does not include churches and other social and fraternal groups that occasionally become involved in educational lobbying. The Masons, for example, have reportedly opposed recent voucher-plan legislation that would aid parochial schools. Groups also spring up around specific issues and then wither away, such as those formed to combat sex-education courses.[34] Similar groups have appeared to oppose busing and to fight for or against a slate of school board candidates.

School-oriented groups operate in different ways and for different purposes. They appear to be more influential in urban than in rural districts. The largest volunteer organization in the nation is the National Congress of Parents and Teachers, which has existed since 1897 "on behalf of public education." Critics of the PTA call it the "puppet of the educational establishment" or deride it as the "tea and cookies lobby." While the PTA seeks to work with the local administration, it is not without power to challenge the status quo. Floyd Hunter identified it among the top 20 most influential national organizations.[35] The PTA influences schools through its local units, but it can operate at the state level, as demonstrated by the example of the New Mexico Congress of Parents and Teachers' militant campaign in 1957 to change the state constitution so as to create an elected state board of education.[36] It is not strange to find that the White Book manual for 1960 of the John Birch Society urged its members to infiltrate the PTA: "Join your local PTA at the beginning of this school year, get your conservative friends to do likewise, and go to work to take it over. You will run into real battles against determined leftists who have had everything their way" (p. 27). It is the policy of local PTA chapters to appoint observers for school board sessions, include board members in their programs (except at election time), take positions on issues, request clarification of existing school practices, present surveys, and make recommendations to the board or the administration. All of these are political activities.

The Council for Basic Education serves as the organizational focus for critics of public education who think schools neglect the fundamental intellectual disciplines and wrongly emphasize social adjustment. In focusing its attack upon John Dewey and progressive education, CBE has formed ideo-

[33]Wirt and Kirst, *The Political Web of American Schools,* esp. pp. 50–59.

[34]Mary Breasted, *Oh! Sex Education!* (New York: Praeger Publishers, Inc., 1970), p. 5.

[35]Floyd Hunter, *Top Leadership, U.S.A.* (Chapel Hill: University of North Carolina Press, 1959), pp. 14–16.

[36]Tom Wiley, *Politics and Purse Strings in New Mexico's Public Schools* (Albuquerque: University of New Mexico Press, 1968).

logical alliances with such prominent conservatives as Max Rafferty and Russell Kirk. CBE appeals to laymen, insisting that the teaching profession is awash with progressivist principles. Having no local units, CBE operates nationally to form opinion, distribute literature, sponsor and encourage investigations, and otherwise influence education. Like the PTA, CBE participation appeals primarily to more prosperous middle-class Americans.

Citizens for Educational Freedom seeks tax support for nonpublic schools. Founded by a Catholic priest and composed principally of Catholic laymen, it has support from other religious denominations that endorse its program. By emphasizing alternatives to public education, CEF functions as a critic of the "public school establishment."

Patriotic organizations have a more varied membership, unified by a concern with the loyalty of schools and colleges to their members' perception of American traditions. Textbooks have been a principal concern of such groups as the Daughters of the American Revolution, the American Legion, Pro-America, America's Future, and United Daughters of the Confederacy. In the period 1958–62 alone, one-third of the states saw such groups mobilizing attacks in their legislatures upon textbooks. Scrutiny of public school library holdings led, in 1969, to removal of John Hersey's *Hiroshima* from Orange County, California, school libraries; school officials of Drake, North Dakota, had offending books burned in 1973. Patriotic organizations have sponsored essay contests on Americanism, model-government assemblies of high school students, retaining ROTC training in the colleges and universities, teacher loyalty oaths, and investigation of suspected subversive activity. World War I and resistance to immigration date the intense scrutiny of American public education for signs of "un-Americanism." The American Protective League began to accumulate files on teachers in 1918. At its first convention, in 1919, the American Legion lobbied for citizenship courses in all schools and soon thereafter extended its interests to urge loyalty oaths for all teachers. The Legion has been the most active of the patriotic societies.

Minority-group organizations take extreme and controversial positions that such broad-based organizations as the PTA normally avoid. Groups like the National Association for the Advancement of Colored People have pursued tactics not normally associated with pressure groups, such as demonstrations, strikes, boycotts, and court suits. Since moderation became less popular in the civil rights movement in the mid-1960s, and as minority-group spokesmen became determined to combat racism with militancy, inexperienced educators have had to respond as strategists in ways foreign to their conception of pressure politics.

Taxpayer associations represent groups concerned primarily with expenditures, rather than with curriculum or philosophical issues. Public education is the largest nonmilitary item of public spending; 30 percent of all civilian governmental employees work in local public schools. Associations of taxpayers have helped organize public opposition to tax increases and to school bond proposals, particularly in states heavily dependent upon local financing of schools and among lower-income white groups. In other instances these associations have allied themselves with various educational groups to increase state aid to education and to equalize the tax burden.

Civic associations claim to speak on behalf of general public interest, objective and rational study, and expertness in the examination of public issues. The larger associations hire paid executives who may compete with elected officials in speaking for the city. It has been predicted that as white metropolitan regions become progressively more estranged from the black central cities, civic associations will try to exercise a degree of suburban influence upon the affairs of the inner city. Because civic association functionaries are likely to favor master planning, regional government, and local connections with federal agencies and programs, they bring a perspective that is seemingly at odds with the separated, insulated, and localized traditions long dominating educational planning.

School administrators do not confront categories of interest groups; they deal with individuals and specific organizations, some of which cannot even be located clearly within the above categories. The Massachusetts school superintendents whom Neal Gross interviewed reported encounters with groups and individuals as shown in table 3. Interestingly enough, the superintendents reported that such pressuring was less troubling than was community apathy. And, despite occasional stories of community-imposed censorship and witch-

TABLE 3   The sources of political pressure, as reported by school superintendents

Individuals or Groups Who Exert Pressure	Percentage of Massachusetts Superintendents Reporting Pressure[a]
Parents or PTA	92
Individual school board members	75
Teachers	65
Taxpayers' association	49
Town finance committee	48
City Council politicians	46
Business or commercial organizations	45
Individuals influential for economic reasons	44
Personal friends	37
The press	36
Old-line families	30
Church or religious groups	28
Veterans' organizations	27
Labor unions	27
Chamber of Commerce	23
Service clubs	20
Fraternal organizations	13
Farm organizations	12
Welfare organizations	3

[a]Total number of superintendents reporting: 105.

Source: Neal Gross, *Who Runs Our Schools?* p. 50. Copyright, 1958, John Wiley & Sons, Inc.

hunting crusades, a national survey found only one teacher in twenty who gave "concern about community conditions" (a category broader than "pressure") as a reason for transferring to another district.[37] The reason may be that many schools may be doing precisely what most people in their communities want them to do.

The Profession as an Interest Group

Many citizens believe that teachers and administrators retain more power (and more decisive power) than many professions would admit having. Moreover, citizens frequently disclaim their own competence to wield more authority.[38] One 1967 statewide poll of citizen opinion reported that only 11 percent thought public opinion was influential in shaping educational policy. Seventy percent of those polled thought that the professional educator was best equipped to set the curriculum and run the schools. Persons critical of present education are slightly more likely (39 percent) to participate actively in school affairs than are school supporters (36 percent). Finally, the poll showed that a higher proportion of respondents (71 percent) voted in the last statewide election than in the last school election (51 percent). This sample shows the extent to which the public considers itself uninvolved in educational matters.

The sociologist E. C. Hughes has made a distinction between *license:* the right to do things others do not do, and *mandate:* telling society what is good for society and for the individual. Medical doctors possess much of both, but teachers are given too little, especially of mandate,[39] although they possess a considerable license in the handling of children, if only by default. Each day many thousands of hallway doors close upon the separated classrooms of thousands of schools, leaving the teacher sovereign of that most critical and decisive phase of the entire operation. Community groups that seek to wrest teacher selection from school board jurisdiction recognize this power. Similarly, faculty power in the colleges and universities is well known to those who have studied the structure of higher education in America. Indeed, it has been said that college trustees have *only* extraordinary power: the ability to step in when there is general internal acknowledgment that the institution is in a mess.

[37]"Teacher Mobility and Loss," *NEA Research Bulletin,* 46 (December 1968):120. Zeigler found that teachers perceived organized groups as threats much less often than "local cranks," parents, and other school officials; see *The Political Life,* pp. 128–29. See also the case studies in Robert Bendiner, *The Politics of Schools* (New York: New American Library, Inc., 1970); and David W. Beggs and R. Bruce McQuigg, *America's Schools and Churches: Partners in Conflict* (Bloomington, Ind.: Indiana University Press, 1965).

[38]*San Francisco Chronicle,* January 2, 1968. This article also reported the results of the poll cited below, carried out by the Field Research Corporation for the State Committee on Public Education. See also Wirt and Kirst, *The Political Web,* pp. 216–18.

[39]*Men and Their Work* (New York: The Free Press, 1958), pp. 79, 85–86.

In the past, when the parents of millions of schoolchildren were unschooled immigrants, teachers and administrators were more awesome. Today, when the educational level of the American public is much higher than it was in 1900, this professional advantage seems reduced. It is probably not entirely lost, however, for evidence suggests that any form of expertise is most highly regarded by the educated. Members of school boards, who are themselves better educated than the community at large, and well-educated residents of middle-class school districts are most likely to defer to the "expert" judgment of the school superintendent. He functions somewhat like a professional city manager, whose "expert" credentials enhance his political leadership at the expense of elected officeholders.[40]

THE LIMITS OF LOCALISM

Although a teacher organization, an interest group, or a school board has a local base and membership, none of these bodies is essentially "local" in its characteristic concerns, its policies, and in the techniques it employs. There are state or national headquarters, advisory committees, and organs of communication to counsel any individual or group having an interest in education. Issues of taxation, citizenship training, racial equality, competent management, scholarship, building standards, professional integrity, and student discipline all normally transcend the boundaries of any single community. This fact is now well recognized by teacher organizations, which have been trying to create a unified professional association that can bargain over the heads of local school boards with state and federal government. So, too, the Catholic bishops seeking financial aid for parochial schools address their appeals and exert their influence directly upon state legislators, governors, and the president of the United States.[41] Modern technological demands affect the curriculum across district lines. Thus, although largely unrecognized in law and tradition, publicness in American education is far less local and much more centralized than is generally admitted.

[40]A study of the role adopted by skillful superintendents in getting curriculum innovations accepted in Pennsylvania and West Virginia public schools is reported in Richard O. Carlson, *Adoption of Educational Innovations* (Eugene: Center for the Advanced Study of Educational Administration, University of Oregon, 1965).

[41]Myron Lieberman, "The Union Merger Movement," *Saturday Review* (June 24, 1972):50–56; Louis R. Gary and K. C. Cole, "The Politics of Aid and a Proposal for Reform," *Saturday Review* (July 22, 1972):31–33.

DIVERSITY

Diversity is a state of difference, unlikeness, and heterogeneity. Some find it synonymous with "freedom," "choice," "opportunity"; to others it means "chaos," "confusion," and "conflicting claims." To an extent, diversity exists in every society, especially when social change operates too rapidly for the social order to effect smooth integration of the new elements and reintegration of displaced populations, beliefs, and other cultural artifacts.

A universal and ageless tension appears between certain pressures toward unity, conformity, and integration, and those toward diversity, variety, and individuality. A healthy society depends upon some balance between unity (oneness) and diversity (multiplicity). Too much social cohesion spells totalitarianism; too much pluralism means anarchy. The possibility of reaching a permanent balance point, or synthesis, seems remote, for each society must continue to be pushed along a continuum by the vagaries of historical events —sometimes moving toward diversity, other times encouraging conformity, frequently seeking both at the same historical moment.

Despite the need to temper order with freedom, liberty with loyalty, America is ideologically committed to diversity. The ethos of individualism is a basic belief of this culture. Diversity is facilitated, but not guaranteed, by decentralized government, the absence of an established church, an unfettered press, and free-enterprise economics.

Much of America's educational structure and important parts of the context surrounding educational debate stem from two principles. The first is essentially *monopolistic:* schools are more likely to be democratic institutions and to serve the public good if they are publicly run as well as publicly supported. Horace Mann argued in the 1830s that a multiethnic and multisectarian society faces mortal danger in divisive antagonisms—a danger best mitigated by enrolling all children in public schools, where common learnings and experiences will transcend partisan interests, and build a cultural consensus and enduring friendships. This idea was later reflected in the Oregon initiative of 1922, which required that all children attend public institutions, and it appears in the form of a certain distrust of private schooling and in the widespread belief (even in private-school circles) that such schools must serve public purposes as well as gratify the private desires of their clientele.

The second principle reflects an antigovernment bias whose thrust is *antimonopolistic* and resistant to standardization: schools are more likely to serve the unique needs of individual students and particular communities when developed and run by local authority. What is particularly feared is the "federalization" of standards and "usurpation" of local control by the central government. Institutional life and social forces generate constant pressures either toward unity or toward diversity.

PRESSURES TOWARD UNIFORMITY AND CENTRALIZATION

Society has used three major institutions to achieve and maintain national unity. Government is the most obvious instrument for achieving cohesion in a pluralistic society. Its means include laws, political parties, special access to the mass media, economic controls, the civil service, and the armed forces. Organized religion has been important in certain nations (e.g., Spain) and in times past (medieval Europe, Puritan New England) for assuring social unity. America's many sects and today's intellectual climate, which is suspicious of centralized and highly disciplined churches, work against religious cohesion. Education is another avenue to unity. Schools operate not as instruments of state or church but provide social direction out of their own resources of talent and imagination. Over the past half-century, however, developments within education itself have supported certain tendencies toward uniformity and standardization. These tendencies include "ecumenism," professionalization, the influences of accrediting associations and the textbook industry, teacher and student migrations, and equalitarianism.

Ecumenism

The term *ecumenism* ordinarily connotes the interdenominational cooperation of religious organizations and the search for commonalities among the sects—both in matters of creed and of social policy. Ecumenism is an apt term to describe uniformist tendencies among institutions of higher education. Whether such institutions were founded by Protestant denominations, Catholic orders, Jewish congregations, or secular officers, their diversity of origins has given way to a commonality of form, means, and ends. Speaking of the hundreds of colleges founded by Protestants, for example, Jencks and Riesman write, "Diversity led to the establishment of an inordinate number of separate colleges, but ecumenism then led most of these colleges to emphasize their collegiate rather than their sectarian side, seeking faculty and students of all persuasions and becoming annually more like one another."[1] Ecumenism refers here to a process of imitation, adjustment, and accommodation.

The tradition of Judaism, Jencks and Riesman point out, has also failed to maintain an educational form distinct from the generalized "American breed" of college. "What stands out among Jews . . . is the inability of even a relatively cohesive and very education-conscious ethnic group to create a distinctive pattern of higher education differing in any significant respect from all-American norms."[2] The past century shows considerable initial diversity among college founders and diverging beliefs about the means and ends of higher education followed by a subsequent convergence toward a modal type, the significant variance being the differing success of the colleges in matching themselves to that model. Expansions of federal funds for higher education should further discourage what diversity remains.

On one side ecumenism is mere imitativeness dictated by lack of imagination and status-consciousness. On the other it resembles professionalism—probably the chief force behind the ecumenical movement in education.

Professionalization

One hallmark of professions is the professional association. These associations exist to disseminate information, represent the group's interests to government and public opinion, publish journals, discipline the membership, and reinforce the group's sense of identification. They are significantly unlike lodges, clubs, unions, and other mutual-benefit societies. One finds professional associations in education for teachers (by level taught and by field), school and college administrators, private school headmasters, school board members, deans of admissions, and countless other educational personnel categories. The tiny Association of American Universities links the nation's most prestigious and powerful universities, while the National Education Association calls itself the world's largest professional organization. Without formal connections with government, these many organizations are national in their reach.

Professionalization is also advanced by preprofessional training, which tends to reduce diversity of characteristic behavior, beliefs, norms, and preferences within the profession. In subtle ways—through informal communication and imitation—members of the professions of education become more uniform in outlook and action.[3]

[1]Christopher Jencks and David Riesman, *The Academic Revolution,* © 1968 (New York: Doubleday & Co., Inc.), p. 314. See also John S. Brubacher and Willis Rudy, *Higher Education in Transition: A History of American Colleges and Universities 1636– 1968,* rev. ed. (New York: Harper & Row, Publishers, 1968), esp. chap. 18.

[2]Jencks and Riesman, *The Academic Revolution,* p. 320.

[3]In relating an incident at Seaford (Delaware) High School, observers point out that administrators have developed essentially uniform responses in dealing with student protests: Marc Libarle and Tom Seligson, eds., *The High School Revolutionaries* (New York: Random House, Inc., 1970), esp. p. xvii.

Accrediting Associations

In the late nineteenth century, rapid growth of high schools and the absence of centralized educational authority created a dilemma for colleges: without personal knowledge of the adequacy of the secondary education of their applicants, most colleges could not examine all prospective freshmen according to each institution's own standards. The college-bound student also objected to the diversity among institutions in their admission requirements and qualifying procedures. To obtain a more rational and efficient basis for admitting students, various colleges and secondary schools entered into cooperative arrangements to approve *(accredit)* member schools, standardize admission requirements, and otherwise improve the articulation of secondary to higher education. By 1970 over thirteen hundred four-year colleges were accredited in America.

Because most college-bound youth enrolled in colleges near home, these first associations were regional bodies. Today's six regional accrediting associations exemplify that policy of voluntary cooperation in standard setting. When state governments make denial of state funds a penalty for loss of accreditation, however, the voluntary aspect is gone. It is also lost when states tie accreditation to requirements that do not otherwise exist. For example, although only 16 states require teachers in any nonpublic schools to possess regular teaching licenses, over half the states make state accreditation of private schools contingent upon private school staffs' meeting the same specifications as public school teachers.

The ancient guilds took the position that they alone possessed the legitimacy and competence to pass judgment and set standards for the performance of an art or craft. When a modern day accrediting team—composed of individuals representing the member institutions of the association—visits an institution to examine staff qualifications, the adequacy of its libraries and other facilities, and its graduates' performance, and then confers or denies accreditation, it acts in that same spirit of professional expertness. But this form of private regulation may well have defused pressures for governments to step in and impose more rigorous standardization.

The Textbook and Testing Industries

In 1969 a committee on public education reported to the governor of Texas that textbook use occupied 75 percent of a pupil's classroom time and 90 percent of his homework time. The practice of state governments to "adopt" certain books, buy them, distribute them to local districts, and require their use is well known. Particular groups often object to a given selection and condemn the adoption system for imposing a single viewpoint, contravening the local-control principle by centralizing decisions about critical materials, and failing to consider local needs. Challenges to state textbook selection have come mostly from right-wing groups and from those objecting to racist and sexist bias in school readers and history texts.

School books act to reduce diversity even in those states that do not subsidize local schools by distributing free textbooks. The reason is that virtually all textbook publishers seek a national market to recover the high costs of developing a successful product in a highly competitive field. A graded series of elementary school "readers" may cost $20 million to produce; the investment requires both vigorous salesmanship and a noncontroversial content appealing to the widest possible audience of teachers, students, and selection committees across the nation.[4] The demonstrable "sameness" of school books in all American schools (including those operated overseas for military dependents) stems from this need for enormous sales. So also does the bland "tameness" found in college and university texts, where—in the better institutions, at least—each professor selects the books for his classes. Official requirements to use certain texts are not, then, necessary to standardization: the force of the marketplace is quite sufficient. As long as textbooks are relied upon as heavily as they have always been in the United States, they shall be a powerful agent of uniformity.

The formation of the College Entrance Examination Board in 1900 had the explicit aim of standardizing procedures for administering entrance requirements for the eastern colleges. Its history is instructive of important trends in the standardization of American society.[5] When the Scholastic Aptitude Test was first given by the Educational Testing Service (1926), a private corporation, only eight thousand students took it; thirty-five years later, the SAT had 800,000 annual takers. Publication of standardized tests has been important in the lower schools since the 1920s. Nationally available examinations and scholarship competitions (such as the National Merit Scholarships) create informal standards for secondary schools and college admissions, even if they are not formally enforced. Many expect the results of the National Assessment to have a similar effect.

The products of book publishers are sometimes called "software." During the 1960s a new development was expansion into the "hardware" line, or the marriage of software firms (such as Time, Inc.) and hardware producers (like General Electric) to create such new promotions as the General Learning Corporation. While impact cannot yet be detailed, the very high development, manufacturing, and replacement costs of teaching machines and computerized lessons also mandate nationwide marketing. The implications for reducing diversity are obvious.

Teacher Mobility

Teachers are as transient as any group in America. In any year approximately one in ten teachers will change schools—half of these going to other

---

[4]Jeanne Chall, *Learning to Read: The Great Debate* (New York: McGraw-Hill Book Co., 1967); James M. Reid, *An Adventure in Textbooks, 1924–1960* (New York: R. R. Bowker Co., 1969).

[5]Michael S. Schudson, "Organizing the 'Meritocracy': A History of the College Entrance Examination Board," *Harvard Educational Review,* 42 (February 1972):34–69.

districts or other states.[6] Such movement disseminates ideas and practices, and means that teachers (and students) may enter a school nearly anywhere in the United States with little sense of strangeness. Relationships among teachers and administrators, patterns of teacher-student interaction, and role expectations vary little in obvious ways except, perhaps, in the remotest areas or where the student population is isolated from American culture, as in certain Indian reservation schools.[7] It must, nevertheless, be noted that the same surface environment can obscure important differences in the ways in which rules are interpreted, how the achievement standards are accepted, the amount of time spent on instruction as compared to discipline, and other factors that appear to vary consistently among schools, according to the social class of the student body.

Another consequence of teacher mobility is lessened loyalty to the local institution. Alvin Gouldner has categorized college faculty into two primary types: "locals" and "cosmopolitans."[8] "Locals" identify with the institution in which they teach, internalize its traditions, and involve themselves deeply in its activities. "Cosmopolitans" identify with the disciplines in which they teach and do research, reaching outward to the national scientific and scholarly organizations representing their fields; frequently away from their campuses, the career attachments of cosmopolitans to their institutions are ordinarily minimal, lessening their involvements in local traditions and the surrounding community. While locals preserve institutional separateness and diversity, cosmopolitans promote uniformity.

Student Migrations

America was settled by the movements of masses of people, and rootlessness continues to shape its culture. Americans move for many tangible reasons and generally accept the intangible presumption that any change (of residence, jobs, cars, mates) will likely be "a change for the better." (Hence two opposite responses to racial desegregation pressures—flight to the suburbs and "busing"—are both much in the American tradition.)

Students in elementary and secondary schools normally move because their

[6]The younger, less-experienced, less well-paid, married, elementary school, and female teachers are the more likely to move: "Teacher Mobility and Loss," *NEA Research Bulletin,* 46 (December 1968):118–26. See chap. 6 for a fuller discussion. The *NEA Research Bulletin,* which ceased publication in 1973, has been the most regular source for national and state school statistics of this sort.

[7]The author once taught in an American-run private school in Latin America whose teachers and students were drawn from every section of the United States. A school handbook, prepared for parents, stated that, at this school, "Your child will receive an American education." The director reported that *no* parent or teacher had ever asked him the meaning of "an American education." What adjustments teachers and students had to make were to the climate, the outside-school culture, and (to a lesser extent) to the sizable (40 percent) non–North American segment of the student body; adjustments to curricula, materials, roles, and "social climate" were not necessary.

[8]Alvin W. Gouldner, "Cosmopolitans and Locals: Toward an Analysis of Latent Social Roles," *Administrative Science Quarterly,* 2 (December 1957):281–306; 2 (March 1958):444–80.

parents choose to relocate. Since most migrants belong to the 15–34 age group, hundreds of thousands of parents cause their offspring to become agents of change, moving schools in the direction of uniform expectations, aspirations, and school culture. Such obvious accommodations as statewide mandated curricula and state-adopted textbooks, record-keeping systems, transcripts, and allowances for transferred credits may pale beside less consciously made accommodations. Student migrations would have even greater effect if it were not for the fact that social class factors condition relocations. Poor children usually move to new neighborhoods and schools of relatively low status, and middle-class children usually move to middle-class environments. Hence, while movement may greatly affect the experiences of individual children, it seldom appreciably alters relative class status—although enough movement, especially in transitional urban neighborhoods, may change a school's population and school culture very quickly.

The campus protest movement of the 1960s illustrates the potential impact of migrating students upon higher education. Beginning with Berkeley, where out-of-state students played a disproportionate role among the activist supporters of the "free speech movement," transfer students repeatedly acted as live carriers of ideas and tactics from campus to campus—although the mass media were undoubtedly even more potent at spreading student protest. Apart from political activity, migrating students probably have contributed significantly toward the homogenization of the prestigious colleges and universities, especially their graduate divisions—all of which are extralocal institutions drawing students from across the nation and the world. Like their counterparts on the faculty, these student cosmopolitans are instruments of uniformity.

The Ideal of Equality

"Equality" recently has implied equal treatment of the races. Current evidence shows, however, that variations in educational quality between regions often exceed those between predominantly white and predominantly black schools. Some educators and public figures have long sought to remedy such inequities in the quantity and quality of schooling available to American children. Educational disparities within cities were in part responsible for the post–Civil War movement to repeal the ward system of school boards. Rural-urban inequities worried political and educational reformers from the Populist through the Progressive eras. The effect of the Depression was to obliterate geographical distinctions; all schools became agencies of government responsible for the welfare of all the people.[9] In recent years much has been learned about whole groups of children, such as children of migrant workers, or handicapped children, actually excluded from schools.[10]

[9]Henry J. Perkinson, *The Imperfect Panacea: American Faith in Education, 1865–1965* (New York: Random House, Inc., 1968), esp. pp. 209–10.

[10]In Boston children of cultural minorities, the handicapped, pregnant girls, or others who were forced out or allowed to be absent from school numbered between 4,000 and 10,700: Task Force on Children Out of School, *The Way We Go to School: The Exclusion of Children in Boston* (Boston: Beacon Press, 1971).

Federal activity in public education has been directed toward raising the minimum standards of quality, and reducing the great inequities of educational opportunity caused by decentralization and diversity. Philanthropic foundations have underwritten local attempts to raise quality, have matched local expenditures in attempts of schools to upgrade themselves, and have supported scholarships for the poor. Such private and governmental energies have borne some fruit. The 1960s showed the greatest percentage increase in college enrollments to be among freshmen from families in the nation's bottom quarter on the income scale.[11] Although equality need not mean "sameness," the drive to eliminate inequities in education, when successful, also promotes uniformity.

TENDENCIES TOWARD DIVERSITY

The years of peak immigration to America lasted from 1900 to 1913. Many then thought of the American experience as a "melting pot" that reduced difference to some unique American type. But a few articulate writers professed an alternative ideal: cultural pluralism. They saw American society as an assemblage of diverse cultures existing as harmoniously together as the rich hues and contrasting patterns of an oriental rug. Philosopher Horace Kallen especially disputed the presumption that the schools' function was to transmit a fixed, consensual cultural tradition.

Never a popular movement, cultural pluralism had a fitful existence and seemed doomed to extinction. The idea, if not the language, has been revived with the Afro-American crusade, the fad of American Indian styles that first appeared among the hippies, and the reassertion of Latin cultural themes in Mexican-American communities. The youth of these minorities created a "Third World" movement and argued for ethnic studies departments in high schools and colleges. While many Third Worlders wish most for the articles of middle-class, WASP culture, others profess disdain for prevailing majoritarian values, styles, and artifacts—what they call the "plastic" world.

The influence of Third World communities was extended by those affluent, white college protesters whom Edward Sampson calls the "Fourth Worlders"[12] who try to emulate the music, dress, expressions, and other styles they think characteristic of blacks, American Indians, or Chicanos. Where many of the Third Worlders argue for diversity and accountability through neighborhood control of the public schools, many of the Fourth Worlders espouse alternative, or "free," schools.

We cannot yet measure the effect of these new drives for diversity. In the meantime one major cause of whatever diversity exists among American

[11]United States Office of Education study, reported in *The Chronicle of Higher Education*, 3 (March 10, 1969):1–8.

[12]Edward E. Sampson, "A Modern Sisyphus Goes to College." Paper read before the American Psychological Association, San Francisco, September 1968.

schools seems sure to remain: differences in ability to pay for education. Compared to this factor, local wishes and prejudices, the educational level of the community, the imagination and talent of the staff or the school board, the intensity of public interest, and all other imaginable causes shrink in importance.

Taxes supporting local elementary and secondary schools come overwhelmingly from assessments upon real property within the school district. The presence of flourishing businesses and industries and high value residential property permits a low tax rate. Such a locality garners more revenue for schools than a neighboring district without such a tax base, or one having many more children to educate. In 1972 wealthy Locust Valley, New York, spent $1,722 per child in school, on a tax rate of $22.70 per $1,000 of property valuation; neighboring blue-collar Levittown could spend only $955 per child, although taxing itself at the much higher rate of $35.60 per $1,000. Districts having more "problem" children to educate encounter higher costs. Thus, New York City alone has 74 percent of the state's children on Aid to Families with Dependent Children ("welfare") and 65 percent of those scoring two or more years below grade level on statewide achievement tests.[13] Traditional systems of school support that rely upon local property taxation have been widely challenged in the courts.[14]

Aside from securing judicial remedies, practical difficulties beset financially weak school districts. If a poorer district increases its tax rate to raise more revenue it can have bad effects: high rates encourage businesses and residents to move away or to avoid improving their property and discourage incomers. In recent years suburban property values have grown two and a half times faster than city values (and six times faster in the Midwest). If cities impose steadily higher rates on these lower property values, a taxpayers' revolt is inevitable; voters will repel the rate increases and turn the offending school board out of office. Another problem is that state equalization funds do not equalize district resources. Many equalization formulas are outdated, and the greater political influence of high-income communities prevents true dollar equalization through an additional taxing of the rich to help the poor.[15]

[13]Joel S. Berke, Robert J. Goettel, and Ralph Andrew, "Equity in Financing New York City's Schools: The Impact of Local, State, and Federal Policy." Unpublished paper: "Maxwell School Reports to its New York Alumni," New York City, October 28, 1971, p. 18.

[14]See Charles Benson and Thomas A. Shannon, *Schools Without Property Taxes: Hope or Illusion?* (Bloomington, Ind.: Phi Delta Kappa Educational Foundation, 1972). An accessible reprinting of *Serrano* v. *Priest* (1971) is found in *Harvard Educational Review*, 41 (November 1971):501–34. The five to four decision of the justices of the United States Supreme Court in *Rodriguez,* handed down on March 21, 1973, left the issue in doubt. The decision was both close and narrowly based, i.e., leaving it to state legislatures and not to itself to reform school-finance laws that even the majority of justices declared badly in need of change.

[15]Suburban middle-class districts with relatively high per capita income, but lacking industry, sometimes are classified as "low-wealth" districts and receive more "compensatory" state funds than do urban industrialized areas. In 1968–69 the suburban Mt. Diablo (California) Unified School District received 49.8 percent of its operating funds

While a decentralized structure allows differing economic resources to be reflected in school spending, such diversity is also possible in a functionally centralized system. The Soviet Union, for example, does not support schools equally.[16] Its famed boarding schools may cost seven times the sum that operates regular schools. Moreover, while salary schedules are uniform throughout, the simple concentration of younger and less experienced teachers in the remoter regions automatically reduces expenditures there, allowing for the kind of rural-urban diversity in spending often found in the United States. A second, and stupefying, consideration for planners and policy makers is that differences among schools in quality, as measured by dollar inequities, are not significantly related to differences in student achievement— at least not according to present evidence. An inability to prove a *causal* relationship between spending level and pupil-achievement level will not, however, lessen struggles to attain dollar equalization: in this money-conscious society, the conviction remains that, in education as elsewhere, "you get what you pay for."

The Dilemma of the Cities

America's city schools are supported well above the national average; the typical teacher's or administrator's salary is above the norm,[17] such auxiliary personnel as remedial-reading specialists, counselors, and full-time librarians are more common, and materials are more likely to be free to students. The explanation is both historical and sociopedagogical: cities have always led in education, and the dense populations of cities concentrate and expose problems, causing educational costs to rise accordingly. The one deaf or psychotic child in a small town must be ignored educationally or schooled with normal children; in large cities the numbers of such children create

---

from the state; the figure for the urban, heavily black Richmond district was 34.1 percent: Lillian B. Rubin, *Busing and Backlash* (Berkeley: University of California Press, 1972), p. 31n. Federal aid, which tends to favor cities having concentrations of poor people, cannot compensate for the suburban advantage coming from state aid formulas. Despite massive infusions of federal aid to Detroit schools from 1955 to 1970, the share of costs paid by the local property tax declined only from 52.8 percent to 51.1 percent. See Joel S. Berke and James A. Kelly, "The Financial Aspects of Equality of Educational Opportunity," testimony presented to the Senate Select Committee on Equal Educational Opportunity, September 22, 1971 (mimeo); Select Committee on Equal Educational Opportunity, United States Senate, *Federal Aid to Public Education: Who Benefits?* (Washington, D.C.: U.S. Government Printing Office, April 1971), 92nd Congress, First Session, Committee Print; David K. Cohen, "The Economics of Inequality," *Saturday Review* (April 19, 1969):64–65, 76–79; John E. Coons et al., *Private Wealth and Public Education* (Cambridge, Mass.: Harvard University Press, 1971); Arthur E. Wise, *Rich Schools, Poor Schools* (Chicago: University of Chicago Press, 1968).

[16]Herbert C. Rudman, *The School and State in the USSR* (New York: Macmillan, 1969), p. 69.

[17]In levels of *maximum* teachers' salaries suburban systems located adjacent to large metropolitan areas rank first: "High Scheduled Salaries, 1967–1968," *NEA Research Bulletin,* 45 (December 1967):99–102.

expensive special classes staffed by costly specialists. Efforts to reach and teach the problem learner, to retain the potential dropout, to compensate for deficient or different preschool experiences, and to achieve racial desegregation disproportionately increase educational costs. Schools, unlike eggs or pencils, are not cheaper by the dozen. And for schools and other public services, the cities have assumed heavy tax rates, often one and a half to two times the rate of their suburbs. Only Providence and Houston, of the nation's largest cities, paid less in taxes as a percentage of personal income than did their suburbs. Baltimore's figure was 9.1 percent versus 4.4 percent for its non-urban environs; Columbus, Ohio, 4.8 percent versus 3.9 percent; Denver, 6.5 percent versus 5.0 percent. The financial desperation of most cities stems from population changes.

Since World War II, more than twenty million poor people have migrated into central cities. Many of these poor are black. The single-decade increase in Detroit's public schools during the 1960s was from 46 to 64 percent black enrollment; the cost to local taxpayers for public schools increased by 450 percent in the quarter-century following World War II, during which time Detroit's population was declining. Chicago school officials estimated that 4⅔ city blocks changed each week from primarily white to black residents. Many of the poor are white, however; reports for Chicago indicate that there are three times more white than black residents whose income qualifies them for public housing.[18] In 1970 more than 10 percent of big-city residents required welfare assistance.

Progressive giving of more city land to the housing and service needs of the poor further depresses the tax base. Industrial establishments compound the problem when they depart the cities. The 1929 to 1959 decline in urban manufacturing employment for 12 large cities ranged from 49 percent to 66 percent. Increases in deteriorated housing, rundown commercial establishments, and industrial relocation erode the tax base, even while land values remain high. Again Chicago is a dramatic example: in 1966 in one-third of the city's total land area, one-half or more of the school children lived in public housing; in lieu of property taxes, the city contributed to the schools $10 per child, although school tax contributions in other areas of the city approached $600 per child.[19] The city must also pay for its cultural advantages with lost tax revenue, as the case of Boston illustrates. Forty-five percent of city land is occupied or owned by tax-exempt churches, hospitals, private schools, universities, museums, and parks—forcing the city to levy one of the nation's highest tax rates upon its remaining real estate.[20]

[18]"The Group Life Report: National Project on Ethnic America" (New York: American Jewish Committee), No. 2 (January 1972):6.

[19]Benjamin C. Willis, *Social Problems in Public School Administration* (Pittsburgh: University of Pittsburgh Press, 1967), pp. 20–21.

[20]Peter Schrag, *Village School Downtown: Politics and Education, A Boston Report* (Boston: Beacon Press, 1967), p. 46. Estimations are that one-third of all potentially taxable land in the nation receives some form of tax exemption; much of this land is in

School buildings in the central city are frequently antiquated, overcrowded, and unsafe. The problem of adequate educational facilities is not unique to the cities, of course. Thousands of communities required one or more additional schools every few years since 1945, as the school-age population swelled. Scottsdale, Arizona, passed 29 bond issues between 1950 and 1970 to finance school construction. Milwaukee increased its school buildings from 97 in 1950 to 147 in 1965—a 65 percent increase—while school enrollments were growing by 50 percent. The cities have the additional problem of replacing obsolete buildings at extravagant cost for construction and land ($100,000 per acre in Detroit, compared to $6,000 per acre in its suburbs), compounded by the explosive social and political problems that come with displacing residents and relocating youngsters. Between 1945 and 1965 New York City added 261 new schools, constructed additions to 102 others, and upgraded 165.[21] A newer city, like Los Angeles, has less to replace, but Los Angeles had to add school facilities at a cost of $60 million annually before declining birth rates and less in-migration eased the problem.

Capital construction usually proceeds with revenue from school bonds, and the voters had been cooperative in a way that has aroused the envy of those seeking municipal bonds to build or remodel other public facilities. During the years 1957–64, nearly three-quarters of school district indebtedness measures passed.[22] More recently, however, the national success rate has fluctuated around the 50 percent figure. In fiscal 1973, the voters rejected 90.5 percent of school bond issues in Washington State and 83 percent in Kansas.

Cities are more likely to have older, tenured teachers; this raises instructional costs, since pay scales are based partly on experience. Moreover, teacher unions are strongest in the cities, and their militancy in demanding better pay, paid preparation time, the cost of aides and other assistance, and smaller classes drives up urban educational costs. So does the higher cost of school secretarial, janitorial, and maintenance services. Given the erratic fluctuations in federal school aid—from 1965 to 1968, nearly half the metropolitan

---

the cities. Albany and Ithaca, New York, lose half their potential tax revenue by exemptions; Washington, D.C., Pittsburgh, New York City, and Montpelier, Vermont, lose one-third: Alfred Balk, *The Free List* (New York: Russell Sage Foundation, 1971). The trend is upward as retirement homes and veterans' exemptions have increased exempted properties.

For evidence of diversity of tax rates among 122 American cities of 100,000 population or more (1960 census), see "Property Taxes and the Schools," *NEA Research Bulletin,* 46 (October 1968):92–95. Cf. John Callahan, *Metropolitan Disparities: A Second Reading* (Washington, D.C.: Advisory Commission on Intergovernmental Relations, January 1970).

[21]George B. Brain, "Pressures on the Urban School," *The Schoolhouse in the City,* ed. Alvin Toffler (New York: Praeger Publishers, Inc., 1968), p. 41.

[22]U. S. Department of Health, Education, and Welfare, *American Education* (Washington, D.C.: U.S. Government Printing Office, 1965), p. 20. The Department of Health, Education, and Welfare publishes summaries and detailed reports in a regular series, "Bond Sales for Public School Purposes."

areas received less in the last year than earlier in the period—planning is made a shambles.

No more telling example of the bleak financial prospects for urban education exists than Newark, New Jersey. A governor's investigative committee concluded that Newark's school system was in an "advanced state of decay," threatening the educational well-being of 76,000 students. Newark schools were already $250 million in arrears in capital construction needs and had reached the legal bonding limit. Moreover, 30 of its 75 buildings predated 1900 and 44 more were built before 1918; these old facilities were also beset by overcrowding, 70 percent of the elementary schools functioning at 101 to 151 percent of capacity.[23]

Schools in the Suburbs

Suburbs have become increasingly popular since World War II. Buying a house in the suburbs has become a sign of "making it." Veterans' benefits of no-money-down mortgages and general prosperity encouraged millions of former city renters to become suburban home owners, far from their places of work.

The social scientists studying "Crestwood Heights," a typical suburb, commented upon the "massive centrality" of the schools—both because of the impressive school buildings and because the schools were so important to the community. One explanation is financial: compared with the cities, suburbs are not as burdened to support such nonschool services as public health, public housing, and welfare; moreover, these services cost more in the cities. Suburbs consequently can spend a higher proportion of their resources for education. A 1967 project of the United States Office of Education reported that cities spend 65 percent of their public expenditures on nonschool needs and 35 percent on education; the proportions are reversed in the suburbs.[24]

Such an educationally renowned suburb as New Trier, Illinois, spent over $1,000 per school child in 1961, nearly twice the nonsuburban national average. But there are suburban communities that do *not* conform to the suburban stereotype of life-style and education. These are blue-collar tracts, peopled by teamsters and manufacturing workers, that have modest and rather crowded homes. The educational background of these persons' parents is usually of high-school level. Obviously, diversity exists within the suburban

[23]Each year 28 percent of Newark students were leaving for parochial or suburban schools, their places taken by black migrants from the South or Puerto Ricans abandoning New York City: Governor's Select Commission on Civil Disorder, *Report for Action* (Trenton, N.J., February 1968). For a more general account of population trends, see D. N. Alloway and Francesco Cordasco, *Minorities and the American City* (New York: David McKay Co., Inc., 1970).

[24]These are averages; the variance between particular communities is often greater, *viz.* nonmetropolitan Pennsylvania towns spent 22 percent of local tax funds for nonschool purposes, when Philadelphia spent 58 percent: Harold Howe, "The City as Teacher," in *The Schoolhouse in the City,* ed. Toffler, p. 13.

type.[25] Nevertheless, the suburbs as a type contribute disproportionately to the nation's college population. According to one survey, 5,000 of America's 26,500 high schools produce 82 percent of all college students. Many parents resolutely explain a move to the suburbs (or transfer to a nonpublic school) as meaning a better educational opportunity for their children.

THE DIMENSIONS OF DIVERSITY IN EDUCATION

No unit of education is too small for diversity. It exists within a single individual whose performance varies from task to task, within a class, and between classrooms in a single school. There is often significant diversity within a school district; indeed, the early campaigns against de facto racial segregation concentrated upon such diversity. The contrast in reading achievement scores of the three junior high schools in one small city provides an example. The city-wide average of reading achievement was at the eighty-eighth percentile (i.e., these eighth-graders made scores higher than 88 percent of a national sample of other students tested); what this average concealed is that one school's average was at the ninety-ninth percentile, one was at the seventy-ninth, and the third school ranked at the sixteenth percentile. Neighboring school districts vary in annual expenditures per student. In 1964, for example, Cleveland spent $450 per student and Shaker Heights spent $850; in 1967 Oakland spent $860 and Berkeley spent $1,460. Because each state is constitutionally sovereign, and because most of the data are reported by states or by regions, we will focus upon diversity as manifested in comparisons of state statistics.

Diversity in Structures and Administrative Units

Mississippi's chief statewide policy agency for public education has 3 members; Ohio's State Board of Education has 23 (one for each congressional district). There is also variation among the states as to the number of local school districts that receive delegation of state powers. Such obvious state characteristics as the relative proportion of rural to urban dwellers, total population or total area, or years of statehood do not explain the great differences in the number of school districts. As the decade of the 1970s began, the range extended from Hawaii's 1 statewide district to Nebraska's 1,461 districts.

[25]A blue-collar suburb, "Milgrim," is one of the school communities studied in Carl Nordstrom et al., *Society's Children* (New York: Random House, Inc., 1967). This book describes its high school as having high aspirations for its students; "a modern, progress-oriented, college-focused" institution, in this case one at odds with the values of its community. See also "Suburbia: The New American Plurality," *Time* (March 15, 1971):14–20.

Diversity in Expenditures

One index of diversity is *state* support of public school costs; as indicated above (chapter 1, table 2), the regions vary considerably. Variations among states are greater still: Delaware, North Carolina, New Mexico, and Hawaii each provided for over 70 percent of costs in 1970, but Massachusetts, Nebraska, South Dakota, and New Hampshire averaged under 21 percent.[26]

Ranges of spending per pupil are greater within states than are the averages between states; in even the low-expenditure states some localities spend above the national average. In 1971 the between-states range extended from $438 in Alabama to $1,237 in New York; but the range within Texas was from $243 per pupil to $2,087 per pupil. Here are typical ranges from other states: Arizona, $436 to $2,223; Missouri, $213 to $1,699; Idaho, $474 to $1,763; Florida, $593 to $1,036; Vermont, $357 to $1,517; and Tennessee, $315 to $700.

Despite these great intrastate variations, interstate diversity has been important in enlisting federal aid. Title I of the Elementary and Secondary Education Act (ESEA) apportions federal funds to a state according to its percentage of children certified as coming from families earning under $2,000 or on welfare. In 1965–66 Title I contributions were 15 percent of Mississippi's education budget (where 40 percent of all school children qualified), 6.5 percent of Texas's school budget (where 16 percent of school children were still in poverty), and 2 percent of California's school budget (8 percent eligible children).[27]

Eliminating the most unrepresentative districts often leaves a variation in school spending of *four to one*. While spending figures change each year, diversity may be illustrated by the statistics of any given year. During 1966–67, national spending averaged $564 per pupil. With the exception of Alaska, whose cost of living differential distorts its standing, New York State ranked first, at $912 per pupil, and Mississippi ranked last, at $315—a difference of nearly three to one.

If we relate school spending to state income it is possible to determine which states make a greater (or lesser) educational effort by giving schools

[26]In 1920 the national average for state government support was about 14 percent of total costs; by 1955 it reached 37 percent, near the present figure. The range in 1955 was as great as now: Delaware and New Mexico contributed 80 percent of school operating funds; Nebraska and New Hampshire, under 10 percent. For 1970 rankings see *Estimates of School Statistics, 1969–70* and *Rankings of the States* (Washington, D.C.: National Education Association, 1969 and 1970).

[27]Francis Keppel, *The Necessary Revolution in American Education* (New York: Harper & Row, Inc., 1966), p. 73. Expenditures per pupil may be influenced by many factors. In some large cities school operating costs may be raised by the hiring of numerous specialists—"support personnel"; in prosperous communities costs per pupil may rise as a result of very small class size or above-average teacher salaries; in such largely rural states as Montana costs rise as a result of low enrollments in small towns and the high costs of transporting children from many low-density areas to consolidated schools.

TABLE 4   Educational effort in the prosperous states

State	Income Rank[a]	School Expenditure Rank (as Percent of State Income)
Connecticut	1	37
Illinois	4	43
New York	5	15
California	6	10
Massachusetts	9	49

[a]Per capita income, U.S. Department of Commerce, 1965
Source: Adapted from data in *NEA Research Bulletin,* 45 (March 1967): 10, 31

a higher (or lower) proportion of their total resources. In 1965 Connecticut ranked first in per capita personal income, with $3,401, but ranked thirty-seventh in school expenditures *as a percent of its total income.* Mississippi, the nation's poorest state (a 1965 per capita income of $1,608), ranked twentieth in expenditure effort. Clearly, wealthy Connecticut makes a *lesser* sacrifice for public schooling than does poorer Mississippi; Connecticut's prosperity nevertheless allows it to outspend most other states. The wealthier states can all make this smaller effort (see table 4), although they differ among themselves in discrepancy between income rankings and expenditure rankings.[28] Proposals to dispense expanded federal school aid to the states as a proportion of the tax amounts collected by each state would not bring equalization; the wealthier states would receive disproportionately larger shares, widening the present fiscal gaps in school spending between the states.

Outside the South, the conventional view is that the poverty afflicting Southern education reflects insufficient effort and the uneconomical mainte-nance of racially separate school systems. Yet, as table 5 shows, every state in the South (except Kentucky) ranks higher in the percentage of its income devoted to education than it ranks in available income. As for the existence of segregated systems, the important effect has been less economic than social and psychological. Uneconomical duplication and waste would result only if the two school systems had been equal, and if both white and black schools were located in all communities. In fact, white schools have historically received more funds than black schools; the white schools were as good as they were only because black schools were as bad as they were. If Southern

[28]Some of the same complexities apply in the support of public higher education. In 1970, for example, two states of roughly equal income (each about 11 percent of the nation's total)—California and New York—were expected to spend considerably differ-ent sums; California spent $1,867 million for current operating expenses and $676 mil-lion for capital construction; New York spent $643 million and $325 million on current and capital outlays, respectively. This difference exists despite constricting of California spending because of a hostile state administration and, in New York, a massive expan-sion program for public higher education. Neither of these wealthy states made the effort to support higher education of the mountain states that depend almost entirely on *public* higher education: "The University as a Major Influence in the State" (Berkeley: Univer-sity of California, 1967), pp. 6–7.

TABLE 5   Educational effort in the poorer states

State	Income Rank[a]	School Expenditure Rank (as Percent of State Income)
Tennessee	46	37[b]
Alabama	47	33
South Carolina	48	20[b]
Arkansas	49	37[b]
Mississippi	50	20[b]

[a]Per capita income, U.S. Department of Commerce, 1965.
[b]Tied in rankings.
Source: Adapted from data in *NEA Research Bulletin,* 45 (March 1967): 10, 31.

white children have received an inferior education, it has not been because of equal sharing of resources with black children. Moreover, white and black residents are not evenly distributed geographically. Instead, the important causes of underfinanced schools in the South are its concentration of the nation's lowest-income states, a higher-than-average ratio of children per adult wage earner, and an unfavorable out-migration that depletes these states of some of their better-educated, higher-earning residents.

Turning again to public school expenditures as a percent of state income (the United States average being 4.3 percent), Utah made the greatest effort, allotting public schooling 6.4 percent of total income; Massachusetts and Rhode Island ranked lowest, at 2.9 percent. Utah's standing appears due to high educational consciousness where Mormon influence has been politically strong. The case of the two lowest-ranking states demonstrates other sociopolitical factors. First, New England stands low in state school funding to supplement locally-raised resources. Local effort has been unable to compensate for a low level of state participation in financing, especially given the presence of a second element: the long and vigorous tradition of elite private schooling and the high proportions of school children enrolled in Catholic schools. Strong nonpublic schools appear to depress interest and effort in supporting public education, at least when statewide spending analyses are made.

Diversity in Class Size

Because teacher salaries constitute the largest item in school budgets, a favorite economy measure is to increase class size; when voters disapprove school bonds that would add classrooms, class size goes up further. While consistently small classes (under 20 pupils) are not typical of even prosperous districts, class size is distinctly related to district financial status.

Although many private schools stress small classes, the very large classes (50 or 60 students) once found in church-operated schools caused the average nonpublic school class to enroll 32.3 pupils in 1966; the mean public school class in the United States was 24.9. (In 1970 the class size in the parochial schools of San Bernardino, California, was 29, down from 38 in 1964; in the local public schools, it was 25.3, down from 27.6.) Regional variations in teacher-pupil ratios ranged in 1966 from the Northwest, which had 12 percent of its pupils in classes over 36, to the Southeast, where that proportion was 24 percent. A teacher in Albuquerque could expect one more pupil than the Detroit teacher, two more than found in the typical classroom in Kansas City or Dubuque, three more than in Duluth, Milwaukee, or Pueblo, Colorado—and six more than in Green Bay, Wisconsin.[29]

Student complaints of excessive class size are commonplace. Everyone has heard that impersonal lectures to mass student audiences contribute to alienation on college campuses, and the chief satisfaction of students in many independent schools is that they receive more personal attention. Teachers are, if anything, even more preoccupied with class size. A 1967 poll by one statewide teacher association reported that large classes disturb teachers more than does any other single irritant—well ahead of inadequate teaching materials, district fiscal problems, pressure group interference, excessive clerical duties, or pupil disrespect. A 1968 survey undertaken by the National Educational Association found over two-thirds of American teachers dissatisfied with their own class size. That several generations of researchers have failed to establish consistent relationships between class size and student achievement is immaterial: as long as students, teachers, and parents feel that class size adversely affects performance and well-being, large classes will be decried.

The *Urban Education Task Force Report* identified patterns of diversity in class size favoring suburban communities over their central cities: when Chicago's average class size was 28, Evanston's was 18; Detroit 31, Grosse Pointe 22; Philadelphia 27, Lower Merion 20; St. Louis 30, University City 22. Even the unusually low urban figure of 20 in New York City (1970) was above suburban Great Neck's 16-student average.

Diversity in Providing Instructional Aids and Services

Also a function of differing abilities to pay are variations in the provision of free textbooks and special services to pupils and teachers. Even where "tradition" seems to explain variation, the root cause often rests in the soil of relative poverty and its accompaniment, fiscal conservatism.

Aids and services provided by the nation's largest school districts in the late 1960s varied greatly. Los Angeles and San Diego provided all books, materials, laboratory supplies, and field trips free to all pupils through grade 12. Chicago furnished only textbooks and home economics supplies. Indiana-

---

[29]Martin A. Larson, *When Parochial Schools Close: A Study in Educational Financing* (Washington, D.C.: Robert B. Luce, Inc., 1972).

polis had a "means test," distributing free textbooks and materials only to needy pupils. Milwaukee charged high school pupils for books and supplies. Special provisions for mentally, physically, or emotionally exceptional children are far commoner in urban districts and in wealthier districts, as are science consultants, remedial-reading specialists, school librarians, and other auxiliary staff. Data in the Coleman Report indicate that there were language laboratories for 48 percent of black and 72 percent of white high school students in the urban South in 1965; in the urban Far West the comparable figures were 95 percent and 80 percent respectively. While such early-childhood programs as Head Start were highlighted for promoting school success for the underprivileged preschooler, nearly one child in three in America lived in a district without public school kindergartens—and the voters of the university town of Eugene, Oregon, rejected taxes to pay for kindergartens by a three-to-one margin.

Diversity Concerning Teachers

Salaries are the largest part of functional expenses for schools. Diversity begins with the enactment of minimum salary laws. In 1965 only 31 states possessed a minimum salary standard for qualified, licensed public school teachers. Mean salaries in America's largest districts were nearly 20 percent above the national average in 1970. Selected suburban districts surpass the cities, especially in setting higher maximum salaries.

TABLE 6 Variations in professional salaries, by regions[a]

Region	Technical Fields	Nontechnical Fields
East	100.0	101.3
Midwest	100.9	102.0
Southeast	97.8	101.7
Southwest	99.5	94.0
West	101.8	100.4

[a]Mean salary for all male college graduates employed: 100 (index number)
Source: *NEA Research Bulletin*, 40 (December 1962): 101.

In 1967—when the average American public school teacher earned $6,905 —the range by state (except Alaska) extended from California's $8,450 to Mississippi's $4,650; such diversity also characterizes the private school sector.[30] While small cost-of-living differences do exist between regions, regional variations in salaries have virtually disappeared in all professional fields—except teaching. Table 6 reports these small occupational variations,

[30]Otto F. Kraushaar, *American Nonpublic Schools* (Baltimore: The Johns Hopkins University Press, 1972).

TABLE 7   Variations in teaching salaries, by regions and decades[a]

School Year	Highest-Paying Region (Far West)	Lowest-Paying Region (Southeast)
1939–40	144.4	57.1
1949–50	124.8	74.6
1959–60	122.8	79.6

[a]Mean salary for all male college graduates employed: 100 (index number)
Source: Adapted from data in *NEA Research Bulletin 40*, December 1962): 103.

in contrast to the marked salary diversity in teaching, shown in Table 7; both tables use 100.00 as an index number representing the average salary of all male college graduates. The fiscal dependence of public education upon unequal local property resources accentuates and perpetuates this diversity.

The typical salary schedule for teachers is based upon professional preparation and years of classroom experience. Secondary school teachers, who traditionally possess more education and remain longer in teaching, consistently earn more, even in unified districts having a single salary scale covering both elementary and secondary teachers. Male teachers earn more than their female counterparts for the same reason, men being twice as likely to have a master's degree than women, and proportionately more men than women teachers intend to make education a career.

Eighty-five percent of the nation's public school teachers in 1960 possessed a college degree; in 1966 the figure was 93 percent. The 1966 average concealed, however, an astonishing range: from 95 percent in Oklahoma to 16.7 percent in North Dakota. Advanced degrees are more common among teachers in the high-ranking states, like Oklahoma. They are also prominent in Indiana, whose state universities have awarded hundreds of advanced education degrees, and in Hawaii, which imports teachers with the highest educational qualifications. The private school sector also has diversity. While only 4 percent of independent school teachers lacked the bachelor's degree in 1970, this figure was much higher in the church-run schools: 13 percent in Catholic, 14 percent in Protestant, and 21 percent in Jewish schools, where noncollegiate rabbinical training is important in teacher qualifications. Thus the origins of diversity in teacher preparation are multifaceted.

Diversity Characterizing Students

The student bodies of schools are also different, and pupil variations subtly affect the practices of their teachers. Some Long Island and suburban Chicago public high schools graduate virtually 100 percent of their students, and 95–98 percent enter college. Certain big-city and rural high schools graduate 40–50 percent, and only 5 percent pursue further schooling. Even among the largest cities there is diversity. New York City has nearly twice Los Angeles's 26 percent dropout rate. A high-achievement school culture positively affects even students from disadvantaged backgrounds, encouraging more to attend local colleges than would normally be expected. Conversely, high-potential students seem to be negatively influenced by enrollment in low-achievement schools, although the negative effect is not as strong as the positive one.

One index of educational functioning is a school's "holding power." In 1965 71 percent of American students who began the ninth grade remained to graduate. Here, too, there is diversity: Wisconsin graduated 88 percent, Georgia 57 percent. By ethnic background, too, there is diversity: in the American Southwest, 86 percent of white students graduate from high school, but only 60 percent of Mexican-American youth do. The educational level of a state's total population is a long-term consequence of its schools' holding power. The average adult American shows a steady rise in the number of years of schooling completed, from 8.4 years in 1940 to 10.6 years in 1960 and 12.2 years in 1970. The spread in 1960 was, however, a significant three and a half years when South Carolina's average (8.7 years) was compared to Utah's (12.2 years).

Although functional literacy and years of schooling are but loosely related, failure rates on Selective Service literacy tests parallel state dropout statistics. From 1958 to 1965 armed forces inductees from Mississippi failed at the rate of 57 percent; failures from Washington State averaged 6 percent. Statistical analysis by race shows dramatic correlations with state educational standings. Blacks schooled in Mississippi failed at an 80 percent rate, blacks from California at 49 percent, and blacks from Washington State at 25 percent; whites from Mississippi failed at a 53 percent rate, California whites, 17 percent. General adult illiteracy data show a range from Utah's 3.3 percent to Louisiana's 24.9 percent illiterate. Still, in the last analysis, it appears that individual variations within any one school in pupil achievement can show a larger range than is found in school to school, state to state, or region to region comparisons—or when comparing students of different ethnic or racial backgrounds.

Such achievement measures as college-bound figures, dropout rates, or test scores are the easiest student data to assemble. Information about other characteristics of student bodies—their morale, alienation, self-confidence, social attitudes, independence—is scarce and ill-organized. What David Boroff calls the "vibrant reality of a particular college" is largely the product of its student body, many of whose subtle but crucial characteristics are not adequately measured by social and behavioral scientists.[31] Nevertheless, these characteristics could prove ultimately to be more important to the quality of American life and to the national future than the traditional achievement measures. We must assume that here, too, there is diversity aplenty.

[31]David Boroff, *Campus U.S.A.: Portraits of American Colleges in Action* (New York: Harper & Row, Publishers, 1958), p. x.

THE CASE OF HIGHER EDUCATION

In most of the world the sector of higher education remains small, selective, and homogeneous. Consequently, the remaining diversity of American higher education, of its almost three thousand colleges and universities, is most astounding to non-Americans. The fast-growing community, or junior, college category embodies in itself such a great diversity of aims, programs, and clients that its very identity is ambiguous to its participants and frequently the subject of internal conflict.[32]

Many American institutions of higher education have passed successively from one type to another during their individual histories. Such "regional universities" as Western Michigan University or the Albany campus of the State University of New York originated as subcollegiate normal schools, became teachers' colleges, and emerged as multipurpose colleges or universities. Numerous two-year colleges have become four-year institutions.

Higher education is more "democratic" or "popular" in the United States than in other societies, in part, at least, because it represents such an upward extension of universal elementary and secondary schooling. This is shown in the growing proportions of college-bound youth, reaching some 46.7 percent of 18- to 21-year-olds in 1970. It appears also in the curriculum, where demand and institutional responsiveness have caused engineering, education, and business departments to enroll half of all undergraduates.[33] In Europe, for example, such subjects are not taught in the universities. The land-grant university, which first specialized in agriculture and technical education and has extended to hotel-management courses and to archeology, is indigenous to the United States, as is the junior college; both are institutional creations of the democratizing impulse in American higher education. The idea of the "extended university" is yet another of its manifestations, although Britain pioneered here.

Harvard, America's first college, founded in 1636, imitated the British colleges. Unlike the European universities—collections of essentially impersonal faculties of law, medicine, and theology (along with a faculty of "arts")—the British college was a residential institution dedicated to unified general education, to character development, and to communal values. This tradition appears today in countless small, single-degree, small-town, undergraduate liberal arts colleges. The tradition also lives on in the general education requirements of the bachelor's degree programs of today's multipurpose universities, in dormitory and fraternity life, in athletics and other cooperative efforts, in yearnings for "meaningful relationships" with other students and with faculty,

[32]Burton R. Clark, *The Open Door College* (New York: McGraw-Hill Book Co., Inc., 1960).

[33]In 1970 about 10 percent of American students pursuing postsecondary schooling were enrolled in proprietary, profit-making schools, receiving trade training for secretarial careers, computer programming, modeling, medical assistance, electronics, and scores of other fields.

and in the belief that character-building is still education's business. When a university tries to solve such problems as mass teaching, institutional impersonality, and research dominance by inaugurating "cluster colleges," putting resident faculty in student housing, and awarding prizes for teaching, it reflects this tradition.

There is, however, another model for American higher education: the research university dedicated to science and scholarship, specialization, advanced degrees, academic freedom, and intellectual skepticism. This is the legacy of the nineteenth-century German university. Born of the growing influence of science and technology, the modern university symbolized secularism. It centered teaching and learning upon lectures and seminars and put students into laboratories and libraries. The college's professing-teacher gave way to the university's researching-teacher, challenging the known by exploring the unknown.

Most American institutions of higher learning embody elements of both models. As prestigious a private research university as Harvard retains its undergraduate liberal arts Harvard College, with its "house system." Meanwhile, in even the smallest populist or tightly governed church college there broods the professor who yearns to raise standards, lighten his teaching "load," cease monitoring the private lives of the students, and "do research." The graft of these divergent traditions has been troublesome. Participants in higher education tend to polarize its various elements: teaching versus research; the transmission of accepted wisdom versus the extension of uncommon knowledge; general education versus specialized training; the communitarian, disciplinary, and paternalistic versus the privatistic, secular, and individualistic. Nevertheless, it seems probable that American higher education will remain that awkward but familiar blend of sometimes-competing features that it has become.

Diversity among institutions of higher education today issues from differing mixes of these various possible features and from uneven changes in emphasis—as the campus portraits drawn by Boroff amply suggest. Diversity also issues from an unequal ability to imitate the nation's most prestigious colleges and universities. Some institutions are simply limited by inadequate pools of outstanding students, productive professors, gifts, and endowment. Even America may have too many colleges (over twenty-seven hundred, half of them unaccredited) for its resources of intellect, energy, and money. The University of Berlin stimulated Johns Hopkins, Cornell, and Harvard Universities in the 1870s and 1880s. Today, Harvard, Berkeley, Swarthmore, and Reed stimulate such institutions as Fordham to commission studies that recommend loosening its ties with the Catholic church, increasing non-Catholic enrollments, and reducing prayer and religious symbolism.[34] Some

---

[34]Walter Gelhorn and R. Kent Greenwalt, *An Independent Fordham? A Choice for Catholic Higher Education* (New York: Fordham University Press, 1968).

of this retreat from diversity based on sectarianism stems from a desire to share in public funds. But much issues from the ecumenist belief that such institutions should be colleges first and church schools second.

Protestant colleges now constitute one-quarter of all private institutions but enroll only one Protestant student in seven. Catholic institutions educate a minority of all Catholic college youth. Nevertheless, church-run colleges will continue to lend some diversity to higher education. One reason is that conservative parents prefer their relatively greater "safety," not only from campus revolutionaries but also from the ordinary hazards of leaving family influence. Second, there remains a pious, sometimes fundamentalist body of American youth that prefers church colleges. Third, there exists some likelihood that church-related schools will secure greater public financial support. Barring this, the entire private sector of higher education will profit where aid is allowed through tax rebates or tuition waivers granted to college students as individuals.

Some 100 (4 percent) of the nation's colleges are predominantly black colleges. In 1970 they enrolled 34 percent of America's black undergraduates. This is not a homogeneous group of institutions. Among the 40 primarily small institutions that belong to the United Negro College Fund are schools that ranged in enrollment in 1971 from Talladega College (502 students) to Tuskegee Institute (3,062) and that vary in total annual costs per student from Miles College ($602) to Fisk University ($2,485).[35] Except for the fact of race, these colleges have not yet added appreciable new dimensions of diversity to American higher education. Most were founded by religious groups, and some still resemble Protestant white colleges. In their closed-campus style, classical preferences, and self-limited responsiveness most have reflected the collegiate orientation of the American South, where virtually all are located. Nevertheless, they have played an important role in shaping the middle class of the Southern black community, and they were of considerable value to upward-mobile individuals. In the recent past the black colleges (like other institutions near the academic bottom) contributed to variety primarily by their impoverishment and inability to imitate the "better college," and the difficulty they have in acquiring the all-Ph.D. faculties they sought; between 1950 and 1960 these colleges declined in expenditures per student. In 1970 their best-known institutions (including Fisk, Tuskegee, Howard, Spelman, Hampton) ranked no higher than the middle among collegiate institutions, using traditional measures. While the future role of the black college in the black revolution remains in doubt, there are those who think it could be significant.[36]

[35]United Negro College Fund, Inc., "Toward a Decade of Excellence: A Report on the Year 1971," (New York: The Fund, 1971), pp. 6–7. See also "The Traditionally Black Institutions" in Fred E. Crossland, *Minority Access to College* (New York: Schocken Books, Inc., 1971).

[36]Jencks and Riesman, *The Academic Revolution*, pp. 406–79. This book's highly pessimistic analysis of the black colleges, while controversial, has not been convincingly

INDICES OF DIVERSITY

The states differ enormously in their support of public higher education and in the proportion of their youth attending colleges and universities. A single state, California, was expected to account for 20 percent of the nation's gross expenditures for operating all public higher education in 1970 and for 15 percent of total outlays for construction and capital improvement.[37] In per capita spending for public higher education Alaska ranked first and Massachusetts last, the strength and reputation of private institutions again being a negative factor in the Northeastern states. In New Jersey, as late as 1970, support of public higher education was so minimal that over half of its youth seeking college studies had to leave the state. The usual process of state teachers' colleges becoming general colleges had not prevailed there.[38] The existence of many private colleges and the degree of autonomy allowed many public institutions make comparisons of institutions more relevant than state standards in assaying diversity. The three items discussed below exclude countless other indices of such diversity.

Regularity of Progress

While a four-year undergraduate sequence has become progressively less common, colleges differ markedly in whether their students graduate "on schedule." In the mid-1960s 80 percent of Princeton students did; at Hollins College the figure was 53 percent, and at the Universities of Iowa and Georgia the figures were 37 percent and 35 percent, respectively. Social-class factors matter greatly, but so do institutional or statewide policies governing grading, probationary status, and "expected rate" of flunking. In the nation as a whole, half of all premature leavers are freshmen, but only one in four students survives Iowa's first year—when the real selection process operates. Harvard selects *before* admission, and its far fewer dropouts scatter over the four years.[39] Where public universities are required to accept all high school graduates applying, each freshman class is decimated by forced withdrawals; where states or municipalities provide the alternatives of junior colleges or other public higher education, the university's freshman-year ax

---

refuted. Cf. T. J. LeMelle and W. J. LeMelle, *The Black College* (New York: Praeger Publishers, Inc., 1969). For a brief, popular discussion, see "Black Mood on Campus," *Newsweek* (February 10, 1969):53–59; for a report of foundation aid to predominantly black colleges, see Reginald Stuart, "Ford in Black Higher Education," *Race Relations Reporter*, 4 (March 1973):22–28.

[37]Council of State Governments, "Public Spending for Higher Education," reported in *The University as a Major Influence in the State* (Berkeley: University of California, 1967), pp. 6, 8.

[38]E. Alden Dunham, *Colleges of the Forgotten Americans* (New York: McGraw-Hill Book Co., 1969), pp. 57–61.

[39]Lawrence A. Previn et al., eds., *The College Dropout and the Utilization of Talent* (Princeton, N. J.: Princeton University Press, 1966), p. 8.

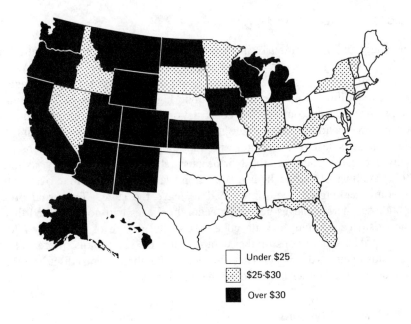

Under $25
$25-$30
Over $30

	Appropriation per capita	Rank		Appropriation per capita	Rank		Appropriation per capita	Rank
Alabama	$16.56	45	Louisiana	$26.93	22	Ohio	$16.48	46
Alaska	42.80	1	Maine	18.50	44	Oklahoma	21.37	40
Arizona	33.65	10	Maryland	21.67	39	Oregon	33.92	8
Arkansas	22.25	38	Massachusetts	12.80	50	Pennsylvania	22.64	37
California	33.70	9	Michigan	30.09	16	Rhode Island	24.43	32
Colorado	35.45	7	Minnesota	28.88	18	South Carolina	15.18	47
Connecticut	20.87	41	Mississippi	20.62	42	South Dakota	26.35	26
Delaware	26.90	24	Missouri	24.59	31	Tennessee	18.56	43
Florida	25.86	29	Montana	35.65	6	Texas	24.07	34
Georgia	25.17	30	Nebraska	23.38	35	Utah	32.75	11
Hawaii	42.74	3	Nevada	27.85	20	Vermont	25.92	28
Idaho	29.39	17	New Hampshire	14.64	48	Virginia	24.37	33
Illinois	27.58	21	New Jersey	13.57	49	Washington	42.76	2
Indiana	28.61	19	New Mexico	31.29	13	West Virginia	27.17	22
Iowa	31.25	14	New York	26.72	25	Wisconsin	37.04	4
Kansas	30.42	15	North Carolina	22.85	36	Wyoming	35.65	5
Kentucky	25.99	27	North Dakota	32.50	12	Total U.S.	$25.56	—

Per-capita spending of tax funds to operate colleges and universities and ranking of the states, based on current appropriations and the July 1, 1968, population estimates of the U.S. Bureau of the Census.

Redrawn from M. M. Chambers, for The Chronicle of Higher Education, *3, No. 3 (Oct. 14, 1968): 8. By permission.*

FIGURE 1   What the states spend, per capita

is less bloodied since much of the "cooling out" function has been performed outside the university.[40]

Student Culture and Values

Public impressions of campus life ignore significant variation among colleges in student subcultures. Drug use, for example, is commonest in "progressive" liberal arts colleges that have close student-faculty relationships and that place great value on the academic independence, intellectual interests, and personal freedom of students. It is less common in technical schools, teachers' colleges, community colleges, and church-run institutions.[41] Variance of student opinion is probably even more marked than that of behavior, and table 8 reports the beliefs of a national sample of freshmen, grouped according to type of institution attended. While students typically become less conservative as they proceed through school, such a change is so uneven among institutions that variance between schools can be greater among seniors than among freshmen.

Academic Status

Most high schools capture within their student bodies most of the possible intellectual diversity, so that they resemble one another intellectually even if they differ in demonstrable achievement. Such achievement tests as the College Boards indicate that the lowest quarter of the student body at certain colleges exceeds the top quarter at other institutions.[42] But many colleges do not even overlap in this respect. Because colleges *tend* to draw from different pools of students, the growth of any one college does not much affect the standards of any other. Consequently no strong body of opinion yet exists to oppose the enrollment growth of higher education or the multiplication of institutions. An example is the women's colleges. Educational discrimination against women students and women faculty helped to create a few women's colleges, mostly drawing from the same social class and offering the same curriculum as did the leading men's colleges. The result was a small group of academically superior, nationally attractive women's institutions. Their standing has been unaffected by the subsequent swelling of independent women's colleges (to 298); many of these newer colleges reflect the educational ambitions of Catholic orders of nuns, and are mainly academically

[40]See Clark, *The Open Door College,* chap. 5.

[41]Kenneth Keniston, "Heads and Seekers," *The American Scholar,* 38 (Winter 1968):98.

[42]One study of freshman variability on ACE test scores showed the *mean* scores of institutions in the North Central states ranging from 94 to 123. In the predominantly white colleges of the South the institutional average score ranged from 68 to 123: T. R. McConnell and Paul Heist, "Do Students Make the College?" *College and University,* 35 (Summer 1959):442–52.

TABLE 8   Opinions and aims expressed by the college class of 1972

Questions to Freshmen about Their Objectives and Their Opinions	2-Year Colleges		Technical Insts.	4-Year Colleges				Universities	
	Public	Priv.		Public	Nonsect.	Prot.	Cath.	Public	Priv.
I. Objectives considered essential or very important:									
To be an authority in my field	54.1%	53.5%	62.5%	58.4%	61.2%	59.3%	62.3%	60.5%	61.7%
To obtain recognition from peers	33.4%	34.0%	45.3%	36.7%	40.2%	36.6%	38.7%	38.1%	41.9%
To be very well-off financially	45.0%	39.5%	44.8%	38.3%	37.5%	34.9%	37.4%	41.7%	40.4%
To help others in difficulty	53.0%	63.6%	49.5%	60.5%	65.5%	67.0%	71.1%	56.5%	62.6%
To join the Peace Corps or VISTA	14.9%	16.7%	10.7%	19.0%	24.7%	21.0%	27.2%	17.8%	21.3%
To become an outstanding athlete	13.4%	11.3%	16.3%	12.1%	13.9%	13.4%	11.6%	8.9%	10.0%
To contribute to scientific theory	8.0%	7.0%	27.5%	8.6%	10.4%	9.6%	10.2%	13.2%	14.5%
To write original works	8.8%	9.3%	11.0%	12.4%	18.8%	14.4%	15.6%	14.2%	17.7%
To not be obligated to people	24.2%	23.7%	24.4%	24.1%	23.2%	24.0%	18.8%	23.3%	22.8%
To develop a philosophy of life	75.3%	83.0%	83.4%	83.1%	87.8%	86.8%	89.1%	84.0%	87.8%
II. Agree strongly or somewhat that:									
Student should have major role in design of curriculum	90.1%	89.8%	79.9%	90.2%	90.0%	88.7%	88.9%	90.4%	89.5%
All science findings should be published	53.9%	51.6%	56.4%	53.2%	56.7%	52.8%	52.4%	55.0%	56.7%
Individual cannot change society	34.6%	31.0%	33.8%	31.8%	32.0%	30.3%	28.5%	31.1%	30.9%
Benefit of college is monetary	70.7%	61.8%	51.1%	58.4%	45.5%	53.4%	47.4%	54.4%	42.8%
Faculty promotions should be based in part on student evaluations	60.9%	61.2%	61.4%	63.4%	62.4%	61.9%	63.1%	65.7%	65.8%
Student publications should be cleared by college officials	63.6%	68.5%	49.7%	59.4%	44.5%	60.6%	54.0%	51.7%	39.0%
Marijuana should be legalized	18.5%	12.0%	21.8%	16.2%	27.3%	15.5%	17.8%	21.1%	29.6%
College has right to ban speakers	35.9%	40.8%	33.3%	32.1%	24.1%	32.8%	31.6%	29.2%	22.9%
Disadvantaged students should get preferential admission treatment	46.2%	47.1%	30.3%	41.6%	42.0%	43.5%	39.5%	38.2%	36.0%
Colleges have been too lax on student protest	58.0%	60.3%	64.4%	54.2%	46.6%	56.1%	53.3%	53.1%	45.9%

Source: Data gathered by the American Council on Education and reproduced in *The Chronicle of Higher Education*, 3 (December 23, 1968): 8.

and financially weak, local institutions. Between 1960 and 1972, however, high costs and disinterest in single-sex colleges caused 152 to close down or to become coeducational schools. The fate of the survivors may rest largely on federal antidiscrimination policy.

The predominant European attitude about higher education (and about the select secondary schools feeding the universities) is that "more means worse," that expansion lowers standards everywhere. But it is historically demonstrable that the academically strongest American colleges and universities have *raised* their standards, especially since World War II, as more youth have gone to college. No longer having to accept very many of the dull offspring of the rich, they select their students overwhelmingly from the academically-able of the upper and middle classes, leading to a further differentiation of themselves from the intellectually average and weakest institutions, further heightening this kind of diversity.

THE IDEOLOGICAL AND POLITICAL FOUNDATIONS OF DIVERSITY

A National Assessment of Educational Progress is a project to evaluate elementary and secondary education. It originated in the 1960s with the encouragement of the United States Office of Education (a federal agency) and two private foundations, the Carnegie Corporation and the Ford Foundation Fund for the Advancement of Education, and it became an activity of the Education Commission of the States. Staff members constructed tests covering various curriculum fields for large samples of school children at four age levels. According to its director—Ralph Tyler, a renowned research administrator—the program will inventory the state of American education. Although the program's administrators made clear that they would not identify individual students, teachers, or school systems, the education profession offered angry opposition. A writer in *Educational Forum* called the program "a recipe for control by the few." A former leader of the National Education Association implied that daily classroom assessments by teachers are sufficient. Officials of the Council of State School Officers, American Association of School Administrators, and Association for Supervision and Curriculum Development stated that a national assessment portended a national curriculum and federal control. Certain school superintendents refused to cooperate with the project.

Some of the opposition undoubtedly reflects anxiety about the findings, indicating an insecurity and defensiveness about how well schools actually perform. It also represents a generalized, automatic animosity toward any national program, a fear of centralization, pro-states'-rights sentiments, and a lingering suspicion of federal aid to education evident even within the United States Office of Education. This professional dread of federal influence has a companion in nonpublic school objections to governmental monopoly.

The two together constitute the major political bulwark of our present diversity.

When the Teacher Corps program—which sends federally selected and paid teachers into slum schools to augment regular faculty—was renewed by Congress in 1967, it required that administrative responsibility pass from Washington into local and state hands. This illustrates how the virtually unquestioned need for federal aid is accommodated to the engrained hostility to central government.

Another example is the habitual dispensing of Washington dollars for limited, special purposes ("categorical aid") selected by Congress, instead of "general aid" to education, usable in any manner selected by the localities or states—sometimes called "put it on the stump in the dark of night and run" money. As a result of the categorical approach, the governor of Colorado complained in 1967 that his small state was administering 10 federal programs for construction, 56 for instruction, 35 for teacher training and student aid, and 11 for research. Still, with all the programs, in 1970–71, federal aid was paying only from $22 to $50 of school costs per pupil.

Authorization for federal support of education comes from the "general welfare" clause of the United States Constitution. Consequently national "defense" needs (broadly defined) and other national objectives appear frequently in the language of federal bills. While the schools' share of each federal dollar remains small—2 percent, as shown in figure 2—ample precedent for future congressional legislation or presidential action exists in acts that date from 1785.[43] The few "milestones" of federal involvement below are only the more obvious choices.

The Morrill Act (1862) granted federal lands to the states for the "endowment, support, and maintenance of at least one college where the leading objectives shall be, without excluding other scientific and classical studies and including military tactics, to teach such branches of learning as are related to agriculture and the mechanic arts. . . ." All the states took advantage of the act. Some, like Michigan and Texas, founded new "A and M" colleges—facetiously called "cow colleges" or "Silo Tech" by their detractors. Such private universities as New York's Cornell and New Jersey's Rutgers assumed the Morrill program. Still other states, like California, created a combined land-grant and state university system. Massachusetts divided its grant between a state agriculture college (now the University of Massachusetts) and the private Massachusetts Institute of Technology. Ra-

[43]For more on the forgotten years see George N. Rainsford, *Congress and Higher Education in the Nineteenth Century* (Knoxville: University of Tennessee Press, 1972).

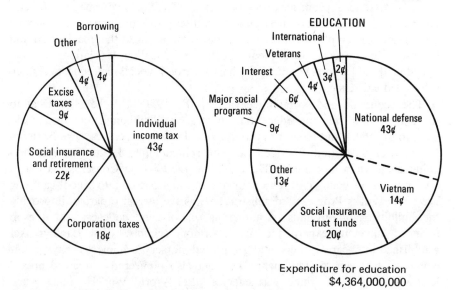

WHERE THE DOLLAR COMES FROM   WHERE THE DOLLAR GOES

Expenditure for education
$4,364,000,000

Bureau of the Budget data, reported in NEA Research Bulletin, 45 (May 1968):56. By permission.

FIGURE 2   The federal dollar—fiscal 1969 (estimate)

cially separate systems of land-grant schools appeared in the South.[44] Land-grant institutions helped to push other colleges toward nonclassical studies, applied research, technology, and public service. Their contributions to American agriculture and engineering have been outstanding. Moreover, they helped extend higher education outside the Northeast, while democratizing college student bodies in an unprecedented manner. Founded in a day when *public* higher education consisted of a few traditionalist state universities and the normal schools for training elementary school teachers, they were eventually so successful that public institutions now enroll an ever-increasing majority of those persons attending college.

The Smith-Hughes Act (1917), directed at the high schools, promoted vocational education (primarily in agriculture, home economics, and industrial arts). At this time secondary schools were under pressure to offer useful courses, since the majority of their students would get no further schooling. This federal law gave states the responsibility for devising and administering

[44]Sixteen black land grant colleges were founded in the border and southern states. In 1970 they ranged in size from Delaware State College (1,000 students) to Southern University A and M ·College in Baton Rouge, Louisiana (10,000 students), site of the deaths of two students in demonstrations in 1972. See Peter H. Schuck, "Black Land-Grant Colleges: Discrimination as Public Policy," *Saturday Review* (June 24, 1972): 46–48.

programs and invented the requirement that states match federal funds; today the typical state appropriates for vocational education five times the federal contribution. Despite its timely and innovative provision, however, economic growth and the employment revolution have outdistanced the imagination and resources of the act. Subsequent vocational education legislation, like the Vocational Education Act of 1963, has not saved vocational education from a troubled existence.

The economic and social upheavals of the 1930s led the New Deal to push legislation affecting education. At least $17 billion in emergency aid went to the states and territories through new laws and agencies. The National Youth Administration provided student scholarships, health, testing, and guidance services in schools. The camps of the Civilian Conservation Corps took millions of young men, and many camps later passed into school-camping use. The Works Progress Administration was the largest program, improving the buildings and grounds of numerous schools and colleges, and it even financed university experiments in "laboratory schools." The Lanham Act established day-care centers and supported nursery schools by paying unemployed teachers to staff them. This act also pioneered "impacted areas" legislation, more of which was enacted after World War II: under such legislation, districts whose school costs are raised by the enrollment of the dependent children of employees of shipyards, defense contractors, and military bases, and of residents of federal housing projects, receive reimbursements of federal funds. The Federal Surplus Commodities Corporation helped supply school cafeterias, anticipating the National School Lunch Act of 1946.

A new approach was to aid the individual, who would continue his education under the Serviceman's Readjustment Act (1944). This "G.I. Bill of Rights" had momentous direct effects. In the first five months, a half-million veterans applied; hundreds of nearly extinct institutions, depleted of students by the war, prospered. The veterans' presence, in turn, affected all higher education in unforeseen ways. The older, more serious veteran changed campus culture. His presence subtly encouraged many professors to reject student discipline and custodial care as their responsibilities. The collegiate "fun culture" and dormitory and fraternity life declined in many institutions. What the veteran began has since been continued by growing numbers of older graduate students. The total impact has been incalculably great, and studies of student revolt and educational unrest must consider these unanticipated consequences of the "G.I. Bill."

Following the Russian Sputnik launching, Congress passed the National Defense Education Act (1958). This act stimulated school science, mathematics, and foreign language teaching, and provided counseling services, summer institutes for teachers, and low-interest loans for college students planning teaching and other "national interest" careers. A far broader conception of schools underlies the Elementary and Secondary Education Act

(1965), the most important of 60 education acts passed during the presidency of Lyndon Johnson. Under Title I, financial assistance went to local districts for the education of poor children; Title II authorized appropriations for libraries, textbooks, and other materials; Title III supported supplementary educational centers and model programs; the United States Office of Education was strengthened by Title IV's authorizations of expanded functions in stimulating educational research and research training; and Title V made grants to strengthen state departments of education. Several approaches prevail in ESEA: aid to individuals (those with research plans or those undergoing training), to local districts and independent institutions (bypassing the states), and direct grants to the states themselves. Moreover, ESEA illustrates the complex politics of federal aid legislation.[45] Most prior attempts at fairly comprehensive aid were killed by "Red, Religion, or Race" issues. On the "red" fear (federal control), the political balance in 1965 overwhelmingly favored "big government" views. President Johnson's defeat of a Republican conservative had elected an additional 80 liberal Democratic congressmen pledged to aid education. Liberals assumed a two to one control of the House Education and Labor Committee, and Harlem's Adam Clayton Powell became chairman. Moreover, President Johnson unleashed the power of his office to ensure passage.[46] An ecumenical spirit, furthered by Vatican II and the Kennedy presidency, blunted religious hostility. Prior passage of the Civil Rights Act (1964), outlawing school segregation, slightly shifted emphasis from race to the problems of poverty and inner-city decline. Yet the results of Johnson-administration legislation were profoundly disappointing to those who saw federal aid as a means to equalize educational expenditures. Because federal aid has no systematic provision for equalization, poor states and poor localities are aided no more often by the totality of federal programs than are wealthier states and communities.

[45]Stephen K. Bailey, *The Office of Education and the Education Act of 1965* (Indianapolis: Bobbs Merrill, 1966); Philip Meranto, *The Politics of Federal Aid to Education in 1965* (Syracuse, N. Y.: Syracuse University Press, 1967); S. J. Trachtenberg's review of Meranto in *Harvard Educational Review,* 38 (Winter 1968):185–89; "ESEA and Intergovernmental Relations," in Frederick M. Wirt and Michael W. Kirst, *The Political Web of American Schools* (Boston: Little, Brown, 1972), pp. 153–172; Frank J. Munger and Richard Fenno, *National Politics and Federal Aid to Education* (Syracuse, N. Y.: Syracuse University Press, 1962), pp. 184–85.

[46]The vote in Congress on the Elementary and Secondary Education Act was:

	Senate		House of Representatives	
	Yes	No	Yes	No
Republicans	18	14	35	96
Southern Democrats	15	4	31	53
All other Democrats	40	0	197	4

THE ISSUE OF MONOPOLY

In 1970 11 percent of the nation's elementary and secondary school population, 5,600,000 students, attended nonpublic schools. In most other nations the distinction between "public" and "private" schools is less sharp than in America. State aid to church schools is common in Canada, England, Germany, Latin America, and much of Asia. If religious or other private schools serve a public function they become, in theory at least, public institutions. In some new nations church schools are prestigious and are involved in a network of power and influence through their alumni in government offices; the Catholic schools of India's Karala state are an example.

American attitudes toward nonpublic schools derive from several traditions. One is a dislike of privilege of any kind. Another is the related belief that segregated schooling (whether religious, racial, or economically based) deprives individuals by limiting contacts in the formative years of childhood. Third, there is the historical specter of religious bigotry and divisiveness fostered by churches given governmental sanctions, and churches sponsor the majority of nonpublic schools.

Strictures against public aid to nonpublic schools are pervasive but not complete. Tax exemptions on private school property furnish considerable indirect aid. Under various laws and court rulings many students in nonpublic institutions share in public health services, school lunch programs, free transportation, state college scholarships, the use of certain public facilities, textbooks, and test and guidance programs. States with historically low levels of support for public higher education, like New York and Pennsylvania, have taken substantial steps to underwrite private colleges, making them quasi-public institutions.

In 1970 some 87 percent of all elementary and secondary school youngsters were enrolled in public schools. While there has been an increase in secular private school enrollments, the very large Catholic school sector could not maintain its earlier growth; it appears that the nonpublic share in American education seems to have peaked, at least over the short run. Meanwhile, the newest, most populist type of institution, the community (junior) college, surpassed private college enrollments (25 percent of the total) in 1968, enrolling 30 percent of the students in higher education.

The Secular, Independent Schools

America's nonpublic schools emerged from a European past, where virtually all education was private—except for scattered provisions for public aid in educating paupers and orphans, and a few "town" schools. With growing commitments to public responsibility for schooling in the nineteenth century, and stricter provisions against use of public funds for nonpublic purposes, many private schools disappeared altogether or passed into the public domain. A few, however, weathered the loss of monies and students, severed their religious connections (despite "compulsory chapel"), gained a new clientele and endowment, and prospered. By 1970 there were some twenty-four hundred such institutions in the United States, 71 percent of them secondary schools; most of the strongest belong to the 780-member National Association of Independent Schools. They educated over a million students, less than 1 percent of the nation's total enrollment in elementary and secondary schools.

Diversity flourishes here, too. There are military academies, the so-called segregation academies established to forestall racially desegregated schooling, academically feeble finishing schools and custodial institutions for the unmanageable offspring of the wealthy, college-preparatory schools of almost-unequaled accomplishment, such as Phillips Exeter, which had 73 National Merit Scholars in a recent senior class (topping all other secondary schools), or the ancient Roxbury Latin School in Boston, founded in 1645.

Some of the most famous independent schools are boarding schools in rural or small-town America, but the trend is strongly toward day schools in metropolitan areas; indeed, the suburban "country day school" has furnished the urban upper-middle class an educational escape from the city school and the city neighborhood for decades. Independent schools predominate in the Northeast, partly because its older cities have been more deeply afflicted by urban blight—a factor that favors private school development. Between 1950 and 1960, for example, New York City lost 1¼ million middle-class whites and gained 800,000 Puerto Ricans and blacks, many of whom were poor; in Manhattan some overcrowded independent schools must reject eight of every nine applicants. In Philadelphia and Chicago more white children attend private or parochial schools than the public schools.

Aside from this urban factor, the East leads in the influence of its endowed schools for two other reasons. This region was settled before any public education was widely accepted, and public higher education still lags badly behind demand. Unlike America west of the Mississippi River, the prevailing attitude in the East is that public institutions are second choices. The Northeast also is disproportionately home to many private institutions of higher education, especially the type of selective college and university toward which many independent secondary schools are oriented. Consequently, the academic demands of these prep schools tend to be greater than most of their counterparts in the South. Because nonpublic schools are both more numerous and more accepted in the Northeast, state regulations there tend to be minimal. New England, for example, looks only to their safety and sanitation, while nonpublic schools in the Midwest must meet detailed state specifications covering their teachers, curricula, and attendance policies.[47]

Although recent college admission and achievement studies show public

[47]See Donald A. Erickson, *Public Controls for Non-Public Schools* (Chicago: University of Chicago Press, 1969).

high school graduates performing ahead of the alumni of the better independent schools, prep schools still have the image of academic superiority. Their status advantage rests partly in historical connections with the upper classes, a tradition still strong in England.[48] Status also derives from selective, restrictive admissions policies (once very strong against Catholic and Jewish students), guaranteeing parents a degree of social-class exclusivity. Their student bodies tend, therefore, to be socially more homogeneous than those in many public schools. Some of these schools, which have large scholarship programs and alumni recruiters scouring the South and Northern working-class neighborhoods for prospective students, are more "democratic" than are certain upper-class suburban public school districts. But such democratization is shallow, limited inexorably by high tuition (ranging from $1,500 to $4,000 annually) and other costs, and the fact that most scholarships are still won by middle-class youngsters.[49] It is not surprising that Kraushaar found that under 1 percent of independent-school students came from poverty-stricken families; most of these were concentrated in the Northeastern schools, which had the greatest will and resources to recruit such students.

Endowed schools, though less vulnerable than public institutions, are far from impervious to the social and intellectual currents influencing the whole society. They have a special appeal to philanthropic foundations that finance educational experiments taxpayers would be loath to underwrite in public schools, preferring to use public funds on the known rather than the unknown. Despite faculty-student ratios as favorable as 1:9, however, most such schools have not pioneered in new approaches to teaching and learning or in curriculum departures. Exceptions have been a few radical or "progressive" (mostly elementary) schools and occasional university laboratory ("demonstration") schools—schools that tend toward increasing conservatism with age. The best prep schools get very good results with conventional methods,

[48]For a brief discussion see G. William Domhoff, *Who Rules America?* (Englewood Cliffs, N. J.: Prentice-Hall, Inc., 1967), pp. 16–17; for a different perspective, see James McLachlan, *American Boarding Schools: A Historical Study* (New York: Scribner's, 1970). Three variations of nonpublic schools are described in Ellen Frankfort, *The Classrooms of Miss Ellen Frankfort: Confessions of a Private School Teacher* (Englewood Cliffs, N. J.: Prentice-Hall, Inc., 1970).

[49]See the extensive discussion of all aspects of the independent schools in Kraushaar, *American Nonpublic Schools.* While ghetto recruitment has "heated up" since *Time* published its survey on prep schools (*Time*, October 26, 1962:76–82), the situation has not changed drastically from the days when the annual tuition of New Jersey's Lawrenceville School was $3,000 and most of its graduates expected to go to Princeton, or when Andover, which had 28 percent of its students on scholarships, awarded half of these to youngsters from families whose earnings placed them in the nation's top 15 percent in income and gave the sons of alumni an advantage in the stiff competition for admission.

On questions of inequality, racial separation, and community participation as shown in recent state plans to aid nonpublic schools, see the criticisms of Stephen Arons, "The Joker in Private School Aid," *Saturday Review* (January 16, 1971):45–46.

and their patrons seem satisfied.[50] It is ironic that educational innovation will occur not where the resources (or even the goodwill) abound, but where the problems of teaching and learning are, by traditional standards, so great or the clientele so disaffected that change is forced into being.

Church-Operated Schools

Church-school enrollment, at its peak in the mid-sixties, had these components: Roman Catholic, 5,600,000 (4,550,000 elementary; 1,050,000 secondary); Lutheran, 210,000 (195,000 elementary; 15,000 secondary); other Protestant denominations, 212,000 (176,000 elementary; 36,000 secondary); and Jewish, 63,000 (52,000 elementary; 11,000 secondary).[51] The Roman Catholic church still operates over 80 percent of all nonpublic schools, and perhaps 90 percent of all schools run by churches. Declining enrollment in the Catholic schools has not been offset by growth in the schools sponsored by younger evangelical Protestant sects, rapid increases in Jewish day schools, and steady expansion of Episcopal elementary schools.[52]

As with secular independent schools, there are pronounced regional variations among the church-operated schools. In North Carolina 1½ percent of all school children attended church-run schools in 1965; in Wisconsin the figure was 26 percent; in Rhode Island, 28 percent. By 1970 the range had narrowed from about 1 percent in Alaska and Utah to some 17 percent in Pennsylvania. Such variation by city is greater: in the 1960s, the figure for Boston, New Orleans, Chicago, and Milwaukee was 33 percent; Pittsburgh,

[50]Kraushaar, *American Nonpublic Schools, passim.* Given the conventional character of almost all prep and parochial schools, it seems likely that no more than 1 percent or so of America's schoolchildren attend the flexible and innovative schools that the private school lobby includes in its justifications for public assistance to the nonpublic sector of education. See George R. La Noue, "The Politics of Education," *Teachers College Record,* 73 (December 1971), esp. pp. 306–8.

[51]David W. Beggs and R. Bruce McQuigg, *America's Schools and Churches, Partners in Conflict* (Bloomington, Ind.: Indiana University Press, 1965), pp. 68–69. In 1970 Catholic schools accounted for 82.8 percent of all nonpublic school enrollments; for the range, by states, see *Church and State,* 26 (March 1973):12–13. The other churches with large numbers of schools are the Seventh-day Adventists, Episcopal, Lutheran, and Christian Reformed churches. The small Amish sect (60,000 members), which built its first school only in 1925, had 16 schools by 1950 and 300 by 1970 (estimated enrollment 10,000). Urbanization and modernization, which the Amish found threatening to their own socialization of their children prompted this growth: John R. Hostetler and Gertrude E. Huntington, *Children in Amish Society* (New York: Holt, Rinehart & Winston, 1971).

[52]For a discussion of the noneconomic reasons for the decline in Catholic school enrollments (20 percent decline, 1968–72) see Louis R. Gary and K. C. Cole, "The Politics of Aid—and Proposals for Reform," *Saturday Review* (July 22, 1972):31–33. By the 1970–71 school year some 1.2 million former parochial school children had enrolled in public schools as a result of school closings; 4.9 million remained. A study that claims to refute the argument that parochial school closings would create intolerable problems for local public schools is Larson, *When Parochial Schools Close.*

42 percent; Manchester, New Hampshire, 52 percent; Dubuque, Iowa, 61 percent (although this figure declined to 35 percent by 1971). In ethnic neighborhoods a church's educational role may be of primary importance. In Boston the parochial school system influences the conduct and policies of public education. School board members and public school teachers (and their children) are often themselves parochial-school educated; complaints about the age and condition of public school buildings, of their large class size, of seemingly insuperable problems in teaching and maintaining order are commonly deflected by admiring references to the parochial schools' undeniable authority and discipline under similarly difficult circumstances. In the South many Catholic schools enroll large numbers of black students, but overall only about 4 percent of their enrollment is black and about 4½ percent Mexican-American.[53]

Church schools have kept educational costs per pupil at about half the national average, largely by use of teachers from religious orders or of the minister's wife, and by using few extra personnel, large classes, a rather circumscribed curriculum, and an absence of "frills." The Old Order Amish emphasize one-room schools staffed by teachers having an eighth-grade schooling themselves. The much larger church-run school systems face the likelihood of more state regulation as their traditional frugal methods become obsolete.[54] The cost of a lay teacher is from two to four times greater than that of priests, brothers, or nuns. Yet, from 1960 to 1970, the proportion of paid, lay teachers in parochial schools doubled (from 25 to 50 percent). This was the result of moderate growth, decreasing numbers of religious vocations, the diversions of some priests, nuns, and brothers to further education or to other work, and certain successes in reducing class size. In 1970 parochial high school tuition was raised to $700 annually in Brooklyn and to $400 in Philadelphia. Hence church schools have become primarily middle class institutions, facing articulate parental demands for small classes, kindergartens, better-prepared lay teachers (more than half lacked a college degree in 1965), and improved college-preparatory programs. Lay teachers are increasingly articulate—in a few instances forming unions and striking the system for higher wages and a voice in policy making.[55]

---

[53]Schrag, *Village School Downtown*, pp. 20–22; Kraushaar, *American Nonpublic Schools*, p. 240. Unlike Mexican-Americans, under 2 percent of American Catholics are black, so other than religious reasons motivate those black parents who select parochial schools for their children.

[54]An example of greater dependence on lay teachers is the situation in Duluth; in 1950 there were 119 religious and 5 lay instructors in the parochial system; in 1965, 125 and 45 respectively; in 1970, 57 and 54: Larson, *When Parochial Schools Close*, p. 66. For the implications of more lay teachers and their mounting militancy and experimentalism, see Caryl Rivers, "When the Apple Hits the Teacher's Toupee, and Other Stories," *Saturday Review* (July 22, 1972):27–31.

[55]*System* is an inaccurate term for Catholic elementary school control because of the typical localization of authority in the individual parish. Secondary schools, however, are ordinarily controlled by a diocesan administration or by religious orders. A useful

Some financial relief for church schools, especially those serving low-income neighborhoods, has come through the Elementary and Secondary Education Act. Agreements between church schools and local public school districts have led to "sharing," and the courts have not barred this as contrary to the First Amendment's prohibition against state support of religion, which they did do when the United States Supreme Court voided the parochial school aid plans passed by the legislatures in Pennsylvania and Rhode Island, in the *Lemon* v. *Kurtzman* (1971) decision. Acceptable practices include parochial school use of public school facilities (such as gymnasiums and laboratories), enrolling church-school students in certain public-school classes, and sending publicly paid educational specialists to nonpublic schools. In 1969 300 communities reported some such "shared-time" programs. When visiting parochial school students do take public school classes, they usually select such subjects as the doctrinally neutral industrial arts and driver-education courses; less frequently (10 percent of the cases) they take classes in chemistry or foreign language; and rarely do they study other subjects.[56] A 1964 survey found shared-time programs in 6½ percent of all Indiana districts, involving instrumental music, vocational training, and physical education exclusively. As yet, ESEA and shared-time compacts have been too little used by doctrinally sensitive educators to remedy the financial maladies afflicting church-run schools.

Proponents of tax aid to nonpublic schools articulate two basic principles: that such schools serve public (civil) as well as private (religious) purposes, and that it is possible to separate the former from the latter, giving aid to the first alone. The first is a substantive and the second is a tactical or implementing principle. The overarching argument, however, is ideological: that government ought not to possess a monopoly on education, that as long as there are parents who believe that education must be rooted in religious values, the state must not thwart their preference. This position, sustained by particular religious and moral traditions, has received support in recent years from certain minority groups and political radicals who argue for their own tax-supported alternatives to existing public schools.

---

reference tool is Harold A. Buetow, *Of Singular Benefit: The Story of U.S. Catholic Education* (New York: Macmillan, 1971).

Mary Ryan, *Are Parochial Schools the Answer?* (New York: Holt, Rinehart & Winston, 1964) revealed dissent among Catholics about the place of parochial schools in America. From the perspective of higher education, see the assessment of parochial schooling in James Trent and Jeanette Golds, *Catholics in College* (Chicago: University of Chicago Press, 1967); from the perspective of the lower schools, see Andrew M. Greeley and Peter Rossi, *The Education of Catholic Americans* (Garden City, N. Y.: Doubleday & Co., 1968).

[56] *NEA Research Bulletin,* 45 (October 1967):90–92; Beggs and McQuigg, *America's Schools and Churches,* pp. 81, 224; and George La Noue's exposé of the "nonsectarian" subjects as treated in church schools: "Religious Schools and 'Secular' Subjects," *Harvard Educational Review,* 32 (Summer 1962):255–91.

THE PRESENT-DAY DEMAND FOR DIVERSITY

Community Control

Assimilation-minded blacks—discontented with existing public schools and convinced that all-black schools are invariably inferior—have concentrated their efforts on attempts either to desegregate all schools or to enroll their own children in parochial or other nonpublic desegregated schools. By 1966 reportedly 40 percent of all black white-collar workers had taken this latter step.

Black separatists prefer another course of action: the establishment of all-black schools in the ghetto areas, under exclusively black control, and the opportunity to create an educational program and teaching methods based on their own perceptions of black culture and the contemporary black requirement of schooling.

The most publicized case of community control was that of New York City. In 1967 the city board of education agreed to delegate certain administrative authority to three special community districts—in Harlem and the Lower East Side, in Manhattan, and in Ocean Hill–Brownsville, in Brooklyn. The Ford Foundation aided the experiment by supplying a planning grant. In 1968 the Ocean Hill–Brownsville board's attempt to transfer out 19 teachers and supervisors precipitated an acrimonious strike. Nevertheless, an influential study (the Bundy Report) has proposed that the city be divided into 60 or more autonomous school districts, each representing an integral community and governed by a parent-dominated local board. By 1972 there were 31 elected, nine-member boards responsible for the city's elementary schools. Detroit achieved a measure of "decentralization" through adding to the district's governing board five persons from each of the city's eight regions.[57]

Alternative Schools

Another model for extending educational diversity came with the "free university" structures that appeared following the first campus uprising of the 1960s. Disillusioned with colleges as they knew them, many informal student groups established their own courses, recruited faculty of their own choosing, and otherwise devised parallel institutions of varying permanence and importance. Even less conventional examples have come from the encounter groups, T-groups, and sensitivity training sessions that appeal to some alienated white middle-class youth. Such alternative schools are far

[57]The plan's inadequacies in furthering community self-determination are indicated in Alan A. Altshuler, *Community Control: The Black Demand for Participation in Large American Cities* (New York: Pegasus Press, 1970). See also George La Noue and Bruce Smith, *The Politics of School Decentralization* (Lexington, Mass.: D. C. Heath & Co., 1973).

more common in the populous, urban states, but the free school in Aspen, Colorado, has the same purposes. As Sylvia Ashton-Warner describes it, the Aspen school is committed to "openness," "freedom," and "spontaneity," eschewing "authority," "imposition," even "teaching." So, too, is Murray Road School, part of the Newton, Massachusetts, public school system—a school without an administration, grades, attendance or curriculum requirements.[58]

Another alternative comes from the other end of the organizational spectrum, from the often highly successful and massive training programs of the corporations and the armed forces.[59] These educational operations alternate paid work and study. More pragmatic than many formal education programs, these schemes make the most of the practical or materialistic motives of their students. It is as yet unclear whether formal educational structures will imitate these successful programs, although several school districts did exploit the profit motive during the 1960s in an attempt to upgrade the public schools. These districts contracted with private corporations to take over one or more schools or to teach certain subjects. Some of these experiments—called "performance contracting," because payment schedules were based upon student performance—were underwritten by the federal Office of Economic Opportunity. Unfortunately, the initial results have been disappointing: students made little or no improvement over previous public school performances.[60]

The Education Voucher Plan

Regular public school systems assume that elected or appointed officials will determine what education school children will receive. Performance contracting makes the same assumption but looks for better means of achiev-

---

[58]Sylvia Ashton-Warner, the author of *Teacher,* an account of her experiences with Maori children in New Zealand, writes poetically of her culture-shock in teaching in an American free school: *Spearpoint: Teacher in America* (New York: Alfred A. Knopf, Inc., 1972). The range of types of free schools and a critique of their indirectness are provided by Jonathan Kozol, *Free Schools* (Boston: Houghton Mifflin, 1972). Kozol's criticisms are given importance by his solid credentials as a teacher-rebel. Additional descriptions of diversity among free schools appear in Stephen Arons et al., *Doing Your Own School* (Boston: Beacon Press, 1972); Center for New Schools, "Strengthening Alternative High Schools" and Alan Graubard, "The Free School Movement," both in *Harvard Educational Review,* 42 (August 1972):313–73. On the Murray Road School see Evans Clincy's account, in *High School,* ed. Ronald Gross and Paul Osterman (New York: Simon & Schuster, 1971), pp. 235–47.

[59]The Defense Department reportedly spends more on post-secondary education than what is appropriated for such education by all the state legislatures combined, and the largest corporations have educational budgets exceeding that of the middle-size university. See Jencks and Riesman, *The Academic Revolution,* pp. 506–7.

[60]The results from 18 sites are reported in "Performance Contracting—OEO Experiment," *NEA Research Bulletin,* 50 (March 1972):9–10. A discussion of these results is part of Charles Blaschke, *Performance Contracting: Who Profits Most?* (Bloomington, Ind.: Phi Delta Kappa Educational Foundation, 1972).

ing specified results. Decentralization, or community control, shifts the responsibility to recognized community groups or to explicitly parental representatives. Most alternative schools—those outside the public sector or the board-of-trustees structure of the established endowed schools—also place control in groups of parents and teachers and, frequently, students. A different principle underlines the voucher system: that every parent may make an independent decision about the schooling of his or her child. The proposal that each child's "share" of available tax resources for schooling—local, state, and federal dollars—be transferred annually to his or her parents, in the form of a voucher, can secure the endorsement of a variety of individuals and interests: church-school supporters who seek to preserve their own school systems, like Father Virgil Blum; proponents of a free-enterprise capitalism in education, like economist Milton Friedman, who thinks public schools should simply have to compete in the open market for students; liberals and even radicals, who despair of otherwise improving the schools; and racial or class segregationists, who would evade court-ordered changes in the composition of school student bodies.[61]

If a movement toward publicly supported but independently controlled schools, colleges, and universities develops beyond present discussion, it will repudiate a cardinal theme of educational development in the United States. The historic commitment has been to the belief that social cohesion and equality of educational opportunity depend upon educating *together* all of the children of all of the people. The new commitment would recognize an urgent need for educational diversity far beyond what a common school system would accommodate.

[61]David L. Kirp, "Vouchers, Reform, and the Elusive Community," *Teachers College Record,* 74 (December 1972):201–7; Christopher Jencks, *Education Vouchers* (Cambridge, Mass.: Center for the Study of Public Policy, December 1970); George La Noue, ed., *Educational Vouchers: Concepts and Controversies* (New York: Teachers College Press, 1972).

Voucher-supported schools could function to force eventual reconsideration of existing ways of doing things; see Dan C. Lortie, "The Cracked Cake of Educational Custom and Emerging Issues in Evaluation," in *The Evaluation of Instruction: Issues and Problems,* ed. Merlin C. Wittrock and David E. Wiley (New York: Holt, Rinehart & Winston, 1970), pp. 149–64.

UNIVERSALITY

Universal education—the experience of schooling for everyone's child—has long been argued as a necessary condition for an open society. While the term *open society* has a social-science modernity about it, the ideals and conditions that define it have been central to the American experience since the Republic's earliest days. The two essentials of an open society most important for understanding American education are the parallel commitments to equality and to social mobility.

The Meaning of Equalitarianism

Among the various possibilities of expressing equalitarian commitments, two stand out: equality in social relationships and equality of opportunity.

Social equality means a tolerant permissiveness in the arena of social relationships. The conditions of life in early America and the peopling of the land by successive generations of newcomers strengthened the belief that men (white men, at least) were equal in sharing a common humanity and experiencing problems in common. Democratic man, Plato observed, is imbued with the desire to accommodate himself to others, which shows itself in generosity and a reluctance to offend. The American writer John Jay Chapman described this phenomenon in 1898: "This desire to please graduates at one end of the scale into a general kindliness, into political benefactions, hospitals, and college foundations; at the other end it is seen melting into a desire to efface one's self rather than give offense, to hide rather than be noticed."[1]

As a corollary, taboos exist against "pulling rank." Authority is disguised by such social conventions as calling the top man a "leader," not a ruler, and by expressing orders as "requests." As no man is inevitably another's superior, neither are any man's interests and ideas. This social and intellectual parity (some call it "leveling"), often named "Jacksonianism," appears in American educational thought and practice on many fronts: the

---

[1]Quoted in Seymour M. Lipset, *America, the First New Nation* (New York: Basic Books, Inc., 1964), p. 109.

support for "sociability" as a school aim, challenges to the authority of teachers and books, curricula flavored with new subjects and popular interests, schools discouraged against "failing" anyone, and school power struggles disguised as human relations exercises.

Equality of opportunity was a particularly apt characteristic of a frontier society, giving individuals access to undeveloped resources for their own profit. From a national perspective it worked well, and equality of opportunity became the most highly espoused form of equalitarianism. In the comfortable belief that most wealth and power are *earned* by those who possess them, Americans condone great disparities in riches and influence and demonstrate insensitivity to such inequalities. It is not simple callousness; as George Santayana perceptively observed of the American, "His instinct is to think well of everybody, and to wish everybody well, but in a spirit of rough comradeship, expecting every man to stand on his own legs and be helpful in his turn. When he has given his neighbour a chance, he thinks he has done enough for him; but he feels it is an absolute duty to do that."[2]

Social Mobility: The Myth and the Reality

Social mobility is the second essential to the ideal of the open society. Although the rate of individual mobility in the United States is not appreciably higher than in other industrialized Western nations, the myth of considerable upward movement is strong. This strength may stem, in part, from three tendencies. The willingness, even eagerness, of those who do spring from lowly origins into prestigious positions in business, politics, and entertainment to trumpet their rise, giving publicity to their ascent, keeps the myth alive; in traditionally status-conscious Europe, those from once-humble station are more reluctant to talk of what many successful Americans brag about. A second source of the myth is the inclination of even moderately successful Americans to create a story of personal rise where little, in fact, exists—to impute to a comfortable, middle-class background some hardship (selling newspapers as a boy, sharing a bedroom, holding a job while in college) to certify the rise from "decent poverty"; the insertion of the log cabin into the politician's campaign rhetoric or the stockroom experience into the executive's saga are only extensions of an exaggerated social mobility that has colored popular culture from Ben Franklin and the Horatio Alger stories through

[2]George Santayana, *Character and Opinion in the United States* (New York: W. W. Norton and Co., 1967), p. 171. For one analysis of evolving meanings of "equal opportunity" see James Coleman, "The Concept of Equality of Educational Opportunity," *Harvard Educational Review*, 38 (Winter 1968):7–22. For the consequences of focusing upon equality of opportunity, rather than actually reducing inequalities in matters like income, see Christopher Jencks and Mary Jo Bane, *Inequality: A Reassessment of the Effect of Family and Schooling in America* (New York: Basic Books, Inc., 1972) and Murray Milner, Jr., *The Illusion of Equality: The Effects of Education on Opportunity, Inequality, and Social Conflict* (San Francisco: Jossey-Bass, Inc., 1972).

Time magazine.[3] Finally, we often make the mistake of crediting individual rise with what is actually group mobility—in a nation that offered a chance "to get ahead simply by standing still," as Ginzberg puts it. The United States has enjoyed net upward mobility throughout its history. More people have moved up than down in life-style and "life-chances." Technological change has raised the entire nation's standard of living and increased the percentage of professional, technical, and managerial jobs, while decreasing the need for unskilled positions. More room at the top has resulted also from different reproduction patterns; the lower birth rate of the upper-middle classes creates vacancies attracting ambitious lower-class aspirants. Rapid population growth has expanded the economy and generated new middle-class positions. Immigration of unskilled workers served to elevate indigenous working-class white Americans to positions that the culturally unassimilated could not fill. The Irish, German, and Scandinavians benefited from the later immigrations of Italians, Greeks, and Slavs—who, in turn, profited from Oriental, Mexican, Puerto Rican, and American Negro population movements. Far more mobility has resulted from expansion of opportunity and from assimilation (partly via schooling) than from the exercise of sheer talent, will, ambition, and hard work by the scrappy individual who rises by seizing another man's place.

Anxiety in the Open Society

Society's commitments to equality of opportunity and social mobility are certified by success and by proof of individual attainment that *all* should seek, regardless of the accidents of origin and circumstances. This ethos challenges each man to put his talents into competition with others. Anxiety accompanies this competition.

But the concomitant pledge to the dignity of "Everyman" imposes a moderating, and even conflicting, influence. Schools receive and perpetuate two norms: the achievement-oriented "need-to-do-well" and the equalitarian-oriented "need-to-respect-others," including those of lesser abilities.[4] Anxiety arises when the balance between the structures of competition and sociability

[3]Irvin C. Wyllie, *The Self-Made Man in America: The Myth of Rags to Riches* (New Brunswick, N.J.: Rutgers University Press, 1954); Eli Ginzberg et al., *The Optimistic Tradition and American Youth* (New York: Columbia University Press, 1962), esp. pp. 72–73.

Ralph H. Turner has made the distinction between *sponsored mobility* (as when established elites select or recruit for future elite status) and *contest mobility* (as when an individual competes openly and takes the prize through his own efforts). The latter is preferred in the American ethos. "Sponsored and Contest Mobility and the School System," *American Sociological Review*, 25 (December 1960):855–67.

[4]John Gardner, *Excellence: Can We Be Equal and Excellent Too?* (New York: Harper & Row, Publishers, 1961); Seymour M. Lipset, *The First New Nation: The United States in Historical and Comparative Perspective* (New York: Basic Books, Inc., 1963).

is threatened—as the debate about whether ability and achievement are caused by heredity or by opportunity, a controversy now labeled "Jensenism." In school there is strong pressure to maintain the balance, causing Erving Goffman to say that the teacher runs a "tension-management" system. One device is to censure both the nonaggressive student (not necessarily a nonachiever) because he "doesn't try," and the overly aggressive student who seems to hate his competitors too openly. Competing "goods" beset the school. Should the school promote high standards or keep open the door to opportunity? Should it admit selectively and promote leadership or serve humanity by "uplifting" all who will come?

The permissive society disavows *ascribed status* (who you are) in favor of *achieved status* (what you have done). Therefore, clear proof of ascribed status is "inadmissible evidence." A genetic explanation of the differences among individuals or groups is outrageous, because it denies the possibility of equal conditions, *and* it holds that equality of opportunity will never reduce inequality. It is thoroughly in the American tradition of liberalism to believe that environmental engineering—including the diffusion of unparalleled universalistic opportunities for schooling—is basic to the open society.

Cartoon by Edward Frascino. Copyright 1970 by Saturday Review, Inc.

"Take advantage of every opportunity to enjoy yourself before you get into kindergarten, Brian. That's when they start breathing down your neck."

TABLE 9   School enrollments and projections, by regions of the world

Region	Percent of Age Group Enrolled	
	1965	*1970*[a]
AFRICA		
First Level (primary grades)	51	71
Second Level (secondary schools)	9	15
Third Level (postsecondary and university)	0.35	0.55
Percentage of Gross National Product Invested in Formal Education	5.78	6.96
LATIN AMERICA		
First Level	91	100
Second Level	22	34
Third Level	3.4	4.0
Percentage of Gross National Product Invested in Formal Education	4.52	5.43
ASIA		
First Level	63	74
Second Level	15	19
Third Level	3.4	4.1
Percentage of Gross National Product Invested in Formal Education	3.69	4.26

[a]Projected enrollments.
Source: From Unesco document 14 c/10, 1966. Reproduced by permission of Unesco.

SCHOOLING "ALL OF THE CHILDREN OF ALL OF THE PEOPLE"

In a world of revolutions—the scientific-technological revolution of the Old and New Worlds, the industrial and nationalistic revolutions of the "Third World"—expansion of formal education is a worldwide principle of planning.[5] This universalization of schooling is true of pre-industrial India, where 50 percent of the 6–14 age group attended school in 1961; industrialized Japan has already achieved university expansion to include 17 percent of the age group. In the Philippines educational expenditures in 1970 consumed one-third of the nation's budget. No Latin American nation keeps more than a quarter of its youngsters past grade six, nor graduates more than 1 percent from the universities, but not from lack of effort: annual school appropriations have ranged from 18 percent to over 30 percent of the total national budgets. Table 9 illustrates recent growth and shows the extent of worldwide commitment to education.

Notwithstanding unprecedented school expansion, population growth and heavy school dropout and failure rates have actually increased the world's

[5]Ivan Illich, "The Futility of Schooling in Latin America," *Saturday Review* (April 20, 1968):59; Philip H. Coombs, *The World Educational Crisis: A Systems Analysis* (New York: Oxford University Press, 1968); James S. Coleman, ed., *Education and Political Development* (Princeton, N.J.: Princeton University Press, 1965).

illiteracy by an estimated 20–25 million persons annually. The underdeveloped nations of Asia, Africa, and Latin America contain some 500 million of the world's more than 783 million illiterate adults (1970 figures). It requires four or five years of continuous instruction to establish permanent literacy skills, and the task seems hopeless in Brazil, where nearly all who enter first grade leave by grade five, or in India, where two-thirds are lost.

Youth in emerging nations aspire to schooling, especially to secondary and university educations, which are historically associated with higher status and with "clean," "inside" jobs. Yet neither jobs in the "modern sector" nor opportunities for further schooling keep pace with these aspirations.[6] Studies in Africa show that 65–90 percent of primary school graduates will be disappointed. The explosive consequences are unemployment, underemployment, and frustration. Accordingly, Tanzania resorted to limiting primary schooling to 50 percent of the age group so as to allow expansion of secondary and higher education with rigorous admissions standards. Three reasons support this policy: it improves the present one in ten chance that a primary school graduate may continue his schooling to a more functional level; it increases motivation to complete, and compete in, the primary school; and it recognizes the accelerative effect of secondary and university graduates on economic growth.

As part of its "Great Leap Forward," the People's Republic of China maintained constant enrollments in higher education in nontechnological subjects but increased its engineering school enrollments by 300 percent in five years and pushed its illiteracy rate down to 15 percent.[7] The developed nations are also convinced that educational expansion means economic growth. England managed with two universities for seven hundred years before adding the University of London and several "red brick" provincial institutions in the nineteenth century; by 1965 there were thirty universities. There were still not enough places, and 25 percent of all qualified applicants were refused; of the 8 percent of British youth receiving some postsecondary education, only half are in universities. England was also busied correcting a dropout problem that removed 60 percent of its secondary school students before age 16. Figure 3 illustrates growth in secondary schooling—traditionally a small,

[6]See Philip Foster, *Education and Social Change in Ghana* (London: Routledge & Kegan Paul, 1965); M. Nash, *The Golden Road to Modernity: Village Life in Contemporary Burma* (New York: John Wiley & Sons, Inc., 1965); Arthur Porter, "Africa," in *Essays on World Education: The Crisis of Supply and Demand*, ed. G. Z. F. Bereday (New York: Oxford University Press, 1969), pp. 225–43; Don Adams and Robert M. Bjork, *Education in Developing Areas* (New York: David McKay Co., 1969); G. Skorov, *Integration of Educational and Economic Planning in Tanzania*, African Research Monographs, No. 6 (Paris: UNESCO, 1966).

[7]Carlos P. Romulo, "Symposium on Asian Education," in Bereday, *Essays on World Education*, p. 250; C. T. Hu, ed., *Aspects of Education in Communist China* (New York: Teachers College Press, 1970); Rhea M. Whitehead, "How the Young Are Taught in Mao's China," *Saturday Review* (March 4, 1972):40–45; Albert H. Yee, "Schools and Progress in the People's Republic of China," *Educational Research,* 2 (July 1973):5–15.

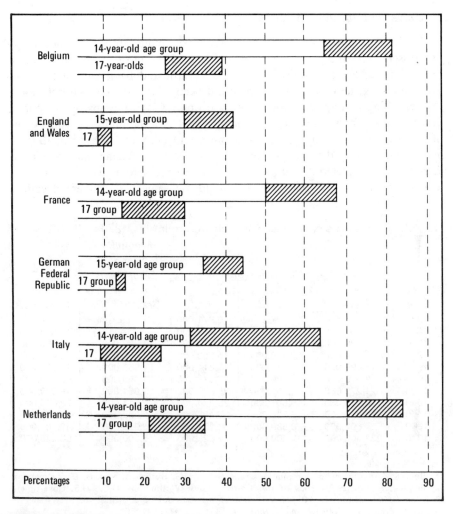

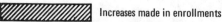 Increases made in enrollments

Adapted from R. Poignant, L'Enseignement dans les Pays du Marché Commun *(Paris: Institut Pédagogique National, 1965), p. 82. By permission.*

FIGURE 3 Percentage of full-time students by age group, and increases c. 1950–c. 1960

elitist sector—in Western Europe during the expansive 1950s, before the still more expansive 1960s. In 1957 France had 175,000 university students; a decade later the number was 500,000—a growth rate that contributed to the subsequent explosion of student unrest.

Universal Education, American Style

In the mid-nineteenth century, a Swede examining American schools was impressed that "the popular schools are one of the most prominent subjects of national pride and satisfaction. . . ."[8] Little did he dream that, within four or five generations, education would become this nation's largest industry, enrolling more than a fourth of its people. Given the absence of public interest in secondary and higher education in 1850, the undistinguished quality of America's mostly private academies and colleges, and the limiting of mass schooling to the primary level, it is especially amazing that the United States has completed the move from elite to mass to universal secondary education in but 120 years and might do the same with higher education.

TABLE 10   Elementary and secondary school enrollments, 1870 to 1970*

School Year	Public Day School Enrollments			Nonpublic Schools Enrollments (Kindergarten & Grades 1-12)	Total All Schools
	Kindergarten & Grades 1-8	Grades 9-12	Total		
1870	n.a.	n.a.	6,871,000	n.a.	n.a.
1880	9,757,000	110,000	9,868,000	n.a.	n.a.
1890	12,520,000	203,000	12,723,000	1,757,000	14,480,000
1900	14,984,000	519,000	15,503,000	1,352,000	16,855,000
1910	16,899,000	915,000	17,814,000	1,558,000	19,372,000
1920	19,378,000	2,200,000	21,578,000	1,699,000	23,278,000
1930	21,279,000	4,399,000	25,678,000	2,651,000	28,329,000
1940	18,832,000	6,601,000	25,434,000	2,611,000	28,045,000
1950	19,387,000	5,725,000	25,492,000	3,380,000	28,492,000
1960	27,692,000	8,589,000	36,281,000	5,900,000	42,181,000
1970	32,400,000	13,600,000	47,625,000	5,600,000	53,225,000

*Numbers rounded.
n.a. Not available.
Sources: Adapted from compilations reported in U.S. Bureau of Census, Department of Commerce, *Historical Statistics of the United States* (Washington, D.C.: U.S. Government Printing Office, 1960), p. 207, and *Continuations and Revisions* (1965), p. 31; "Facts on American Education," *NEA Research Bulletin,* 49 (May 1971): 47–55.

In 1970 some 58 million students were enrolled in public and nonpublic elementary and secondary schools and in degree programs in higher education. There were 2,400,000 full-time faculty and administrators. The annual school operating cost was some $55 billion.[9] Moreover, in the 1960s more under-

---

[8]P. A. Siljeström, *The Educational Institutions of the United States: Their Character and Organization,* trans. Frederica Rowan (London: John Chapman, 1853; New York: Arno Press, *New York Times,* 1969), p. v.

[9]"Facts on American Education," *NEA Research Bulletin,* 49 (May 1971):47–54, and "Public-School Statistics 1971–72 and 1970–71," *NEA Research Bulletin,* 50 (March 1972):30, which show continued growth in spending but report somewhat lower dollar totals than I calculate.

TABLE 11   United States: enrollments in relation to age groups, by decades

Year	Enrolled in School as Percent of Relevant Age Group[a]					
	Elementary School (Ages 5–13)	Secondary School (14–17)	Graduated from Secondary School (17)	Higher Education (18–19)	Higher Education (18–21)	Completed 4-Year College (25–29)
1880	n.a.	n.a.	3	n.a.	2.7	n.a.
1890	n.a.	7	4	n.a.	3	n.a.
1900	n.a.	11	6	n.a.	4	n.a.
1910	74	15	9	n.a.	5	n.a.
1920	79	32	17	n.a.	8	n.a.
1930	84	51	29	11	12	n.a.
1940	84	73	51	13	15	6
1950	86	77	59	23	27	8
1960	90	87	65	42	37	11
1970	97[b]	94	79	50	45	16

[a]Figures rounded in most cases.
n.a.Not available or not sufficiently reliable.
[b]Estimated.
Decennial Census figures for the 14–17 age group and 18–19 age group "in school" are much higher for the years 1920–50, reflecting the presence of "overage" pupils, held back because of rigid nonpromotion policies.
Sources: Adapted from data in U.S. Bureau of Census, Department of Commerce, *Historical Statistics of the United States* (1960), pp. 207, 210, 211, and *Continuations and Revisions* (1965), p. 31 (Washington, D.C.: U.S. Government Printing Office); "Facts on American Education," *NEA Research Bulletin,* 49 (May 1971): 47–55.

graduate and graduate degrees were awarded in education than in any other field; thus, education as a subject of study was itself taking up academic space. The growth of schooling at all levels and the decreasing number of the foreign-born in America[10] meant that the average American has become highly schooled, and illiteracy was reduced in the population, as figure 4 illustrates.

Popularizing Schools in America

The sophisticated European who witnessed the spread of "common schools" —public institutions, principally of elementary grade—in nineteenth-century America recognized the phenomenon. Ambitious nation-building following the Reformation and the French Revolution had also generated moves toward

[10]The influence of the foreign-born upon illiteracy statistics is suggested by these comparisons (figures rounded):

	Percent Illiterate	
Year	White, Native-born	White, Foreign-born
1880	9	12
1900	5	13
1920	2	13
1940	1	9

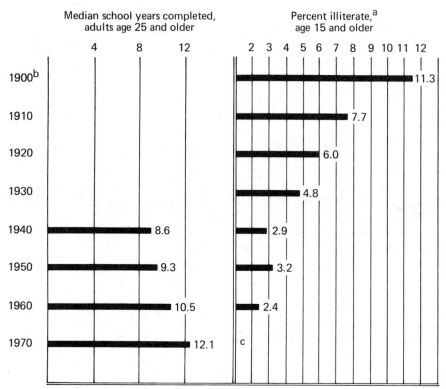

U.S. Bureau of Census, Historical Statistics of the United States *(1960)*
and Continuations *(1965) (Washington, D.C.: U.S. Government Printing
Office).*

FIGURE 4   Average educational attainment and illiteracy data for American adults

state systems of schools in Prussia and France; indeed, those nations possessed plans, unlike the seemingly haphazard American development. In the rhetoric of "education for citizenship" and for economic self-sufficiency, in the forms and diversity of institutions, and in the modes of instruction, there was much in America that smacked of European developments. Yet even then the challenges of a new environment created subtle differences that increasingly distinguished American educational experiences from those of England and the Continent. Popularization is the key.[11] When Americans linked school control to popular decision, they gave new meaning to "public"

[11]"The genius of American Education—its animating spirit, its distinctive quality—lies in the commitment to popularization.": Lawrence A. Cremin, *The Genius of American Education* (New York: Random House, Inc., 1966).

education. Consigning the content of schooling to the influence of public opinion gave schooling the diversity and breadth it still manifests. The democratization of educational opportunity committed schooling to universality, a more challenging concept than mere mass education.

As written histories of American education marvel, every decade from 1880 witnessed a doubling of enrollment in secondary education, principally in public high schools. Boston had provided one, in 1821, as an alternative to its Boston Latin Grammar School (founded in 1635) for youth who did not need classical studies as college preparation. The private, or quasi-public, academies that had previously supplied most secondary schooling declined as state legislatures over the next half-century authorized high schools. Michigan had over one hundred high schools in 1874 when its Supreme Court ruled that the Kalamazoo school board did indeed have the right to maintain a high school to

> furnish a liberal education to the youth of the state in schools brought within the reach of all classes [since] . . . education, not merely in the rudiments, but in an enlarged sense, was regarded as an important practical advantage to be supplied . . . to rich and poor alike, and not something pertaining to culture and accomplishment . . . [for] those whose accumulated wealth enabled them to pay for it.[12]

Other courts concurred, and the way was legally cleared to assemble an institutional ladder of educational opportunity, from common school to high school, to rearrange and modify existing units into a continuous "system" of schools. The four themes of improvisation, pragmatism, opportunism, and benevolence furnish keys to understanding the history of American education, and of other American institutions as well.

Improvisation is one key. No master plan guided this development; the states and localities proceeded at different rates, using different means, and arrived at somewhat different points.

Pragmatism was everywhere evident. The comprehensive high school sprang not from the ideological determination to educate all children together but from the cultural disinclination to make tidy distinctions among students and out of practical unwillingness to support a dual system—one school for college preparation, another for "terminal" students—where one could suffice. Philosophical justification came afterwards.[13]

Opportunism has turned marginal organizations into majoritarian social institutions. It was not unassisted "technocratic" development that doomed

---

[12]*Charles E. Stuart and Others* v. *School District No. 1 of the Village of Kalamazoo and Others,* 30 Michigan 69 (1874).

[13]For example, James B. Conant, *Education and Liberty* (Cambridge, Mass.: Harvard University Press, 1953), and *The American High School Today* (New York: McGraw-Hill Book Co., 1959); and Henry S. Commager, "Our High Schools Have Kept Us Free," *Life,* 29 (October 16, 1950):46–47.

the high school dropout to a marginal existence in the "expert society," or turned the middle-class youth who does not go to college into a "dropout from society." At least as responsible is that proschool conditioning of parents, of employers, and of society at large, which turned education from a "privilege" into a "right," into an "obligation"—creating a spiral of what Martin Trow calls "educational inflation." Some who exploited the opportunity were the academically able, who could compete without fear of being crushed underfoot. More important, the multitudes took advantage of educational opportunism, motivated as they were by the spirit in the nation that "causes every one . . . to be constantly on the look-out for improvements, and to adopt with fervour every opportunity. . . ."[14] The readiness that led people to emigrate, then move from town to frontier to city to suburb, to leave the East for the West and return again, to change spouses or jobs, and to found new sects also led increasing numbers into schools and colleges, until even the academically torpid in society were entangled in educational expectations.

Benevolence and *self-serving* worked together to make America the "diploma society." Conservatism supported schools to protect the status quo, while reformism saw schools as bringing needed change. Those motivated by sheer generosity, those with a romantic or liberal faith in "Everyman," and those assured of their own superiority all contributed to providing and expanding schools. To some proponents, schools were merely another welfare agency, like orphanages, almshouses, or poor relief. To others, they were substitutes; "open a school and close a prison" went the slogan.[15] Conservatives, such as Daniel Webster in 1820 and Max Rafferty in 1960, variously envisioned public schools as purifiers of community morality, civilizers of alien ways, defusers of radical ideas, sources of patriotic regeneration, and leaven to the leaden mass. Others who supported the public school system preferred tax-supported to private schools because they wished the public to subsidize the education of their own children, knowing full well that family culture and economic circumstances favored their children as the predominant school-users.[16] With every passing year, however, the schools became inexorably less the exclusive preserve of the already-privileged, although citizens without strong educational interests, whose children will not attend college or will drop out early, remain "invisible" even today to many school officials.[17]

---

[14]Siljeström, *Educational Institutions of the United States,* pp. 403, 409.

[15]Rush Welter describes the growing consensus supporting public education in the nineteenth century as "anarchy with a schoolmaster": the substitution of schooling for other social and political services: *Popular Education and Democratic Thought in America* (New York: Columbia University Press, 1962), p. 200.

[16]Michael B. Katz, *The Irony of Early School Reform* (Cambridge, Mass.: Harvard University Press, 1968), esp. p. 92.

[17]Robert E. Agger and Marshall N. Goldstein, *Who Will Rule the Schools: A Cultural Class Crisis* (Belmont, Calif.: Wadsworth Publishing Co., 1971), p. 59; Maurice Craft, ed., *Family, Class and Education: A Reader* (New York: Fernhill House, 1970). The public sector in education still spends more on the rich than on the poor. Middle-class children enroll earlier, stay longer, and are more likely to use the public colleges than are the children of the poor. Considering school expenditures over an entire life-

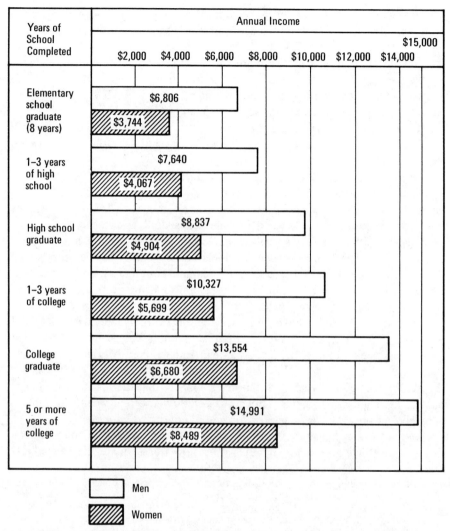

Adapted from NEA Research Bulletin, 48 (May 1970):61.

FIGURE 5 Average money income (1968) in relation to years of completed schooling

The Educational Standard of Living

Americans failing to participate fully in universal education often bear the brunt of economic uncertainty and social marginality. Every summer the "stay in school" message tells them what figure 5 shows: that more education

time, Christopher Jencks estimates that a child from the top income quarter receives twice the educational tax subsidy of a child in the bottom income quarter: *Commentary* (September 1966), p. 16.

is consistently associated with higher annual income.[18] (It does not mention, however, that white working women and black men "profit" less from additional schooling than do white men and black women—evidence of the interaction of "educational discrimination" with sex and race discrimination.) Some who drop out, who fail to go on to the next level, who experience chronic failure, or who are functionally illiterate despite their diplomas, experience lowered self-esteem and "social tarnish," even if they somehow escape economic penalties. Yet there are now some signs that internalizing failure, or the quiescent acceptance of such inevitable penalties by the most affected groups, may become less prevalent.

Our times are marked by what Warren Bennis calls "arribismo"[19]—the "unbridled desire to rise." It is seen in a self-conscious assertiveness evident among those who know, or sense, subjugation, as in such traditional victims of discrimination as blacks, Mexican-Americans, Indians, women, and homosexuals, and in such rebels against conventional mores as open drug-users and draft resisters. Persons inside schools and colleges who feel imprisoned by excessive or irrelevant educational demands on their time—those who rebel against what Paul Goodman calls "compulsory miseducation"—manifest this assertiveness.[20] Nevertheless, there are many more in America who demand more schooling, exposure to programs with higher standards, and the opportunity to attend quality institutions. Although such underrepresented groups as blacks, Puerto Ricans, American Indians, and Mexican-Americans made gains in the 1960s, they are still educationally deprived.[21] It will not be acceptable to ambitious "education have-nots" that the market for college graduates might be shrinking—not in a society whose real wealth has grown steadily, and not *just as their turn for higher education has come.*

American social history has shown the successive effect of education on its various ethnic groups.[22] The Irish were slow to assimilate, as their educa-

---

[18]Some assume that more education *causes* higher earnings because it makes one "worth more" in employment. Another interpretation is that those who will earn more *anyway* (because of talent, family connections, or other attributes) will also seek education. Another interpretation stresses the greater likelihood that the educated will seek work, find work, work full-time and work consistently, gaining advancement. See Samuel Bowles, *Planning Educational Systems for Economic Growth* (Cambridge, Mass.: Harvard University Press, 1969), and Richard H. P. Kraft, "Technological Change and the Need for Educational Adjustment," (Ph.D. diss., University of California, Berkeley, 1967).

[19]A Peruvian word, used by Bennis in *The Research Reporter,* 5:3 (1970):2 (Berkeley: Center for Research and Development in Higher Education, University of California). We are speaking here of what planners call "social demand" reasons for making certain kinds of policy decisions; there are also (and sometimes conflicting) "manpower" and "cost-benefit" approaches: Guy Benveniste, *The Politics of Expertise* (Berkeley, Calif.: The Glendessary Press, 1972), p. 180.

[20]Paul Goodman, *Compulsory Mis-education* (New York: Horizon Press, 1964).

[21]Fred E. Crossland, *Minority Access to College* (New York: Schocken Books, Inc., 1971); chap. 3, "The Importance of Being Equal," in Donald R. Thomas, *The Schools Next Time* (New York: McGraw-Hill Book Co., 1973), pp. 48–87.

[22]Nathan Glazer and Daniel Moynihan, *Beyond the Melting Pot* (Cambridge, Mass.: M.I.T. Press and Harvard University Press, 1963); Herbert Gans, *The Urban Villagers*

Cartoon by John G. Stees. Copyright © Baltimore Sun.

"We're loaded with PhD's, BA's, and MA's. What we need is a couple of good body and fender men."

tional reactions have shown. But now Irish-Americans attend college in the same proportions as the general population. This may soon be true of Italian-Americans. Investigators report virtually as much emphasis on schooling, encouragement, and assistance in Mexican-American homes as in other families, although Chicano aspirations and achievement are not yet equalized. The Puerto Rican and black populations that Joseph Lyford studied were less marked by anti-establishment militancy than by the achievement standards and values ordinarily described as "middle-class." The minority-group parental demands of lower-class persons can be higher and more anxiety-producing than those imposed by middle-class majoritarian America.[23] Such demands are at great variance with both the parents' own abilities to help their children realize these expectations and the realities of frequent (but not invariable) lower-class academic retardation.

(New York: Free Press, 1962); Estelle Fuchs and Robert J. Havighurst, *To Live on This Earth: American Indian Education* (Garden City, N.Y.: Doubleday & Co., 1973); Henry S. Johnson and William J. Hernandez, eds., *Educating the Mexican Americans* (Valley Forge, Pa.: Judson Press, 1971); Joseph P. Lyford, *The Airtight Cage: A Study of New York's West Side* (New York: Harper & Row, Publishers, 1966); Francesco Cordasco and Eugene Bucchioni, eds., *The Puerto Rican Community and Its Children on the Mainland* (Metuchen, N.J.: The Scarecrow Press, Inc., 1972).

[23]Irwin Katz, "Academic Motivation and Equal Educational Opportunity," *Harvard Educational Review*, 38 (Winter 1968):57–65.

EDUCATION: POPULAR, BUT NOT UNIVERSAL

If the term *universal education* means an education that operates, by various means, to permit every individual to realize himself fully, then American society does not yet offer universal education. If we limit the definition of universality to providing an equal opportunity for each individual and every social group to be schooled to the limit of personal desire and social need, the negative evidence is still weighty. A nation's educational structure may be free (tax-supported), compulsory (to limit exploitation of youth by parents or employers), comprehensive, under public control, and democratic in its aims—and still fail consistently to meet many legitimate aspirations. Let us consider some of these failures.

The School and the Immigrant

Some observers see the present inability of American schools to reach and to teach large segments of America's minority populations as an element of continuity with yesterday's schools.[24] Today's problems, especially in large urban centers, had their counterparts in the big-city schools of the 1890s, when most of the lowest classes were white immigrants. In Cleveland 38 percent of the white population in 1890 was foreign-born; in 1966 one-half of the elementary and one-third the secondary enrollments were from foreign-language homes.[25] Similar figures pertained elsewhere. So did the consequences associated with the mutual response of school and immigrant child: high nonpromotion figures (40–65 percent of students were "repeaters"—held back 1–5 years behind their age group); high dropout rates (50–60 percent of those who even reached high school in the 1920s and 1930s)[26]; widespread reading retardation; and placing language-deficient children in the "backward class."

The upward extension of compulsory schooling intensified failure in the high schools. It prompted the assignment of poor achievers (consistently overrepresented by children from poor families) to vocational and general

[24]Michael Katz, *Class, Bureaucracy, and Schools: The Illusion of Educational Change in America* (New York: Praeger Publishers, 1971). For a less extreme view see the survey of research by David K. Cohen, "Immigrants and the Schools," *Review of Educational Research,* 40 (February 1970):13–27; Timothy Smith, "Immigrant Social Aspirations and American Education," *American Quarterly,* 21 (Fall 1969):523–43; or the case study approach, such as Humbert S. Nelli, *Italians in Chicago, 1880–1930: A Study in Ethnic Mobility* (New York: Oxford University Press, 1970).

[25]Herbert Adolphus Miller, *The School and the Immigrant* (Cleveland: Survey Committee of the Cleveland Foundation, 1916; New York: Arno Press, *New York Times,* 1970). A 1908 study of the United States Immigration Commission found that 58 percent of the school children in the 37 largest cities were of foreign parentage.

[26]Writing of the dropout of 50 years ago, Edgar Z. Friedenberg notes that many took existing unskilled jobs. "They weren't a dropout problem; they were the working class." In "An Ideology of School Withdrawal," *Profile of the School Dropout,* ed. Daniel Schreiber (New York: Random House, Inc., 1967), p. 16.

tracks.[27] American schools may have widened the differences between the middle and bottom social classes, increasing economic segregation. They often acted less effectively to equalize than to confirm different futures for their students.[28]

The school's failure to meet the child of the immigrant on his own terms meant several things. First, it showed the public school's commitment to cultural homogeneity, a continuous inability to condone cultural difference— whether carried by the Irish, the lower-class Jew, the migrant worker's child, or the ghetto black. Perhaps since the English colonists' first fumbling attempts to convert and educate the Indians, American education was fated to attempt to erase differences, to "acculturate" diverse groups, to integrate the many into the one.[29] Such cultural nationalists as Noah Webster clearly stated such a purpose, and Jefferson's objections to a foreign education implied it. A writer in *The Massachusetts Teacher* worried aloud in 1851 that the Irish immigration, like the muddy Missouri contaminating the clear waters of the Mississippi, might "spread ignorance and vice, crime and disease, through our native population." Short of barring such immigration, "the remedy is education. The rising population must be taught as our own children are taught." As the Boston School Committee cautioned in 1858, the school day must become

> hours of instruction, of active exercise of the mind, and of the personal
> influence of the teacher on both the mind and the heart of every pupil . . .
> taking children at random from a great city, undisciplined, uninstructed, often
> with inveterate forwardness and obstinacy, and with the inherited stupidity of
> centuries of ignorant ancestors; forming them from animals into intellectual
> beings; giving to many their first appreciation of what is wise, what is true, what
> is lovely, and what is pure. . . .[30]

Whether cultural variety originated in religion, ethnicity, race, or social class, the schools—and those social groups that most influenced them—were concerned with "Americanization," with "molding character," with teaching

[27]Edward A. Krug, *The Shaping of the American High School, II* (Madison, Wis.: University of Wisconsin Press, 1972), esp. chap. 5.

[28]Robert H. Wiebe, "The Social Functions of Public Education," *American Quarterly,* 21 (Summer 1969):147–64; Henry J. Perkinson, *The Imperfect Panacea: American Faith in Education, 1865–1965* (New York: Random House, Inc., 1968), esp. pp. 144– 59; Sol Cohen, "The Industrial Education Movement 1906–1917," *American Quarterly,* 20 (Spring 1968):95–110.

[29]Carl F. Kaestle, *The Evolution of an Urban School System: New York City, 1750– 1850* (Cambridge, Mass.: Harvard University Press, 1973).

[30]Quoted in Katz, *School Reform,* pp. 169–72. A leader of the kindergarten movement reportedly characterized slum children as "little savages from three to five, the pests of the street, their mouths full of profane and obscene language": in Marvin Lazerson, "Urban Reform and the Schools: Kindergartens in Massachusetts, 1870–1915," *History of Education Quarterly,* 11 (Summer 1971):121n.

SECTARIAN BITTERNESS.

Thomas Nast, "Sectarian Bitterness" (wood engraving), Harper's Weekly,
14 (February 26, 1870):140.

values. Caught between conflicting cultures, the child successful in school
often paid the price of estrangement from family.

The cultural bias of middle-class, anti-urban, Protestant, "old-American"
stock was also operating against the religious and ethnic character of the
later immigrations. It was from this earlier population that most teachers
and administrators came, and as Kenneth Eble puts it succinctly, "Teachers
like students who are like themselves."[31] This period was also one of intense
interest in heredity, eugenics, and race. Hence, ethnocentrism sometimes
showed itself in a contemptuous skepticism of the innate abilities of the new
masses. Quite possibly the upturn of interest by the Protestant upper-middle
class in going to college, which coincided with this immigration, was a way
of marking one's group apart and gaining some "status insurance"—reinforced, if necessary, by institutional quotas on Catholic and Jewish student
admissions.

The "immigrant question" remains germane to considering the modern
urban educational dilemma. First, the responses of students or systems
encountered in such recent history can recur. Second, immigration, although
much reduced, continues to introduce "strangers in the land," especially
since the Immigration Act amendment of 1965, when very large increases
in annual immigration rates began among Italians, Greeks, Chinese, and
Filipinos. Still more important are the birthright Americans—the Puerto
Rican, black, and Appalachian white migrants who arouse hostile responses
in the neighborhoods (and probably in the schools), and who themselves
react appreciably as did earlier immigrants.[32] Third, the descendants of those

[31]*Professors as Teachers* (San Francisco: Jossey-Bass, Inc., 1972), p. 147.

[32]Oscar Handlin, *The Newcomers: Negroes and Puerto Ricans in a Changing Metropolis* (Garden City, N.Y.: Doubleday & Co., 1962). See also Don Spiegel and Patricia
Keith Spiegel, *Outsiders U.S.A.* (San Francisco: Rinehart Press, 1973).

very groups of immigrants that so often fared poorly in yesterday's school constitute much of today's white working class. Many are economically and socially insecure, resentful of other groups' demands on what have been their neighborhoods, their jobs, and their schools. Moreover, they have felt overlooked in the much-publicized drive to secure equal educational opportunities for minorities, especially for black Americans.

The unions, which represent many of the descendants of the immigrants, have been concerned far less with social mobility than with improving working conditions and economic security at their members' present social levels; their jealously guarded apprenticeship programs are preparation for the trade, not out of it. One example of union activity in increasing educational opportunity may illuminate the situation. In 1966 the International Brotherhood of Teamsters established an annual college scholarship program; the Teamsters Union is the largest single labor body in the United States, having over two million members. Annually, *eight* sons and daughters of Teamster members are awarded the James R. Hoffa Scholarship, two from each of the four "conference" areas (regions) of the United States. The selection committee, composed of college admissions directors, considers "scholastic aptitude, financial need, high school average, rank in class, honors and awards, participation in extracurricular activities and counselor recommendations."[33] Four of the eight 1969–70 winners were also National Merit Scholarship finalists, and another won the award; all were already prime candidates for college admission and for other sources of scholarship aid. Hence, in both number of award and selection criteria used, the national Teamsters' scholarship program could not itself expand the educational opportunities of its members' children.

The Case of Black Americans

The Negro and the Schools, a scholarly and comprehensive study of segregation in education, was published on May 16, 1954. It was sponsored by the Ford Foundation's Fund for the Advancement of Education.[34] The book was destined to gain wide attention, for, on May 17, the United States Supreme Court ruled against the racially segregated schools maintained by the Topeka, Kansas, school board. The pursuit of equal educational opportunity for black youth aimed at overturning powerful traditions of educational discrimination —beginning with legal prohibitions against teaching slaves to read. In the waning years of the nineteenth century, a Georgia governor expressed what

[33]*The International Teamster,* 67:6 (June 1970):19–21. Various Teamster locals also may award scholarships. For example, Local 142 (Gary, Ind.) awarded 16 college scholarships in 1972, totaling $4,300: *The International Teamster,* 69:12 (December 1972):23.

[34]Harry S. Ashmore, *The Negro and the Schools* (Chapel Hill: University of North Carolina Press, 1954).

was undoubtedly a widespread opinion, saying: "I do not believe in the higher education of the darkey. He must be taught the trades. When he is taught the fine arts, he is educated above his caste, and it makes him unhappy."[35]

As the twentieth century unfolded, the black student commonly found himself headed toward the lower-class future of many immigrant youth. When not encouraged into vocational education, the nonachievement "culture" typical of his school had the same result—but without giving him a modicum of job training. When combined with outright discrimination in hiring and promotion, and with failure to achieve the improvement in relative economic status enjoyed by much of the white working class through union activity, the result was a massive concentration of blacks in unskilled employment: as porters, elevator operators, and janitors, as laundresses and charwomen. As this sector of the job market constricted, black economic and social insecurity relative to whites actually worsened: in 1939 white and black proportional unemployment was nearly equal; by 1972 the black rate was over twice that for whites. The racial differential in family income actually increased slightly after 1970. From 1940 to 1960 black infant mortality increased from 70 percent higher to 90 percent higher than the comparable figures for whites. The proportion of black families headed by a woman grew from one-fourth in 1968 to more than one-third in 1972.

Table 12 shows pertinent comparative standings midway through the turbulent civil rights decade of the 1960s. In addition to the marked racial differences on virtually every index, three other facts are especially important. First, a larger proportion of blacks are of school age. (Whereas blacks, Chicanos, Native Americans, and Puerto Ricans constitute 15 percent of the total population, they are about 18 percent of the 18–24 age group.) This means that the massive problem of securing educational parity will not vanish with time. It also means that reversing the educational underinvestment in black youth has considerable potential for future social and economic development. Second, these data do not give the lie to Kenneth Clark's assertion that schools have intensified class distinctions—in this case, between the races. Unless schooling can be massively employed to compensate for discriminatory employment practices and any other handicaps that may be associated with race in a multiracial society, current conditions effectively block the economic

---

[35]In *Atlanta Journal*, April 24, 1901. Much historical work should be done on Negro education, but see Henry Allen Bullock, *A History of Negro Education in the South, from 1619 to the Present* (Cambridge, Mass.: Harvard University Press, 1967); Louis Harlan, *Separate and Unequal* (Chapel Hill: University of North Carolina Press, 1958); Charles Dabney, *Universal Education in the South* (Chapel Hill: University of North Carolina Press, 1936); Horace Mann Bond, *The Education of the Negro in the American Social Order* (New York: Octagon Books, Inc., 1966); Henry L. Swint, *The Northern Teachers in the South, 1862–1870* (Nashville, Tenn.: Vanderbilt University Press, 1941).

TABLE 12 United States: comparative statistics of white and black populations, 1966

Item	WHITE			BLACK		
	Men	Women	Total	Men	Women	Total
Total population	83,302,000	87,472,000	170,774,000	10,355,000	11,153,000	21,508,000
Residential distribution:						
Metropolitan areas			63.8%			68.8%
Cities			27.2%			56.1%
Suburbs			36.6%			12.6%
Nonmetropolitan areas			36.2%			31.2%
Moved in previous year			18.8%			22.9%
Age distribution:						
Under age 18	36.8%	33.7%	35.2%	47.2%	43.2%	45.1%
Years of schooling, age 25 and older:	12.0	12.1	12.1	8.7	9.5	9.1
less than 5 years	5.7%	4.7%	5.2%	23.2%	14.0%	18.3%
4 yrs. high school or more	51.3%	53.0%	52.2%	25.8%	29.4%	27.8%
1 or more yrs. college	22.5%	17.1%	19.7%	8.6%	9.1%	8.9%
Occupational distribution, age 18 and older:						
White-collar workers	42.3%	63.0%		14.8%	23.2%	
Professional, technical, managerial (nonfarm)	28.8%	20.2%		7.0%	9.9%	
Clerical, sales, and kindred workers	13.5%	42.9%		7.9%	13.3%	
Manual workers, craftsmen, foremen, and kindred workers	20.6%	17.3%		10.3%	15.8%	
Operatives and kindred workers	20.2%			31.0%		
Laborers, non farm and mine	5.0%	0.3%		22.4%	1.0%	
Service workers	5.9%	17.4%		15.0%	58.5%	
Farm workers	6.0%	2.0%		6.5%	1.5%	
Median family income			$7,251.			$3,886.

Source: U.S. Bureau of Census, "Negro Population, March 1966," *Current Population Reports*, Series P–20, No. 168 (Washington, D.C.: U.S. Government Printing Office, Dec. 22, 1967).

95

mobility of blacks in the "diploma society."[36] But American blacks are not yet getting even as much schooling; if anything, the "years of schooling" statistics probably disguise even greater educational retardation. Finally, at every level black women complete more schooling than do black men, a female advantage found in no other group in America. Several factors seem to cause this phenomenon: job and wage discrimination is less severe against black women than against men, encouraging women realistically to persist in school; more education is a special advantage to women who are heads of households, a common pattern in the black community; and the family socialization received by black girls gives them some sort of advantage over their brothers in coping with schools.

What Happened to the Coed?

The emphasis of school culture upon neatness, quietness, conservatism, and inaction has led observers to call it "feminine." These attributes apparently issue partly from the nature of school tasks and partly from the preponderance of women teachers, especially in the formative primary grades; even in universities, where women faculty are small minorities, some persons claim that male professors have always succeeded in schools by becoming "feminized males."[37] The existence of compulsory schools—"female enclaves in a man's world"—frequently constricts the opportunities and positive self-images not only of the lower classes, by being middle-class institutions, but also of male students, by their feminine climate and reward system. Hence there is a tendency for lower-class males to be academically maladjusted.

Social science research on learning sex roles, educational and occupational studies of enrollment and employment trends, and cultural history give some support to such theories of sex-typing and its often dysfunctional effects.[38]

[36]Recent dramatic increases in the level of schooling completed by American blacks, relative to whites, have *not* been matched by a narrowed gap in income between the two races: "The Effects of Education on the Earnings of Blacks and Whites," *Review of Economics and Statistics,* 52 (May 1970):150–59; U.S. Census Bureau, "The Social and Economic Status of the Black Population in the United States, 1972" (Washington, D.C.: United States Government Printing Office, 1973).

[37]Patricia Sexton, *The Feminized Male* (New York: Random House, Inc., 1969), esp. pp. 29–39.

[38]Beverly I. Fagot and Gerald R. Patterson, "An In Vivo Analysis of Reinforcing Contingencies for Sex-Role Behavior in the Preschool Child," *Developmental Psychology,* 1 (December 1969):563–68. See also Arthur L. Stinchcombe, *Rebellion in a High School* (Chicago: Quadrangle Books, Inc., 1964), pp. 36–40; Nancy Frazier and Myra Sadker, *Sexism in School and Society* (New York: Harper & Row, Publishers, 1973); Patrick C. Lee, "The Early Classroom Experience: Masculine or Feminine?" *Perspectives on Education* (New York: Teachers College, Columbia University), Fall 1973, pp. 10–15.

Boys have *more to do* in this society than do girls, busying themselves with athletics, cars, hobbies, and other "outward-oriented" pursuits; girls are forced to concentrate upon the personal attributes of appearance—clothes and "good looks": James S. Coleman, *The Adolescent Society* (New York: The Free Press, 1961).

The fact that intellectual and cultural pursuits are made "womanly" creates yet another arbitrary discrimination, sexual ascription. As Van Wyck Brooks once observed, in America the men are busy trying to collect all the money in the world, and the women all the culture. The larger society, which is male-dominated, compensates for its academic estrangement by distrusting schooling that is not patently vocational and "no nonsense" training. Failing to equip girls to cope, psychosexually, with what the society considers maleness, schools also deprive themselves, female students, and society of developed

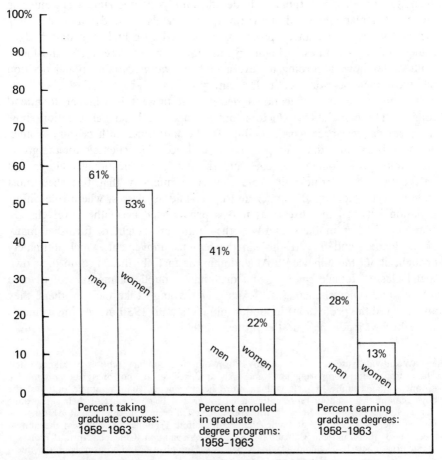

Adapted from Laure M. Sharp, "Five Years After the College Degree: Part I: Graduate and Professional Education" (Washington, D.C.: Bureau of Social Science Research, Inc., 1965), mimeo. (Findings subsequently published in Laure M. Sharp, Education and Employment: The Early Careers of College Graduates *(Baltimore: Johns Hopkins University Press, 1970). By permission.*

FIGURE 6 Men and women college graduates: their academic plans (United States college graduates, class of 1958)

talent in what have been the more "masculine" fields of science, mathematics, and engineering.

Common sense supposes that, if school culture favors girls, they will show less dissatisfaction, succeed more often, achieve more, and persist longer. Studies comparing male and female high school students on standardized achievement tests and grades earned in secondary and higher education, for example, find that females do better, supporting the sexual-bias thesis.[39] Yet women, on the average, fall behind in not pursuing higher education as often; tending to drop out of college with greater frequency, when compared with male students of comparable aptitude and family income status; not entering the more demanding (and status-rewarding) fields of study; and persisting less in completing advanced programs associated with higher income and/or leadership opportunities.[40] Figure 6 indicates some of these facts; and figure 7 illustrates how, according to several indices, women's educational position relative to men has worsened in this century.

The most decisive educational decision at present is whether to attend college. Those social-class factors that affect educational participation show some sexual variances worth noting. In the late nineteenth century women began to break into the male preserve of colleges. The clientele for the growing numbers of women's colleges and the newly coeducational colleges and universities came principally from the same minority that furnished most male college students: the upper and upper-middle classes, where role differentiation between the sexes was not as pronounced as in the lower classes. These coeds' own mothers, and later they and their daughters, furnished many of the leaders and the "troops" in the feminist movement, which ultimately brought about the Nineteenth Amendment, de facto birth control in their own social classes, female smoking and drinking in public, a measure of divorce reform, and other challenges to sexual stereotyping. Like their brothers, they also entered the professions in modest numbers until 1930, increasing women's share in law, medicine, and the professoriate.[41]

---

[39]Worldwide studies show that boys drop out of secondary schools at higher rates. Therefore, studies comparing boys and girls at this level are not analyzing *comparable* groups; i.e., a sample of girls will be more heterogeneous than a sample of boys, the boys remaining in school representing a narrower and brighter part of their sex group: Carol N. Jacklin and Eleanor E. Maccoby, "Sex Difference in Intellectual Abilities: A Reassessment and a Look at Some New Explanations." (Paper presented at the annual meetings of the American Educational Research Association, Chicago, April 1972.)

[40]Christopher Jencks and David Riesman, "Feminism, Masculinism, and Coeducation," *The Academic Revolution* (Garden City, N.Y.: Doubleday & Co., Inc., 1968), pp. 290–311. See also David Riesman, "Some Continuities and Discontinuities in the Education of Women," *Abundance for What? and Other Essays* (Garden City, N.Y.: Doubleday & Co., 1964), pp. 324–48; Cynthia Fuchs Epstein, *Woman's Place* (Berkeley: University of California Press, 1971). A study conducted by the American Council on Education, and reported in the *New York Times* (August 26, 1973) indicates that, despite considerable federal and feminist pressures, over a three-year period the proportion of college faculty who were women rose only from 19.1 to 20 percent.

[41]Full-time college and university faculty positions had gone to women in these percentages: 1900: 20 percent; 1930: 37 percent; 1970: 20 percent. See Jesse Bernard,

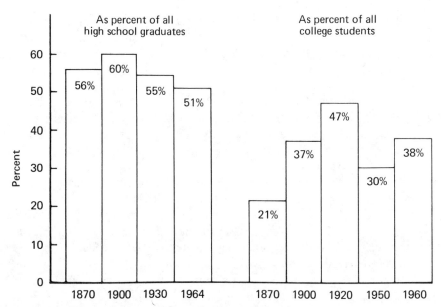

Adapted from data in U.S. Bureau of Census, Historical Statistics of the United States, Colonial Times to 1957 *(1960) and* Continuations to 1962 and Revisions *(1965) (Washington, D.C.: U.S. Government Printing Office).*

FIGURE 7   Women in the school population: historical perspective

As more middle-class persons went to college, girls kept pace with their brothers. One contributing factor was the long-standing tradition of teaching careers for women of middle-class origins.[42] But the explosion of college-going after 1945 left the coed behind. One-third of America's 11 million veterans enrolled in colleges and universities, using G.I. Bill benefits; most were middle-class or higher. Without such financial aid, their sisters could not attend in such numbers. The new cultural ethos, emphasizing early marriage and large families, also removed women from the earlier generation that had gone off to college in the spirit of female uplift and personal freedom.

Although class-related factors have progressively less influence on high school graduation, they remain strong in determining college entrance and the college graduation decision; in fact, social class seems most to affect the academically marginal student and women students.[43] Indifferent students

---

The Academic Woman (University Park: Pennsylvania State University Press, 1964); Eleanor Flexner, *Century of Struggle* (Cambridge, Mass.; Harvard University Press, 1959), on the story to 1920; Anne Firor Scott, ed., *The American Woman: Who Was She?* (Englewood Cliffs, N.J.: Prentice-Hall, Inc., 1971), esp. pp. 11–58.

[42]In 1966 38 percent of women and 26 percent of men majoring in education came from homes where family income was $10,000 or more: *NEA Research Bulletin,* 47 (December 1969):105. (See chap. 6 for a fuller discussion of the social characteristics of American teachers.)

[43]See "Social Stratification and Mass Higher Education" in Jencks and Riesman, *The Academic Revolution,* pp. 61–154.

who enter college usually find their studies arduous and unpleasant; some are dismissed and more leave voluntarily. Women students face the additional obstacle that daughters ordinarily have less claim than their brothers on college dollars when middle-income families have several children to educate.

In every region of the world, although not in the United States, illiteracy rates for women are markedly higher than for men—40.3 percent to 28 percent in 1970; male illiteracy rates also drop more quickly. In America there are cultural, religious, or ethnic groups in which the status of females has traditionally been low, and in which boys and girls operate under markedly different norms; the educational opportunities of sons and daughters in these groups will be even more sharply differentiated than in the rest of the society. Such a factor may help explain why males so predominate among Oriental undergraduates. There is also less social support to continue her schooling if the woman student of any social class marries while in college—or so the data on married students suggest.

When one speaks of working-class families, financial and moral support for a daughter's advanced education, and for the longer and more expensive programs therein, become problematical indeed[44]—excepting perhaps in the case of the black woman, who has an advantage over her brother. Compound these problems with the strong prejudice in many graduate schools against women students, the numerous "put downs" experienced by ambitious women, and it becomes clearer why militant women often liken their status to that of black Americans.

FACTORS AFFECTING EDUCATIONAL ACCESS, SUCCESS,
AND PERSISTENCE

The previous section concentrated upon three populations that do not participate equitably in the nation's educational systems or in its economic and cultural life. These groups—each with its own history—have been marked off by difference of ethnicity, race, or gender. There are several other characteristics, whether of the educational system or carried to it by students, that have been found to impinge upon both any individual's (or group's) opportunity to use the system to his and society's advantage, and the system's ability to become or remain universal.

These factors are cost and availability of educational slots, student ability, personality, previous academic achievement and school experience, and cultural-family factors; social class influences all of these factors. We will focus this discussion upon higher education because this is the level now "in

---

[44]On sex roles and relationships in the stable working class, see Mirra Komarovsky, *Blue-Collar Marriage* (New York: Random House, Inc., 1962). Komarovsky found that while educational level increases book reading among men, it does not among women. (Three-fifths of those interviewed never read books.)

limbo" between "mass" and "universal" characteristics, and this is now the locus of critical personal decisions. (In 1970, 50.5 percent of all high school graduates did not enroll in post-secondary schooling, while the figure for those who attend college but do not complete their course has remained stable at about 50 percent.)

Financial Barriers to Exercising Educational Options

By 1973 the cost of attending college ranged from $1,635 per year for average commuter students attending public institutions to $3,280 for resident students at private institutions, according to a survey by the College Scholarship Service of the College Entrance Examination Board. Among college costs, economists also include wages unearned because of school attendance—a critical factor for lower classes and for groups that reproduce the immigrant pattern of sixty years ago requiring that children beyond compulsory school age become employed to pay the family debt, help the family become established, and finance the immigration of relatives left in the Old Country. The new Portuguese immigration illustrates this: in New Bedford, Massachusetts, with a large concentration of the newly arrived, the high school dropout rate is 95 percent for all 16-year-old Portuguese youth (compared to 24 percent nationally in 1970).[45]

Not even those nations that restrict higher education to a fraction of the youth population and commonly aid most or all who are admitted go far toward opening university doors by reducing economic inequality. In the Soviet Union authorities estimate that three-quarters of those enrolled in higher educational institutions receive stipends. These stipends vary greatly in adequacy, and are differentially used also to develop government-favored fields of study.[46] The United States, lacking national planning authority for education, and having a mixed system of public, private, state, local, and federal institutions, has improvised in the student-aid area. To date, much of the aid effort has been limited to tuition and other instructional costs, hardly sufficient for students from poor homes, who attend college without adequate clothing, supplies, and spending money.

Scholarships   English colonists imported the tradition of scholarships. For several reasons, this aid has only a limited effect in furthering opportunity. Too few scholarship monies are available. In 1966–67 private collegiate institutions allocated only 5.7 percent of their current-fund expenditures for

---

[45]"Immigrants of a Feather . . . ," *Christian Science Monitor*, March 24, 1970. A national poll found one of five black families with a high school dropout; one out of three reported financial reasons: *Newsweek*, 63 (July 29, 1963), p. 18. While financial reasons are often unsupported by research as the "real" factor in college dropouts or in going on to graduate school, it seems more creditable when speaking of the high school dropout—who is concentrated in the unstable lower class.

[46]Herbert C. Rudman, *The School and State in the USSR* (New York: Macmillan, 1969), p. 71.

student aid (including emergency grants, tuition waivers, etc.), while in public institutions, with their larger share of poorer students, the figure was 3.0 percent.[47] Grants and cash prizes awarded by foundations, organizations, businesses, unions, governments, and individuals are also inadequate. The size of the typical award is inadequate except to supplement other income; undergraduate scholarships rarely exceed tuition charges in value. The competitive or restrictive nature of most scholarships limits their function as a "breakthrough" for new student populations. Scholarships tend to be awarded to those already predisposed to college careers, although they may "make a difference" in many individual decisions. Scholarship opportunities (and work provisions) are unevenly distributed across fields; law and medical school scholarships lag behind, for example.

Loans   Since 1967 federally insured, deferred-payment bank loans for students have supplemented other loan arrangements; in three years the government program stimulated 1.2 million loans, exceeding $1 billion. How much such loans materially widened educational opportunity remains uncertain. Loans have some of the same limitations as scholarships, and the federal program is restricted to full-time students. Dael Wolfle earlier found that most loans are taken out by those already planning for college—not by lower-class youth whose family credit was poor and whose expectations for borrowing covered consumer items but not investment purposes like college education, nor by women unwilling to saddle a future husband with such a debt or doubtful of their ability to repay it if they marry.[48]

For most students, especially those who attend community or state colleges, cost is a major factor in determining choice of an institution and deters altogether many other youth from pursuing further schooling. It is probable that the relative lack of really low-income students in higher education partly explains why studies show that financial status does not account for most of the lack of persistence in college.[49] Jencks and Riesman probably assessed the contributing effect of lack of money realistically:

> Getting through college without help from home requires more interest in college than many students feel. . . . One is hardly likely to go if few of his friends go, if college life strikes him as being different from anything he has experienced

---

[47]*NEA Research Bulletin,* 48 (May 1970):40–41. College-going costs increased by two-thirds or more in the 1960s, rising faster than family income or levels of available student aid. On the scholarship situation in tuition-based schools, see Otto F. Kraushaar, *American Nonpublic Schools* (Baltimore: The Johns Hopkins University Press, 1972), pp. 248–51.

[48]Dael Wolfle, *America's Resources of Specialized Talent* (New York: Harper & Row, Publishers, 1954); Anna Hawkes, "Factors Affecting College Attendance," in *The Education of Women,* ed. Opal D. David (Washington, D.C.: American Council on Education, 1959), p. 31.

[49]James W. Trent and Leland Medsker, *Beyond High School; A Psycho-Social Study of 10,000 High School Graduates* (San Francisco: Jossey-Bass, Inc., 1968); Bruce K. Eckland, "Social Class and College Graduation: Some Misconceptions Corrected," *American Journal of Sociology,* 70 (July 1964):36–50.

to date, and if he is going to have to work long hours after school and live in penury to make it. Money, in short, is seldom an insuperable problem when taken in isolation, but it may be decisive for the student who is ambivalent anyway.[50]

Witness the situation confronting many a middle-class black youngster. His family's aspirations, perhaps his parents' college education, the chance that some of his friends are college bound, and his own drive push him toward college. He will probably go—given inexpensive community colleges, black colleges in the South, and minority-designated scholarships—despite his family's unfavorable economic rank. For the working-class youngster of whatever race, on the other hand, the financial obstacles typically become insurmountable by being combined, as they often are, with too many other depressants on fragile college ambitions.

Availability of Institutions

Does the accessibility of institutions promote their use and encourage universality in education? From America's earliest days the answer seems to have been "yes, somewhat." Rural-urban differences and historic regional variations in the availability of schools appear to have been related to literacy, median educational level, college-going, intellectual activity, and various other pertinent characteristics—although other factors were surely operating, and the cause-effect relationship seems a circular one. Although New England historically enjoyed disproportionate college-going because of its concentration of many private colleges, sparsely settled Vermont, with its problems of winter travel and weather, has the nation's lowest proportion of high school graduates in college. California, with several decades of rapid growth in various kinds of public higher education, has led the nation in percentages of young people attending college. Before high schools were widely available in rural areas, many students attended the state normal schools, some to train themselves to teach school, others to secure a secondary education; they used what was available. Data for 1966–67 indicated that 51 percent of high school graduates in metropolitan areas, where colleges and especially universities are more generally available, entered college; the comparable figure for nonmetropolitan communities was 40 percent.[51] Table 13 suggests that equality of opportunity depends partly upon where one lives.

---

[50]*The Academic Revolution,* p. 119.

[51]An example is Bishop College—a "traditionally black," small town private institution—which tripled its enrollment in a decade by relocating in Dallas, Texas, despite raising both its admissions standards and tuition fees: Crossland, *Minority Access to College,* p. 123. A study of 1966 high school graduates in Illinois and North Carolina, however, disputes any conclusion that college proximity *per se* importantly affects college-going rates; the only exception seemed to be students of lower ability who were positively affected by the presence of a local community college: Vincent Tinto, "College Proximity and Rates of College Attendance," *American Educational Research Journal,* 10 (Fall 1973):277–93.

TABLE 13 "Free-Access"[a] Colleges by State, 1970

Regions and States	Pop. in Millions (1967)	No. of Colls.		Pct. of Pop. within Commuting Distance of Free-Access Colls.				Ratio of Coll. Freshmen[b] to High School Graduates			
		Total	Free-Access	Total	White	Black	Sp. surname	Ratio	Pub.	Pri.	Out-of-State
NORTHEAST	48.2	647	92	38%	38%	37%	—[c]	.59	.28	.15	.16
Connecticut	2.9	47	13	87%	87%	90%	—	.67	.26	.13	.28
Maine	1.0	22	0	0%	0%	—	—	.35	.19	.05	.11
Massachusetts	5.4	105	13	52%	53%	25%	—	.66	.24	.28	.14
New Hampshire	0.7	20	2	44%	44%	—	—	.45	.21	.08	.17
New Jersey	7.0	57	10	38%	36%	59%	—	.59	.20	.09	.30
New York	18.3	206	34	36%	38%	23%	36%	.71[d]	.39	.18	.14
Pennsylvania	11.6	155	16	25%	24%	41%	—	.43	.21	.12	.10
Rhode Island	0.9	15	1	41%	40%	60%	—	.67	.30	.19	.18
Vermont	0.4	20	3	41%	41%	—	—	.34	.15	.07	.12
SOUTH	61.4	821	312[e]	50%	50%	52%	—	.52	.37	.08	.07
Alabama	3.5	50	24	56%	57%	54%	—	.47	.35	.06	.06
Arkansas	2.0	23	12	43%	43%	42%	—	.55	.39	.08	.08
Delaware	0.5	6	2	35%	35%	44%	—	.49	.23	.08	.18
D.C.	0.8	19	3	82%	82%	81%	—	n.a.	n.a.	n.a.	n.a.
Florida	6.0	59	26	64%	62%	72%	—	.65	.49	.06	.10
Georgia	4.5	56	14	30%	33%	24%	—	.41	.28	.06	.07
Kentucky	3.2	47	17	52%	51%	69%	—	.49	.35	.08	.06
Louisiana	3.7	27	15	48%	49%	47%	—	.49	.42	.03	.04
Maryland	3.7	50	19	57%	59%	47%	—	.52	.32	.05	.15
Mississippi	2.3	46	26	65%	67%	63%	—	.64	.52	.07	.04
N. Carolina	5.0	92	29	68%	69%	67%	—	.41	.25	.12	.04
Oklahoma	2.5	36	16	31%	31%	26%	—	.62	.49	.08	.05
S. Carolina	2.6	52	12	56%	58%	53%	—	.39	.18	.13	.08
Tennessee	3.9	55	16	41%	39%	52%	—	.46	.31	.09	.06
Texas	15.9	113	54	38%	37%	43%	40%	.61	.49	.08	.03
Virginia	4.9	63	15	50%	52%	40%	—	.47	.26	.07	.14
W. Virginia	1.8	27	12	54%	53%	59%	—	.42	.31	.06	.05
MIDWEST	55.1	740	193	33%	33%	39%	57%	.55	.39	.08	.08
Illinois	10.9	125	41	56%	56%	59%	57%	.68	.43	.11	.14

TABLE 13 (continued)

Indiana	5.0	52	0	0%	0%	0%	—	.46	.32	.08	.06
Iowa	2.8	58	18	39%	29%	52%	—	.53	.30	.12	.11
Kansas	2.3	50	21	43%	43%	59%	—	.64	.49	.08	.07
Michigan	8.6	88	29	40%	41%	33%	—	.51	.41	.06	.04
Minnesota	3.6	54	21	29%	30%	24%	—	.52	.39	.07	.07
Missouri	4.6	67	15	41%	39%	60%	—	.56	.41	.07	.08
Nebraska	1.4	28	8	16%	16%	0%	—	.56	.42	.07	.07
N. Dakota	0.6	16	8	30%	30%	—	—	.62	.52	.02	.09
Ohio	10.5	116	7	12%	12%	19%	—	.51	.35	.08	.08
S. Dakota	0.7	16	3	12%	12%	89%	—	.56	.39	.09	.08
Wisconsin	4.2	70	22	47%	47%	89%	—	.48	.38	.05	.05
WEST	33.0	388	192	51%	51%	48%	55%	.69	.58	.05	.06
Alaska	0.3	10	8	31%	31%	—	—	.46	.17	.06	.23
Arizona	1.6	14	8	38%	39%	42%	30%	.97^f	.88	.01	.08
California	19.2	187	86	60%	60%	48%	66%	.75	.66	.05	.04
Colorado	2.0	29	15	42%	41%	58%	48%	.61	.50	.02	.09
Hawaii	0.7	11	5	48%	48%	—	—	.64	.41	.06	.17
Idaho	0.7	11	6	40%	40%	—	—	.62	.38	.12	.12
Montana	0.7	12	8	31%	31%	—	—	.59	.44	.04	.11
Nevada	0.4	2	0	0%	0%	0%	—	.53	.37	.00	.16
New Mexico	1.0	16	8	22%	24%	38%	16%	.50	.37	.02	.11
Oregon	2.0	38	13	49%	49%	75%	—	.64	.50	.06	.08
Utah	1.0	12	5	20%	19%	—	—	.57	.45	.09	.03
Washington	3.1	39	23	51%	51%	53%	—	.73	.63	.05	.05
Wyoming	0.3	7	7	43%	43%	—	—	.70	.55	.00	.15
TOTAL U.S.	198.0	2,596	789	42%	42%	47%	47%	.57	.39	.09	.09

[a]Colleges accepting all or most high school graduates and charging no more than $400 annually in tuition and fees.
[b]Degree-credit students only.
[c]Dash used when base too small for reliable estimate.
[d]Ratio for New York probably high by 15.
[e]Actually lower because of segregation.
[f]Ratio for Arizona probably high by 10 or more.
Sp.: surname: Mexican-Americans, Cubans, Puerto Ricans.
n.a.:Not available.
Source: *The Chronicle of Higher Education*, 5 (October 19, 1970): 5.

Type of Institutional Arrangement Locally Available

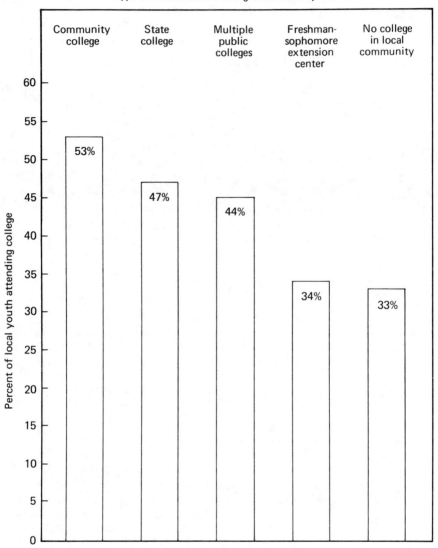

Adapted from data gathered longitudinally from 1959 to 1962, on sample of 10,000 high school graduates in 16 communities: James W. Trent and Leland Medsker, Beyond High School (San Francisco: Jossey-Bass, Inc., 1968), p. 27. By permission.

FIGURE 8   College enrollments in relation to presence of public college opportunities in home community

Is availability related to the distribution of students across a range of institutional types? The answer is in part "yes," since once history has made certain types of institutions characteristic of a region, they tend to be attractive in that region. Hence, students from the Northeast are more likely to attend private colleges, at home or elsewhere, than are students from other regions; meanwhile, Western and Midwestern students enroll disproportionately in public institutions. The answer is partly "no," however, in that propinquity operates most for students of limited information and choice. Factors other than locality better determine whether a given high school graduate at Amherst, Massachusetts, attends local Amherst College (small, private), the local University of Massachusetts campus (large, public), geographically accessible Harvard University (large, private), or Reed College, 3,000 miles away (small, private).

By itself, the existence of a rigorously selective "national" institution in one's home town will not appreciably affect local college-going (or graduation rates), nor will it attract distant talented youth from families to whom colleges are unknown institutions. But as figure 8 indicates, the relative "openness" of an educational institution has importance. Nonselective community colleges have the most apparent impact on their communities. Other data indicate, however, a selective effect: students of high socioeconomic status are little affected by availability; they will go to college somewhere, especially if they are also bright. The principal beneficiaries of extending the availability of public institutions are bright students of working-class backgrounds, as a comparison of figures 8 and 9 indicates.

The small-town, cloistered residential college—still powerful in the American imagination as the "typical" college—has declined in importance throughout the twentieth century. The movement of America to urban-suburban complexes (see table 12), the expansion of places for commuting students by the spread of community colleges and the locating of new campuses of state universities in cities, the ubiquitous automobile, and the freeway had made over half of all college and university students commuters between parental home and campus by the 1960s. Since the 1930s migrations to colleges in other states had held steady at 19 percent, but the rate dropped to 17 percent in 1968.[52] The stay-at-home movement seems likely to continue, for a number of reasons. First, there is a growing push toward college by the working class. Costs have risen higher than incomes in the lower economic strata, and resistance to expanding public support of higher education at past rates continues to increase (the costs to taxpayers of a year of college are almost five times that of a primary school year).[53] Recent economic

[52]"Migration of College Students, Fall 1968," *Chronicle of Higher Education,* 5 (October 26, 1970):4–5.

[53]As early as 1964, government estimates of projected educational expenditures predicted a "flattening curve": Kenneth Simon and Marie Fullan, *Projections of Educational Statistics to 1973–74,* U.S. Department of Health, Education, and Welfare (1964). Quoted in Coombs, *The World Educational Crisis,* pp. 202–3.

Type of Institutional Arrangement Locally Available

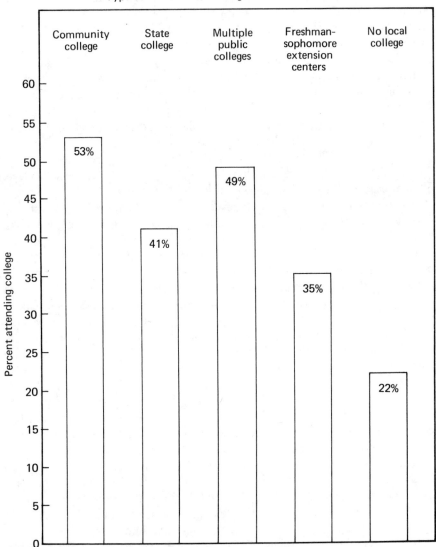

Adapted from data gathered longitudinally from 1959 to 1962, on sample of 10,000 high school graduates in 16 communities: James W. Trent and Leland Medsker, Beyond High School (San Francisco: Jossey-Bass, Inc., 1968). By permission.

FIGURE 9 The enrollment of high ability–low SES students in relation to presence of public college opportunities in home community

and political uncertainty—which in one year expands federal and state aid to students and institutions and in the next curtails this aid sharply and emphasizes private effort—will encourage stay-at-homes, as will the trend toward requiring out-of-state students to pay the full cost of their higher education in public institutions. Finally, there is a long-standing parental suspicion (strongest in the lower-middle and working classes) of away-from-home experiences.

The Ability Factor

It seems realistic to predict that "high-cost programs for low-aptitude students" will be hard to sell.[54] The high attrition rate in California's community colleges and the fact that under 10 percent of these students eventually transfer to a four-year college provoked the governor to suggest that too many academically unpromising youth were present; the "open door" had become an expensive "revolving door." At the same time another prominent politician objected to an "inevitable" lowering of standards and a debasement of college degrees as the City University of New York embarked on its open admissions plan in 1970. Present relationships of aptitude to educational status and the probabilities in future recruitment merit some discussion.

Investigation shows a rough positive relationship between persistence in high school and manifest ability to do the work that schools demand. Since nearly everyone graduates from high school, however, the issue of academic ability has moved to postsecondary education.[55] Most of the academically superior *do* go directly to college from high school. At more modest levels of ability, one large study found, 60 percent of high school graduates in the upper 40 percent of ability immediately entered college, compared to under 10 percent from the bottom 40 percent in ability.[56] These figures mean that a wide range of aptitude is present in America's college population and in the majority of institutions. A comparison of relative aptitude and social status, shown in table 14, demonstrates that social class is nearly as important in determining college-going as is academic aptitude.[57] Academically selective

[54]Jencks and Riesman, *The Academic Revolution*, p. 130; W. Lee Hansen and Burton Weisbrod, *Benefits and Costs of Public Higher Education in California* (a report prepared for the Joint Committee on Higher Education of the California Legislature, November 1967); "Open Admissions: American Dream or Disaster?" *Time* (October 19, 1970):63–66.

[55]This generalization does not hold true for all groups in America. Despite recent gains the American Indians and Mexican-Americans still attend college only in tiny proportions. In Boston, Puerto Rican youth (1970) dropped out of high school before grade 10 in 90 percent of the cases: Jonathan Kozol, *Free Schools* (Boston: Houghton Mifflin, 1972), p. 41; Fuchs and Havighurst, *To Live on This Earth*, esp. pp. 260–72.

[56]John C. Flanagan et al., *Project Talent: The American High School Student* (Pittsburgh: University of Pittsburgh, 1964), table 11–1. See also Trent and Medsker, *Beyond High School*, pp. 24–25.

[57]Rogoff found talent more decisive in the larger and social origin more influential in the smaller community: Natalie Rogoff, "Public Schools and Equality of Opportunity," *Journal of Educational Sociology*, 33 (February 1960):252–59.

TABLE 14   Percent of high school graduates going to college the following year, by scholastic aptitude, social class, and sex in 1960[a]

	Socioeconomic Status:[b]					All Classes
	Low	Lower-Middle	Middle	Upper-Middle	High	
Academic Aptitude:						
Males:						
Low	10	13	15	25	40	14
Lower-Middle	14	23	30	35	57	27
Middle	30	35	46	54	67	46
Upper-Middle	44	51	59	69	83	63
Upper	69	73	81	86	91	85
All males	24	40	53	65	81	49
Females:						
Low	9	9	10	16	41	11
Lower-Middle	9	10	16	24	54	18
Middle	12	18	25	40	63	30
Upper-Middle	24	35	41	58	78	49
Upper	52	61	66	80	90	76
All females	15	24	32	51	75	35

[a]Students delaying college entry, not reported. With lower-status males predominating here, long-term class bias would be lessened slightly.

[b]Since aptitude is not distributed equally among social classes, cell sizes are unequal.

From *The Academic Revolution* by Christopher Jencks and David Riesman, copyright © 1968 by Christopher Jencks and David Riesman. Reproduced by permission of Doubleday & Company, Inc.

(and socially elite) colleges typically have proportionally fewer withdrawals than do nonselective institutions. But ability and socioeconomic class seem less important in determining why students drop out than a complex of attitudinal and family (cultural) factors.[58] Since aptitude and privilege already operated in selecting the college population, other attributes are more free to show themselves in selecting among collegians. To those who most cherish colleges as intellectual citadels, it is distressing that large proportions of very able students are found among both college dropouts and campus protesters.

The universalization of higher education may not be in the national self-interest (e.g., as manpower or "cost benefit" analysts figure it). It may not even be important in promoting self-esteem—although it will be hard to convince many people of that. But for now, looking from "inside" education, the pertinent question is: Are efforts to recruit into colleges more of the college age group likely to lower the average level of aptitude in higher education?

[58]Trent and Medsker, *Beyond High School.*
Students who leave college for lack of goals or for personal reasons (including military duty), however, are found more likely to graduate eventually than are those who quit for scholastic or financial reasons, for marriage, for job offers, or for lack of interest: Laurence A. Previn et al., eds., *The College Dropout and the Utilization of Talent* (Princeton, N.J.: Princeton University Press, 1966), p. 56.

The answer seems to be "no"—as long as so many able students (some 40 percent of the brightest high school graduates) do not even begin college. Some of these are the very able children of the educationally poor: the 13 percent of all boys and 22 percent of all girls in the top 10 percent in ability that stop with high school. Youngsters from the bottom half of the social ladder who are above average in academic ability (e.g., scoring higher than 60–80 percent of their peers) make an even larger potential pool; in 1960 under one-half of the males and under one-third of the females from this large group entered college.[59] Increasing their presence in higher education will not lower the "academic tone" of the colleges. The phenomenal expansion of higher education over the past century was principally the accomplishment of middle and upper-middle ability students, who are far more numerous than students of top ability.

Many changes have overtaken American colleges between 1776 (when there were 3,000 living graduates of the 13 colleges) and 1971, when 816,000 collegians went to their commencements (or boycotted them!). This expansion allowed certain famous colleges to transform themselves from bastions of social prestige to intellectual redoubts. Yet, for every one institution that purified itself of the outrageously indolent playboys in its student body and raised its entrance requirements, one or several more nonselective ones were founded. Nevertheless, a massive upgrading of the entire system accompanied the transformation of a number of institutions into places of intellectual stimulation virtually unknown on the nineteenth-century collegiate landscape, so that the lowest 25 percent of all institutions today probably academically equal or exceed the median institution of one hundred years ago. (This is an admittedly impressionistic conclusion, since statistical confirmation, or refutation, is lacking.) Without going so far as to claim that educational expansion has created intelligence, it seems to have tapped it, beyond the power of pessimists to believe.[60] And this can continue to happen.

Personality Traits

Most studies of factors associated with educational status have focused upon such "objective" determinants as test scores, family income, and father's

[59]"It is the high schools' inability or unwillingness to encourage these students to attend college that accounts for the increasing importance of class background in determining which high school seniors go to college": Jencks and Riesman, *The Academic Revolution*, p. 131. This implies that social class was less important in the past. I do not believe that this is known for a fact. What is probably true is that, before high schools became universal institutions and when high school seniors were a more academically *self*-selected group, social class factors may have been less important in picking the colleges' *freshman* class—since many high school graduates (including upper-middle-class students) did not find it "necessary" to go to college.

[60]Today's *dropout rate*—approximately 50 percent of those entering—seems to be about what it was earlier; it may even now be lower. Theodore Caplow, in *The Sociology of Work* (Minneapolis: University of Minnesota Press, 1954), put the matter succinctly: "Each enlargement of opportunity has disclosed a new population of students, fully as competent as those who were educated before" (p. 80).

education. In recent years, however, personality inventories have been expanded as descriptive research instruments, to determine, for example, whether personality and cognitive patterns distinguish student activists or religious conservatives from the general college population. Clues to such factors as "dissatisfaction" have appeared in such studies as Joseph Kahl's much-cited comparison of academically able working-class boys who chose or rejected college. Motivational studies emphasizing psychological factors have analyzed college dropouts and underachievers.[61] Research is also pursuing the possibility of differential effects of personality traits in homogeneous versus diverse groups and in males versus females.

Social psychologists and educators have written considerably of low self-esteem, negative self-image, and fatalism as detrimental to school achievement and persistence. Thus, Lyford predicted better prospects for Puerto Ricans than for their neighbors in the New York ghettos because of their more favorable self-concepts and less "adjustment" to injustice.[62] The literature on this subject, both objective and subjective, is eloquent and extensive.[63] Recognizing the existence of self-hate ("When I grow up, I'll be white") has spurred campaigns to raise group pride and feelings of power and the creation of ethnic studies programs to give American minorities a sense of greater historical identity and worth. As more students once locked in caste attend integrated schools and colleges, they will be testing both their self-esteem and that of members of the majority—some of whom have built into their self-concepts ideas of racial, cultural, or sexual superiority to be challenged by the exposure to a shared experience.

PREVIOUS ACHIEVEMENT AND EDUCATIONAL EXPERIENCE

Achievement does have predictive power; failing in the first, second, ninth, or tenth grade strongly identifies the potential high school dropout. High

---

[61]Joseph A. Kahl, "Educational and Occupational Aspirations of 'Common Man' Boys," *Harvard Educational Review,* 23 (Summer 1953):186–203; Elizabeth Dowan and Carol Kaye, "Motivational Factors in College Entrance," in *The American College,* ed. Nevitt Sanford (New York: John Wiley & Sons, Inc., 1962); Alfred B. Heilbrun, "Personality Factors in College Dropouts," *Journal of Applied Psychology,* 49 (February 1965):1–7; Alexander W. Astin, "Personal and Environmental Factors Associated with College Dropouts Among High Aptitude Students," *Journal of Educational Psychology,* 55 (August 1964): 219–27; John L. Holland and Ruth C. Stalnaker, "Descriptive Study of Talented High School Seniors: National Merit Scholars," *Bulletin of National Association of Secondary School Principals,* 42 (March 1958):9–21; Trent and Medsker, *Beyond High School,* pp. 6–9, 36–37.

[62]*The Airtight Cage,* p. 37. Cf. Cordasco and Bucchioni, eds., *The Puerto Rican Community and Its Children on the Mainland.*

[63]Stephen M. Joseph, ed., *The Me Nobody Knows: Children's Voices from the Ghetto* (New York: Avon Books, 1969); Jay David, *Growing Up Black* (New York: Pocket Books, Inc., 1969); James A. Banks and Jean D. Grambs, eds., *Black Self-Concept* (New York: McGraw-Hill Book Co., 1972). For a survey that stresses both the controversies and the research, see Harry L. Miller and Roger R. Woock, *Social Foundations of Urban Education* (Hinsdale, Ill.: The Dryden Press, Inc., 1970).

school grades have long had modest predictive power in determining educational futures. Those high school graduates whose average grade is C+ or above have slightly better than one chance in two of gaining some college experience; for the rest, the odds drop to one in three.[64] Two explanations are obvious: grades, first of all, are both rewards (or punishments) and sources of information about one's accommodation to the educational system; although some uncertainty persists, students expect their future school experiences to be roughly similar to the past and are encouraged to apply (or discouraged) by what has already happened.[65] Second, college admissions officials do not like to guess wrong about those whom they admit. Hence, they typically give great weight to previous grades, since they believe them fair measures of a student's work habits and attitudes toward academic duties, and previous grades predict college grades better than do aptitude tests. This is why community colleges, and other "second-chance institutions" that do not screen on the basis of grades, enroll more students with poor academic records than they enroll children of the poor.

From the early school years, grades perform multiple functions. Grades have been used to admit or exclude students from electives, special programs, accelerated courses, and extracurricular activities (including student councils, class offices, and safety patrol) and even to regulate access to the regular curriculum (as when a B in chemistry is prerequisite to taking physics). In elementary schools they function, with achievement tests, to assign pupils to different instructional groups within a single classroom or across a grade level. In secondary schools they may be a basis for "tracking" students—channeling them into "general mathematics" or algebra, into "basic science" or chemistry, or simply into "fast," "average," and "slow" sections in history or English. Grades inform counselors, parents, and students about choices between general, vocational, and college-preparatory majors. Tracking and counseling practices are highly political issues in light of today's concern for extending more educational opportunities to minorities.[66] Surveys of black parents, rather than finding the desire to eliminate testing and grading systems,

---

[64] Based on a study of 1965 high school graduates who began college within one and a half years: *NEA Research Bulletin*, 47 (December 1969):107. That only 53 percent of above-average, and as much as 34 percent of below-average, students went on is indicative of the *other influences* being discussed. On the problems of the high school dropout see Lucius F. Cervantes, "The Dropout," in *Outsiders USA*, eds. Spiegel and Keith-Spiegel, pp. 173–202.

[65] Participation in formal adult education programs is also heavily influenced by previous education. College graduates participated in adult education in 23 percent of the cases, high school graduates in 10 percent, and those with 5–8 years of schooling in 6 percent of the cases according to one large study: Jack London et al., *Adult Education and Social Class* (Berkeley: Survey Research Center, University of California, 1963).

[66] When California adopted its Master Plan—differentiating available types of higher education institutions according to the high school record of the student—the proportion of brown and black students at four-year San Francisco State College actually declined from 11 percent (1960) to 3 percent of the student body in 1968: E. Alden Dunham, *Colleges of the Forgotten Americans* (New York: McGraw-Hill Book Co., 1969), p. 52.

show an insistence that their children, too, be equipped by schools to pass the tests and get the necessary good grades. Such parents resent school officials who sponsor "black dialect" lessons in lieu of drill in "standard" English, or who tell students that the "three Rs" are outdated and that college-going is unnecessary. If improved opportunities allow Northern, urban blacks to surpass their brothers in the rural South in the vital area of language facility, they ask, why cannot the schools give even better opportunities and erase racial differences in achievement? (See figure 10.) Such parents live in a world of books, labels, forms, instructions, advertisements,

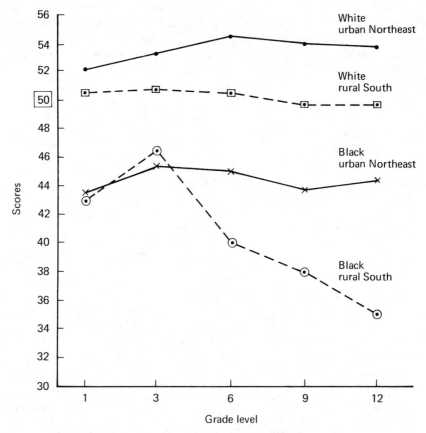

aNational mean score at each grade level: 50.

Data gathered by James Coleman for U.S. Office of Education, Equality of Educational Opportunity (Washington, D.C.: U.S. Government Printing Office, 1966). As reproduced in Coleman, James, "The Concept of Equality of Educational Opportunity," Harvard Educational Review, 38, Winter 1968, p. 20. Copyright © 1968 by President and Fellows of Harvard College.

FIGURE 10   Achievement in verbal skills,[a] by grade levels, race, region

and want ads—unlike the migrant worker parents whom Coles found expressing no need of reading and writing.[67]

It is common to find a gross disproportion between enrollments in the academic and terminal programs in ghetto high schools.[68] A not atypical Harlem high school graduating class of 325 may award 50 academic diplomas and 275 general diplomas.[69] In New York City as a whole in 1967, nonwhites constituted 40 percent of the high school population, 36 percent of the enrollment and 18 percent of the graduates of the academic high schools, and 60 percent of the enrollments in the vocational high schools.[70]

Family and Cultural Factors

The term *culturally deprived* was used commonly a decade ago to describe the lower educational status of American minorities and to explain its causes.[71] Observers noted caustically that no human living in society *can* be culturally deprived since, by definition, to live in a group is to have a culture; moreover, they said, use of such a designation constitutes evidence of racism. The phrase *culturally disadvantaged* received similar criticism, especially from groups promoting race pride and cultural pluralism and from those critical of American "middle-class culture." The more relativistic term *culturally different* became common. Some settled for *children of the poor,* which shifts the emphasis from the sensitive area of "culture" (but often meaning "race") to the more neutral one of income; those embarrassed about being caught "looking down" on another group's culture are happy to decry poverty—in whose blessings few Americans believe. But the "culture of poverty" remains at issue.

The Family as Educational Strategist

The United States is a competitive society. The race to the top is not a sprint but a marathon "in which victory goes to those who train the longest

[67]Robert Coles, "What Migrant Farm Children Learn," in *Knowing the Disadvantaged,* ed. Staten W. Webster (San Francisco: Chandler Publishing Co., 1966), pp. 236–43. See also the essays in Arnold B. Cheyney, ed., *The Ripe Harvest: Educating Migrant Children* (Coral Gables, Fla.: University of Miami Press, 1972).

[68]In 1965 78 percent of the students in the college preparatory program and 22 percent in all other curricula went to college: *NEA Research Bulletin,* 47 (December 1969):107. Trent and Medsker report that few of those in their sample who had become employed after high school graduation would take vocational courses if they could repeat high school: *Beyond High School,* p. 258. While some of this is conventional self-deception (as in "If I had it to do over again, I'd never quit my piano lessons"), it also signifies a legitimate sense of lost opportunity.

[69]Sixty percent of that high school's enrollment also read *below* a sixth-grade level: Mary F. Greene and Orletta Ryan, *The Schoolchildren Growing Up in the Slums* (New York: Pantheon Books, Inc., 1965).

[70]Board of education figures reproduced in Paul Lauter and Florence Howe, "How the School System Is Rigged for Failure," *New York Review of Books,* June 18, 1970.

[71]Frank Riessman, *The Culturally Deprived Child* (New York: Harper & Row, Publishers, 1962).

and care the most."[72] The family's importance in the open society lies not only in socializing youngsters for family roles and participation in those subgroups to which the family belongs but also in providing an adequate orientation to and understanding of the competitive culture as a whole. The family whose answer to the ambitious child is, "So! You think you're better than your dad?" teaches one kind of lesson. The family that nurtures such ambition teaches another. When a society's resources are not divided equally among all its family units, those with more assets generally also have the edge in socializing for this competition; their children have a head start from birth and are supported by a staying power of family action. Indeed, the modern middle- and upper-class family may have come to specialize in acting as an educational and social strategist for its children. It is not, then, simply a matter of money, for many parents of low or modest income have helped their children to learn, and hence to succeed in school.

The universalization of schooling means that the upper- and middle-class family has educational sophistication to pass on to its children. Research has consistently demonstrated the positive relationship of father's education (and, in some cases, of mother's education) to the educational futures of their off-spring. Indeed, as America expanded school enrollments and the social and economic influence of formal education, family educational status has become more a statistical determinant of who goes to college and more a real determinant of who graduates than was true 50 years ago. While many lower-class youth and their parents, especially in minority groups, do articulate a desire, and even an intention, of going to college, it is overwhelmingly middle-class youth whose parents know best how to implement their aspirations: who help with homework, meet the teacher regularly, make plans and save for college, consult catalogues and write to colleges and, very importantly, support their articulated expectations with cultural experiences compatible with the culture of the schools.[73]

Family Culture as Artifact of Social Class

When educators and social reformers considered the "immigrant problem," their explanations alternated between views of the immigrant as "depraved" or "deprived"—to use Michael Katz's language. Today the same may be

---

[72]Jencks and Riesman, *The Academic Revolution*, p. 133. That similar family characteristics transcend racial differences among college-oriented adolescents is shown in Albert J. Lott and Bernice E. Lott, *Negro and White Youth* (New York: Holt, Rinehart and Winston, Inc., 1963).

[73]Robert Panos and Alexander Astin, "They Went to College: A Descriptive Summary of the Class of 1965," *American Council on Education Research Reports,* 2:5 (Washington, D.C.: ACE, 1967); Craft, ed., *Family, Class and Education: A Reader.* Trent and Medsker, *Beyond High School,* found that the amount of serious reading reportedly done by parents is somewhat more important for predicting college entrance than is the amount of reading done by students themselves.

Reprinted by permission of Universal Press Syndicate. Copyright, 1971, G. B. Trudeau.

said of analyses of the social and educational positions of various American nonwhite populations. As already indicated, however, environmental explanations have predominated, supported by a general cultural optimism, the specific ethos of opportunity and self-improvement, the revulsion against the consequences of racist theories of Nazi Germany, scientific doubts of the viability of the very concept of race, and the unwillingness of social institutions to believe that they *cannot* create improvements in people.[74]

The environment of the home and, to a lesser extent, of the neighborhood have received much attention. One focus remains on the structural integrity of the family in the ghetto. Since the politically controversial appearance of Daniel Moynihan's 1965 report on the "breakdown" of the black family, much has been written of its assumed contributions to school failure, delinquency, and further poverty. The proportions of homes without fathers, of children raised by mothers or other female relatives, are rising. James S. Coleman found that only one-half of all black ninth-graders reported their natural fathers living at home, and another survey showed one-half of all nonwhite urban poor children living in households run by women.

The educational consequences of an absent father need not be deleterious. Although there may be negative personal and social effects, neither Coleman nor Alan Wilson found that the absence of the father correlated much with school achievement.[75] The economic effects are more sure; because of economic discrimination, families headed by women (and by the elderly) fall below the national mean income. Such departures from the accepted norms as illegitimacy, common-law relationships, and abandonment indicate social-class rather than racial peculiarities. One finds these factors among white Americans living in poverty, and today about one-third of poor white children in cities also live in households run by women. Conversely, the higher the social class and educational level of the home, the more "normal" is its structure.

The black middle class illustrates the relationship of "family culture" to the attributes of social class. By defining "middle class" broadly, one parent in white-collar employment, the black middle class becomes one-third of America's black population. Ginzberg's study of middle-class black college students found: family origins of higher education levels than white averages

---

[74]The turbulent events following the publication in 1969 of Arthur Jensen's highly controversial article reaffirming primarily hereditary causes of racial differences in conceptual intelligence are briefly recounted in Berkeley Rice, "The High Cost of Thinking the Unthinkable," *Psychology Today,* 7 (December 1973):89–93—a description and analysis sympathetic to researchers under political fire.

[75]Coleman's data have been reinterpreted by others to reveal such a correlation with school achievement; see, however, Alan B. Wilson, "Educational Consequences of Segregation in a California Community," *Racial Isolation in Public Schools,* II (Washington, D.C.: U.S. Government Printing Office, 1967). Salvador Minuchin et al., *Families of the Slums* (New York: Basic Books, Inc., 1967), finds the absence of fathers more a predisposing than a sufficient factor in delinquency.

(parental college educations frequently received in black colleges); their fathers, and especially their mothers, at occupational levels above the national mean; 80 percent of the students living with both natural parents, in small family units; students oriented toward a "career," not a "job"; longtime parental assumptions of college-going; and family financial support as the chief source of aid, even though family income levels fell below the white middle-class mean.[76] Like their white middle-class counterparts, these families provided verbal models, examples of problem solving, and those attitudes that the educationally effective family contributes to their children's schooling.

Family Culture and School Approaches

In the flurry of controversy and consternation that followed publication and discussion of the Coleman report, some were ready to downgrade the schools by asserting that life chances depended principally upon the pupil's own family background and that of his schoolmates, upon personality traits, even upon accident.[77] Some others insisted that schools *do* "make a differ- ence," in that they teach what is not likely to be learned elsewhere. "Children don't think up algebra on their own," observed Mosteller and Moynihan. At the very least educators had an increased disposition to acknowledge that it is difficult for existing schools entirely to "undo" family influence (either positive or negative) and to look anew at policy and strategy decisions called for when home and school were not in apparent congruence.

There are three positions one could take on the subject of how schools should operate where children lack cultural experiences that support and rein- force schooling. Although these positions are different, their acting out in educational programs may, however, erase all distinctions between them.

The Combative Approach   Schools fail many children of the lower class and of culturally different backgrounds, it is sometimes argued, because they approach these students with a curious combination of idealism, ignorance, and prejudice. Rather than combat the "pedagogical power" of the home and neighborhood, teachers timidly follow the book, blindly assuming motiva- tion where little is visibly present. Student achievement affects teacher morale, and repeatedly frustrated teachers may seek transfer (the individual "solu- tion"), or collectively may demand the right to evict "disruptive" children from the classroom—a feature of the United Federation of Teachers contract demands in the New York City school strike of 1967.[78] To ease teacher frustration larger school districts began using federal funds to help train

[76]Eli Ginzberg et al., *The Middle-Class Negro in the White Man's World* (New York: Columbia University Press, 1967).

[77]Gerald Grant, "Shaping Social Policy: The Politics of the Coleman Report," *Teachers College Record,* 75 (September 1973):17–54; Jencks, *Inequality.*

[78]Gerald Levy, *Ghetto School: Class Warfare in an Elementary School* (New York: Western Publishing Co., Inc., 1970), esp. chap. 3.

teachers to be more effective by counseling individuals, paying their tuition in courses in nearby colleges, preparing material, or running workshops.

The Compensatory Approach   This is a more common position, easier to assume than the combative one, since it is, after all, politically and practically difficult to "wage war" on the family, even when the warfare is only pedagogical. Most thinking about compensatory education has been directed toward nonwhite school children, even though the classic pattern of a poor fit between home and school (manifested partly in below-average achievement test scores) is equally evident in the all-white poor neighborhoods of Duluth, Minnesota, or Philadelphia.[79] Operation Head Start began in 1965 as an attempt to provide very young children with experiences of a kind that more privileged preschoolers receive in the natural course of events: storytelling, finger painting, and zoo trips. The rationale was simple: "If a three- or four-year-old child can be stimulated in a pre-kindergarten to learn the simple things he does not learn from his parents . . . he may get a headstart on later success in school."[80] The deceptively simple program—the annual cost per pupil was $1,000–$1,200—was confounded by the finding that gains were often lost after children had entered the regular kindergarten. Nevertheless, Head Start was intensified and reinforced by a Follow Through program designed to continue the program into the grades. Many parents simply did it on their own: between 1963 and 1970 the percentage of black youngsters attending nursery schools went from 11 percent to 21 percent.

New York City had already established the small, experimental Higher Horizons project for older students. Its achievements in raising intelligence test scores and college-going through "cultural enrichment" received enthusiastic attention in the early 1960s. Expanded to include more children, it was joined by the More Effective Schools project, which sought to reduce class size and to provide special services (psychologists, psychiatrists, social workers, a breakfast club, and remedial reading classes) in 21 slum schools. Other cities, large and small, followed suit on a more modest scale; Baltimore, Detroit, Chicago, Cleveland, New Haven, and Washington, D.C., approved or began MES plans by 1970. The New York State Legislature became the first to augment the beginnings of federal compensatory aid with a state program, "Project Able." The California Office of Compensatory Education had two staff positions in 1965; in 1966 there were authorizations for 68 positions as

---

[79]Dick Hubert, "The Duluth Experience," *Saturday Review* (May 27, 1972), pp. 55–58. Duluth, which is 97 percent white, was chosen by the Minnesota State Board of Education as the site of interschool transfers to achieve social-class integration in order to improve academic performance in the lower-class schools. Murray Friedman, "Kensington, U.S.A.," in *Overcoming Middle-Class Rage*, ed. Murray Friedman (Philadelphia: The Westminster Press, Inc., 1971), pp. 56–65, reports how certain poor white districts in the city score lower than the city's nonwhite districts in the tests of basic school skills.

[80]U.S. Office of Education and Office of Economic Opportunity, *Education: An Answer to Poverty* (Washington, D.C.: U.S. Government Printing Office, n.d.), p. 20. See the discussion of evaluation findings in Miller and Woock, *Social Foundations of Urban Education*, pp. 220–49.

a result of receiving funds from the Federal Elementary and Secondary Education Act (1965); in 1970 the chief of that office was elected state superintendent of public instruction.

Enthusiasm for compensatory education declined as educators learned more about its effects. In 1966 the Higher Horizons project was ended, its early successes lost after its expansion. The cost of the More Effective Schools program—nearly one-half million dollars annually per elementary school—had become harder to justify, since pupil achievement only slightly surpassed that of students in similar schools without special services; while pupils and teachers were reported happier and parents were more involved, pupil performance after two years in MES was following the classic pattern of progressively greater retardation with each year in school.[81] Yet growing skepticism about the effectiveness of compensatory education programs must be tempered by the knowledge that misallocation and misappropriation of funds have been so widespread as to raise the question whether compensatory education has been fairly tested. Much of the money under Title I of the Elementary and Secondary Education Act was diverted from the core of the curriculum presented to poor children into ancillary programs or system-wide general usage. Testimony before a Senate committee exposed monies spent in "a superficial veneer of fragmented programs or new equipment, rather than in an integrated, high impact intervention to achieve major educational change."[82] Estimates of expenditures necessary to make compensatory education "really effective"—$100–$160 *billion* over the next ten years—are high, and the programs' supporters must contend with the uncertainty of public commitment, the political balance of the heredity-environment debate, and the nation's economic situation at any given moment; all will help determine future federal policy on aid.

Critics of American public education support the challenges of compensatory education as defined. Frank Riessman writes, for example, that awarding special stimulation cannot be a substitute for "changing the schools themselves."[83] Since nonwhite children typically fall farther behind grade norms as they stumble through the grades, how, they ask, can help come from what is really only "more of the same"? High school antidropout

[81]D. J. Fox, *Expansion of the More Effective Schools Program* (New York: Center for Urban Education, 1967). Cf. Simon Beagle, "Evaluating MES" (Washington, D.C.: American Federation of Teachers, n.d.), 8 pp. (Pamphlet No. 319).

[82]Select Committee on Equal Educational Opportunity, United States Senate, "Federal Aid to Public Education: Who Benefits?" (Washington, D.C.: U.S. Government Printing Office, April 1971, Committee Print), p. 5. Meyer Weinberg, "The Suspension of Reality: Thinking About Race and School" (paper presented in a series sponsored by the Department of Sociology and Anthropology, Mississippi State University, March 18, 1971), pp. 3–8; Marilyn Bernstein and Joseph Giacquinta, "Misunderstanding Compensatory Education," *Harvard Educational Review,* 39 (Summer 1969):5.

[83]"Ebb and Flow in the School Integration Movement," *Integrated Education,* 4 (October–November 1966):8–17. Schools have continued to believe that America's various subcultures are inferior and have operated on that assumption; this is the message of Stanley Charnofsky, *Educating the Powerless* (Belmont, Calif.: Wadsworth Publishing Co., Inc., 1971).

campaigns operating on that premise have not worked, either. The racial integrationists have also been skeptical. Some believe that the "social lessons" of integrated education are simply more important than other measures of learning. Those who believe that conventional academic achievement cannot be gotten in predominantly minority schools—no matter how "culturally enriched"—think that compensatory education is a dodge, distracting attention from achieving racially mixed schools.

Support for this belief comes from a third group, those who have accepted the conclusions of the research in the Coleman report: the social-class integrationists. Children who lack the cultural resources of the middle-class home are affected positively by these resources when the resources are brought to school in the persons of their schoolmates. When disadvantaged children are taught in stable middle-class schools, they do better than under any other conditions—and without academic disadvantage to their middle-class peers. Before Coleman, Ralph Turner noted that, among seniors in ten Los Angeles high schools he studied, ambitions to be upwardly mobile were most common among those students attending schools in neighborhoods where the prevalent family background was higher than their own.[84] Since, as the Colman report concluded, facilities, curriculum, and even teacher quality are less related to school achievement than is the social background of one's fellow students, improvement in any of the former cannot match the effect of improvement in the latter.[85] And since nonwhites are concentrated in the lower classes, only seldom can an all-black, all-Filipino, or all-Chicano school be a middle-class school. So, to achieve social-class integration will normally require racial integration as well; the educational consequences of racial desegregaton will be positive, provided that the resulting school "mix" is strongly middle-class.

The Disregard-the-Family Approach   In *Dark Ghetto,* Kenneth Clark questioned the "cultural deprivation" theory.[86] He did not disagree that family cultures vary, but he wondered whether the theory did not merely shift the blame to families when it belonged instead upon teachers who do not believe their students can learn, do not expect them to learn, and do not help them to learn. If a child's motivation is, to some extent, set by his teacher, then teachers with low expectations, who view teaching as custodial care plus discipline, doom him to failure.[87]

[84]Ralph H. Turner, *The Social Context of Ambition* (San Francisco: Chandler Publishing Co., 1964), p. 61.

[85]For a readable critique of the Coleman report and its implications, see Bureau of Educational Personnel Development, Office of Education, *Do Teachers Make a Difference?* (Washington, D.C.: U.S. Government Printing Office, 1970). A more technical analysis, largely supporting the report's conclusions, is Frederick Mosteller and Daniel P. Moynihan, eds., *On Equality of Educational Opportunity* (New York: Random House, Inc., 1972).

[86](New York: Harper & Row, Publishers, 1965).

[87]Former U.S. Commissioner of Education Francis Keppel noted that teachers in many slum schools may doubt "the most basic premise of education: the capacity of the child to learn": *The Necessary Revolution in American Education* (New York: Harper & Row, Publishers, 1966), p. 15. Cf. Robert Rosenthal and Lenore Jacobson, *Pygmalion in the Classroom* (New York: Holt, Rinehart and Winston, Inc., 1968); and Robert L. Thorndike, "Review of *Pygmalion in the Classroom,*" *American Educational Research Journal,* 5 (November 1968):708–11.

Let us extend Clark's position somewhat and propose that family culture per se should be irrelevant, and that schools should pay much less attention to cultural reparations than to the business of being schools. There are examples of groups whose educational experiences obliquely support the limited contention that the cultures of the home and of the school need not always match—as presumably is the case in the majoritarian American middle class.

The spectacular educational success of the Jewish minority may be one such example. A significant part of Jewish immigration after 1880, from ghettos in Eastern Europe to lower-class ghettos in America's Northeastern cities, faced discrimination on many fronts, including restrictive quotas on Jewish students and faculty in colleges. Nor were all Jews of one culture; they brought elements of the various cultures of the lands from which they came, language differences, and religious differences among themselves. Nevertheless, many have succeeded, persisted, and prospered in the world of the American school and college—probably because of a tradition of learning ("The Religion of the Book") and perhaps because of another tradition, that of coping with a non-Jewish world on its own terms.[88]

The second example is the Japanese-American. Like Jewish students, when Japanese-Americans are compared with other students of similar intelligence, they are found to have received better school grades and achieved a higher average occupational status. In 1940, when American-born white children on the Pacific Coast had a median schooling of 10.1 years, the Nisei (American-born Japanese) already averaged 12.2 years. William Caudill and George DeVos have analyzed the phenomenon from the perspective of cultural anthropology.[89] They hypothesize that the Nisei have approximated middle-class American educational and occupational standards through elements in their own distinct culture—not because they have "taken on" or are motivated by American middle-class culture. Without a similarity of the social structure, customs, or religion of Japan and the United States, elements of Japanese culture have functioned well in American schools; politeness, neatness, respect for authority and for parental wishes, diligence, and an emphasis on keeping

[88]On most indices of academic success, Jewish students are overrepresented. In 1961 Jews were about 4 percent of the U.S. population, but over 5 percent of all college students, 8 percent of the college graduating class, usually 15 percent or more of the student bodies of some of the more prestigious colleges and universities, 24 percent of all AB's planning to enter medical school, and they were also overrepresented on honor rolls and in F.B.I. records on campus protesters. On the more mundane statistics see James A. Davis, *Great Aspirations: The Graduate School Plans of America's College Seniors* (Chicago: Aldine Publishing Co., 1964), table 1.2. See also Nathan Glazer, "The Jewish Role in Student Activism," *Fortune* (January 1969):112–13, 126, 129. The achievements of many American Jews have obscured those Jews who live in poverty; the Jewish are the numerically third-largest group of the very poor in New York City, and some of the Orthodox groups within Judaism do not fit the educational stereotype of Jewish academicism. See the sympathetic account of the Hasidic community in Brooklyn in Ellen Frankfort, *The Classrooms of Miss Ellen Frankfort* (Englewood Cliffs, N.J.: Prentice-Hall, Inc., 1970).

[89]William Caudill and George DeVos, "Achievement, Culture, and Personality: The Case of the Japanese Americans (1956)," in Webster, *Knowing the Disadvantaged*, I, pp. 208–28.

up appearances and on the personal achievement of long-range goals have characterized the Japanese-Americans.

THE DISTRIBUTION OF EDUCATIONAL OPPORTUNITIES IN A UNIVERSAL SYSTEM

It is often assumed that education is itself "the great equalizer," reducing the differences among people. This may be truer of a mass educating experience such as watching the same television programs or participating in the same youth culture. It is not what happens during instruction in the classroom. A group of children, no matter how heterogeneous on the first day of school, receive new dimensions of difference by its school experiences. Preschoolers who score within two or three months of one another on a reading-readiness test may be five years apart in reading mastery after grade three, and nine or more by grade six. Schools multiply the opportunities to spread children apart—in academic achievement, adjustment, self-concept, and labeling by teachers, parents, and peers. The more the school is tailored to every child's uniqueness, the more differences in outcomes are inevitable.

An educational system may officially recognize, ignore, or seek to compensate for the consequences of this differentiation—depending upon its own and the society's view of the function of schools. We will discuss three theoretically distinct options.[90] In practice, however, most systems are not "pure"; some examples, and a little further reflection, will indicate that education in the United States contains elements of all three of the following.

The Supportive Option

When education functions to confirm and maintain the existing system of social stratification, to reserve schooling for the "haves" and deny it (or furnish inferior brands) to the "have-nots"—there the supportive function operates. In hierarchical societies this is done by limiting education to those whose parents can pay. In democratic nations, where universal schooling is publicly supported, the mechanisms of privilege are more covert and complex; they are powerful, nonetheless, for in this basically competitive society most parents want to pass on to their children a *better than equal* chance to succeed.

One means of using schools both to educate and to permit inheritance of educational advantage is the elite private school. Its alumni gain easier entrée into the prestigious colleges, law schools, corporations, and exclusive clubs.[91]

---

[90] For the conception of these issues in this form I am indebted to Professor George Z. F. Bereday of Teachers College, Columbia University.

[91] Early in this century, when several elite private schools began to "come into their own," the tuition at St. Paul's School and Groton was $600 annually—a sum *not* earned annually by two-thirds of American male adult workers: James McLachlan, *American Boarding Schools* (New York: Scribner's, 1970), p. 11. This system of privilege is discussed in C. Wright Mills, *The Power Elite* (New York: Oxford University Press, 1956);

TABLE 15 Characteristics of the American college student, class of 1972[a]

Father's education:		Estimated parental income last year (all sources before taxes):	
Grammar school or less	10.4%		
Some high school	17.2%	Less than $4,000	6.3%
High school graduate	30.1%	$4,000–$5,999	10.3%
Some college	17.8%	$6,000–$7,999	15.5%
College degree	16.0%	$8,000–$9,999	16.9%
Postgraduate degree	8.5%	$10,000–$14,999	27.2%
		$15,000–$19,999	11.2%
Mother's education:		$20,000–$24,999	5.3%
Grammar school or less	6.6%	$25,000–$29,999	2.5%
Some high school	15.1%	$30,000 or more	4.8%
High school graduate	43.4%		
Some college	18.8%	Major sources of financial support during freshman year:	
College degree	13.6%		
Postgraduate degree	2.5%	Personal savings or employment	27.8%
		Parental or family aid	52.1%
Father's occupation:		Repayable loan	13.6%
Artist (including performer)	0.8%	Scholarship, grant, or other gift	18.2%
Businessman	30.1%		
Clergyman	0.9%	Major influences in deciding to attend this college:	
College teacher	0.7%		
Doctor (M.D. or D.D.S.)	2.0%	Parent or other relative	48.1%
Educator (secondary)	1.9%	High school teacher or counselor	22.6%
Elementary teacher	0.3%	Friends attending this college	15.2%
Engineer	7.0%	Graduate or other college	
Farmer or forester	6.6%	representative	12.2%
Health professional (non-M.D.)	1.1%	Counseling or placement service	4.7%
Lawyer	1.2%	Athletic program of the college	6.0%
Military career	1.6%	Other extracurricular activities	4.7%
Research scientist	0.6%	Social life of the college	7.7%
Skilled worker	13.0%	Chance to live away from home	14.6%
Semi-skilled worker	8.8%	Low cost	24.6%
Unskilled worker	4.2%	Academic reputation of the	
Unemployed	1.1%	college	43.2%
Other	18.3%	Most students are like me	8.8%
		Religious affiliation	5.6%

[a]Responses of freshmen to questionnaire study.
Source: *Chronicle of Higher Education,* 3 (December 23, 1968): 8.

While American prep schools lack the power in determining social place enjoyed by the English public schools, they do operate to restrict intimate social contact to those of similar origins and to teach the sons of the rich the manners and expectations appropriate to an assured social position—to be gentlemen taught neither to "drop out nor sit in."[92]

Since most Americans are the graduates of public schools—including many in high positions in corporations, the professions, and politics—one must also look there for signs that, like the characters in *Animal Farm,* "some are

G. William Domhoff, *Who Rules America?* (Englewood Cliffs, N.J.: Prentice-Hall, Inc., 1967); and E. Digby Baltzell, *Philadelphia Gentlemen* (New York: The Free Press, 1958). Cf. the analysis of status based on ancestry combined with status based on learning appropriate manners in elite schools and the "comradeship of the 'old school tie,'" in Ian Weinberg, *The English Public Schools* (New York: Atherton Press, 1967).

[92]McLachlan, *American Boarding Schools,* p. 15.

more equal than others." In many public schools one finds repeated association of social background with activities likely to determine future schooling, career, and life-style: in the curriculum pursued, school activities, organizations joined (including such social clubs as sororities and fraternities), friendships formed, and levels of absenteeism and dropout. Table 15 summarizes some of the attributes of social class belonging to the college class of 1972.

The racial desegregation struggle is also entangled in exploitations of social privilege and inequity. The erection of the neighborhood school into an ideological symbol supports the status quo; so does middle-class flight to suburban enclaves.[93] When the school year began in New York City in 1964, a new open-enrollment plan offered 110,000 students the opportunity to transfer to schools in other neighborhoods, and 1,800 (of the 2,000 who applied) were actually transferred.[94] Fears of the unknown, of social ostracism, and uncertainty of ability to compete kept most at home.

The Selective Option

Modern societies protest the use of education solely, or primarily, to confer an unearned superiority. Today people demand that education provide opportunity for equitable competition and select students only on some "just basis"—on the relevant criterion of academic ability. Educators, believing that ability is far more equitably distributed than is social and economic power, have accepted standardized tests as fair selection devices. England created a tripartite system of secondary schools in 1944; assignment depends upon results of an examination (the Eleven Plus) taken at the completion of primary school. The master plan for public higher education in California is also somewhat hierarchical: nonselective community colleges, a system of state colleges for the more able (based on high school class rank), and the state university's campuses for the academic elite.

The selective option would create a meritocracy, based on the belief that an intellectual elite is more socially responsible than a property-based elite. This is a "negative equalitarian" social philosophy: negative in accepting social stratification, equalitarian in wanting to "open up" the social structure to change, fresh views, and new talent. In the late 1950s, when secondary education was virtually universal and the colleges were being pressed to expand, the meritocratic view dominated. These are a few of the meritocracy measures from that period: an upgrading of the counseling function "so appropriate programs would be selected" and "no talent lost"; creation of courses

---

[93]Before 1970 the following large cities had a majority of nonwhite (and heavily lower-class) pupils in their public schools: New York, Washington, Chicago, Cleveland, Detroit, Philadelphia, St. Louis, Baltimore, and San Francisco. In 1965 Chicago's nonwhite population was 28 percent of the total but 52 percent of its school population—a disparity due to age distributions (the nonwhite population being younger on the average); family composition (more nonwhite children per adult); and heavier white enrollments in parochial and other nonpublic schools.

[94]Marilyn Gittell, *Participants and Participation: A Study of School Policy in New York City* (New York: Center for Urban Education, 1967), p. 93.

for the gifted and advanced-placement programs;[95] grading on the curve; severe competition for college places (the cutoff point for admission to the intellectually renowned City College of New York went from a high school grade average of 72 percent [1920] to 78 percent [1950] to 85 percent [1960]); and expansion of opportunities through scholarships, fellowships, and great growth in public higher education. The fact that the majority of the most able male students was attending college by 1970 has been offered as proof that the commitment to equal opportunity for talent was working.[96]

Yet opposition to meritocracy mounted. Although dividing the critics into two categories is somewhat a distortion, it may clarify the issues. Practical critics contend that inevitable imperfections in the selection procedures and inequalities in home advantages frustrate meritocratic intentions.[97] In France, with its public universities and nationally administered examination system, the child of a professional has a 59 percent chance for a university education, and an agricultural worker's child has less than a 2 percent chance. While tests are only as class-biased as are the programs and schools that they serve, the minority selected is already motivated and relatively affluent. Hence the supportive scheme (which chooses those already privileged by social position) and the selective (which chooses those already privileged by ability) make too few inroads into America's still untapped reservoirs of talent and energy.

Ideological critics doubt that educational competition is necessary or that government by the cleverest is a democratic safeguard. Some object to any system of compulsion, any system that creates the "involuntary student"— whether he is in school because his parents' position requires it, because the system has selected him as a winner, or because "it is in the best interests of society." Others contend that meritocracy—the British call it "creaming" —is socially dangerous.[98] They worry most, perhaps, about the "leftovers" in the selective system. "Society pays a heavy price for depriving its children of hope and self-esteem."[99]

[95]See the indictment in Bruno Bettelheim, "Segregation: New Style," *School Review*, 68 (Autumn 1958):251–72.

[96]A 1963 study of the New York *Social Register* listings showed considerably fewer sons following their fathers into Yale, Harvard, and Princeton; the influence of family name and wealth mattered less in college admissions: Robert Trumbull, *New York Times*, March 14, 1964. Charles Reich describes belief in a meritocracy as a characteristic of "consciousness II" in his popular *The Greening of America* (New York: Random House, Inc., 1970), esp. pp. 73–78.

[97]In Sweden—"a capitalist welfare state"—in 1960 the professional class (5 percent of adult male population) commanded 35 percent of the university places; the "worker" class (55 percent of the population) had 14 percent of the university places: Coombs, *The World Educational Crisis*, pp. 32, 190.

[98]See Michael Young's anti-Utopian novel of England in the twenty-first century: *The Rise of the Meritocracy* (New York: Random House, Inc., 1959).

The Labour Party and the National Association of Labour Teachers favored comprehensive schools as a corrective to the class bias pervasive in the present system of grammar schools (largely upper and upper-middle class) and the secondary modern schools (largely working-class): Michael Parkinson, *The Labour Party and the Organization of Secondary Education, 1918–65* (London: Routledge & Kegan Paul, 1970).

[99]Bereday, "School Systems and Mass Demand: A Comparative Overview," *Essays on World Education*, p. 101.

The Equalitarian Option

This "positive equalitarian" social philosophy for education follows the liberal principle of stretching traditional patterns as much as necessary in order to observe the ideal of equality. A lack of intellectual endowment is not accepted as a reason to penalize people and to deny them opportunity, any more than is any other attribute (racial, cultural, or sexual) that is not the fault of the individual. Lyman Bryson articulated this position when he stated that selection denies, ahead of time, certain experiences to certain people because it presupposes that certain things are suited or unsuited to them; in truth, everyone is the "keeper of his own excellence," and must have his own chance to decide what is worth having, knowing, and enjoying.[100]

Equalitarianism means grading students for achievement relative to their ability, rewarding them for "effort" and cooperativeness; it means having the elementary school unsegregated by tracking, and having a comprehensive high school. The equalitarian, like the sociologist, recognizes that, even in the expert society, opportunity often depends upon whom you know as well as what you know; long before the Coleman report, educators realized that the mixing of children of different social classes gave opportunity to learn the social skills that facilitate individual mobility.

Other evidences of the equalitarian option at work are antidropout campaigns, graduation irrespective of reaching minimum achievement standards, late deadlines for selecting-out students, the diversity of colleges, and open admissions in previously selective institutions.[101] Easy access is emphasized since, while good college grades benefit one in graduate school admissions, grades matter little in the job market. Appropriate in the legendary "land of the second chance" are policies such as the City University of New York's proviso that a failing student may continue so long as his teachers think he is progressing. At Chicago's Malcolm X Community College no student faces academic dismissal; the lowest grade given is "Incomplete." Such adjustments in academic tradition take education part of the way from *access* (the assumption of fitting students to the system) to *accommodation*: the determination to change the system to fit all students.[102]

---

[100]Among Bryson's many books see *The Next America* (New York: Harper & Row, Publishers, 1952) and *The Drive Toward Reason* (New York: Harper & Row, Publishers, 1954).

[101]Evidence that the more *retentive* is the school system (keeping students in the system), the more equitably are the various social classes represented in the upper grades, is reported in Torsten Husén, "Social Structure and the Utilization of Talent," in *Essays on World Education,* ed. Bereday. The open admissions plan at City University of New York resulted in an increase of Puerto Rican and black youth among the freshman class from 2 percent (1962) to 33 percent (1970): Crossland, *Minority Access to College,* p. 113.

[102]That the accommodation is still mostly rhetorical is suggested by the fact that, while the community colleges have increased the proportion of high school graduates in college, the proportion that earns the B.A. degree has probably not increased: Jencks and Riesman, *The Academic Revolution,* p. 489n.

4

BREADTH

Nearly five years before Sputnik, Arthur Bestor's *Educational Wastelands* asserted that American school reform must begin with the courageous judgment that the various subjects and disciplines of the curriculum are *not* of equal value.[1] The implications of Bestor's reductionism were serious indeed, since expansionism, a basic trait of the American character, has supported popular and universal schools with broad content and purposes. Moreover, equalitarian America is suspicious of notions of priorities and selectivity and jealous of preserving the formal prerogatives of public opinion to set school curricula.

The authors of the schoolbooks that dominated the nineteenth century were of the people; their books were not the products of scholars and intellectuals, but of printers, journalists, small-town lawyers, ministers, and teachers. (College professors did write many of the high school texts, but these left most Americans untouched.) In this century, supported by a culture whose bent is more technical than philosophical, educational psychology has far outdistanced educational philosophy in influence; the criterion of what the child *can* learn appeared more compelling, in practice, than some principle of what he *should* learn. Not even higher education has been immune from the political and consumer powers of the American people. It is not true, as Sidney Hook claims, that curriculum decisions in American higher education were historically based on purely intellectual considerations of "what is the best education for modern men and women."[2] Put harshly, "wisdom still comes from below, making education no better than a compromise between academic competence and the wishes of Main Street."[3] The claim of having

[1] Arthur Bestor, *Educational Wastelands* (Urbana: University of Illinois Press, 1953).

[2] Sidney Hook, *Academic Freedom and Academic Anarchy* (New York: Dell Publishing Co., Inc., 1969), p. ix. Cf. Frederick Rudolph, *The American College and University: A History* (New York: Random House, Inc., 1965).

[3] Peter Schrag, *Voices in the Classroom: Public Schools and Public Attitudes* (Boston: Beacon Press, Inc., 1965), p. 131. For a different view—that educational decisions are made by, and for the benefit of, various elites, see Clarence J. Karier, "Business Values and the Educational State," in Karier et al., *Roots of Crisis: American Education in the Twentieth Century* (Chicago: Rand McNally & Co., 1973), pp. 6–29.

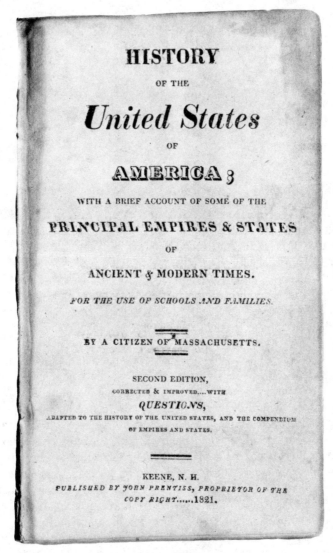

Lessons from an early United States History textbook

"academic competence" has given educators considerable discretion in tinker-ing with the narrowly conceived academic skills and subjects; the vocational, health, and social-civic courses represent the wishes of the public. It is largely by the latter that today's breadth of goals and programs in schools was achieved.[4]

[4]Or so the experience of one state suggests: Robert E. Cralle, "The History of Legis-lative Prescriptions Regarding Elementary School Subjects in California" (M.A. thesis, University of California, Berkeley, 1926).

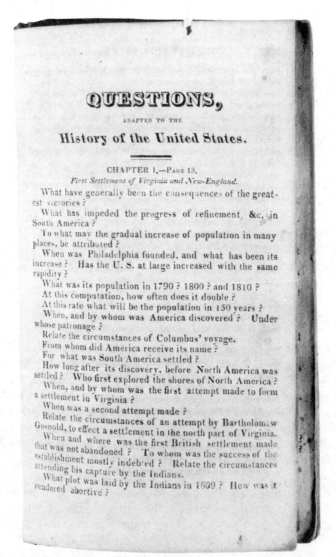

QUESTIONS,

ADAPTED TO THE

History of the United States.

CHAPTER I.—PAGE 13.

First Settlement of Virginia and New-England.

What have generally been the consequences of the greatest victories?

What has impeded the progress of refinement, &c. in South America?

To what may the gradual increase of population in many places, be attributed?

When was Philadelphia founded, and what has been its increase? Has the U. S. at large increased with the same rapidity?

What was its population in 1790? 1800? and 1810?

At this computation, how often does it double?

At this rate what will be the population in 150 years?

When, and by whom was America discovered? Under whose patronage?

Relate the circumstances of Columbus' voyage.

From whom did America receive its name?

For what was South America settled?

How long after its discovery, before North America was settled? Who first explored the shores of North America?

When, and by whom was the first attempt made to form a settlement in Virginia?

When was a second attempt made?

Relate the circumstances of an attempt by Bartholomew Gosnold, to effect a settlement in the north part of Virginia.

When and where was the first British settlement made that was not abandoned? To whom was the success of the establishment mostly indebted? Relate the circumstances attending his capture by the Indians.

What plot was laid by the Indians in 1609? How was it rendered abortive?

Lessons from an early United States History textbook (continued)

THE BEGINNINGS OF BREADTH

In his 1842 annual report as chief administrator of Connecticut's public schools, Henry Barnard reiterated the accepted proposition that schools should be more than mere places of learning: "Every school-house should be a temple, consecrated in prayer to the physical, intellectual, and moral culture of every child in the community, and be associated in every heart with the earliest and strongest impressions of truth, justice, patriotism, and religion." Let us examine how the schools met some of these demands.

Religious and Moral Literacy

Unlike the modern church school, which does not represent the secular spirit of the whole society, the nineteenth-century public school partook of a Protestant culture. Its links with colonial (especially Puritan) educational purposes—learning to read so as to have access to God through the Bible—were weakening but not yet broken. Ministers remained influential in school and, especially, in college affairs. The man who served as headmaster from 1902 to 1966 of Massachusetts' famed Deerfield Academy acknowledged that his school's reputation was made in moral and not academic education.[5] Compulsory daily chapel long persisted in many nominally secular colleges—to 1910 at the University of Minnesota; more important, a college education often retained its antebellum emphasis upon character training, not intellectual development. The continual reappearance of state legislation prescribing "manners and morals" courses in public schools and the issuance of "moral education guidelines" for teachers suggest a durable public interest in character formation.

Education for Citizenship

In a nation conceived in the belief in divine sponsorship, religious and nationalistic purposes were complementary. Noah Webster explicitly linked them in his 1805 school *Reader*: "How little of our peace and security depends on REASON and how much on *religion and government*."[6] Love of country, patriotism, the blessings of liberty, and manifest destiny were everywhere proclaimed in the schoolbooks. Eclectic readers, such as McGuffey's, featured the speeches of patriots and the documents of state, providing new reading materials to replace the Bible and much of the classical materials used theretofore. Through his spellers, readers, and dictionary, Webster differentiated American from English spellings and pronunciations, defined words through American referents, and created a national idiom as a force for cultural unity.[7] New school subjects were created out of the stuff of national identity: English grammar and spelling, United States history, state and regional histories, American literature, and civics. Geography glorified

[5] John McPhee, *The Headmaster: Frank L. Boyden, of Deerfield* (New York: Farrar, Straus & Giroux, Inc., 1966), p. 17.

[6] Noah Webster, *An American Selection of Lessons in Reading and Speaking* (Salem, Mass.: Cushing and Appleton, 1805), p. 147. See Ruth Miller Elson, *Guardians of Tradition: American Schoolbooks of the Nineteenth Century* (Lincoln: University of Nebraska Press, 1964); Clifton Johnson, *Old Time Schools and Schoolbooks* (London: Macmillan, 1917); Monica Keifer, *American Children Through Their Books, 1700–1835* (Philadelphia: University of Pennsylvania Press, 1948). That American political, religious, and educational traditions are hostile to intellect is argued in Richard Hofstadter, *Anti-Intellectualism in American Life* (New York: Alfred A. Knopf, Inc., 1962).

[7] Henry Steele Commager, ed., *Noah Webster's American Spelling Book* (New York: Teachers College Press, 1958), p. 4.

© 1970 United Feature Syndicate, Inc.

physical America. Schoolbooks ignored controversy and left the social order unquestioned—something still largely true of schools.[8] Schools helped Americans to acquire a complacency which ill prepared them for signs of disunity, charges of oppression, and large-scale protest.

Educators found formal instruction in "the American way of life" increasingly necessary because of the continuous process of immigration. The Civil War was another challenge to unity that schools were asked to counter. Through their lessons, student councils and other civic exercises, and probably most importantly through indirect teachings, schools became influential in shaping the political attitudes of American youth.[9]

A Curriculum of Useful Knowledge

Ruth Elson has noted that schoolbook portrayals of American heroes emphasized nonintellectual traits: Jefferson's cultured ways were overshadowed by Daniel Boone's exploits, by the manly courage of Washington, and by the practical energies of Franklin. Bookish children were a cause of concern; they were admonished to "go out and play." Caleb Bingham's popular *The Columbian Orator* proudly explained European and American educational differences as originating in "democracy":

> Our government and habits are republican; they cherish equal rights, and tend to an equal distribution of property. Our mode of education has the same tendency to promote an equal distribution of knowledge, and to make us emphatically a "republic of letters": I would not be understood adepts in the fine arts, but participants of useful knowledge. . . . The spirit of our habits and government tends rather to general improvement in the useful, than partial perfection in the amusing arts.[10]

[8] A poll conducted for *Life* magazine in 1969 found 27 percent of parents sampled believing that race relations should be fully discussed in the classroom; the proportions of students and teachers so believing approached 50 percent: Bayard Hooper, "The *Life* Poll: Conflict in the High Schools," *Life,* May 16, 1969, p. 29.

[9] Robert D. Hess and Judith V. Torney, *The Development of Political Attitudes in Children* (Chicago: Aldine Publishing Co., 1967); Byron G. Massialas, ed., *Political Youth, Traditional Schools* (Englewood Cliffs, N.J.: Prentice-Hall, Inc., 1972). See also the issue on political socialization: *Harvard Educational Review,* 38 (Summer 1968).

[10] Caleb Bingham, *The Columbian Orator,* 8th ed. (Boston: Caleb Bingham & Co., 1817), p. 299.

Unlike England's rhetoric texts, American composition books presented practical writing exercises. Arithmetic and handwriting earned their places in the curriculum on utilitarian grounds, as preparation for future clerks and tradesmen. The appeal of broadening vocational education was heightened by claims that the apprenticeship system was inadequate to the nation's needs for skilled labor. Industrial interests supported trade training at taxpayer expense. Some labor leaders decided that educated and trained workers would be less vulnerable to exploitation by employers and more drawn to unions. Most important, Americans approved the appearance of shorthand, bookkeeping, homemaking, and manual arts in many of the urban eight-year elementary schools, and eventually they patronized the broadened high schools. As Martin Trow has reminded us, "People are more concerned with liberal opportunities than with liberal education." Many educators assumed that comprehensive high schools, with vocational programs to attract working-class youth, were democratic—and hence superior to separate trade schools or the occasional manual-training ("manual arts") high schools that appeared before 1900.

The comprehensive high school's concessions to a more utilitarian curriculum were grudging and partial.[11] While the common schools were teaching state and national history and American literature, for example, the secondary schools before 1900 emphasized ancient and world history and English literature.[12] Passage of the Morrill Federal Land Grant Act in 1862 forced greater breadth in the even more resistant college. A creation of middle-class exponents of advanced agricultural and technical education, not of the ordinary farmer or mechanic, the new engineering and "cow colleges" authorized by the Morrill Act were built before a large clientele thought them needed. For years they faced both indifference and hostility. While the established colleges scoffed at the "take anyone" admissions policies practiced by the "A and M" colleges in order to acquire students, their own catalogues became inflated by adding the physical sciences, modern languages, modern history, and economics to the curriculum. Abandoning the pretense of being a community of educated men united by a common body of studies, they adopted the "elective system." They surrendered to such creations of their student bodies as the fraternity-sorority system and intercollegiate athletics—the "fun culture" that no trustees' decision called into being. Such popularization of higher education eventually forced nearly every academic to the realization that virtually every student comes to college for practical reasons: social, familial, or vocational.[13]

---

[11]Edward A. Krug, *The Shaping of the American High School, II* (Madison, Wis.: University of Wisconsin Press, 1972); John H. Martin and Charles H. Harrison, *Free to Learn* (Englewood Cliffs, N.J.: Prentice-Hall, Inc., 1972), pp. 108–28.

[12]John A. Nietz, *The Evolution of American Secondary School Textbooks* (Rutland, Vt.: Charles E. Tuttle Co., 1966), p. 249.

[13]Lawrence Dennis and Joseph Kauffman, *The College and the Student* (Washington, D.C.: American Council on Education, 1966).

A Special Place for the Sciences

When North America was first colonized by Englishmen, a consensus about the appropriate studies for a learned man united the educators of the West. Ancient Greece had contributed both the ideal of a liberal education and some of the very books studied by the early classes at Harvard College. Roman civilization contributed its language, literature, and emphasis upon orations. The Catholic Middle Ages glorified reasoned logic and philosophical disputations, while the Renaissance revived parts of classical learning theretofore lost and shifted emphasis to the concept of the humanities. The Protestant Reformation promoted Hebrew and Biblical studies. University students all over Europe, and then America, read the same books, used the same languages, were taught by the same methods, and participated in the same academic rituals, constituting a slowly expanding historical community of scholarship that stretched, nearly unbroken, from the twelfth to the eighteenth century.

The culture that had supported liberal education was, however, preindustrial; more important, it was prescientific.[14] By the nineteenth century the currents of modernism were transforming various social institutions, including education. The influential Englishman Herbert Spencer typified the new enthusiasm for science. In an 1860 essay, "Education: Intellectual, Moral, and Physical," he identified the goals of modern education: to maintain health, earn a living, be an effective parent, learn civic duty, production and enjoyment of the arts, and self-discipline. He concluded that science was "the knowledge of most worth" in realizing these goals. In America, despite the objections of traditionalists that admitting science students would lower the intellectual tone of higher education, most colleges promoted a curriculum of science in the last third of the nineteenth century.

Increasingly, the states prescribed various forms of science instruction for the lower schools: applied science, such as "laws of health" or "principles of hygiene"; formal science, such as physics or chemistry—sometimes later dropped for lack of school science equipment; and "interdisciplinary" science, such as "nature study" or "animal life." By the end of the century lessons in science were common, although moral lessons drawn from nature continued to be prominent in schoolbooks. Laboratory work was rare; classroom experiments were virtually all teacher-demonstrations. That the average high school of 1910 had but one or two teachers meant that successful innovations came first to a few big-city schools.

A Curriculum of Chaos

The piecemeal addition of subjects was made easier by educators anxious to reach and teach all children in schools that were at once both terminal

---

[14]Mortimer J. Adler and Milton Mayer, *The Revolution in Education* (Chicago: University of Chicago Press, 1958), p. 106.

for some students and preparatory (for the next level of schools) for others. The Massachusetts General Court required 8 subjects in the high schools of 1827, but added 12 more by law by 1857. One state entered this century with 14 mandated elementary school subjects and added 17 more in the next 20 years. Additions so outran removals that when Scott Nearing visited Indiana's one-room rural schoolhouses in 1915 he found the teachers struggling with a school day of 45 teaching periods, permitting just 13 minutes per recitation. Schools commonly added subjects at all levels without additions of teachers, supplies, and equipment—and without coordination with the offerings of higher or lower schools. Since many schoolbooks were ungraded (the fifth-grader and college sophomore could well be assigned the same English text), both duplications and gaps were commonplace. Yet schools expected students to progress systematically through the grades, and from one level of schooling to the next.

Charles McMurray, a leading educator, posed the dilemma succinctly in 1892. Happy that "the old classical monopoly is finally and completely broken," he now worried that the common school course had become a "batch of miscellanies," a "superficial hodgepodge" that overloaded pupils without educating them.[15] Reform lay in reorganizing the curriculum, so that order, system, uniformity, progression, and mastery might once more prevail. The solution was to locate some organizing principle—social, psychological, or philosophical—appropriate to the needs of modern society and of diverse individuals.

The schools tried a number of such principles. "Concentration" meant selecting some subject or topic as the central focus for learnings from various fields. The central subject might be history, literature, or geography.[16] "Correlation," more popular still, was believed to be compatible with the way the child's mind grasps and assimilates knowledge as a whole. Correlation might be as simple as studying frontier history and the geography of the West at the same time in the school year. "Fusion" occurred when once-discrete fields were incorporated as broad fields: history, geography, and civics became "social studies"; reading, writing, spelling, and grammar formed "language arts." "Minimum essentials" were the basic materials of education, selected after consultation with historians and economists, businessmen, publishers, and other experts to become the new curriculum, permitting the exclusion of useless, inert information and skills.

Each of these devices reflected the desire to make knowledge, and the methods by which it is acquired, more "lifelike." Each was also a manifestation of a larger philosophical view of education and society. First called

[15]Charles McMurray, *The Elements of General Method: Based on the Principles of Herbart* (Bloomington, Ill.: Public School Publishing Co., 1892), pp. 16–17.

[16]A satirical summarizing of the thinking that often marks curriculum change is Merrill Harmin and Sidney B. Simon, "The Year the Schools Began Teaching the Telephone Directory," *Harvard Educational Review*, 35 (Summer 1965):326–31. For a survey of curriculum theories since the late nineteenth century see Lawrence A. Cremin, "Curriculum-Making in the United States," *Teachers College Record*, 73 (December 1971): 207–20.

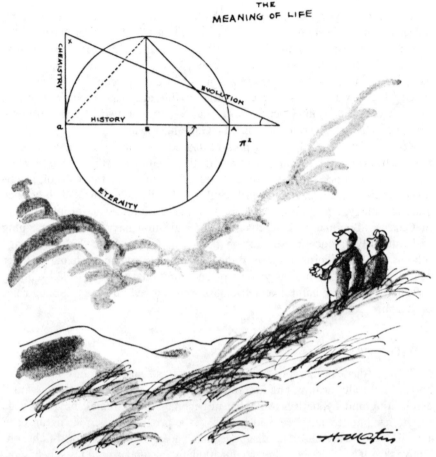

Cartoon by Henry R. Martin. Copyright 1971 by Saturday Review, Inc.

"I just wish I could see the faces of all my old students who kept asking me what good would their geometry be."

the "new education," it became known worldwide by the second decade of the century as "progressive education"—and the United States was its chief host.[17]

THE PROGRESSIVE EDUCATION MOVEMENT

Romanticism

One trait of progressive theory and practice was the romanticizing of the past as a simple, more understandable and humane, idyllic era. This provided a reason for studying history and the cultures of simpler societies. Looking

[17]Lawrence A. Cremin, *The Transformation of the School* (New York: Alfred A. Knopf, Inc., 1961).

backward also partook of an anti-urban bias strong in American culture, reflected earlier in Jefferson's "perfect democracy" of yeoman farmers, in pastoral art and poetry, and frontier legends.[18] A nostalgia for simple village life grew in the schoolbooks of the late nineteenth century and in the kindergarten movement's attempt to create a "children's garden" as an antidote to city life. "A few days in the country at this age has raised the level of many a city child's intelligence more than a term or two of schooltraining could do without it," wrote the romantic G. Stanley Hall.[19]

Romanticism also appears in present-day educational criticism, again supported by various cultural phenomena: the flight from the city and from "bureaucratic work," the vagabond life, the commune, the cult of primitivism so like that of the eighteenth century, the disenchantment with science and technology, and even the ecology movement. In moderate form it appears in Charles Silberman's claim that today's education has "lost" the meaning and authority it once presumably had and in his calls for "informalizing" schools.[20] Romanticism's more radical contemporary spokesman is Peter Marin, who sees children as victims of an "emotional plague" called schools, deflected from their natural social relations and forced into the crippling roles of "teacher" and "student."[21]

Naturalism

In its Rousseau-like proposition that such social inventions as schools corrupt naturally healthy human tendencies and teach such unnatural "skills" as cheating and hypocrisy, romanticism becomes the extreme, subjective side of another intellectual force evident during the progressive period: naturalism. (At its other extreme, naturalism meant an excessive veneration of the objective "truth" of science—shown educationally in standardized tests, behavioristic psychology, and education as "social engineering.")[22]

A variation of venerating the past, which is the younger present, is to venerate childhood. The idea of a school based on the "simple creed of childhood, delight and liberty" was in keeping with other movements which marked off the special qualities of innocent childhood: "enlightened parenthood," children's courts, orphanage reform, child-labor legislation, and similar affirmations of the "rights of childhood"—including birth-control advocate

---

[18]Morton and Lucia White, *The Intellectual versus the City* (Cambridge, Mass.: Harvard University Press, 1962).

[19]*Aspects of Child Life and Education* (New York: D. Appleton & Co., 1921), quoted in Marvin Lazerson, "Urban Reform and the Schools: Kindergartens in Massachusetts, 1870–1915," *History of Education Quarterly*, 11 (Summer 1971):115–42.

[20]Charles E. Silberman, *Crisis in the Classroom* (New York: Random House, Inc., 1970).

[21]Peter Marin, "Children of the Apocalypse," *Saturday Review* (September 19, 1970): 71–73, 89.

[22]The archetype of this kind of "naturalist" was the educational psychologist, Edward L. Thorndike. See Geraldine Jonçich, *The Sane Positivist: A Biography of Edward L. Thorndike* (Middletown, Conn.: Wesleyan University Press, 1968).

Margaret Sanger's "right to be a wanted child." By 1920 Freudianism began to add a special new emphasis on early experience. A few celebrated private schools interpreted this mixed legacy to mean that education should guard against "unnatural" restraints and repressions that might warp personality and should promote self-expression and joy, especially in social relations and the arts. These new goals became more important than conventional knowledge and academic achievement.

But the naturalism of such laissez faire schooling faced numerous obstacles, both ideological and practical. First, the majoritarian culture was worried more about idleness, playfulness, sin, and bad habits than about thwarting what Rousseau had called the "loveable instincts" of childhood. Hence, it was the rare school that reflected "extreme permissiveness." Second, psychologically oriented school reformers found the child's latent capacities far more pedagogically and socially significant than his expressed needs and interests. This split the ranks of the progressive campaign between those who espoused childhood and those who studied and tested it. Third, many teachers, while believing in the principles of growth and maturation, wanted a larger role than that of passive observer or "expediter" of learning. The result was, at best, a compromising of childhood interests with the directive teacher and the prescribed syllabus. Fourth, there were objections on political grounds. Such progressive theorists as George Counts saw schools as a potential instrument of social reform; Counts concluded that "child-centered," expressive schools were bastions of self-centered individualism. Finally, as Robert M. Hutchins chided latter-day progressives, to identify a need on the student's part does not automatically identify a necessity for the curriculum.[23] By their expansive commitment to "the whole child," and to a definition of curriculum as "all the experiences which the student undergoes under the school's auspices," progressive education laid itself open to charges of irresponsibility.

The Campaign Against Formalism

When John Dewey spoke of curiosity, activity, spontaneity, creativity, and dramatic tendencies as natural motivators to be capitalized upon by the progressive teacher, he struck a note also sounded by progressive child-rearing theorists. In *Up Through Childhood* (1904), G. A. Hubbell cautioned parents that "You say to the child, 'Do not,' and his whole nature says 'Do.' Every nerve and muscle within him calls for action, and yet you say, 'Sit still and be good,' but action is the law of life. . . ." When the physician-turned-muckraker Joseph Mayer Rice toured America's schools in the 1890s, he found them frozen in ritual and worthless practices, operating against this "law of life." Children were punished for such actions unrelated to their lessons as failing to stand rigidly when reciting, their teachers ritualistically

---

[23]*The Conflict in Education in a Democratic Society* (New York: Harper & Row, Publishers, 1953), p. 30.

reprimanding, "How can you learn anything with your knees and toes out of order?"[24] When a mother visited Dewey's school at the University of Chicago, she reported seeing no books, although the classroom held a live alligator, an Indian blanket, fruit and sandwiches, and a teacher and children in virtually endless conversation.[25]

When state legislatures or school districts added a course in duties of citizenship or local civil government they were responding to the campaign against formalism. So, also, with senior problems or family life units, excursions and field trips, exhibits collected by the students, and student-written dramatic programs in place of spelling bees, and the introduction of school "industries"—weaving, the classroom "store," butter-making, crafts, and the school garden. Today's expressions of the same reform impulse are the open classroom, schools without walls, schools within schools. The degree of *informalization* proposed—to use Silberman's term—ranges from his own moderate but unspecific concept of a balance between pupil-spontaneity and teacher-encouragement, with multiple centers of activity in any classroom, to Ivan Illich's radical plan for a "deschooled education."

Schooling for an Industrial Society

A cultural revolution took place between 1830, when the common school movement began to popularize a commitment to universal public education, and 1890, when the progressive education movement began to seek school reform. Despite his rural Vermont background, John Dewey was animated by the spirit of an increasingly industrial society. He knew that schools had yet to come to terms with the secular, urban, industrial world. The management of an industrial economy in the interests of the whole community could not be accomplished by the "industrially illiterate": those without understanding of the machine civilization and those unable to see beyond their own machine-tending.

It appears perplexing, then, that vocational courses remained so marginal. Home economics enrolled more students than all the other vocational programs, and high schools never gave the American work force its predominant job training. One contributing factor was the progressive's disinterest in trade training per se. His attitude toward the industrial arts was of a liberal arts kind: a first-hand experience in manual work, to build awareness of the work world and to cultivate empathy with those who labor with their hands, and an intellectual understanding of the moral, social, and economic

---

[24]Joseph M. Rice, *The Public School System of the United States* (New York: The Century Company, 1893).

[25]Laura Runyon, "A Day with the New Education," *Chatauquan,* 30 (March 1900): 589–95; John Dewey, *The School and Society* (Chicago: University of Chicago Press, 1899), pp. 47–48.

dimensions of the industrial order.[26] Reform meant "teaching for meaning." Therefore, it required finding more school time for social, health, and recreational, as well as vocational, programs. A 1910 survey reported 17 percent of the school day devoted to study of the fundamentals ("mechanics") of arithmetic—despite research that showed that such time allotments did not secure better results than those obtained in schools doing much less of it. But change was resisted; a 1925 study found three-fourths of the school day still devoted to the three R's.

Their reformist struggles often placed the progressives in the position of seeming to oppose the traditional academic subjects, as well as the classics for which very few Americans cared, to espouse "utilitarian" at the expense of "cultural" outcomes; and to favor transitory interest at the expense of intellectual discipline. The progressives might answer that Latin, for example, first entered the curriculum on utilitarian grounds (as the international language of religion, law, scholarship, medicine, science, diplomacy, and literature); only when it ceased to have practical importance did the classicists "discover" that it "disciplined the mind, perfected sensibilities, and developed the will."

Education for Change

Survival was the overriding aim of the instruction and imitation of elders, which constituted education in earlier societies. The curriculum provided certain rudimentary vocational, domestic, and protective skills (including religious magic) designed to equip one to cope with each day as it came. The oftentimes "chancy" nature of existence also fostered authoritarian relationships between the teacher and the taught. As recently in educational history as the Middle Ages, there was more of the survival than the ornamental element to education. Indoctrination persisted, and knowledge was "authoritative." Hence reading existed to serve memory of the things learned by rote, to aid recognizing what was already known—rather than to discover the new.[27] Yet books have also opened doors to new experiences, have supplemented what is known through direct experience with what is experienced vicariously through having learned to read. In an "information-poor" America of small towns linked only by dirt roads, before the days of electronics media, the schools could indeed expand one's horizon despite their few books and

---

[26]"The problem of the educator is to engage pupils in these activities in such ways that while manual skill and technical efficiency are gained and immediate satisfaction found in the work, together with preparation for later usefulness, these things should be subordinated to *education*—that is, to intellectual results and the forming of a socialized disposition": John Dewey, *Democracy and Education* (New York: Macmillan, 1916), p. 231.

[27]Philippe Ariès, *Centuries of Childhood* (New York: Alfred A. Knopf, Inc., 1962), p. 138.

meager offerings. Today's school, argues sociologist James S. Coleman, has had that function taken away from it permanently, since information dispensing is more efficiently and effectively done by television and films. The rapid and complete revolution in communications has stripped the school of a principal function, and left it groping for purposes beyond that of certification giving.[28]

One such possible new function, Coleman contends, is equipping youth with strategies for dealing with, interpreting, and using what they are taught outside schools and colleges. We hear also of education for "self-renewal"— an idea of psychic survival in a world whose primary law is change. Thus, John Gardner writes, "If we indoctrinate the young person in an elaborate set of fixed beliefs, we are ensuring his early obsolescence. The alternative is to develop skills, attitudes, habits of mind and the kinds of knowledge and understanding that will be the instruments of continuous change and growth. . . ."[29]

The key elements in the philosophy of progressive education were change and intelligence operating in the endless resolution of problem-solving situations. The progressive defined education as growth—whose goal is still more growth. The pupil was to be faced with "real" problems that would develop his potentialities cooperatively to continue social evolution.

Education for Community

The relationship of school to community had two obvious dimensions in progressivism. The concept of the "community school" was already evident in urban complaints against bureaucratic school administration. This is Jacob Riis's complaint about New York City schools around 1900:

> We asked the Board of Education to make their school playgrounds the neighborhood recreation centres. . . . They listened, but found difficulties. . . . It was the same story when I asked them to open the schools at night and let the boys in to have their clubs there. . . . But it isn't going to keep me from putting in the heaviest licks I can, in the campaign that is coming, for turning the schools over to the people bodily, and making of them the neighborhood centre in all things that make for good, including trades-union meetings and political discussions. Only so shall we make of our schools real cornerstones of our liberties. So, also, we shall through neighborhood pride restore some of the neighborhood feeling, the *home* feeling that is now lacking in our cities to our grievous loss.[30]

[28]"The Children Have Outgrown the Schools," *Psychology Today,* 5 (February 1972): 72–75, 82.

[29]John W. Gardner, *Self-Renewal and the Innovative Society* (New York: Harper & Row, Publishers, 1963), p. 21.

[30]Jacob Riis, *The Making of an American* (New York: Harper & Row, Publishers, 1966, originally pub. 1901), pp. 357–58.

That perception of loss of community in the urban, industrial present led to the second concern, with the school *as* community. In an ever more complex world, the family, church, neighborhood, and work place had been losing both their function of educating—imparting meaningful skills—and of giving youth a sense of identity with some community of shared purposes. The ability to know the social whole was lessened greatly by the specialization that divided the world of work and obscured one job from another. Therefore the study of cultures should help reintegrate society by emphasizing the interrelationships of jobs and how men live together. Beyond learning about holistic cultures, pupils should commit their classroom labors to the good of the "little community of the classroom"—in Dewey's terms—to make each school an "embryonic community life, active with types of occupations that reflect the life of the larger society." From membership within this community, where each is imbued with the spirit of service to others and strengthened in self-direction, "we shall have the deepest and best guarantee of a larger society which is worthy, lovely, and harmonious."[31] This view is far removed from the stereotype of progressivism as concerned with casual sociability and popularity, of the shallower forms of learning to get along together into which many classrooms indeed did lapse.

Its serious-minded pursuit of community, its promise of social amelioration, and its view of the individual linked to his fellows in common pursuits all recommended progressive education to the postrevolutionary Soviet government. A twelve-year experiment with the "activity method" began in Russia with "A Circular Letter of the Commissariat for Public Instruction" in August 1918. It advised that textbooks "should generally be banished from the schools" and replaced by teacher- and student-initiated "projects." This venture ended with another directive in 1930. Even if short-lived, this first Soviet attempt gave one variant of progressive education a widespread trial, never duplicated in the United States. In its own opportunistic style America only selectively incorporated elements of the reform movement known as progressive education.

THE POST-PROGRESSIVE ERA

An editorial in *Saturday Review* (July 5, 1958) opened with the statement that "1958 may go down in history as the year when many Americans first expressed dissatisfaction with two things they had been proudest of: their automobiles and their schools." The analogy was apt in that a "scaling down" marked both the new popularity of compact cars and the campaign for "getting the frills out" of the schools. But the attack on education had

[31]*The School and Society*, p. 44. The multiple "centers of interest and activity" characteristic of many progressive classrooms and the presence of items of common social usage are also evident today in many Head Start classrooms.

Cartoon by John A. Ruge. Copyright 1966 by Saturday Review, Inc.

"We made it over from an old, abandoned progressive school."

actually begun earlier. Large numbers of Americans had been critically appraising schools since the ending of World War II had freed public attention from other matters.

Much of the initial sense of postwar crisis originated in practical matters: inadequate facilities, teacher shortages, and booming enrollments from high birth rates and massive migrations. The controversies over assessments, tax rates, bond issues, and securing teachers that convulsed Levittown, New York, were repeated in some degree in thousands of other places. The National Citizens Commission for the Public Schools was established in 1949. Popular magazines played up a heightening sense of crisis and division, and professional education journals began responding to "the attacks upon our schools" by the "enemies of public education." Progressive education became the chief target.

The Attack on Progressive Education

Polls, although finding public opinion "magnificently inconsistent," showed approval of the curriculum as more useful and worthwhile than formerly. In *Life*'s 1950 survey, 87 percent of those polled upheld vocational education, social skills, character building, and personality development—the contemporary stereotypes of progressivism—and 90 percent accepted "the whole child" as the proper object of school concern. Thus American opinion had not turned its back on breadth. Yet even some of its friends concluded that progressivism had been fine, but was now out of date. Writing in *Fortune* in 1961, Charles Silberman praised progressivism for aiding in the painful transition from agrarianism to industrialism, for absorbing and Americanizing immigrant children, for its concern for human qualities. It was now repudiated "because it badly serves the needs of our own times" which, Silberman optimistically concluded, are for "something never before seen—masses of intellectuals."[32]

Abandoned by their friends, the old progressives fared badly from the pens of their enemies. The attack had two phases, both demanding a return to the fundamentals. The first stressed moral and patriotic values and focused its concern upon elementary education. The second emphasized academic subjects and concentrated its initial attack upon secondary schools.

Return to the Fundamentals: Part I

The occasional linkage in the 1930s of some progressives to communism was reawakened in the Cold War years, amid generalized fears that the American way of life was threatened from within and without. The "little red schoolhouse" came to mean the "soft-on-communism" progressive school and the free-thinking, secular university. Teacher loyalty oaths, subpoenas, censorship, and other attacks on academic freedom were used to root out "subversive influences." Before critics blamed the schools for early Soviet leadership in space, education was the scapegoat for the reportedly corruptible behavior of American prisoners of war in Korea. Sex education was opposed as a plot to undermine the family, and personality tests were called "brainwashing."[33]

This attack on the schools was more than militant anticommunism; a tone of moral indignation was unmistakable. Its deep and wide support lay in a nostalgia for a simpler past, a longing for sturdy virtues, for an absolutist moral system, for the practices of thrift, self-denial, and rugged individualism associated with rural or small-town Protestant America. When President Eisenhower, late in 1957, exhorted every school board and PTA to scrutinize its schools' curriculum and standards, to see "whether they meet the stern demands of the era we are entering," his words communicated concern for the survival of the American system. His person communicated the plain-speaking, unsophisticated, patriotic, and historic virtues that America thought it knew—and feared it might be losing.

Hyman G. Rickover's *Education and Freedom* (1959) specifically blamed

---

[32]Charles E. Silberman, "The Public Business: The Remaking of American Education," *Fortune* (April 1961):125–31, 194, 197–98, 201.

[33]That the linking of sex education and the communist menace outlasted the cold war is shown in Mary Breasted, *Oh! Sex Education* (New York: Praeger Publishers, 1970).

progressive education for sapping the nation's strength to produce leaders and for creating the "bureaucratic mentality" that hampered his efforts to develop an atomic submarine force. But the prime spokesman for patriotic and moral fundamentalism was probably Max Rafferty—the high-powered, politically astute state superintendent of California schools from 1963 to 1971. In *What They Are Doing to Your Children* (1965) he ridiculed teachers who compromised their positions by teaching self-discipline when what the pupil "really needs is a session after school with the ruler." This was an especially popular view, given the punitive climate of opinion aroused by student political activities off campus in the early 1960s and the eruption of the Free Speech Movement on the Berkeley campus in 1964. Newspaper editorials applauded his demand that schoolwork again become a "mighty serious business," forcing children to work and to strive. Objective teaching had no place in an emotional subject such as love of country: "Balancing virtues with vices, belittling the heroes, dwelling unduly upon the scandals of the past—these are the techniques that produce in the minds of children a balanced, bland, tasteless, lifeless image of their country." One of Rafferty's earliest proposals after winning office was to restore the portraits of the nation's heroes to the classrooms, one step in his general plan to foster unashamed worship of country.[34] The progressive concern with the peer group, Rafferty argued, had killed the competitive drive and prepared the mind for "welfare statism." Thus, Rafferty appealed also to the general feeling of powerlessness in a bureaucratic, professionalized society. He spoke effectively for local control, popular will, and family responsibility.

Return to the Fundamentals: Part II

During the first attack on the school curriculum, educators had the support of the liberal and academic intelligentsia, itself under political attack. This changed as the focus of crisis swung to issues of academic standards, subject-matter content, and intellectual skills. The debate, and then the construction of new curricula, centered upon secondary schools, although, by all accounts, the high school had been least affected by progressivism. Its teachers had

---

[34]During Rafferty's tenure as head of the California State Department of Education, "Education in Depth" was its official philosophy. Its principles were that positive, eternal values exist that education is to seek out and teach; the school's principal objective is the teaching of organized, disciplined, and systematic subject matter; the individual is the "be-all and the end-all" of the educative process; memorizing names, places, events, dates, and passages of prose and poetry is a necessary part of instruction; the desirable curriculum provides skills necessary to cultured, productive, patriotic citizenship; individual and national survival requires learning to hold one's own in a highly competitive world; students are to be made "learned," not popular, well-adjusted, or universally approved: Memo (Sacramento: State Department of Education, June 16, 1965). Cf. Max Rafferty, *What They Are Doing to Your Children* (New York: New American Library, Inc., 1965); and William O'Neill, *Readin, Ritin, and Rafferty* (Berkeley: The Glendessary Press, 1969).

"I'm not looking for new techniques of communication with my peer group . . . I just want to learn to read and write!"

more often taken the hard line on discipline, favored discrete courses rather than an integration of subjects, saw vocational programs as dumping grounds for "incorrigibles," let the textbook reign, and were themselves graduates of liberal arts colleges and universities—rather than of those teachers' colleges presumably dominated by progressivism.[35]

By the 1950s the boom in college-going affected the high schools. Some professors claimed that this expansion threatened college standards. A severe competition for places in prestigious colleges pushed up demands for more rigorous standards in the academic curriculum of the high school, including nonpublic schools that found themselves swept up in the same currents. Upper-middle-class parents in affluent suburbs were especially zealous in pushing

[35]"Corporal Punishment: Teacher Opinion," *NEA Research Bulletin,* 48 (May 1970): 48–49.

homework, advanced placement, extra loads, and "college-like" innovations in mathematics, science, and foreign language courses. They expected their schools virtually to guarantee their graduates entrance into selective colleges.

In 1900 the elementary school, the terminal institution for almost all children, was society's last chance to work out its vision of future citizens. As such, it was an omnibus institution, concerned both with those prepared for more schooling and those prepared "for life." By 1950, however, the high school had assumed that position. More parents were now themselves high school graduates and felt able to judge the schools. As the college and university becomes a more familiar personal experience, itself the mass terminal institution, it appears reasonable that debate—about purposes, institutional climate, discipline, methods, quality—will shift upward to the college, and that what are now almost exclusively internal discussions will come to include widespread external participation.

The second type of fundamentalist spoke repeatedly of priorities, "courageous decisions," and "weeding out." One father protested: "Time was when parents took their children to the circus and the teacher taught them to read; now the teacher takes my boy to the circus and I must teach him to read."[36] Others argued that the school consumed precious instructional time in general socialization, which was now better done by the mass media, by better-educated parents, and by the commercial youth culture. Such a sophisticated critic of schools as Arthur Bestor did *not* argue that the academic disciplines and training in how to think were "life"—nor were they even the most important element in life to most persons. They were, he argued, merely the school's *raison d'être,* and if neglected by schools they would nowhere else receive sufficient attention in this culture.

At first this push for curriculum reform had no orthodoxy of its own, partly because its exponents were themselves divided. What unity the movement possessed was that of being against the earlier ideology of progressivism.[37] Within a decade, however, its own slogans emerged: "structure of the disciplines," "the inquiry method," "induction," and "cognitive development." Beginning with the University of Illinois Committee on School Mathematics in 1951, a number of "discipline-centered" curriculum projects were developed, involving teams of university scholars (and sometimes teacher participants), supported financially by such federal agencies as the National Science Foundation, by such private foundations as the Fund for the Advancement of Education, and by textbook publishers anxious to distribute their instructional packages of texts, lab manuals, and films.

Also evident among fundamentalist critics was a naked dislike of the

---

[36]Quoted in Paul Woodring, *Investment in Innovation: An Historical Appraisal of the Fund for the Advancement of Education* (Boston: Little, Brown, 1970).

[37]John I. Goodlad, "Curriculum: A Janus Look," *Teachers College Record,* 70 (November 1968):95–107; and Goodlad, R. von Stoephasius, and F. M. Klein, *The Changing School Curriculum* (New York: Fund for the Advancement of Education, 1966).

Cartoon by Jack Markow. Copyright 1964 Saturday Review, Inc.

"Could you please tell me what I learned today, Miss Tepper? Mother's sure to ask."

"interlocking directorate" (to use Bestor's term) of school administrators, professors of education, and state and federal school officials. Their hostility was returned by a defensive profession that resented hearing itself described as ill educated and anti-intellectual, insulted at being told that no educational improvement could come without lay intercession. Outspoken educators disputed the implication that all schools should model themselves after colleges and use their methods, and that scholars and foundation executives, without personal experience with the problems of elementary and secondary schools, should give direction to public education. Nevertheless, a number of states adopted new curriculum and teacher-certification legislation; the professional component of education courses (what the then-president of Yale University called the "fog of pedagogy") was reduced, and workshops and institutes to "retrain" teachers became a part of curriculum projects.

A diet of academic "solids" in preparation for college represents a kind of career training for the middle class that ran counter to progressivism's general-education aims and to the equalitarian concern that *all* abilities be accommodated. But *all* could not be accommodated except at the expense of excellence, argued such critics as Grinnell College's Harold Clapp. Harvard English professor Douglas Bush complained that, "for asserting that not everyone has a right to be in college," he was called "a Piltdown man, a snob, and a Fascist."[38] Some critics saw in "the notorious dilution of the curriculum"—where Shakespeare, too difficult for some students, is read by none and physics is replaced by a science survey course—the tendency of American culture to seek the lowest common denominator.[39] Robert Hutchins claimed that progressive education, pleasurable and therefore popular, could easily supersede liberal education, which is difficult and even "painful," as Aristotle said real education will be. Other academic critics rejected the idea of a very limited pool, a tiny intellectual elite, for whom Plato must be preserved while the rest get Popeye. Like Rickover, they maintained that under the challenge of universal education, schoolmen simply gave up too easily and sold out the only subjects worth the effort of educating all children.

The Results of Critical Attack

Evidence of success in restricting breadth lay in the several million students using phonics, learning the "new math," and studying the scholars' curricula. It showed in popular articles about "the new high school kids" who combined academic distinction with popularity, in college officials who reported their freshmen better prepared than ever. It also showed itself in the complaints of opponents who found high schools becoming "cramming sessions," education a "grim contest" that forced students to seek fun outside of learning.

The "victory" of the fundamentalists seems to have been both short-lived and incomplete—if not completely illusory. A leader of the Association for Supervision and Curriculum Development, a unit of the National Education Association that most represents latter-day "establishment" progressivism, confidently declared in 1970:

> In the great debates about education we are the ones who have been most nearly right all along. . . . The public . . . and . . . some of the prestigious academicians, have had their silly season of deriding the great progressive gains made from the twenties through the forties. . . . They thought a school system that tried to wrestle with the real problems of life and society was merely soft and

---

[38] Harold Clapp, "Some Lessons from Swiss Education," *Modern Age*, 2 (Winter 1957–58):10–17; Douglas Bush, "The End of Education," *Phi Delta Kappan*, 38 (February 1957):163–66. See also Gottfried Dietze, *Youth, University, and Democracy* (Baltimore: The Johns Hopkins University Press, 1970).

[39] Adler and Mayer, *The Revolution in Education*, p. 81. Rudolph (*The American College and University*, p. 215) has observed, with Tocqueville, democracy's habit of "confusing excellence with privilege and of mistaking quantity for quality."

anti-intellectual. They wanted schools to be rigorously intellectual . . . concerned only with the pure disciplines. . . .

Well, they succeeded—for a while. Until the facts of life caught up with them. . . . In considerable degree they achieved their planned irrelevance, with life deliberately shut out of the classroom. And what did it get them? A perceptive generation . . . went "alienated." They have rejected the concentration on the merely technical. The battle cry of "relevance" is heard from coast to coast, and the great humane values which have been our chief concern are once more being forced upon those who sought to ignore them.[40]

In fact, however, neither side won very much, and talk of change far exceeded performance. Textbooks continued to eclipse both the laboratory inquiries and teaching machines of the latter-day reformers and the discussion groups and field trips of the earlier movement—as they always had. Innovation tended to shift from secondary schools to the early grades in the late 1960s; but the motives seemed specific and practical—to ameliorate the poor performance in basic skills in many urban schools. The accommodations made went in philosophically diverse directions. The National Assessment of Educational Progress was launched, but its first skills tests exemplified familiarly practical outcomes: "the social and business demands of writing," for example. Cautious public opinion supported the fundamentals, but not at the cost of longer school days and shorter vacations. More than ever America wanted to know "what it was getting for its money," but public opinion solidly opposed proposals for a standard test for all high schools as late as 1966. While parents showed overwhelming partiality to grading, some college registrars shifted consideration from academic records to evidence of "all-around" development, and a few colleges dispensed altogether with standardized admission tests.

The scholar's concern with mathematics for developing quantitative thinking was not shared by a public interested in arithmetic skills in everyday applications, insistent that the time and effort their children devoted to any subject have discernible meaning for the lives they would live.[41] Before the "new math" could be tried everywhere, state legislators and newspaper columns attacked it on the grounds that "now the kids can't even add and subtract!" Driver education continued to spread in high schools, and more college freshmen reported earning a varsity letter in high school sports than

[40]Fred T. Wilhelms, "Realignments for Teacher Education: The Eleventh Charles W. Hunt Lecture" (Washington, D.C.: American Association of Colleges for Teacher Education, 1970):22–23.

[41]University professors "tend to regard education as an entirely intellectual affair, whereas long tradition . . . emphasizes moral, physical, and athletic concerns. . . .": Frederick Wirt and Michael W. Kirst, *The Political Web of American Schools* (Boston: Little, Brown, 1972), p. 215. See also Michael W. Kirst and Decker F. Walker, "An Analysis of Curriculum Policy-Making," *Review of Educational Research*, 41 (December 1971):479–509.

Drawing by Ed Fisher; © 1969 The New Yorker Magazine, Inc.

"I'm sorry, Mr. Travis, but even here, at the Freedom University, seven times eight is fifty-six."

claimed membership in a scholastic honor society.[42] As academic standards rose, the market expanded for the books of a new generation of "romantics,"

---

[42]"Class of 1972 Draws Its Profile," *Chronicle of Higher Education,* 3 (December 23, 1968):8. See also "Public School Programs and Practices," *NEA Research Bulletin,* 45 (December 1967):103–26; "Curriculum Change Is Taking Place," *NEA Research Bulletin,* 45 (December 1967):103–26; "Curriculum Change Is Taking Place," *NEA Research Bulletin,* 48 (December 1970):103–5; Robert W. Locke, "Has the Education Industry Lost Its Nerve?" *Saturday Review* (January 16, 1971):42–44, 57; and *Parents' Reactions to Educational Innovation* (Princeton, N.J.: Gallup International, Inc., 1966). Questionnaires distributed in various kinds of nonpublic schools showed that few students complained that their study and homework loads were excessive: Otto F. Kraushaar, *American Nonpublic Schools* (Baltimore: The Johns Hopkins University Press, 1972), p. 131.

such as John Holt, Jonathan Kozol, Edgar Z. Friedenberg, Paul Goodman, and Herbert Kohl. Talk of priorities loses credibility before the fact that in 1970, a state university offered 195 different courses for freshmen and sophomores, and a nearby community college listed 483.

In short, the American curriculum seemed as much as ever compounded of conservatism and liberality, of drudgery and fun-seeking, of formalism and freedom, of vocationalism and humanitarianism—the school being both implacable and innovative, as is the style of this century and of this culture.

WHAT KNOWLEDGE IS OF MOST WORTH?

All men do not agree in those things they would have the child learn. From the present mode of education we cannot determine with certainty to which men incline, whether to instruct a child in what will be useful to him in life, or what tends to virtue, or what is excellent, for all these things have their separate defenders.

These words from the *Politics* of Aristotle appropriately apply to a society as diverse as is the United States.[43] Yet there are various schemes of classification that can bring some conceptual order out of the seeming disarray of opinion. We will present three such schemes that should serve to focus the perspectives of educational debate and also try to explain this debate in new terms.

Before proceeding, however, we should state that the participants in educational enterprise do not much engage themselves in debate about the "purposes" of education and the "nature of man." As table 16 suggests, the most "philosophical" issue—liberal versus professional education—ranks rather poorly in interests, although it surpasses the more technical issues of credits and prerequisites for defining the major field of study. Definably "educational issues" consistently rank well below political issues, dress codes, and related matters in surveys of the causes of high school and college protest incidents.

The Student-Subculture Model

Rather than be concerned with what theorists or reformers *say* about educational values, several sociologists, notably Burton Clark and Martin Trow, have analyzed student behaviors and styles in high schools and colleges.[44] They find in the campus culture as a whole certain types or clusters

---

[43]Cf. Don H. Parker, *Schooling for What?* (New York: McGraw-Hill Book Co., 1970), based on interviews with over one thousand Americans; and the conflicting conclusions of husband and wife, in Nat Hentoff and Margot Hentoff, "The Schools We Want: A Family Dialogue," *Saturday Review* (September 19, 1970):74–77.

[44]Burton R. Clark, *Educating the Expert Society* (San Francisco: Chandler Publishing Co., 1962), pp. 202–70.

TABLE 16   Importance attached to education issues, by different campus groups (in rank order)

	Students	Faculty	Administration	Department Chairmen
Teaching ability	1	7	7	6
Class size	2	1	3	2
Class schedule and teaching load	3	2	1	1
Requirements for degree	4	7	9	5
Adequacy of counseling	5	3	2	4
Teaching methods	6	5	5	7
Availability of counseling	7	6	4	8
Respect of faculty and administration for students	8	7	8	9
Liberal vs. professional-education	9	4	6	3
Requirements for major	10	8	10	10

Source: Preliminary Report, Campus Governance Project of the American Association for Higher Education. In Harold Hodgkinson, "Governance and Factions," *The Research Reporter* (Berkeley: Center for Research and Development in Higher Education, University of California) 3:3 (1968): 5.

of values and behaviors, which can be called subcultures. These appear (in extensive or attenuated form) among student populations on virtually any campus. The following is one such typology of student subcultures:

The collegiate subculture pursues "fun," social information, and the skills of sociability. This is the "interpersonal curriculum" that Coleman found characterizing adolescence. It is at home in the "old-fashioned" activities of athletics, cheerleaders, fraternities, and sororities and lives on in alumni associations and class reunions. It tolerates the formal curriculum (vocational or liberal) by ignoring it as much as possible.

The vocational subculture pursues the diploma. Nonintellectual, like the first, it seeks job-oriented information, technical skills, the credential. It is serious, often hard-driving, and especially prominent wherever the upwardly mobile, in secondary or higher education, seek occupational security through education.[45] It is not a subculture of protest, since the student who "grasps a clear connection between current activity and future status tends to regard school authority as legitimate, and to obey."[46] At best, however, it pays only lip service to the institution's attempts at liberal education.

---

[45]The University of Akron (Ohio) illustrates an institution overwhelmingly vocational in climate. Some 90 percent of its student body is from Akron, mostly living at home. In 1968 30 percent of the male freshmen listed engineering and 26 percent listed business as their probable majors; 1 percent planned an English major: Peter M. Swerdloff, "Hopes and Fears of Blue-Collar Youth: A Report from Akron," *Fortune* (January 1969):148–50, 152. The University of Northern Iowa's student body also sees such careers as public school teaching as "a step up the socioeconomic ladder"; thus the institution is a place for neither intellectual nor bohemian adventures: E. Alden Dunham, *Colleges of the Forgotten Americans* (New York: McGraw-Hill Book Co., 1969), pp. 84–85.

[46]Arthur L. Stinchcombe, *Rebellion in a High School* (Chicago: Quadrangle Books, Inc., 1964), p. 9.

The academic subculture pursues *knowledge* for its own sake. Inside and outside of classes it is attracted by *ideas*. These "serious students" are more evident (but not usually in the majority) in the humanities, in the "hard sciences," and in graduate schools. Unlike the other subcultures, it behaves least like a consumer group and identifies with the faculty and with whatever academic traditions the institution possesses.

The nonconformist subculture pursues identity. Ideas are important, but the alienated group uses off-campus and societal groups as its referents and tests of these ideas. It does not identify with the institution and is at odds with and challenges both the curriculum and the extracurriculum.

The Adler-Mayer Schema

A very different approach to the study of educational values is found in the Adler-Mayer analysis, which originated in a series of working papers for two funds of the Ford Foundation.[47] Using the literature primarily of postprogressive controversy about American education, it attempts to identify the principal variations in perspectives on educational aims, arrangements, methods, and clientele evident in modern American thought, using this schema:

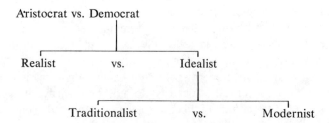

This terminology refers to relative, not to historically fixed, positions. Hence the exponent of an aristocratic position on contemporary American education differs noticeably from the contemporary European educational "aristocrat," or from the ancient "aristocrats" of the educational past.

The aristocrat and democrat division hinges on the issue of compromising equality. The aristocrat accepts the proposition that all men are brothers and equal under the law, and even that all should be educated. Beyond a minimum of universal schooling, however, inequalities in natural abilities should cause most individuals merely to be trained for specific tasks, while the capable remainder are given an extensive liberal education. Not only are the majority less educable, but their dispositions and interests are practical and nonintellectual; fairness requires that this should be recognized and accommodated. The democrat believes that all men are more educable and

[47]Adler and Mayer, *The Revolution in Education*, esp. pp. 71–106.

capable of intellectual arousing than is recognized by American schools. He believes that the longer schools keep all men, the better for them and for society.

The realist and idealist division among democrats hinges on whether accommodations to differences among individuals require differentiation of educational content. The realist-democrat argues that, after some given level of common schooling, varied programs or institutions should predominate— each type of schooling being superior in its own way. This is essentially the position of the tripartite British secondary system and of other tracking practices that envision prolonged universal education. The rejection of separate vocational high schools in America in favor of comprehensive schools, the preference for general courses over divisions into vocational and college-preparatory curricula, and the breadth or general-education requirements in colleges are, however, victories, of sorts, for the idealist-democrat position. While admitting that one must allow for different rates of learning, the idealist urges the abolition of curricular differentiation. Educators must find *methods* for giving all students the liberal education once reserved for an intellectual elite, or one might alter liberal education so that all may partake of it. Therefore, Arthur Bestor argues against teaching two histories, one for the 80 percent and another for the 20 percent. Even such a believer in an intellectual elite as Douglas Bush states that more intellectually nourishing fare could and should be set before poorer students.[48] As an idealist, Robert M. Hutchins decries an education that overly emphasizes individual differences: besides being different, men are also the same, and "the purpose of basic education is to bring out our common humanity."

The traditionalist and modernist division centers on what is contained in that same education for all. Idealists do not necessarily disagree among themselves on the definition of liberal education inherited from the ancient Greeks: an education worthy of a free man, an appeal to man as an intellectual and moral being, a releasing of one's intellectual and aesthetic faculties in the development of thoughtfulness and taste, a preparation for a worthwhile leisure. Bertrand de Jouvenel notes that while the full-time "gentleman of leisure" has disappeared, so has the laborer who is nothing but a "hand"; hence we require an education that expands men, that bestows "the power to multiply and explore choices so that the world ceases to be a little place, trimmed to one's private experiences," in the words of poet Mark Van Doren.[49] The humanities, argues the traditionalist, constitute the superior curriculum to accomplish these ends. The humanities are not impractical, for the thinking

---

[48]Bestor and Bush, in Brand Blanshard, ed., *Education in the Age of Science* (New York: Basic Books, Inc., 1959), esp. pp. 182–83, 216–21.

[49]Bertrand de Jouvenel, "Toward a Political Theory of Education," in *Humanistic Education and Western Civilization: Essays for Robert M. Hutchins,* ed. Arthur A. Cohen (New York: Holt, Rinehart and Winston, Inc., 1964), p. 66; Mark Van Doren, in Dennis and Kauffman, *The College and the Student,* p. 124. Cf. Thomas F. Green, *Work, Leisure, and the American School* (New York: Random House, Inc., 1968).

that persons are most called upon to do is thinking about the human condition —in their family, community, occupational, and political relationships. Between 1930 and 1970 the positions of goods-producing and service-producing occupations were exactly reversed, and people again make their livelihoods in dealing mostly with other people, not with products. Unlike vocational education, which is doomed to irrelevancy by the rapid retraining needs of industry and the dying of the Protestant work ethic, liberal education is learning how to learn; it cannot be made obsolete. Hutchins admits that the late-nineteenth-century revolt against study of the classics contained a valid grievance: liberal education had fallen into the hands of teachers of Greek and Latin who taught as drillmasters, more interested in language than in ideas. But now, Hutchins reasons, democracy requires that liberal education be restored lest civilization be lost; one need not burn the great books, he warns, but merely leave them unread.[50]

The modernist is impatient with such dualisms as liberal and vocational or humanistic and scientific. He believes in integrating many kinds of knowledge and in expanding the received tradition. He is impatient with the idea of a "timeless" curriculum, accepting the sentiment of the Japanese proverb: "Do not follow in the footsteps of the men of old, but seek what they sought." Or, as psychologist B. F. Skinner stated in his critique of Hutchins: "I see no reason why every individual must climb the tree of knowledge all the way from the roots. The Greeks made a lot of mistakes."[51]

The Historical-Functional Approach

The Adler-Mayer schema located philosophical principles around which an educational opinion could be formed. Paul Tillich, taking a more historical-anthropological approach, has distinguished three educational functions (he calls them "aims")—inducting, technical, and humanistic.[52] These educational functions are so universal that they may coexist in time and place. Their elements may also be variously combined.[53] Hence Tillich describes liberal

[50]One of Hutchins's examples is Michigan State University's four-year course leading to a Bachelor of Science degree "with a major in mobile homes"; "As Mobile Homes come in, Civilization goes out," writes Hutchins, in A. Whitney Griswold, *The University* (Santa Barbara, Calif.: Center for the Study of Democratic Institutions, 1961).

[51]Richard I. Evans, *B. F. Skinner, The Man and His Ideas* (New York: E. P. Dutton & Co., 1968), pp. 90–91.

[52]Paul Tillich, *Theology of Culture* (New York: Oxford University Press, 1959).

[53]An educational psychologist, Carl Bereiter, contends that school failures stem from efforts to combine, in one institution (the elementary school) and one person (the teacher), the two distinct functions of inducting and technical training; he calls them respectively *education* (the deliberate development of human personality, the explicit teaching of values and appropriate modes of conduct) and *skill-teaching*. Bereiter advocates, seriously, that schools cease their efforts at education and confine themselves to two kinds of professional services, offered by separate experts: child care and basic skill training in reading, writing, and arithmetic: *Must We Educate?* (Englewood Cliffs, N.J.: Prentice-Hall, Inc., 1973). A brief summary is Bereiter's "Schools Without Education," *Harvard Educational Review*, 42 (August 1972):390–413.

education in the Middle Ages as combining inducting education (into the Christian community) with technical education, whereas modern liberal education combines technical with humanistic components. These functions may also be apportioned differently among the curriculum and extracurricular activities—both under the purview of the school. Thus Bestor has no objection to having athletics, dancing, cooking, driver-training, and other non-humanistic activities in the school, as long as they are confined to nonclassroom time.

The *inducting* function covers what social scientists call "socialization" or "enculturation": the acquisition of traditions, symbols, and appropriate responses to the demands of family and group. Induction education may come spontaneously through participation in group life or may be intentional and intellectualized. Noah Webster and Max Rafferty promoted American history teaching for inducting reasons. When Sidney Hook protests conventional vocational education because it teaches only one's technological responsibilities, not one's social responsibilities, he seems to be seeking after the induction function.

Technical education supplies general skills, such as reading and writing, and the specialist skills of the arts, crafts, and professions. It goes on through imitation, apprenticeship, formalized (even theoretical) instruction, and exposure to the technological or technocratic *esprit de materiel*—as Theodore Roszak argues in *The Making of a Counter Culture* and Charles Reich in *The Greening of America*. The society gives precedence to its industrial demands over its cultural or religious heritage and over intangible individual needs. In our own times manpower and productivity considerations best express the technical aim. But so do demands for better performance in the basic skills. That students in professional departments and schools are the least dissatisfied with their studies suggests that the university is succeeding best in the technical arena.

The *humanistic* function has the ideal of developing all human potentialities, of releasing creativity and discovery. Unlike the first two functions, which *confer* identity, its aim is *creating* self. It demands discipline and imposes criticism, but not subjection of self. When it becomes drained of creative content it becomes formalized and ritualized, as Hutchins described classical teaching in 1900. Secularization has deprived the humanistic function of its religious substance and animating spirit; humanism and the humanistic ideal of education today appear "empty."[54] That students enrolled in the general course in high schools drop out more frequently (18 percent) than those in the two chiefly technical curricula—the vocational-commercial course (13 percent) and college-preparatory course (4 percent)[55]—underscores the

---

[54]Tillich, *Theology of Culture*, pp. 151–52.

[55]Herbert Bienstock, "Realities of the Job Market," in *Profile of the School Dropout*, ed. Daniel Schreiber (New York: Random House, Inc., 1967), p. 121.

Cartoon by William P. Hoest. Copyright 1969 Saturday Review, Inc.

"What's to worry about? They'll teach sex like they do the rest of the subjects and the kids will lose interest."

failures of our current pallid efforts to compound a general education out of elements of induction and humanistic education.

THE "DESCHOOLED" SOCIETY: SOME OPTIONS

Everyone likes the kind of story told of the seven-year-old who, after long staring at the cereal box, marveled aloud: "Once you learn to read, you just can't stop. You just see the letters and you're reading."[56] An intense excitement at learning undoubtedly grips millions of students, at least from time to time. The invariable monotony of the school day and the college year tends to blur substantial personal accomplishment and a quieter sense of satisfaction; autobiography—including the recounting around the dinner table of what one learned in school today—is an imperfect medium for ascertaining this, because it inflates dramatic and colorful moments and obscures the not unpleasant routine that makes up much of any life. It is pure sophistry to claim, as some romantic critics of schooling have repeatedly done, that all young children possess an intense desire to learn, which is invariably dampened

[56]Quoted in Kenneth E. Eble, *A Perfect Education* (New York: Macmillan, 1966), p. 143.

by the environment of the school and extinguished by the meaningless tasks set before students.

Nonetheless, our times are clearly marked by doubts about schooling, doubts issuing from so many varied perspectives that the total effect is a vast uneasiness. Some examples may illuminate the range of diagnoses of what ails the schools. They will also re-introduce the options that would, if pursued, radically "deschool" America or "disestablish" the public education system.

Inadequate learning is in most people's mind the most serious charge leveled at schools, largely on behalf of racial minorities and youngsters from lower-class homes. Dramatic confirmation exists in the account of the educational conference interrupted by a black mother. Angered by the tone of the discussion—which emphasized authentic relationships, emotional warmth and succor, an unstructured classroom—she burst out: "How dare you tell us, parents, that our children need love in school. What they need is to learn. Your job is to teach them, ours to love them; and there's no one better at loving children than a black woman."[57]

Distrust and sometimes fury directed at the public school lurk in the drive toward desegregated schools, in the hiring of more teachers who represent the minorities, in the decentralizing of school control in some cities, in aides and tutoring programs. "Accountability" became a powerful slogan in the late 1960s. The 1970 public opinion survey commissioned by the Kettering Foundation reported that three out of four Americans favored national tests by which their own schools' performance could be measured, two of three interviewed wanted teachers and administrators held responsible for pupil achievement, and 58 percent approved a "payment by results" system of teacher salaries.[58] The appearance of a parallel system of storefront schools in the ghettos is another manifestation of outright rejection of the public schools, shown also by withdrawals to parochial or other nonpublic schools, and by a massive absenteeism that averages 25 percent daily in New York City high schools and 40 percent or higher daily in certain schools in many United States cities, large and small.[59]

Wrongful learning is the most drastic charge leveled against schools and colleges. It holds that youth are taught to do what a frivolous or sick society requires: to conform, cheat, exploit, consume, and produce worthless goods. It is what Edward Sampson calls "the fourth world," the young, white, upper-

---

[57]"I begin by taking the concerns of the parents very seriously. Their anxieties about the behavior and academic progress of their children in school cannot be dismissed as retrogressive or conservative." These are the words of an alternative school worker, Tom Roderick, of East Harlem Day School, quoted in Steven Arons et al., *Doing Your Own School* (Boston: Beacon Press, Inc., 1972), p. 14.

[58]Gallup Poll, "Second Annual Survey of the Public's Attitude Toward the Public School," *Phi Delta Kappan,* 52 (October 1970):97–112.

[59]The malaise affects teachers, too. The New York City teacher absentee rate increased 50 percent from 1967–70, to 7.5 percent daily—twice the city's absentee rate for office workers: "Abandoning the Schools," *Christian Science Monitor,* February 6, 1970.

"You can't dress like that, boy—this is a permissive school."

middle-class, and postaffluent college students, that articulate these charges most forcefully. Their critique is framed not in the statistics of retardation but in such books as *Growing Up Absurd, Summerhill, Death at an Early Age, How Old Will You Be in 1984?, Reach, Touch, and Teach,* and *Teaching as a Subversive Activity.* It may influence even "educationally successful" college graduates to seek alternative vocations in place of conventional careers. It also has generated its own repudiation of the "educational establishment"—in alternative schools and free universities,[60] thought of as options to institutions believed incapable of, or unready for, important change.

"Education is too big" is an objection expressed by a heterogeneous group that includes educators dismayed at a graduate school structure producing 30

[60]Jonathan Kozol, *Free Schools* (Boston: Houghton Mifflin Co., 1972), esp. pp. 31–32; Martin Carnoy, ed., *Schooling in Corporate Society: The Political Economy of Education in America* (New York: David McKay Co., 1972), esp. pp. 11–13, 211–23; Allen Graubard, "The Free School Movement," *Harvard Educational Review,* 42 (August 1972):351–73; Harold W. Sobel and Arthur E. Salz, *The Radical Papers* (New York: Harper & Row, Publishers, 1972).

to 50 percent more expensively educated people than are needed. It lurks in students who find school in general confining or boring, even though they have no particular grievance with their school's character. It is supported by the research of sociologist Ivar Berg, who finds that most jobs formally require far more education than the job actually demands and reports that more education is often associated with more job dissatisfaction and less productivity. It is lived out, at least temporarily, by a mini-movement to skip college; from 1969 to 1972 the percentage of the nation's white males, aged 18 and 19, in college declined from 47.3 percent to 39.6 percent.[61] This body of criticism also influences the behavior of voters in tax and bond elections; politicians who resist proposals to upgrade the educational requirements for occupations licensed by the state; and supporters of the "extended university" or "external degree" plan whereby credits and even degrees may be granted for study away from the campus, by examination and in recognition of other experience.

The most radical spokesman for curtailing schooling is Ivan Illich—a critic of all mammoth institutions. He has broadened his original critique of Latin American efforts to make schooling universal on the American pattern; he now advocates education without schools in the United States.[62] The whole community, including farms and factories, would become again the chief site of education; everyone would be free to teach by sharing his skills with whoever wants to learn them, without licenses or degrees. Even among those who know nothing of Illich, one increasingly hears of proposals to outlaw educational discrimination, to forbid penalizing people for a lack of formal schooling.

Public schools repress choice, some critics assert, in that they would "Americanize" all comers. As instruments of majority rule, schools do violence to minority groups and minority preferences. Church figures, in their concerns for preserving church schools, or in opposition to the inadequate moral instruction they perceive in public schools, have long inveighed against the "Godless" public school "monopoly." The 1960s also expanded ethnic awareness, however, and protests are now heard against schooling that ignores or repudiates a heritage of cultural difference—or that distorts that heritage, which was the complaint of a black high school student who characterized her school's black history course as "colored folks' history."[63]

---

[61]Kraushaar, *American Nonpublic Schools,* esp. p. 141; Ivar Berg, *Education and Jobs: The Great Training Robbery* (New York: Praeger Publishers, for the Center for Urban Education, 1970); *Time* (April 16, 1973):80.

[62]Ivan Illich, *Celebration of Awareness: A Call for Institutional Revolution* (Garden City, N.Y.: Doubleday & Co., Inc., 1970); *Deschooling Society* (New York: Harper & Row, Publishers, 1970). See also Joel Spring, "Deschooling as a Form of Social Revolution," in Karier et al., *Roots of Crisis,* pp. 138–47.

[63]"Who wants to hear about the man (George Washington Carver) and the peanuts!" she exclaimed: In Kenneth L. Fish, *Conflict and Dissent in the High Schools* (New York: Bruce Publishing Co., 1970), p. 4. See also Michael B. Kane, *Minorities in Textbooks: A Study of Their Treatment in Social Studies Texts* (Chicago: Quadrangle Books, Inc., 1970).

© 1971 United Feature Syndicate, Inc.

Again, after years of obscurity, the concept of cultural pluralism finds renewed support as an alternative to cultural monotony, bureaucratization, and depersonalization.[64] These critics speak for *more breadth* in education, although not necessarily for breadth in each institution.

Attempts to institute such diversity have included optional class periods for the study of one's own cultural group and a greater measure of election of activities, giving to students at all levels more of the university's larger personal freedom to pursue eccentricity, variety, and self. Such experiments as Philadelphia's Parkway Program and Chicago's Metro High School could serve such ends, if their drawing upon other community agencies and groups is sufficiently diverse and intensive.[65]

But the most discussed approach is the voucher plan. The sums ordinarily spent upon public schools would be distributed (in a voucher form) to parents who would then shop around among schools, public and private, and spend their voucher in any school they chose. One version of the plan would increase the value of the poor child's voucher, to provide schools with extra incentives to admit and satisfy those whom present schools do not educate satisfactorily. Both opponents and supporters of vouchers note its appeal to characteristic mottos: "free competition," "free enterprise," "the consumer knows best," and "something for everyone."[66]

In voucher plan theory, all dimensions of diversity in practices would obtain—as has happened in American religion under guarantees of freedom of religion. The analogy of freedom of education and the disestablishment of the public school system with our religious experience seems appropriate, given the oft-proclaimed status of public education as this nation's "secular religion."

[64]Seymour W. Itzkoff, *Cultural Pluralism and American Education* (Scranton, Pa.: International Textbook Co., 1969). See, however, John W. Blassingame, "Black Studies: An Intellectual Crisis," *The American Scholar*, 38 (Autumn 1969):548–72.

[65]Parkway is described in John Bremer and Michael von Moschzisker, *The School Without Walls* (New York: Holt, Rinehart and Winston, Inc., 1971).

[66]Christopher Jencks, in *The New Republic*, 151 (November 7, 1964):33–40. See also *Education Vouchers: Final Report* (Cambridge, Mass.: Center for the Study of Public Policy, December 1970); and Theodore R. Sizer, "The Case for a Free Market," *Saturday Review* (January 11, 1969):34–42, 93.

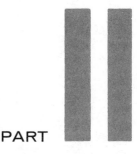

PART

THE PROFESSION OF TEACHING

Sooner or later one must recognize that the outcomes of formal education depend upon what goes on in each encounter between student and teacher. The exponent of subject-matter knowledge as the supreme measure of educational worth must finally measure a school by its teachers: "The student meets the subject in the teacher, and the teacher for that simple reason never ceases to be crucial in the drama of learning."[1] The lesson for educational radicals is the same: "To think differently about schools is to think differently about teachers."[2] The discussion of teaching in the nation's colleges and universities has reached such an insistent level as to suggest that a greater institutional commitment to effective teaching may be under way.[3]

[1]Mark Van Doren, "Teacher's Role in the Drama of Learning," *Educational Record,* 39 (July 1958):199–201. Many of the concerns of these chapters are treated, in a somewhat different fashion, in Robert Dreeben, *The Nature of Teaching: Schools and the Work of Teachers* (Glenview, Ill.: Scott, Foresman and Co., 1970); and Harry S. Broudy, "The Professional Teacher—A Mischievous Illusion," *The Real World of the Public Schools* (New York: Harcourt Brace Jovanovich, 1972).

[2]Dan C. Lortie, "Observations on Teaching as Work," in *Second Handbook of Research on Teaching,* ed. Robert M. W. Travers (Chicago: Rand McNally & Co., Inc., 1973), p. 474.

[3]See Kenneth E. Eble, *Professors as Teachers* (San Francisco: Jossey-Bass Inc., 1972).

5

THE ART AND THE SCIENCE
OF TEACHING

CLASSROOMS WITHOUT TEACHERS: 1950–70

Compared to the Depression years of the 1930s—when public schools probably had the highest proportion of well-educated, experienced, and career-minded teachers in the nation's history—the teaching corps after World War II was numerically depleted and professionally undernourished. Every September one read of huge teacher shortages, overcrowded classrooms, and the issuance of thousands of emergency teaching credentials to those hired without having met minimal state requirements of preparation. Several factors were responsible. First, there was an inadequate teacher supply. Most of the new teachers for postwar schools had to come from the generation born during the Depression, a time of low birthrates. The ravages of war had further decimated the potential teacher population of those born in the twenties. Second, there was intense occupational competition. An expanding economy, the ambition of individuals to compensate for remembered privation by taking better-paying jobs than teaching, the opportunity to use G.I. Bill benefits to prepare for other professions, and the high social approval given to early marriage and large families all made teacher recruiting and retention difficult. The expanding market also was a factor. High postwar birthrates made additional teachers necessary. So did desires for more schooling per individual. Some teachers were lost to the elementary schools as high school enrollments in the late fifties and sixties grew; many prospective high school teachers became new faculty members in an expanding system of higher education, especially in the community colleges. Population displacement, typified by movements of Americans to metropolitan areas, urban and suburban, and to the North and West, created demands in some regions and stagnation in others.[1] During its period of greatest population growth, California *annually* depended upon other states for one-half of its new ele-

---

[1]Population growth in the decade 1960–70 was concentrated in only 25 percent of the nation's counties, while some cities and states lost population: Philip M. Hauser, "The Census of 1970," *Scientific American,* 225 (July 1971).

mentary teachers and over one-half of its new secondary teachers; Florida, Arizona, and the Pacific Northwest had similar needs. Shortages of "regular" classroom teachers, moreover, were exacerbated by the appearance of such federally sponsored activities as the Peace Corps, the Job Corps, the Teacher Corps, and projects to improve schools in the ghettos. The War on Poverty doubtless also diverted some potential classroom teachers into community-development activities. In a September 1966 survey of state departments of education 38 states reported a diminished supply of qualified teachers over the previous year and 44 indicated increased demand; in both cases, the appearance of federal programs was the principal factor reported responsible.[2]

By the latter years of the period, disparity between supply and demand had created a selective and not a gross shortage. The post-Sputnik pressures on high schools to upgrade their programs in the "hard subjects," especially in science and mathematics, meant two things for teacher supply and demand: that more students study these fields, thereby requiring more teachers; and that those teaching without appropriate preparation be replaced by qualified teachers. The second was the more important, notably in small high schools. During the school year just before the Russian space achievement, one state reported that instruction given by high school teachers without either a college major or minor in the subject taught ranged from 1 percent in music and 8 percent in science and industrial arts to 35 percent in mathematics.[3]

In addition, the wishes of colleges and universities, of students, and of prospective employers are not well articulated—partly through adherence to the principle of relative freedom in choosing one's life work.[4] The educational backgrounds of college graduates are not well calibrated to the breadth of the public school curriculum. In recent years about one-third of each year's crop of college graduates were prepared to teach; in 1966 the proportion of all graduates actually entering teaching rose to 38 percent. Women were overrepresented in this group, since teaching has traditionally absorbed 40 percent or more of women college graduates. Consequently, the supplies of prospective elementary teachers and of high school teachers of English, art, speech, foreign languages, home economics, and business education—the teaching areas where women typically predominate—were large. Conversely, on the basis of sex differential alone, the likely shortage fields would be the men's teaching fields: agriculture and industrial arts, mathematics, and

[2]"A New Look at Teacher Supply and Demand," NEA Research Bulletin, 44 (December 1966):117–23; "Teacher Job Shortage Ahead," NEA Research Bulletin, 49 (October 1971):69–74. In 1966 the Peace Corps employed 5,400 teachers overseas, the Job Corps employed 1,720 teachers, and Head Start anticipated a staff of 12,000; the number diverted from regular classrooms by the draft was substantially larger: Time (September 23, 1966):43.

[3]Joseph A. Kershaw and Roland N. McKean, Teacher Shortages and Salary Schedules (New York: McGraw-Hill Book Co., 1962), p. 91.

[4]Staff Report on the Commission on Higher Education, Human Resources and Higher Education (New York: Russell Sage Foundation, 1970).

science.[5] Men educated as teachers are less likely than their female counterparts actually to enter teaching. This further heightens differences in supply. So does variation in likelihood of entry among fields. The annual proportion of prepared graduates who actually entered classrooms has ranged from 53 percent in journalism and 67 percent in the sciences to 80 percent in women's physical education.[6]

A NEW ORDER OF THINGS: 1970–?

The image of students without teachers is a device used to dramatize past shortages more than a description of reality. Students did get teachers, through hiring the technically unqualified, using long-term substitutes, increasing class size, doubling up on study halls, and curtailing programs. But by 1970, two new phenomena were affecting American teachers. The teacher shortage had been turned into a substantial surplus that promises to persist, and a growing professional militancy offers the possibility that many a classroom might indeed be unmanned—as teachers walked a picket line outside schools, district offices, and state legislatures.

From Shortage to "Surplus"

Like certain other college graduates, those seeking teaching positions in the 1970s face the predicament of not enough jobs, a predicament worsened by long-term economic recession. Between 1966 and 1970 the number of states reporting shortages of teaching applicants dropped from 33 to 2, and the number reporting limited or general excesses rose from none to 12. Such a switch occurred without an equalizing of teacher earnings with those of other occupations requiring college graduation, without a noticeable increase in society's opinion of relative teacher prestige, and without significant improvements in working conditions, including greater teacher autonomy. Instead, there were five responsible factors. First, demand stabilized as the nation experienced a lower birth rate after the peak year of 1957. The number of additional teachers required by population growth was only 35,000

[5]Shortage areas can be made quickly into surplus fields by a relatively minor shift in preparation among the very large number of prospective teachers trained annually. Thus, if only 1 or 2 percent of all those in teacher-training programs would switch from social science or general elementary preparation to vocational education, or women's physical education, or speech correction, or elementary school librarianship—the fields of reported unmet demands in 1970—in three or four years' time, the openings reported would be fully subscribed. See Herold G. Regier, *Too Many Teachers: Fact or Fiction?* (Bloomington, Ind.: Phi Delta Kappa Educational Foundation, 1972), pp. 11–12.

[6]"End of General Teacher Shortage," *NEA Research Bulletin,* 49 (March 1971):8–10; James A. Davis, *Undergraduate Career Decisions* (Chicago: Aldine Publishing Co., 1965); Michael H. Moskow, *Teachers and Unions* (Philadelphia: University of Pennsylvania Press, 1966), pp. 83–86.

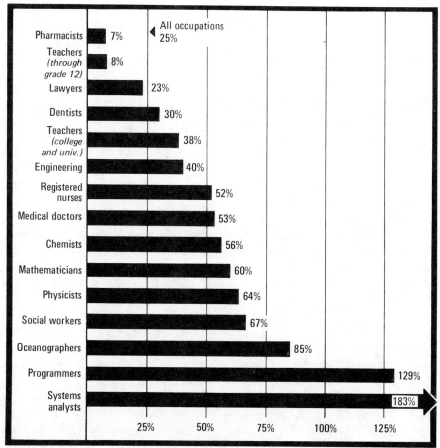

FIGURE 11 Employment needs: percent growth, 1968–80 (projected)

in 1970; this was between one-half and three-fourths the requirements of elementary and secondary schools over each of the preceding 16 years. The projections of additional students in grades kindergarten through 12 for each year between 1970 and 1980 was for small or nonexistent growth, the decade's need for additional elementary and secondary teachers estimated at a mere 3.3 percent.[7] The need for college teachers would continue to

[7]A much-cited survey by the National Education Association offers these estimates of *additional* public school teaching positions projected during the 1970–80 period: 1970–36,000; 1971–19,000; 1972–8,000; 1974–none; 1975–reduction of 1,000 positions; 1976–1,000. In *Teacher Supply and Demand in Public Schools, 1970* (Washington, D.C.: National Education Association, 1970). See also the analysis in Regier, *Too Many Teachers*.

grow higher, given the high birth rates of the 1950s; the differences are included in figure 11. Yet statistics covering those young Americans already born make clear that the number of college-age youth will decline, from 17 million in 1978 to 14 million in 1988. Unless a rising proportion of youth go to college in the future, college enrollments and the need for faculty will drop. Even should college-going rates remain stable or rise somewhat, economic uncertainties and inflationary college costs will cause institutions to adopt a very conservative policy in adding new faculty or replacing those who retire. Even the prestigious colleges could experience such unsettling phenomena as an expansion in the number of interrupted student careers and higher drop-out rates. Meanwhile, many public school districts report declining enrollments, empty classrooms, and a consequent reduction in state funds, and some private school applications have shrunk. Second, a slowing-down in program expansion is a result of state and federal withdrawal of support, taxpayer resistance, and a general questioning of school outcomes. Curtailments of new programs, and the tendency to "think smaller" when it comes to planning which requires more credentialed staff, could cause an overproduction of 100,000 to 150,000 elementary and secondary school teachers annually, according to predictions by the National Education Association. Third, in 1960 the colleges and universities produced 130,000 graduates prepared to teach; that number grew to 290,000 in 1970. It was projected to reach 400,000 by 1980. While the percentage of college graduates was increasing from 1960 to 1970 by 79 percent, public school enrollments grew by only 24 percent.[8] Studies of college undergraduates showed that one-half of all students shift their majors during their collegiate careers; education is both the most retentive field and one that gains more students than it loses. Fourth, the competition from the underemployed has put teachers into competition with professionals in other fields. Affected by economic uncertainty, some scientists, engineers, business graduates, architects, and other professionals have turned to education to find employment. Finally, returning teachers also compete with beginners. Each year 15,000 to 35,000 such individuals wish to return to classrooms; various social and economic factors could balloon those figures. Estimates are that for every four public school teachers at work, there is one (or more) fully qualified, experienced teacher in reserve; 93 percent of these "reservists" are women, half in the 25–35 age bracket. Yet to be determined is whether the specter of a teacher surplus and uncertainty about nonteaching employment opportunities has caused fewer teachers to leave teaching. If so, the need for replacement teachers would be reduced proportionately.

The combination of record low demand and record high output and supply has led to the prediction that by 1980 the percentage of the college graduating

[8]Bernard H. McKenna, *Staffing the Schools* (New York: Teachers College Press, 1965).

class needed for elementary and secondary teaching will decline from 38 percent to 15 percent. The shock to some institutions will be very great, especially those state colleges where 42 percent of the student body, on the average, report plans for public school teaching careers. The historic dependence of educated women upon teaching jobs, and the near-universal agreement that more men should be included in the teaching body,[9] suggest that the woman college graduate will be the most affected.

Classrooms Without Teachers: "On Strike"

While the specter of teachers on strike became an inescapable reality during a period of teacher shortage, the factors involved in greater professional militancy seem certain to persist in the era of surplus. The future promises more of what the 1960s witnessed: intense reexaminations of the public and the self-image of teachers.[10] The bench mark in this movement was probably the one-day strike of twenty-two thousand New York City teachers, more than half the city's teaching force, in April 1961. The strike was successful on several counts: its demands forced additional expenditures for teacher salaries; the state law banning strikes by public employees (passed after a Buffalo teachers' strike in 1947) was shown unenforceable; and the mobilizing effects of the strike were large and long-lasting, as the union that called the strike increased its membership and solidified its position as the teachers' bargaining agent.

Since 1961 teachers in many school districts have effected work stoppages; indeed, strikes have been called against whole states—as in the case of Florida, Oklahoma, and Pennsylvania in 1967–68. In 1971 lay teachers struck the Catholic school systems of New York City and San Francisco—a remarkable and apparently unprecedented sign that unionization had really arrived. Other public employees—municipal, state, and federal—have joined teachers in challenging antistrike legislation. They have sometimes succeeded in overturning statutory provisions in the courts and in simply defying bans and injunctions. The militancy of the union movement increased the reported membership of the American Federation of Teachers from 75,000 in 1962 to 250,000 teachers in 1970. It also forced the National Education Association to accept a strike policy. From 1946 through 1965 there were 22 work stoppages, involving a total of 16,000 NEA members; in 1966 alone there were 11 strikes with 31,000 NEA participants. In the 1969–70 school year

---

[9]Profound sexual bias makes men's occupations "more important," gives men preference over women in virtually all employment, and leads many women to conclude that they can raise the prestige or quality of their professions *only* by recruiting more men.

[10]Alan Rosenthal, *Pedagogues and Power: Teacher Groups in School Politics* (Syracuse, N.Y.: Syracuse University Press, 1969); "Teacher Strikes in Perspective," *NEA Research Bulletin,* 46 (December 1968):113–16; and "Teacher Strikes, 1960–61 to 1969–70," *NEA Research Bulletin,* 48 (October 1970):69–72.

TABLE 17   Public school teacher strikes, July 1960–June 1970

Item	Teacher Strikes		Personnel Involved (Estimated)	
	Number	Percent	Number	Percent
SCHOOL YEAR				
1960–61	3	0.6%	5,080	1.0%
1961–62	1	0.2	22,000	4.3
1962–63	2	0.4	2,200	0.4
1963–64	5	1.0	11,980	2.4
1964–65	12	2.4	15,083	3.0
1965–66	18	3.6	33,620	6.6
1966–67	34	6.8	10,633	2.1
1967–68	114	22.8	162,604	31.8
1968–69	131	26.2	128,889	25.2
1969–70	180	36.0	118,482	23.2
TOTAL	500	100.0%	510,571	100.0%
TYPE OF ORGANIZATION				
Professional association	331	66.2	282,745	55.4
Teacher union	135	27.0	207,838	40.7
No organization	17	3.4	1,079	0.2
Joint union/association	9	1.8	16,731	3.3
Independent organization	8	1.6	2,178	0.4
TOTAL	500	100.0%	510,571	100.0%
STATE				
Alaska	1	0.2%	500	0.1%
California	27	5.4	34,545	6.8
Colorado	4	0.8	3,721	0.7
Connecticut	15	3.0	6,791	1.3
District of Columbia	5	1.0	3,446	0.7
Florida	4	0.8	32,000	6.3
Georgia	2	0.4	98	a
Idaho	1	0.2	300	0.1
Illinois	53	10.6	29,258	5.7
Indiana	14	2.8	28,666	5.6
Iowa	2	0.4	209	a
Kentucky	7	1.4	55,060	10.8
Louisiana	4	0.8	2,607	0.5
Maryland	8	1.6	10,855	2.1
Massachusetts	10	2.0	9,226	1.8
Michigan	125	25.0	45,240	8.9
Minnesota	1	0.2	2,000	0.4
Missouri	11	2.2	3,834	0.8
Montana	2	0.4	818	0.2
Nevada	2	0.4	3,200	0.6
New Hampshire	3	0.6	1,345	0.3
New Jersey	34	6.8	17,261	3.4
New Mexico	3	0.6	3,058	0.6
New York	23	4.6	128,998	25.3
North Dakota	1	0.2	200	a
Ohio	65	13.0	16,500	3.2
Oklahoma	5	1.0	24,822	4.9
Pennsylvania	42	8.4	29,763	5.8
Rhode Island	7	1.4	2,675	0.5
South Dakota	1	0.2	441	0.1
Tennessee	4	0.4	851	0.2
Utah	3	0.6	10,325	2.0
West Virginia	3	0.6	114	a
Wisconsin	8	1.6	1,844	0.4
TOTAL	500	100.0%	510,571	100.0%b

aLess than 1/10 of 1 percent.

bFigures in the column do not add to this total because of rounding.

Sources: Compiled from published and unpublished data of the U.S. Department of Labor, Bureau of Labor Statistics, and the NEA Research Division. Adapted from data reported in *NEA Research Bulletin*, 48 (October 1970): 70–71.

affiliates of the two national teacher organizations called 180 strikes. Table 17 indicates the distribution by sponsoring organization, time, and place for the decade 1960–70.

A Time of Challenge to Stereotypes

We have discussed the appearances of an ostensible teacher surplus and of unprecedented assertiveness by teacher organizations together because both compel some rethinking of the teacher's position in the American educational and social systems. The personal decision to choose teaching and the decision of how to behave as a teacher qua professional will make more demands upon the individual.[11] The response of public opinion to recent teacher strikes includes the extremes of viewing teachers as heretics and as martyrs; the future may well bring a new consensus, one whose outlines are yet indistinct.

The fact that schools exist to transmit culture across the generations, to conserve the past and present, surely means that teaching in the future will not be "a whole new ballgame." Yet a number of new elements may be at work. Class size has long been the favorite issue with teachers. It will be instructive to see if teacher groups use collective bargaining and the projected teacher "surplus" to reduce class size.[12] Will the organized profession actually commit itself to upgrading competence and to developing a leadership that will challenge the tradition of "gifted amateurs" who have been America's educational spokesmen from Jefferson and Franklin, through Horace Mann, to James B. Conant and Charles Silberman? Decisions about recruiting, rewarding, and retaining teachers can become more deliberative. Each reader of this book may take part in those deliberations. What the teaching profession *is,* and how it came to itself, is the concern of this chapter and chapter 6. The present chapter considers enduring issues of what makes for a good teacher and a competent profession; chapter 6 paints a sociological-demographic portrait of those with whom one will teach.

THE TEACHER STEPS FORWARD

Educational theories begin to develop when a society moves from informal to intentional education, i.e., from socialization to schooling. Part of such a theory is its principles of teaching. These ordinarily command little atten-

---

[11]Ronald G. Corwin, "Teachers as Professional Employees: Role Conflicts in the Public Schools," *A Sociology of Education* (New York: Appleton-Century-Crofts, 1965), pp. 217–64.

[12]To reduce average class size to twenty-five students would require *twice* the number of teachers projected by the NEA as the oversupply (1,263,000) produced between 1972 and 1980: Regier, *Too Many Teachers,* p. 13.

Cartoon by Fred Surace. Copyright 1964 Saturday Review, Inc.

"Hello parents, my name is Miss Hadley. I teach the *First Grade*. I *like* to teach the *First Grade. We* have lots of fun . . ."

tion until questioned by new philosophical or psychological postulates, by changing political or religious theories, by upsetting events, or sometimes by the results of research.[13] Thus, new learning theories challenged the teacher's image as "one who pours in knowledge" with that of "one who draws out learning." A secular liberalism undermined the punitive aspects of the teach-

---

[13]Studies of teacher characteristics and teacher effects number in the thousands. A good pre-Coleman introduction to teacher evaluation is Bruce J. Biddle and William J. Ellena, eds., *Contemporary Research on Teacher Effectiveness* (New York: Holt, Rinehart and Winston, Inc., 1964).

"What sort of teaching theory will command interest during a given period of history depends on what sorts of learnings carry a premium in that period," argues Harry S. Broudy: "Historic Exemplars of Teaching Method," in *Handbook of Research on Teaching,* ed. N. L. Gage (Chicago: Rand McNally & Co., 1963), pp. 1–43.

ing role. The presence of cultural minorities revealed unappreciated aspects of teacher characteristics as they affected pupils.[14] Recently university students' protests against the faculty research role have created more interest in the analysis of good college and university teaching and course guides and teaching evaluation forms by the thousands.

It is now fashionable to hear that "there is no such thing as teaching—only learning." Yet a theory that places learning through the intervention of the teacher below that acquired by teaching oneself still must conclude that unassisted learning is too time-consuming and uneconomical for all but the rarest talent, that "most men would have neither the leisure nor the courage to learn all they need to know if teachers did not ease and accelerate the process for them."[15]

Another kind of challenge to the teacher has been posed by Coleman's investigation of school achievement. He concluded that nothing in school—including such characteristics of teachers as their intelligence, education, and experience levels—has as much relationship to a pupil's achievement as his own or his schoolmates' socioeconomic status. To conclude this is not to say anything about how the social class of one's peers operates. Some research indicates that a teacher's expectations influence achievement, and that these vary according to student social class.[16] Other evidence points to the relative proportion of teacher time devoted to classroom management, discipline, and instruction—the latter receiving more attention in middle-class schools. There is the additional matter of determining whether and how teacher characteristics influence learning variations in uniformly middle-class and intellectually homogeneous classrooms. Pending considerably more investigation, we must only conclude that the attributes of teachers that affect student achievement, for good or ill, are more subtle and mysterious than heretofore assumed.[17]

The Search for the Typical Teacher

Studies of teacher characteristics show that teachers both resemble the populations among whom they live and vary consistently among themselves. Thus, on the first count, big-city teachers—like big-city residents generally—differ from the average of all teachers by including more unmarried persons, by being better educated, and, if married, by having smaller families. Second, studies going back to the 1930s have located substantial, systematic varia-

[14]For example, some recent research suggests that the teacher characteristic of "speaks clearly" is less important for white students than for black: Robert W. Heath, "The Ability of White Teachers to Relate to Black Students and to White Students," *American Educational Research Journal*, 8 (January 1971):1–10.

[15]John W. Donahue, S.J., *St. Thomas Aquinas and Education* (New York: Random House, Inc., 1968), p. 83.

[16]Ray C. Rist, "Student Social Class and Teacher Expectations: The Self-Fulfilling Prophecy in Ghetto Education," *Harvard Educational Review*, 40 (August 1970):411–51.

[17]See the post-Coleman analysis in *How Teachers Make a Difference* (Washington, D.C.: U.S. Government Printing Office, 1971).

TABLE 18   Faculty opinions on campus incidents, by age of faculty members

Hypothetical Incident	Percent of Faculty Opposed	
	Faculty Age	
	Under 30	55+
1. A biology teacher spoke out in his class in favor of premarital sexual relations.	30%	63%
2. The student government using student funds invited a well-known social activist to the campus to speak.	8	21
3. A group of students held an anti-draft protest meeting on campus and subsequently picketed the local selective service board.	20	45
4. An unmarried male and female student couple were found to be sharing the same apartment.	17	58
5. A faculty member organized a Black Power group which engaged in some disruptive activities in the local community.	51	80
6. A faculty member participated in a nonviolent sit-in demonstration in the administration building.	30	63
7. The student newspaper carried a series of articles on the use of drugs describing in detail how to use them.	46	72
8. A faculty member conducted classified military research.	30	41

Source: Based on data gathered from fifteen hundred faculty members in various types of institutions, for R. C. Wilson and J. G. Graff, "Faculty Characteristics and Attitudes Toward Students," *Research Reporter* (Berkeley: Center for Research and Development in Higher Education, University of California), 4:1 (1969):3.

tions in the social backgrounds of teachers: between urban and rural, elementary and secondary, male and female teachers, those in (segregated) white and black schools, and among America's various geographic regions.[18]

Even the body of college teachers—a more homogeneous group by virtue of being predominantly male and a less variable group because it is smaller (in 1970 there were 2,062,243 elementary and secondary public school teachers, and only 438,300 teachers in colleges and universities)—is itself diverse. For example, age is a significant index of difference in attitudes on proper student and faculty behavior, as table 18 indicates. To the extent that community colleges recruit less than formerly from secondary school faculties, they will introduce new divisions of faculty values and opinions—as some such colleges have already discovered.

Images of the Teacher

A few years ago one could see a double feature in which both female leads were teachers. The heroine of *The Prime of Miss Jean Brodie* was a teacher in a Scottish girls' school in the 1930s. In the movie she was always

[18]W. W. Charters, "The Social Background of Teaching," in *Handbook of Research on Teaching,* ed. Gage, pp. 715–813. Note that little study has been made of other than public school teachers, e.g., those in private and commercial ventures, Sunday schools, music and art institutes—as Lortie observes in *Second Handbook of Research on Teaching,* ed. Travers, p. 494.

with or thinking of her pupils, a buoyant and alive individual charged with the belief that her profession was society's most influential one. On the other hand, the heroine of *Butch Cassidy and the Sundance Kid* was never depicted around her school, or with her students. When she decided to leave her Western town and throw in her lot with fleeing desperados, she explained, "I am 26, unmàrried, and a schoolteacher. I've already hit the bottom of the barrel!"

It would be well to give some attention to historic images of the teacher, including such contradictory stereotypes as these two films reflect. Stereotypes are often erroneous and always exaggerated images of a group, in this case of an occupational group. While stereotypes tend to persist and are hence more a caricature than a description, they are subject to change: witness the ability of television "play-by-play" and "color men" to convince viewers that professional football players are scholars of a complex science of thick, technical playbooks and arcane language. A calculated effort to challenge a stereotype by improving an image seems to be more difficult, however, in the case of a profession as large as teaching; after all, everyone has known teachers at first hand and finds their work less mysterious. One of the reasons that professors typically enjoy a higher prestige than do other teachers—despite the professoriate having its own unflattering stereotypes of absentminded ineffectualness—is that, until very recently, few Americans have ever known a professor or seen one at work.

One of the most famous images of teaching was conveyed in George Bernard Shaw's "He who can, does; he who cannot, teaches!" (Virtually unknown is Shaw's later "recantation," "He who can do, does; he who can think, teaches!") Shaw perpetuated an ancient assumption that teaching attracts those unable to succeed elsewhere.[19] This was the image of the grammar teacher in ancient Greece, and the fact that educated slaves (prisoners of war) were sometimes assigned teaching duties contributed to low status; yet some teachers, including the famous Sophists, had extraordinarily high prestige. In ancient China those who failed the demanding civil service examinations often became schoolmasters, thereby establishing the image of teachers as rejects. The trustees of Franklin's Philadelphia Academy proposed, in 1750, that, "the Country suffering at present very much for want of good Schoolmasters, and obliged frequently to employ in their Schools, vicious imported Servants, or concealed Papists, who by their bad Examples and Instructions often deprave the Morals or corrupt the Principles of the Children under their care," the academy should enroll "a number of the poorer Sort" of students and qualify them to act as schoolmasters. While "poorer sort" probably referred to economic and not intellectual standing, the imagery remains unflattering.

Nineteenth-century America took its time before considering teaching as

[19]Alma S. Wittlin, "The Teacher," in *The Professions in America*, ed. Kenneth S. Lynn (Boston: Beacon Press, 1967), pp. 91–109. Cf. the regrettably superficial analysis in Michael Belok and Fred Dowling, "The Teacher Image and the Teacher Shortage," *Phi Delta Kappan*, 42 (March 1961):255–56.

an avenue of upward social mobility. The poor boy "who knew that he did not want to be a lawyer or a preacher or a doctor, and who had too much ambition to want to be a teacher" pursued opportunity by a career in commerce, manufacture, engineering, or transportation.[20] By the later years of the century, however, the image of the teacher improved, to judge by the more numerous and more favorable references to teachers in American literature.[21] It is probable that this period's sentimental regard for childhood, the broad consensus that schooling was crucial to the nation, and actual small improvements in the recruitment, education, and treatment of teachers were together responsible for a somewhat improved image.

The foregoing suggests some of the elements that affect teacher stereotypes. Here are some other factors believed to cause the difference in images and prestige observed worldwide between elementary, secondary, and university teachers. *The client's age status* affects the image of those working with him. Young children, no matter how much loved, are dependent and subordinate individuals whose care implies a custodial dimension. Both teachers and housewives suffer a degree of lesser prestige by their occupational association with children.

The client's social status also reflects upon professionals. Secondary school and university teachers, historically teachers of a social elite, gain reflected prestige. Where secondary education is also mass education, as in the United States, teaching a prestigious subject (physics) or an intellectual elite (a class of "gifted" children) may confer a differentiated status and support a special self-image. *Depth of scholarship* enhances the secondary teacher's and professor's stereotype. The teacher of the younger child, however, has generalized duties and deals with the basic subjects at elementary levels—which does not connote high intellectuality. Decades ago a pioneer sociologist of education concluded that a sort of split personality develops where "the teacher is forced to say over and over things so elementary that they have no interest for him and . . . part of him must serve as an animated phonograph while another part stands aside and jeers."[22] Yet, repeated polls indicate that teachers themselves feel no special loss of status by the nonscholarly and clerical duties that elementary teachers routinely perform. A heightened public recognition of the crucial early school years could possibly enhance public regard for the qualities required of the elementary school teacher. *Educational status* also favors the secondary and university teacher. He himself has more schooling, and he is likely to have received a more selective university education than a teachers' college graduate. *Sexual discrimination* confers more

---

[20]Frederick Rudolph, *The American College and University* (New York: Random House, Inc., 1965), p. 207.

[21]Don C. Charles, "The Stereotype of the Teacher in American Literature," *The Educational Forum,* 14 (March 1950):299–305.

[22]Willard Waller, *The Sociology of Teaching* (New York: John Wiley & Sons, Inc., 1965; originally pub. 1932), p. 397. For a valuable general work see Theodore Caplow, *The Sociology of Work* (Minneapolis: University of Minnesota Press, 1954).

assertive, ambitious connotations and higher prestige upon men's professions. Indeed, Theodore Caplow maintains that the primary division of labor is that between men and women. It has been noted, for example, that elementary school teachers in Denmark, many of whom are men, approach the greater prestige of high school teachers.

As this discussion demonstrates, stereotypes and status, group image and prestige, tend to become a single issue. This conforms to the social usages of images. Like it or not, unfavorable stereotypes serve to deny quests for improved status, as when nineteenth-century school boards refused to raise a teacher's pay or improve working conditions on the grounds that 16-year-old local girls—the stereotype of the rural teacher—had no right to expect better. But a stereotype has no *necessary* relationship to the social importance of an occupation, or even to public regard for the services performed. A sixteenth-century English educational leader, Richard Mulcaster, lamented the discrepancy between the low estate of teaching and the higher regard for education thus: "Our calling creeps low and hath pain for companion, still thrust to the wall though still confessed good." American commentators three centuries later continually contrasted the noble rhetoric of the school crusade with the humbleness of its foot soldiers—America's teachers. In a day when public schools were daily declared "cornerstones of our democracy," when the ordinary farmhand received $200 plus board, teachers in Iowa's ungraded schools averaged less than $150 per year.

The drive to professionalize teaching took shape in the 1830s and grew with the public school movement. Books for teachers exhorted them to be true to the highest ideals, quoting philosophers, scholars, and divines on the nobility and responsibility of the teaching act. Martin Luther had put teachers second only to ministers. Erasmus had likened them to kings in their service to the state, and Thomas Carlyle would have had them honored as are generals and field marshals.

The Quest for the Competent Teacher

"A teacher affects eternity; he can never tell where his influence stops," wrote the American historian Henry Adams. Despite Adams and countless autobiographical statements about "the teacher who changed my life," a teacher's effect is often hard to determine with precision. The problems are several. Unlike much of the work of the physician or the lawyer (a better example), education lacks clearly defined products by which to test the practitioner's influence. One of the reasons why schools are not "pure" bureaucracies is the vagueness with which educational goals are permitted expression.[23] Many teachers ordinarily contribute (probably unevenly) to a single student's educational experience. Determining the singular effect of

[23]Robert Dreeben, "The School as a Workplace," in *Second Handbook of Research on Teaching*, ed. Travers, p. 453.

any one teacher is difficult, since other teachers may have contributed the crucial "readiness" or the essential "culminating" learning. Out-of-school teaching and learning with peer-group help is education to which everyone is exposed. Teachers may be falsely credited or blamed for what is learned elsewhere. Schooling ordinarily goes on in groups of individuals who have varying interests, aptitudes, and stages of readiness. Should a teacher's competence, then, be measured by the "average" effect on the class, by that on the student who has achieved most or professed himself most satisfied, or by the vote of the least easily taught pupil? Some theorists of teaching speculate that many of the outcomes of teaching, including the more important and permanent parts of learning, show themselves or come to fruition only in later life. Indeed, the quest to keep on learning, which some say is the chief aim of schooling, is interminable.

Extensive efforts to identify the critical personal traits of good teachers and the essential attributes of successful teaching behavior have encountered and clarified the foregoing factors.[24] The methods used have included systematic observations in the classroom, controlled experiments, asking students or other teachers to rate various teachers, before-and-after tests of pupil achievement, and attitude and projective testing of teachers and students. The inconsiderable and inconclusive results of this research may be one reason why teachers continue to be hired and paid on the basis of their professional qualifications (amount and kind of education, training, and experience) and not according to the qualities that they possess or by their measured productivity; the reward system remains "regulated by longevity and course-taking rather than [by] demonstrated effectiveness in the classroom."[25] Lacking proof, statements about what constitutes teaching competence remain speculative, dignified primarily by the "face validity" of common sense.

Before analyzing the content of those speculative statements on the art and science of teaching, which are the legacy of the profession, it might be well to get the flavor of what American schoolmen have asked for in their future associates. Cyrus Peirce, principal of America's first public normal school (founded in Lexington, Massachusetts, in 1839), lectured his first class on these qualities "very desirable to a teacher": good health; a fair reputation and good standing in the community lest your scholars (pupils) disrespect you; a well-balanced mind "free from eccentricities and from the infirmities of genius"; a deep interest in children; patience "to meet the various trials which will beset you"; "mildness, firmness, and perfect self-control"; and a high sense of moral discrimination, responsibility, and accountability.[26] The

---

[24]See especially Part II of Gage, ed., *Handbook of Research on Teaching.*

[25]Don C. Lortie, "Structure and Teacher Performance: A Prologue to Systematic Research," in *How Teachers Make a Difference*, p. 57.

[26]From the journal of Mary Swift (1839), reproduced in *Teacher Education in America: A Documentary History,* ed. Merle Borrowman (New York: Teachers College Press, 1965), pp. 59–60.

state superintendent of public instruction of Michigan put a briefer list in his annual report for 1842: an elementary school required "a female of practical common sense, with amiable and winning manners, a patient spirit, and a tolerable knowledge of the springs of human action" (i.e., understanding of what motivates pupil behavior).[27]

The author of *Teaching a District School* (1908) asked that each prospective teacher conduct a rigorous self-examination. His or her fitness to teach meant affirmative answers to these questions: Is my character righteous and exemplary? Are my motives to do good and excel in the profession? Am I a born teacher, delighting in explaining difficulties and disseminating knowledge? Do I love, in practice, all sorts of children, with the love of wanting to make them better? Do I dedicate myself to the toil and self-sacrifice that is teaching?[28] Nonetheless, teaching, in America and elsewhere, has always attracted its share of those enrolled without such exceptional character or great personal dedication—those who, like the high school teacher in "Middletown" in the 1920s, explain the choice as uninspired: "I just wasn't brought up to do anything interesting. So I'm teaching!"[29]

THE "ART" OF TEACHING

The sixteenth-century laymen "knew" that medicine was *more* than a science, that it also required a "cunning"—an artistry not limited to those formally educated in medical studies. So, too, in teaching. One of the famous American books on teaching is that of the classicist Gilbert Highet—*The Art of Teaching*. Highet likened teaching, for its necessary emotionality, more to composing music, painting a picture, or even planting a garden, than to performing a chemical experiment.[30] Highet's usage of the term *art* suggests a carefully crafted human performance—with its own developed skills, disciplined knowledge, and conscious order. Another connotation of art, and the one we shall unravel here, is a more naturalistic, innate, and spontaneous definition. It is reflected in common lore: "He's a born teacher!" "Teaching is in his bones!" "She's just a 'natural' for teaching"—or "He can't (hah-hah!) ever forget that he's a teacher." It is Karl Menninger's "What the teacher *is*,

[27]Quoted by Wittlin, in Lynn, ed., *The Professions in America*, pp. 96–97.

[28]John Wirt Dinsmore, *Teaching a District School* (New York: American Book Company, 1908). Dinsmore was at the time professor of pedagogy and dean of the normal department at Berea College in Kentucky.

[29]Recommended is the section of four chapters on schools and teaching in the classic sociological study of a Middle-Western American town (Muncie, Indiana): Robert S. Lynd and Helen M. Lynd, *Middletown* (New York: Harcourt Brace Jovanovich, 1929). See also their follow-up study, *Middletown in Transition* (New York: Harcourt Brace Jovanovich, 1937).

[30]Gilbert Highet, *The Art of Teaching* (New York: Alfred A. Knopf, Inc., 1950). One may quarrel with Highet's distinctions of the "warm" arts and the "cold" sciences, however, which seems itself a stereotypic distinction.

is more important than what he teaches." It is the belief that some people have instinctive or inborn traits, or traits so ingrained by upbringing, that training, study, and experience can only approximate them. These supposed personal qualities are better sensed than articulated, but the conventional wisdom includes among them such traits as personal warmth, a liking for young people, idealism, the knack of simplifying or restating things so that they can be better grasped, patience, and a low interest in the material things of this world.

Ours is an age and culture that favors achievement—acquirable skills, abilities, and knowledge—more than it likes ascription. The idea of inborn or ingrained traits seems deterministic: "Either you have it or you don't." It smacks of a "natural elite." Acquired skills, on the other hand, seem more "professional," objective, impartial, and democratic. The medical profession chooses not to talk of the "gifted healer," for preferred professional images center upon *trained competence,* rather than upon charisma or natural artistry.[31] Who would have professional schools limited to locating and recruiting the natural-born teacher, preacher, or lawyer? Still, there remain at least remnants of belief in the "natural teacher," found in such screening devices as the personal interview in teacher-training programs, in some teacher-evaluation forms used by school administrators,[32] among academicians who acknowledge a distinction between the scholar who teaches and the gifted teacher, and in the stubborn evidence of our own experiences with different teachers.

PERSONAL QUALITIES: TRAITS OF CHARACTER

Character, meaning a composite of moral qualities, does not hold its former high place in descriptions of the desired teacher; indeed, the term has an old-fashioned sound in an age that uses the more neutral term *personality.*[33] Nonetheless, the subject has implicit importance to those who believe that an artist-teacher teaches by virtue of his natural instructive talents, and that *what he is* is what is taught. And, in many church schools and colleges and in many communities, the issue of the teacher's character remains explicit and openly acknowledged.

[31]On the presence of the gifted "empiric" in medical practice, in opposition to the "orthodox physician," see Joseph F. Kett, *The Formation of the American Medical Profession* (New Haven, Conn.: Yale University Press, 1968).

[32]John Gauss shows how a standard teacher-evaluation form could be constructed to disqualify Socrates as an effective teacher: "Teacher Evaluation," *Phi Delta Kappan,* 43 (January 1962), back cover; also reproduced in Mary Greer and Bonnie Rubenstein, *Will the Real Teacher Please Stand Up?* (Pacific Palisades, Calif.: Goodyear Publishing Co., Inc., 1972), pp. 50–51, and in Corwin, *A Sociology of Education,* p. 283.

[33]On closer examination, personality traits prove not to be neutral. Consider authoritarianism or submissiveness, which have, in our culture, a negative valence—although they are judged signs of poor mental health rather than of evil or weak character.

As every reader of period novels recognizes, the teacher and preacher have been held to special standards of personal conduct—lest the teacher's moral authority and what is taught be "disrespected." By all accounts, such restraints are largely gone, especially in urban areas where greater anonymity, heterogeneity, and social tolerance pertain. A 1957 survey of American teachers reported that only 2.8 percent felt their personal lives under serious restrictions; a decade later the situation appeared unchanged. In a survey of citizen opinion in New London, Connecticut, 83 percent answered "No" to the question: "Should the standards of conduct for teachers differ from those of other good citizens?"[34] (Note the adjective, however.)

Traces of a double standard do remain. The argument persists that teachers work with the young and impressionable. Teaching remains a sensitive area insofar as a community's moral, political, and social preferences are concerned. Parents commonly not only want their children to *do* better, but many also want them to *be* better persons than they are. They want their children's schools to be better than theirs were, and they accordingly often expect the teacher to be commensurately superior. The codes of ethics, which exist in the various professions, may be thought of as the organizational equivalent of the superior personal character once assumed part of the art of teaching.[35]

Traits of Personality

A study of North Carolina teachers rated as "excellent" by their supervisors, other teachers, laymen, and their own students credited personality as the chief factor responsible—although pupils were more likely than the others to stress the teacher's knowledge and teaching strategies.[36] Investigators have even tried to draw a sort of "personality profile" of the typical teacher.[37]

[34] *The Status of the American Public-School Teacher* (Washington, D.C.: National Education Association, 1957), p. 33; "Teachers in Large School Systems, 1966," *NEA Research Bulletin,* 45 (May 1967):58; Frederic W. Terrian, "Who Thinks What About Educators?" *American Journal of Sociology,* 59 (September 1955):150–58. See also the survey of relevant research in R. K. Kelsall and Helen M. Kelsall, *The School Teacher in England and the United States* (London: Pergamon Press, 1969), esp. pp. 34–51.

[35] The Georgia State Teachers Association is reported to have drafted the first state-wide code of ethics, in 1896. The National Education Association adopted a code for the profession in 1929, since revised several times: Sidney Dorros, *Teaching as a Profession* (Columbus, O.: Charles E. Merrill Publishing Co., 1968), p. 15.

[36] Joseph Daniel, *Excellent Teachers* (Columbia: University of South Carolina Press, 1944).

[37] J. W. Getzels and P. W. Jackson, "The Teacher's Personality and Characteristics," in *Handbook of Research on Teaching,* ed. Gage, pp. 506–82. The large and growing literature on personality and occupational choice includes Gordon W. Allport, *Pattern and Growth in Personality* (New York: Holt, Rinehart and Winston, Inc., 1961; J. L. Holland, *The Psychology of Vocational Choice* (Waltham, Mass.: Blaisdell Publishing Co., 1966); R. A. Schutz and D. H. Blocher, "Self-Satisfaction and Level of Occupational Choice," *Personnel and Guidance Journal,* 39 (March 1961):595–98; C. Sternberg, "Personality Trait Patterns of College Students Majoring in Different Fields," *Psychological Monographs,* 69:403 (1955):1–21.

Such research could be useful in vocational counseling, as well as in determining whether certain personality traits distinguish those who are successful teachers, and more able to grow on the job, for professional recruiting and upgrading. Personality studies could also answer the theoretical question of the relative extent to which an occupation attracts people of like characteristics, or whether the job demands and association with fellow professionals create a fairly homogeneous group.

Two cautions need mention at the outset. First, much of the personality research has tested *prospective* teachers. It is hazardous to generalize to those who actually enter teaching, and especially to those who persist in teaching.[38] Second, explanations for the preponderance of certain traits may be unduly complex. For example, recurring traits noted in the teaching population include passivity and conservatism. Explanations offered have included sex (the high proportion of women), lower-middle-class status, the bureaucratic features of school systems, the psychological climate of teacher training programs, the fact of local school control, the mechanisms of paying and promotion in education, and other factors. A simpler hypothesis is that those who choose teaching, and most of those who remain teachers, liked school themselves, "played school" as children, and have relatively few quarrels with formal education as they have experienced it. "I loved school. . . . All the brightest moments of my childhood were in one way or another connected with school. (At age nine, I wrote 'I want to be a teacher like Anna Ivanovna.')"[39] These words of a Soviet schoolteacher may express feelings of positive identification with one's former teachers that may be exceedingly common to teachers everywhere. Similarly, when the teachers of North Carolina failed to support academic freedom by not speaking out on behalf of John Scopes's teaching about evolution in Tennessee, they were not necessarily showing the personality traits of timidity and resignation. Instead, teachers may simply have shared their communities' prevailing pro-biblical opinions and been expressing their personal satisfaction with teaching religion and science in the schools as these subjects had been taught to them.[40]

A justifiable criticism of the findings produced by personality research on teachers is that they are both inconclusive and pedestrian. It is the "reiteration of the self-evident" to find that good teachers are "friendly, cheerful,

[38]It is probable that teachers whose personality or other characteristics do not "fit" the school culture well enough leave the profession in disproportionate numbers. Thus, several studies indicate that supervisor evaluations of teacher efficiency are in reality often measures of personality compatibility or noncompatibility: Lindley J. Stiles et al., *Teacher Education in the United States* (New York: Ronald Press, 1960), p. 150. Cf. Fred T. Tyler, "The Prediction of Student-Teaching Success from Personality Inventories," *University of California Publications in Education,* 11 (1954):233–314.

[39]Frida Vigdorova, *Diary of a Russian Schoolteacher* (New York: Grove Press, Inc., 1960), pp. 11, 12. Cf. Herbert J. Walberg, "Professional Role Discontinuities in Educational Careers," *Review of Educational Research,* 40 (June 1970), esp. pp. 413–14.

[40]Willard B. Gatewood, *Preachers, Pedagogues and Politicians: The Evolution Controversy in North Carolina, 1920–1927* (Chapel Hill: University of North Carolina Press, 1966), p. 232.

sympathetic, and morally virtuous. . . . For what conceivable human inter-action . . . is not the better if the people involved are friendly, cheerful, sympathetic, and virtuous rather than the opposite?" ask Jacob W. Getzels and Philip W. Jackson.[41] Repeatedly studies have established that prospective teachers seek the schoolroom as a means of associating and identifying with children. The reported greater job satisfaction of elementary school teachers is probably related to lesser frustration of this motivation; the structuring of the self-contained classroom and the lesser emphasis upon absorbing in-formation permit more sustained contacts with youth than is easily possible in the segmented secondary school. For the same reason, university professors may be more fulfilled by their closer relationships with advanced students not simply because they do not like teaching the elementary principles of their field to freshmen, but because they want to teach those whom they can also *know*.

William Arrowsmith argues that teaching has always meant "a care and concern for the future of man, a Platonic love of the species, not for what it is, but what it might be." Idealism, in the sense of a visionary desire to serve people, is a value expressed most often by those choosing careers in teaching, law, medicine, and social work.[42] Among future teachers, however, it is mentioned more often by women and those preparing for elementary school positions, and less frequently by men and secondary school candidates. The interest in this discrepancy is its possible relationship to the greater job satisfaction consistently reported in women teachers and elementary school teachers.[43] Teaching still seems to offer some a realistic opportunity to put their altruistic tendencies to work.

Spontaneous Tendencies

Psychologist John M. Stephens offers an unpretentious but carefully con-structed theory of the "born teacher"—one possessing artistry springing from the automatic, irrepressible exercise of powerful, primitive human tendencies.[44] Several of the tendencies described by Stephens are mentioned below.

---

[41]In Gage, ed., *Handbook of Research on Teaching,* p. 574. Cf. Morris Rosenberg et al., *Occupations and Values* (New York: The Free Press, 1957).

[42]The choosing of a teaching career—out of a desire to be useful and a commitment to "a future that would please me rather than one that would make me wealthy"—is a part of the teaching autobiography of Leonard Kriegel, *Working Through* (New York: Saturday Review Press, 1972), p. 28. A small study at Illinois Teachers College indicated that nearly half the students gave idealism as their reason for choosing teaching; 28 percent, however, mentioned "good job": Richard W. Saxe, "Motivation for Teaching," *Teachers College Record,* 70 (January 1969):313–20.

[43]On the complexities of interpreting occupational values and job satisfaction, see Ward S. Mason, *The Beginning Teacher* (Washington, D.C.: U.S. Government Printing Office, 1961), esp. 71–94.

[44]"Spontaneous Schooling and Success in Teaching," *School Review,* 68 (Summer 1960):152–63. See also Stephens's book, *The Process of Schooling* (New York: Holt, Rinehart and Winston, Inc., 1967).

The compulsion to talk to others about his subject   This urge grips the natural teacher, while the scholar or expert may lack it altogether. Altruism is unnecessary; all that is required is the compulsion to talk that is also displayed by the traveler impelled to tell of his journey, or the parent to talk of his child's doings.

The compulsion to linger over elementary ideas   The underlying cause matters not; it may be "sheer repetitiveness or slowness or love of one's own words." What is essential is that students have the multiple opportunity to react before another idea is paraded before them; thus, a teaching urge satisfies a basic learning need. Jacques Barzun made a similar point when he wrote that the "born teacher" breaks down the new, puzzling situation into simpler bits and leads the beginner, with infinite patience, "in the right order from one bit to the next."[45]

The compulsion to correct   This urge satisfies the psychologist's requirement that the teacher provide "reinforcement"—instantly accepting (or rejecting) the correct (or erroneous) responses that students make. Included are subtle changes in expression on the teacher's face—showing pleasure or relief at progress toward the right answer, puzzlement or hurt at error. Being automatic, these cues are more dependable and effective than are deliberate efforts to correct. Overt correction also comes easily to those made uncomfortable by the presence of error. It is again a widespread human tendency. "In the margin of books no one else will ever read, we pen comments to authors already dead. Teachers correct spelling errors in examination books that are not to be returned."

The compulsion to give others the correct response   "It is seen," writes Stephens, "in the almost irresistible urge of the audience to supply the correct answer for which the quiz contestant is groping," in the frantic handwaving of other pupils as a classmate struggles with a problem, in the "unintentional rhetorical question which we promptly answer ourselves." The natural teacher will have this urge in good measure, although he will often suppress it.

The compulsion to point the moral, to say "I told you so!"   Although restrained outside the schoolroom by social taboos, this urge is irresistible in the successful teacher. Much of teaching, Highet reminds us, consists in explaining. The teacher's "See what happens when you neglect to remove the fractions before transposing" is his instinctive response to a powerful human urge. As with the other tendencies, it best functions spontaneously and compulsively. Hence, "born teachers" find it hard to restrain these traits in after-school hours and away from the company of students. But, advises Stephens, "from teachers more generously endowed with these tendencies we should expect superior classroom performance."

---

[45]Jacques Barzun, *Teacher in America* (Garden City, N.Y.: Doubleday & Co., Inc., 1954), p. 21.

THE SCIENCE OF TEACHING

In *The Affluent Society,* John Kenneth Galbraith pointed out an interesting characteristic of the "new class" to which professionals belong: while the language describing their work is humanistic—self-fulfillment, satisfaction, service—the professional approach is increasingly objective and scientific. Teaching has shared in this larger movement to objectify practice, to supplement or replace the reliance upon "chancy" personal qualities with the greater certainty of trained skills. The foundations of professional practice, which we shall discuss under the rubric of the science of teaching, include advanced education, specialized knowledge, and continuous research.

Advanced General Education

Teachers throughout history have stood before their pupils as examples of educated persons—possessed of the lore they were to impart, masters of the mysteries of the trade, literate when much of the society was illiterate. By all accounts, the typical American teacher in any period—no matter whether ill educated by some absolute standard—was considerably more schooled than the average parents of his pupils. In 1900, when the average American adult had five years of schooling, the average teacher had nine years of schooling in the poorer places and twelve years in the better. In 1970, when the statistical "typical" adult over 25 reached the level of high school graduation, over 96 percent of all public school teachers had a bachelor's degree or more. As the definition of a liberal education changed for other Americans, so it did for teachers—even college teachers. It is rare to find a classically educated teacher among contemporary secondary school and college faculties, unlike the situation in seventeenth-century America.

Teachers around the world tend to be graduates of the level of schooling one unit higher than that at which they teach: elementary school teachers are secondary school graduates, high school teachers are college graduates, and college teachers have graduate degrees. When Henry A. Tappan of the University of Michigan proposed in 1856 that America follow this principle, he appeared Utopian. Nowhere in American education did the average teacher meet this standard. Many local administrators undoubtedly followed the practice observed in Wisconsin of hiring anyone as teacher who could correctly write his name, read a little, and add 5 and 7.[46] Not until 1907 did Indiana become the first state to require that all *licensed* teachers be high school graduates. Despite the propensity of critics of contemporary schools to romanticize the educational past, American teachers in the nineteenth

---

[46]Lloyd P. Jorgenson, *The Founding of Public Education in Wisconsin* (Madison: State Historical Society of Wisconsin, 1956), pp. 159–60. On the educational standing of the contemporary American teacher see "Facts on American Education," *NEA Research Bulletin,* 49 (May 1971):47–55.

century were not, on the whole, well educated. There has been considerable advancement since then, however, in the general education of this country's educators.

Academic Specialization

An advanced general education opens the doors to those wide and lively intellectual interests that many think the good teacher must have. There is virtual unanimity, moreover, that the teacher must also be master of his subject matter. Because knowledge grows, the teacher must like his subject enough that he will continue to learn it—for "to be a history teacher and be bored by history, to teach French and never open a French book at home, that must be either a constant pain or a numbing narcosis."[47]

The twin charge of the post–World War II criticism of American public education was that teachers, in their concern for students' social and emotional development, had lost interest in teaching subject matter, and that too many teachers were teaching subjects in which they lacked adequate study. Both charges contained some truth. The universalization of schooling had brought into classrooms a great many students who had little liking for and less motivation to learn the more abstract elements of the school subjects. Progressive education was a response to this fact, and although Dewey, Boyd Bode, and certain other leaders of progressivism intended that activity programs lead into, or demonstrate, the facts and principles of organized bodies of knowledge, the linkages were not always made. Despite attempts to reassert the primacy of subject matter, the original problem remains. Unless new curricula, teaching innovations including the adaptation of methods developed for television, new reward systems (perhaps including paying children who show progress), and other modifications succeed *both* in showing greater learning and in maintaining the interest of students and teachers, future revolts against subject matter dominance will occur. A revolt in the name of "relevance" has already been mounted.

Another consequence of universalization is that it required great, and sometimes rapid, increases in the numbers of teachers. Some of these new teachers lacked deep interest in the subjects they taught; their own knowledge came from rote learning and was hardly greater than that of their quickest pupils. In fact, as well as in name, many were not "masters" (from the Latin *magister,* akin to "much" or "large," in knowledge); they were "teachers" (from the Old English, meaning "to show," and akin linguistically to the word *token*). Moreover, as the curriculum was broadened, particularly in small high schools, many teachers found that demands for their versatility were greater than for their depth. Although mathematics and science teach-

---

[47]Highet, *The Art of Teaching,* p. 19.

ing was often emphasized (especially after Sputnik), schools offered other fields that were taught by those who lacked any advanced preparation.

The prediction for the future is that public school teachers decreasingly will be compelled to teach several subjects, and without preparation. Three factors appear to support such a prediction: the consequences of the teacher surplus, already discussed; the larger schools formed by district consolidation or urbanization;[48] and financial stringencies that restrict curriculum offerings and that favor the older academic specializations and those subjects offered in depth by most colleges. One might counter with other observations. Looking ahead, there is the trend toward "schools within schools," small units of pupils and teachers that often emphasize a generalist approach to learning, not specialization in discrete bodies of knowledge. If the recent past is any guide to the future, there is the interesting fact that there was virtually no increase from 1956 to 1966 in the percentage (70 percent) of high school teachers who were teaching only in their major field of preparation.[49] Yet that was the decade of intense interest in subject matter—manifested in curricular changes, advanced placement, and other accommodations to the gifted; agitations for the reform of teacher education; and teacher-licensing requirements that tended toward greater academic specialization. It remains uncertain how widespread will become laws requiring that prospective elementary school teachers have a college major and minor in subject matter areas and not in education. The effect of such laws is also uncertain. Without a fuller movement to a departmental or team-teaching organization, such actions only guarantee that a teacher has a better academic preparation in one or two of the subjects of the elementary curriculum, not that he or she will be equally well prepared for teaching the other subjects offered in the self-contained classroom.

Most college teachers are themselves required to master only the subject they are to teach. Whatever they learn of teaching that is not also a part of the knowledge of their subject matter and that they do not know intuitively, is acquired through unsupervised on-the-job, trial-and-error experience. This is what one university president has called the "mystique of amateurism" in college teaching.[50] Yet many acknowledge that teaching skill and scholarship

---

[48]From 1966 to 1971 the size of school faculties rose in all regions and for both elementary and secondary schools—the average growing from 39 to 42 teachers per school: "The American Public-School Teacher, 1970–71," *NEA Research Bulletin,* 50 (March 1972):5.

[49]"Characteristics of Teachers: 1956, 1961, 1966," *NEA Research Bulletin,* 45 (October 1967):88. By 1971, however, the percentage of secondary school teachers teaching 50 percent or more outside their major field of preparation had dropped to 14.7 percent (from 16.7 percent in 1971 and 16.9 percent in 1966): *NEA Research Bulletin,* 50 (March 1972):4.

[50]Bruce Dearing, "The University as Teacher," quoted in Mary Wortham, "The Case for a Doctor of Arts Degree," *American Association of University Professors Bulletin,* 53 (December 1967):372–77. See also Kenneth Eble, *Professors as Teachers.*

are not equivalent, and that college teachers do not necessarily provide models for prospective elementary school and secondary school teachers. Kenneth Eble, director of the Project to Improve College Teaching, gives this example of teaching that also exemplifies the power of knowledge:

> One of my most memorable classroom experiences was watching a college professor bet his brains against the laws of physics. Standing on one side of a cavernous auditorium, he held to his forehead an iron ball attached by a long cable to the ceiling. Then he let it go and stood unmoving as the ball swung across the room and back. It did not, as the laws of physics said it would not, bash his brains out. The students were tremendously impressed, both relieved and faintly disappointed. . . .[51]

Teacher-education programs have been influenced by the belief that a teacher's understanding of his subject matter is unique, and that those with the same vocational interest gain more when studying together. These beliefs justified the normal school—a specialized institution for the training of teachers. There has been a gradual transformation of normal schools into teachers' colleges and then into multipurpose colleges, but a special curriculum, restricted to those intending to teach, still exists. Although they train in specialized institutions or follow a special course of study, today's prospective teachers are probably less segregated from ordinary students than are other prospective professionals.

Teaching shares an educational history with law, medicine, nursing, engineering, librarianship, and other fields. Until 1900 most young persons entered a two-year medical school without any college education; indeed, in nineteenth-century America many people practiced medicine without any formalized professional education, and it would have amused the common man to hear that blood-letting, bone-setting, the administering of paregoric, and the delivery of babies required schooling. Most lawyers, engineers, and clergymen were also innocent of professional education except that received in apprenticeships, although some took college work in the classics as "the mark of a gentleman." In 1900 there were only three tiny college-level schools of business. Hence, when teaching sought to upgrade its training programs, restrict entry to the qualified, and dignify its practice in the public eye, other professions were engaged in a similar upgrading. Were it not for history, we might think it natural for certain fields to enjoy high status and require long years of study; instead we find these to be social conventions. The elevation of pedagogy into a subject of formal study, as a part of the "science of teaching," is another such convention.

[51]*The Chronicle of Higher Education,* 5 (March 29, 1971):8.

Specialization in Pedagogy

The amount of pedagogical preparation received by prospective teachers varies considerably. It is determined by the credential regulations of a given state; whether the preparation is for elementary or secondary school teaching; and whether the preparation is undertaken in a teacher's college, in a multi-purpose university, or in a liberal arts college with a teacher-education supplement. The fact that thousands of teachers have been employed without meeting a state's prescription for pedagogical training has been cited by critics of professional education as evidence of the dispensability of pedagogical training. Since laymen run the licensing establishment (the state boards of education and state legislatures) and form the local boards of education that hire noncertificated teachers, this criticism reflects upon the profession's limited power, but not upon its belief in the necessity of professional knowledge.

Some of the challenges to pedagogy are philosophical—reflecting fundamental disagreements on what teaching is and how good teachers are secured. Some is irrational prejudice, as when an academic department will not consider any preparation in teaching skills for its own graduate students lest it smack of "education."[52] The belief that teaching skill cannot be "taught" but must be learned by apprenticeship, on the job, is also stated by those who oppose professional education on the grounds of priorities: "There is only so much time available for the education of the teacher, and every course taken in the education department means one less in history, English, or sociology." The implication is that, once out of college, one cannot or will not study these academic subjects on one's own but will inevitably learn about teaching. On both philosophical and practical grounds, there are similar controversies in other professional fields.

In addition there are some sociological characteristics of preparation for teaching that deserve mention, to enable the reader to examine his own experiences and perhaps reconsider their value.[53]

The nonrationalized nature of teaching, which makes it difficult to agree on the product of education, also hinders agreement on how to achieve competence in teaching. Social pressures for accountability and performance contracting have implications for those who are preparing teachers that they appear not well equipped to handle. And, like their associates in other fields,

---

[52]Eble, *Professors as Teachers*, p. 104. Teacher-training institutions are also controversial elsewhere. In Soviet higher education circles, for example, critics charge that the pedagogical institutes that train teachers offer a less adequate basic education and poorer preparation in the subject matter specialty of the prospective teacher. It is pointed out, for instance, that under 5 percent of the faculties in such institutes have doctoral degrees: Herbert C. Rudman, *The School and State in the USSR* (New York: Macmillan, 1969), pp. 92–95.

[53]Dan C. Lortie, "The Balance of Control and Autonomy in Elementary School Teaching," in *The Semi-Professions and Their Organization: Teachers, Nurses, Social Workers*, ed. Amitai Etzioni (New York: The Free Press, 1969), pp. 1–53, is helpful.

teacher-educators have disagreed on intensive versus spread-out training, on whether classroom experiences should precede, follow or be interspersed with theoretical analysis, on the relative importance of theoretical understanding versus short-term "survival training," and on other issues.

Those who analyze professions frequently point to the possession of a body of unique knowledge as a justification of professional education. It is said that teaching lacks such knowledge, that the professional courses derive their content from other fields—from the subject matters of history, philosophy, psychology, and sociology; they contribute information and understandings that are not exclusive to teaching purposes. In this sense, teaching is likened to nursing, but not to medicine, where a distinctive body of "medical science" has been accumulated.[54] While this distinction may be valid, it may not be important. The real issue is whether the study of the body of knowledge called "education" actually guides or influences teaching practice. If the professional curriculum does not affect behavior, does not lead to continued professional development while a teacher, or does not strengthen the professionally educated person's commitment to teaching, then something would indeed be amiss. This, rather than "unique knowledge," is the practical concern.

The high school graduate who enters college to prepare for teaching has already had some ten thousand hours of firsthand experience with teachers and with the school routine. Unlike future lawyers, architects, engineers, or nurses, he has already absorbed much precise (if limited) information on his future career, formed judgments on good teaching, and gained considerable general socialization to teaching—all without benefit of an education course.[55] The slow-changing technology of education links the prospective teacher's own childhood classroom experiences to his "methods courses" and his observations of classrooms. As a result, there is a near-limit in the ability of preservice courses to impress students with their fresh content, or to move them toward new views of teaching. The real challenge for professional courses is to expand an immediate student anxiety about "crossing to the other side of the desk" to the larger concerns of education, to provide knowl-

---

[54]"The fragmentation of the colleague group, through spatial isolation and the absence of a written tradition of work reports, makes teaching a very solitary and private kind of work. . . . By implication, this inward-looking perspective on work augurs ill for the cumulative development of a codified body of knowledge about teaching that can be disseminated throughout the occupation": Dreeben, in *Second Handbook of Research on Teaching,* ed. Travers, p. 460. See also Philip W. Jackson, *Life in Classrooms* (New York: Holt, Rinehart and Winston, Inc., 1968).

[55]Lortie contrasts prospective teachers with aspiring lawyers who, even when sons of lawyers, had very unrealistic perceptions of practicing law: in Etzioni, *The Semi-Professions,* pp. 10–11, 49. See Lortie's discussion in *How Teachers Make a Difference,* pp. 51–65; "Teacher Socialization: The Robinson Crusoe Model," in *The Real World of the Beginning Teacher* (Washington, D.C.: NEA, 1966), pp. 54–66; "Shared Ordeal and Induction to Work," in Howard S. Becker et al., eds., *Institutions and the Person* (Chicago: Aldine Publishing Co., 1968), pp. 252–64.

edge and provoke insight that, in other professions, distinguishes the subordinate technician from the autonomous professional.

One may think of professional knowledge as having two sources: the experiences of one's predecessors (empirical knowledge) and basic research. For teaching, the normal school was the institutional embodiment of the first kind of knowledge, and the university department of education has become the principal home of the second.

The Normal-School Tradition

The idea of the normal school was imported to America from Europe in the nineteenth century. As Americans slowly became convinced of the necessity of some special training for teachers, they characteristically sought to use existing institutions by simply adding courses in pedagogy. Normal courses or departments appeared in many academies and in various colleges in the 1840s and 1850s. Opposition to this approach grew within common-school circles, however. First it was charged that the classical prejudices of academy and college faculties were a barrier to effective professional education. Many offerings, "normal" in name only, were really academic courses taught by those without much interest in the common schools. Second, critics also pointed out that academies and colleges attracted something of a social elite and could never supply the nation with sufficient or sufficiently committed teachers for the growing system of public education.

As the century advanced, the zealous campaign for separate normal schools and the relative disinterest of the academies and colleges in teacher education led to the creation of hundreds of normal schools. In 1862 there were 13 state normal schools (in 9 of the 31 states of the union); by 1890 the number of state normals was 103.

The extent and quality of the normal-school curriculum predictably varied. The fact that so many rural youth who never became teachers received an equivalent of a high school education in the local normal school suggests how general the curriculum might be. But their animating spirit was inculcating a commitment to "the calling of teacher." In the words of an Illinois normal school leader in 1865, the idea of future teaching "is the Alpha and Omega of schemes of study and modes of thought."[56] David Page's *Theory and Practice of Teaching* was studied, and the experiences of great teachers since the ancients served to inform and inspire. Students also discussed their own teaching experiences with one another—easy to do since the typical normal-school student before 1900 was a young woman who already had experienced two or three terms of teaching in a district school and came to the normal school to learn how to become "strictly professional."

Yet for all their importance in the drive to professionalize teaching, normal

---

[56]Richard Edwards, quoted in Borrowman, *Teacher Education in America*, p. 24.

schools even in their heyday never touched many teachers.[57] A survey of all teachers in three North Central states in 1891–1892 found that only 10 percent of them were normal school or college graduates. While a low enough figure, it was higher than reported elsewhere. According to the 1903 report of Mississippi's state superintendent of education, 90 percent of the state's teachers had no professional training whatsoever; indeed, three of four teachers had no schooling beyond that received in a rural elementary school.

The University-Research Tradition

Most school children in the world today are taught by teachers educated in secondary-level normal schools, often called "training colleges." In 1965 over two-thirds of all primary school teachers (the largest sector of education) were being prepared in such institutions.[58] In the United States, on the other hand, most future teachers are educated in the liberal arts colleges and multipurpose universities, since the normal schools and state teachers' colleges have passed from the scene; in 1970 only Lewis-Clark Normal School of Lewiston, Idaho, and Kansas State Teachers College at Emporia carried on these names.[59] It is also in the universities, public and private, where the twentieth-century attempt to enlarge the science of education through research takes place.

Some enthusiasts of a new "true science" of education believed that research, especially in psychology, could make teaching skill independent of the natural gifts of the artist-teacher or of the collected "wisdom of experience."[60] Others retained the distinction between arts and sciences. By its

[57]Teaching experience before formal study was a persisting pattern. In 1906 it was estimated that 80–85 percent of normal school students had teaching experience. In 1913 as many high school graduates in New York State went directly into teaching as to normal schools to prepare for teaching. See Kate V. Wofford, *A History of the Status and Training of the Elementary Rural Teacher, 1860–1930* (Pittsburgh: Siviter Press, 1935).

[58]Marion Edman, *A Self-Image of Primary School Teachers* (Detroit: Wayne State University Press, 1968), p. 27.

[59]Over half of America's nearly 3,000 institutions of higher education prepare teachers. Abraham Flexner—author of an influential report on medical education in 1910 credited with provoking reform—in 1954 informed the Fund for the Advancement of Education that he did not believe that similar reform could be effected in teacher education, one reason being that it was being done in so large a number of so many different kinds of colleges: Paul Woodring, *Investment in Innovation* (Boston: Little, Brown, 1970), pp. 125–26.

The great majority of teachers have typically been educated in *public* institutions, about half of them prepared in the so-called regional universities and state colleges, many of which originated as normal schools or teachers' colleges. These institutions, which in 1965 enrolled 21 percent of the nation's collegians, were preparing 47 percent of those eligible for teaching licenses: E. Alden Dunham, *Colleges of the Forgotten Americans* (New York: McGraw-Hill Book Co., 1969). A fact that suggests how much *public* higher education has been committed to teacher preparation is that New Jersey's state colleges still require that their freshmen sign a pledge to teach in the state's public schools.

[60]The pervasive, but false, belief that "if we know how learning occurs, we thereby know how to teach," along with other "truisms" about teaching, is discussed in *Theory and Research in Teaching,* ed. Arno A. Bellack (New York: Teachers College, 1963).

Drawing by Alan Dunn; © 1962 The New Yorker Magazine, Inc.

"Meet the new teacher."

moral and urgent nature, stated the French sociologist Emile Durkheim, education cannot be measured by strict scientific standards: "All that the educator can and should do is to combine, as conscientiously as possible, all the data that science puts at his disposal, at a given moment, as a guide to action."[61]

The teacher is not a scientist any more than the physician is a medical researcher. It was assumed in both cases, however, that the practitioner would continually read the research and apply it in the conviction that he needs it to progress in his service to his clients. In this belief, professors conduct research, teach their students to read research, and award advanced degrees that require original investigation. During the rapid growth of American graduate education in the 1950s and 1960s, one-third of all graduate students and one-third of all doctoral degrees awarded came from university departments of education.

[61]Emile Durkheim, *Moral Education,* trans. E. K. Wilson and H. Schnurer (New York: The Free Press, 1961).

Public school districts and state education authorities emulated the universities in establishing research bureaus. By 1930 a sizable research establishment existed in public education. There were several national research organizations, journals, and other publications operating to assist teachers and other school personnel. Nevertheless, each succeeding year uncovered the discrepancies between the ambitions of educational scientists and the actual effects of research upon teaching. Much of the research yielded inconclusive results, and support for research is shallow. Research spending in education averaged *one-half of one percent* of all public spending on education during the 1960s, despite increases in federal support of educational research; the corresponding figure for industrial research ranged from 5 percent to 10 percent of the total operating budget. It was noted that most university laboratory schools were actually "demonstration schools," not places of scientific experimentation. Most of the research bureaus established by public school districts gathered test data and other information for local use rather than conducting objective studies. State directors of educational research were likened more to public-relations officers than to scientists.[62]

Polls of teacher opinion indicated that the majority found a need for in-service training—both in the use of educational innovations introduced into schools since they began teaching and in the basic sciences of educational psychology and human growth and development.[63] There was a disappointing gap between the expressed opinion and actual in-service participation by teachers; moreover, most workshops operated at a disappointing level. It often seemed, as Waller observed, that "the creative powers of teachers disappear because the teacher tends to lose the learner's attitude," while Lortie intimates that the repetitive demands made on teachers, as on other workers, are overpowering.[64] Those in education most exposed to research—holders of doctoral degrees—published little or no research once they had completed their theses. This suggested that the actual world of education does not require research for the sake of practice as much as for appearance—because it is expected of modern professions that they add to their expertise through continuous research. It was virtually as true in 1970 as in 1870 that the majority of teachers taught as they had been taught, and that their classroom behavior lacked scientific proof of its effectiveness—that, in its empirical base, it more "resembles the treasured store of traditions passed on by one witch doctor to another."[65]

The innovations that have been ordinarily introduced into education have

[62]Geraldine Jonçich Clifford, "A History of the Effects of Research on Teaching," in *Second Handbook of Research on Teaching,* ed. Travers, pp. 1–46.

[63]"Teachers' Needs for Inservice Training," *NEA Research Bulletin,* 46 (October 1968):80–81.

[64]Waller, *The Sociology of Teaching,* p. 394; Lortie, in *Second Handbook of Research on Teaching,* ed. Travers, pp. 485–86, 488–89.

[65]Donald M. Medley and Harold E. Mitzel, "The Scientific Study of Teacher Behavior," in Bellack, *Theory and Research in Teaching,* p. 82.

not sprung from science as much as from community pressures, commercial enterprise, or inspiration. A recent example is the introduction of compensatory education programs for the disadvantaged. Some $5 billion of federal and local funds were spent before the Coleman report and other relevant research was available to guide policy making. Nor is it likely that research that disproves the value of a program can, by itself, stop a popular program once begun. The same complexities, imponderables, and social-cultural forces that we have seen elsewhere in the world of education bring their weight to bear in research on teaching and learning.

EXPERIENCE: THE "TEST" OF ART AND SCIENCE

Experience has been described as the place where reality interacts with the art that is one's personal predilection and the science that is what one has been taught. There are many signs of reverence for experience in education. Teachers commonly testify that their practice teaching was the most valuable part of their professional education. As one first-year teacher noted, "I really do feel I was totally unprepared to teach when I started this fall. I've made so many mistakes, mistakes which only a little experience might have prevented."[66] As is true in other occupational training programs, a period of supervised experience is common and widely accepted. It is the education profession's established policy to reward teachers and other school personnel on the basis of experience—through salary increments, in granting tenure, as credits toward retirement, and in allocating such intangible rewards as not being assigned to teach in the classroom next to the boys' washroom. The concern with "teacher dropouts" is largely with the loss of experience to the profession that occurs when the novice replaces the veteran; all other things being equal, it is generally thought that the more experienced teacher will be the better teacher. Hence also the concern in slum schools that a disproportionate number of the faculty are inexperienced.[67] The age of the teacher has always been a factor in the evaluation of competence—age connoting

[66]She does go on to say, however, "Learning by doing seems an inefficient way of solving my problems": Jean Morris, "Diary of a Beginning Teacher," *Bulletin of the National Association of Secondary School Principals*, 52 (October 1968):6–22. Lortie maintains that, having lost their belief in the existence of "principles of pedagogy," neophyte teachers come out of this experience with "effective devices, 'bags of tricks,' peculiarly suited to their own personalities": *How Teachers Make a Difference*, p. 57. Cf. Wayne K. Hoy, "Influence of Experience on the Beginning Teacher," *School Review*, 76 (September 1968):312–23.

[67]The situation in the multiracial city of Richmond, California, in 1970 exemplifies this. Among upper-middle-class, predominantly white schools the proportion of probationary teachers (those of three years' experience or less) was 24 percent. In lower-middle- and lower-class schools the probationary-teacher proportion was 43 percent in white schools and 63 percent in predominantly black schools: Lillian B. Rubin, *Busing and Backlash* (Berkeley: University of California Press, 1972), p. 45.

years of experience as well as "maturity." The experience (age) of an institution is usually considered a positive factor, and schools and colleges (like other enterprises) advertise their years in business.

It is said of the student teacher, or the college professor in his first faculty position, that his is a time of "role-reversal": instead of taking courses, he teaches them. On the other hand, he does not cease to learn. Indeed, some cynics contend that if anything at all is learned in the classroom during this period, it is learned by the teacher! While a teacher has been formed by years of schooling, he will be further formed by teaching itself. The neophyte learns from the teacher to whom he is assigned, or the one next door. He learns from the unique rhythm and routines of the class period, the school week, and the academic year—for teaching has its own structure that organizes behavior into patterns. One result may be a certain loss of idealism, as has been observed in business school graduates as they accommodated to the corporate structure, and in teachers who abandon (or moderate) their permissive views on "self-control" in favor of the more authoritarian "discipline."[68] While he has overstated the matter, there is some truth in Waller's observation that "the significant people for a school teacher are other teachers," and that a "landmark in one's assimilation to the profession is that moment when he decides that only teachers are important."

Experience has gone unchallenged, and it has not been authenticated objectively. Without denying its beneficial aspects, we would like to signal certain important qualifications that the study of education poses to experience.

First, people obviously profit differently from experience. For one, a brief period of teaching may be sufficient to put everything in place or to perceive the nuances of teaching-learning. For another, practice will never make perfect. Such differences may stem from various factors. Personal factors include the supposition that people who are curious, perceptive, analytical, and not easily satisfied learn more from experience—as from anything else. Hence it is remarked that, while the average teacher avoids repeating the obviously unsuccessful lesson, the learning teacher will not merely repeat the successful. Background factors might include other experiences. When a school district gives teaching credit for work in the Peace Corps, it assumes that such experience transfers to teaching and has made one more competent. Factors in the work situation itself may influence the profit from experience. Thus, the lament of an anthropology student newly teaching in a Harlem school: "My first days on the job left me bewildered and with a sore throat, but with no teaching insights."[69] The amount and quality of supervision

---

[68]Walberg, "Professional Role Discontinuities," pp. 409–20; Waller, *The Sociology of Teaching,* esp. pp. 375–409; Estelle Fuchs, *Teachers Talk: Views from Inside City Schools* (Garden City, N.Y.: Doubleday & Co., Inc., 1969); Edgar H. Schein, "The First Job Dilemma," *Psychology Today,* 1 (March 1968):26–37; Hoy, "The Influence of Experience."

[69]Gerry Rosenfeld, *"Shut Those Thick Lips!": A Study of Slum School Failure* (New York: Holt, Rinehart and Winston, Inc., 1971), p. 11.

provided, the degrees of freedom and encouragement given to experiment, to improvise, to flounder suggest themselves as important variables.

Second, there is probably a law of diminishing returns in the lessons of experience. Certainly the blanket annual pay raise—which rewards a teacher equally for the assumed growth from day 1 to day 180 as for day 1,800 to day 1,980—can be justified on the grounds of administrative convenience far better than on the grounds of logic or of demonstrably equal rises in competence from year to year.

Third, experience may vary in its value according to still other factors. It may be affected by the age or other characteristics of the students or by the level of schooling.[70] Hypothetically, college students are less demanding and hence provoke less teaching experimentation by which the teacher may learn. Experience may be affected by the subject or teaching field. A field in which there are many approved ways of doing things may have more potential for giving wider knowledge from experience, but less for acquiring mastery through repeated experiencing of a limited number of approaches. Even more plausible is the idea that experience assists each teacher unevenly in learning the various roles that the teacher plays. Experience may quickly teach prompt and correct record-keeping but have less demonstrable effect on successful working with parents, which requires considerable insight, empathy, and interpersonal skills.[71]

Finally, there is the fact that some inexperienced teachers are better than many veterans. As perceptive supervisors of student teaching have observed, some novices are highly effective teachers from the first day. Experience should give the novice both self-confidence and the knowledge of what works and what does not work. But if it dampens zeal and induces a mindless routine, then experience is a bad teacher whose effects we would like to see mitigated.

[70]In making a point about the confusion of "causation" with "association," Grant rightly points to the need to ask such questions as this: *If* more years of teaching experience correlate statistically with slightly higher pupil achievement, is it because experience "matters" (causes, or helps cause higher achievement), *or* is it that "teachers with more experience use their seniority rights as leverage in obtaining assignments that enable them to teach brighter [or more motivated] children"?: Gerald Grant, essay review in *Harvard Educational Review,* 42 (February 1972):115. Put differently, the small positive relationship between teacher experience and student achievement appears to "reflect the selective recruitment to overachieving schools rather than the superior effectiveness of experienced teachers": Christopher S. Jencks, "The Coleman Report and the Conventional Wisdom," in *On Equality of Educational Opportunity,* ed. Frederick Mosteller and Daniel Moynihan (New York: Random House, Inc., 1972), p. 102.

[71]For a good view of the multiplicity of tasks and the pressures to orchestrate them with some degree of harmony see Philip W. Jackson, in *The Way Teaching Is* (Washington, D.C.: National Education Association, 1966), pp. 7–27.

THE AMERICAN TEACHER
AND THE ISSUES OF PROFESSIONALISM

Two trends have helped to shape the modern world of work: a multiplication of occupations through the specialization of labor, and the growth of professionalism as production jobs decline while service needs expand. Careers in education have shared in these developments; the present chapter will explore to what extent this is true.[1]

By the mid-twentieth century, with the United States the acknowledged leader in economic development and occupational differentiation, the Bureau of Census's *Dictionary of Occupational Titles* listed over twenty-five thousand occupations at which Americans were working. Some specialization actually preceded the modern period, as shown by the existence of the guilds—mutual-benefit associations of fellow artisans (in the case of smiths or tailors) or of merchants (such as fishmongers). In the older professions specialization and status differentiation were marked. Medical practice was apportioned among physicians, surgeon-barbers, apothecaries, chemists, and druggists—although the distinctions often broke down in practice. The orders within the English legal profession ranged from the prestigious barristers, through attorneys and solicitors, to the lowly scriveners and notaries who drew up and attested to wills and contracts.

In modern times licenses and approved training and apprentice programs continue to protect specialization and are being extended to new occupations. Those professions most affected by scientific advances tend toward ever-greater division of labor—as a moment's reflection on medicine or engineering will show. In education, enough occupational specialization has now occurred to question whether it remains a single profession. The American school

[1] See especially Dan C. Lortie, "Observations on Teaching as Work," in *Second Handbook of Research on Teaching*, ed. Robert M. W. Travers (Chicago: Rand McNally Co., 1973), pp. 474–97.

principal or college president is rarely the "head teacher" that he was in the nineteenth century; his duties are more administrative, regulatory, and oriented toward public relations than instructional. In even a moderate-size school district or college there are administrative specialties in finance, academic planning, student affairs, and personnel. Counselors, school psychologists, supervisors, remedial reading and speech therapy specialists, and more recently social workers, now work in schools. Whereas previous experience in a regular classroom was once an invariable prerequisite for most other educational careers, this has become progressively less the case. Even among teachers there are divisions. Elementary teachers seldom speak professionally with secondary school teachers, or public school teachers with their cohorts in the nonpublic schools. Subject matter specializations divide teachers into many separate organizations, and the fact of being a teacher of geography or mathematics, rather than of music or biology, creates strong factions (along department lines) within the faculty in much of American higher education.

The introduction of teacher aides—analogues to the medical technician, dental hygienist, or nurse's aide—began seriously in the 1950s, with foundation support.[2] In theory such a secondary occupation arises when some portion of professional knowledge becomes so routine that it can be learned and used by those with less training and status. In education, paid or volunteer aides (paraprofessionals) in growing numbers assume nonteaching duties (clerical tasks, playground monitoring, etc.), or act as tutors in the rudimentary skills. But they have also been used to discipline students whom teachers feel unable to control and as ambassadors to the community in minority-group neighborhoods; even in the high schools, aides are more commonly found in schools serving urban cores.[3] The fact that teachers have heretofore been given little voice in the selection of aides further obscures their place in occupational differentiation.[4] Their part in defining the future role of teachers remains to be determined.

PROFESSIONALIZATION

A century ago in the United States, three-quarters of those claiming to be professionals were found in just four fields: medicine, law, teaching, and the

[2]Paul Woodring, *Investment in Innovation* (Boston: Little, Brown, 1970), pp. 146–49, 221–22. Despite opposition by organized teacher groups, predicted growth was from 45,000 school aides at work in 1965 to nearly 1 million part-time assistants in 1972.

[3]Half of working-class schools employ a sizable number (11 or more per school) of adult paraprofessionals, compared to one-third of the middle-class schools: Robert J. Havighurst et al., *A Profile of the Large-City High School* (Washington, D.C.: National Association of Secondary School Principals, 1970), p. 10.

[4]"Teacher Aides in Public Schools," *NEA Research Bulletin*, 45 (May 1967):37–39; "Helping Teachers with Teacher Aides," *NEA Research Bulletin*, 50 (May 1972):60–63; James A. Cooper, ed., *Differentiated Staffing* (Philadelphia: W. B. Saunders Co., 1972), pp. 65–74.

clergy. Now over two thousand service occupations require such advanced theoretical training as to claim professional standing—and a dozen more appear each year.[5] From 1950 to 1960, when the total occupational growth rate was 15 percent, there was a 47 percent increase in professional-sector employment. Despite this fact, some deny that such occupations as teaching, nursing, advertising, public administration, and pharmacy will ultimately reach the levels of knowledge and social service characteristic of the "traditional professions"—no matter how much they gain in prestige and income.[6]

Of what import is it that one's occupation receives "professional" recognition? The idealistic prospective teacher, "anxious merely to help youth," is especially prone to ask this question and to be impatient with the whole issue. Here are four brief explanations of the American emphasis on professionalism:

First, occupational status in the American social order has assumed much of the importance attached in other societies to family or clan, to residence, to ethnic or religious affiliation, or to other status conferers. Relatively speaking, Americans acquire much of their identity through occupation.

Second, occupational position profoundly affects one's life-style and life-chances. It sets gross income possibilities and the limits on material possessions. It expands or circumscribes one's choices in matters of leisure time, residence, and personal associations. Many teachers have expressed frustration at the discrepancy between their buying power and the desires for travel, self-cultivation, the advanced educations of their own children, and other personal expectations that they have received by their education and occupation.[7]

Third, the teaching profession is a reference group for other aspiring occupations, especially in public employment. White-collar workers in government, social workers, librarians, and others seeking an improved position and greater group-esteem have an interest in the continuing campaign of teachers to secure clear recognition as professionals.

Finally, intrinsic rewards are especially powerful in the professional class. Professionals are people who work at things they like, paying "for the privilege of working harder and [sometimes] cheaper than other people."[8] The amount of honor, prestige, and authority, the sense of public confidence,

[5]Earl J. McGrath, *Liberal Education in the Professions* (New York: Institute of Higher Education, Teachers College, 1959), p. 2.

[6]William J. Goode, "The Theoretical Limits of Professionalization," in *The Semi-Professions and Their Organization,* ed. Amitai Etzioni (New York: The Free Press, 1969), pp. 266–313. Cf. Howard M. Vollmer and Donald L. Mills, eds., *Professionalization* (Englewood Cliffs, N.J.: Prentice-Hall, Inc., 1966). For some of the concerns of this chapter treated more as exposé, see Myron Brenton, *What Happened to Teacher?* (New York: Coward-McCann, Inc., 1970).

[7]Jacob W. Getzels, "Conflict and Role Behavior in the Educational Setting," in *Readings in the Social Psychology of Education,* ed. W. W. Charters, Jr., and N. L. Gage (Boston: Allyn & Bacon, Inc., 1963), pp. 309–18.

[8]Jacques Barzun, *Teacher in America* (Garden City, N.Y.: Doubleday & Co., Inc., 1954), p. 29.

the possession of sufficient autonomy to do the job well, high motivation—all these lead, it is argued, to improved performance and greater job satisfaction.[9] Professional spokesmen have long maintained that the recruiting and retention of able people, and the continual progress of the service performed, require the perquisites and privileges that society confers upon the recognized professions.

TEACHING AS A PROFESSION

One of the more succinct summaries of the characteristics of professions is Abraham Flexner's:

1. Professions involve essentially intellectual operations, with large individual responsibility.
2. They derive their raw material from science and learning.
3. They apply this material to a practical and definite end.
4. They possess an educationally communicable technique.
5. They tend to self-organization.
6. They become increasingly altruistic in their motivations.[10]

These points may be clarified by some examples. By using the first and fourth traits alone, we find that secretaries are not professionals, according to Alexander Carr-Saunders, because their skills rest on "trained common sense." Historically, apothecaries were lesser professionals than physicians because they were merchants rather than advisors who attended their clients.[11] Because they are "tradesmen," the professionalization of modern advertising men is suspect; and radio and television broadcasters believe that it demeans their professional image when they must interrupt their reportage and commentary to plug the product themselves. The brutal, manual requirements of primitive surgery once undermined surgeons' claims to membership in a "learned" profession—a situation changed by modern medical science. The altruism expected of the modern professional means that his every decision rests on his sense of what is right, not on his estimate of what is profitable; unlike the relationship of buyer to seller, that of the (naive) client to the (expert) professional is one of trust.[12] Flexner's requirement of practicality

[9]"Are Teachers Happy?" *NEA Research Bulletin,* 46 (May 1968):40–41.

[10]Abraham Flexner, "Is Social Work a Profession?" *School and Society,* 1 (June 26, 1915):904.

[11]W. J. Reader, *Professional Men: The Rise of the Professional Classes in 19th Century England* (New York: Basic Books, Inc., 1966), p. 40; Joseph F. Kett, *The Formation of the American Medical Profession: The Role of Institutions, 1780–1860* (New Haven, Conn.: Yale University Press, 1968).

[12]T. H. Marshall, *Class, Citizenship, and Social Development* (Garden City, N.Y.: Doubleday & Co., Inc., 1964), pp. 145, 147.

distinguishes professions from the academic disciplines; while the scholar can ordinarily justify knowledge for its own sake, the professional cannot.

The foregoing illustrations also suggest why interested historians and sociologists prefer the term *professionalization* to *professions*. It denotes an ongoing, dynamic process, for an occupation may become more or less professional as a result of its actions and historical events. The realistic defining of professions by multiple characteristics also means that an occupational group may be more professional in one trait and less so in another.

A few years ago the general secretary of Britain's National Union of Teachers, who was also president of the World Confederation of the Organizations of the Teaching Profession—a body that links organized teacher groups worldwide, argued: "If teachers . . . are to help themselves to achieve more favorable status in their own eyes and in the eyes of the general public, they will need more adequate training in their preparation for teaching, more stimulating leadership from their professional organizations, and more understanding of the importance of their role from society in general."[13] We indicated the relationship of preparation for teaching to professionalization in chapter 5. Here we will consider briefly the extent of social recognition as expressed in licensing, and the recourse to organizations to protect and promote group interests.

The License to Practice

In the days when formal education was an important instrumentality of organized religion, the church controlled teaching through licensing of teachers and regular inspections of schools. In modern America the dual process continues, with the state having assumed these functions. It awards licenses (credentials), which authorize teachers and other school personnel to practice, and it uses accreditation to award institutions state approval—basing its judgment partly on the qualifications of the institution's faculty.[14]

The forces that perpetuated society's control through licensing, yet changed its locus from church to state, deserve mention. In those American colonies where Church of England influence was strong, there were efforts to follow English licensing practices. In New England, however, church government was local (congregational). Furthermore, because early Massachusetts was a church state, magistrates participated with ministers in selecting school-masters. This pattern of local determination became the prevailing system. Secularization steadily decreased the minister's influence and the formal im-

---

[13]Sir Ronald Gould, quoted in Marion Edman, *A Self-Image of Primary School Teachers* (Detroit: Wayne State University Press, 1968), p. 291.

[14]Accreditation has had lesser influence on teacher preparation than on medical education—where, because of accreditation, 80 percent of those medical schools once operating were closed: Corinne Gilb, *Hidden Hierarchies: The Professions and Government* (New York: Harper & Row, Publishers, 1966), p. 59.

portance of the "religious test" in the hiring of public school teachers. Other interests became predominant: the farmers' viewpoint in rural areas, and the merchants' or politicians' in the towns and cities.

Still, most hiring was casual—as it was for industrial workers. The typical procedure for teacher hiring long remained an oral examination of the applicant, devised and administered by the local school board. Board members were often academically unfit to conduct a worthwhile examination. Standards varied greatly from year to year and from place to place. The desire of poverty-stricken or stingy officials to take the cheapest candidate often prevailed. Vacancies might not be announced—except to interested relatives of the school committeemen. Teachers were victimized by employment agencies. Bribery was commonplace and, even in the twentieth century, prospective teachers were advised to watch out for the widespread practice of demanding a portion of one's salary or a quart of whiskey or an agreement to board with a committeeman's relative in exchange for a teaching post.[15]

Such abuses reinforced demands for centralization—a trend already evident elsewhere in educational planning. For centuries professionalism favored greater uniformity as a means of raising standards. Professions have sought to achieve such uniformity both through self-controls exerted by their own associations and by recourse to government, by way of licensing laws and examination boards. A certain uniformity in certifying American teachers, through centralizing the examination process, began at the county level, as Indiana's experience illustrates. In the 1870s, monthly during the "hiring season," each county superintendent held an announced public examination of teaching candidates; the questions came from the state superintendent's office. On the basis of performance, the county issued a license certifying eligibility to teach in that county's public schools for 12, 24, or 36 months. In 1899 the Indiana legislature gave applicants the option of sending their examination papers to the state department of public instruction for grading; the resulting license was a state certificate, enabling its holder to teach in any county in the state if hired locally.

Across the nation professional preference for uniformity and centralization gradually caused several developments: eliminating county licenses in favor of state certification; replacing an examination system by the issuance of credentials for completing a specified teacher-training program; substituting a system of probationary and regular certificates for the previous "first," "second," or "third-class license"; and extending licensing to new school personnel—supervisors, principals, school psychologists. Through such measures, the organized profession affirms the principle that its members

---

[15]"No school-director who is worthy of his place will accept a bribe, and no man is worthy of the high calling of teacher who will offer one or submit to any dishonest proposal. This practice of bribery is a blot upon the profession": John Dinsmore, *Teaching a District School* (New York: American Book Co., 1908), p. 18; see also Willard S. Elsbree, *The American Teacher* (New York: American Book Co., 1939).

form the most competent group to specify the qualifications necessary in its membership.

One important function of certification is still denied the education profession: using the state's powers to control the supply of professional manpower. First, many teachers are not covered by credential requirements. During shortage periods, "emergency" credentials are issued. Moreover, licenses are normally not required of teachers in nonpublic elementary and secondary schools or of faculty members in four-year colleges and universities. Thus, teachers in some of the nation's most prestigious schools stand exempted. Second, teachers are not represented in state licensing bodies. Unlike physicans, lawyers, or dentists, whose licensing boards are limited to members of that profession in all the states—or even unlike beauticians and barbers, who typically must be the majority membership of their licensing boards— laymen control certification practices in teaching. In only five states are teachers assured priority on such boards, and in ten states professional educators are, by law, excluded from eligibility to sit on licensing boards.[16]

Organizing Teachers

Professional organizations operate as organs of communication with state legislatures and the Congress, civic leaders, and the press. They are instruments for applying pressure—used alike by the legal profession to gain more influence in appointing judges and by teaching groups to try to influence curriculum change.

The "apolitical myth," which shrouded American education, disguised the essentially political nature of such professional organizations as the American Association of School Administrators, the National Education Association, and the Missouri Teachers Association, under the rubric of "public relations."[17] Teachers were ordinarily unaware of their own organizations' political activity; and only a minority of teachers listed political reasons for joining a teachers' association.[18] Such innocence is now ebbing. Polls show teachers increasingly interested in working as individuals in partisan politics. The willingness of some teacher organizations (especially union locals) to endorse and help finance political campaigns exemplifies collective political behavior.[19]

[16]*Occupational Licensing in the States* (Lexington, Ky.: Council of State Governments, 1952); Myron Lieberman, *Education as a Profession* (Englewood Cliffs, N.J.: Prentice-Hall, Inc., 1956); T. M. Stinnett and A. J. Huggett, *Professional Problems of Teachers,* 2nd ed. (New York: Macmillan, 1963).

[17]Case studies of teachers' association politics in three states—Missouri, Michigan, and Illinois—are drawn in Nicholas Masters et al., *State Politics and the Public Schools* (New York: Alfred A. Knopf, Inc., 1964).

[18]Harmon Zeigler, *The Political Life of American Teachers* (Englewood Cliffs, N.J.: Prentice-Hall, Inc., 1967), p. 19.

[19]*NEA Research Bulletin,* 46 (October 1968):76; Tom Wiley, *Politics and Purse Strings in New Mexico's Public Schools,* 2nd ed. (Albuquerque: University of New Mexico Press, 1968), pp. 163–64.

While it is unlikely that any major American teachers' organization will engage in the vigorous politicking characteristic of France's Fédération de l'Education Nationale, the political possibilities of professional associations promise to become clearer in the days ahead.[20]

Unlike other professionals—who had recourse to such English models as the Royal College of Physicians, Company of Apothecaries, or Inns of Court—the earliest American teachers inherited no tradition of professional associations. The earliest effort to found such a body may have been the Society of Associated Teachers formed in New York City in 1794, but significant organizing awaited the common-school movement of the nineteenth century.[21] Local teacher groups appeared after 1830. County teachers' associations conducted workshops and inspirational meetings—"institutes" —that provided many a rural teacher with the only "professional" knowledge or guidance he or she ever obtained. Ten state associations of teachers called the convention in 1857 that formed the National Teachers' Association; it opened its membership to women teachers in 1866 and was renamed the National Education Association in 1870.

The reorganization of the older professions and the initial assembling of an American teaching profession required organizational activity. One need was gaining enough members so that the association could convincingly claim to speak for the profession. The American Medical Association claimed to represent 50 percent of all physicians in 1912 and 90 percent by 1957. The American Bar Association grew from representing 3 percent of all attorneys in 1910 to 46 percent in 1960. The National Education Association more resembles law than organized medicine in this respect: its 1917 membership was 8,500 (when American teachers numbered some 500,000) and first reached 1,000,000 in 1966. Even this accomplishment leaves teaching organizationally scattered. One-half of all teachers do not belong to the NEA, although some belong to one of its state affiliates.

Until recently the NEA and its state affiliates have paid lesser attention to local issues affecting teachers. For one thing, political efforts of education associations have been prominently tied to influencing legislation. There is also the experience of finding legislators more sympathetic and deferential toward claims of professional expertise than are many local school board members. School jobs are not ordinarily seriously endangered by national or state politicking but may be jeopardized by vigorous local agitation. The trend in labor negotiations is generally away from local bargaining and toward collective and large-scale (inclusive) efforts—e.g., to establish a statewide minimum salary scale, tenure law, or grievance procedure.

[20]James M. Clark, *Teachers and Politics in France: A Pressure Group Study of the Fédération de l'Education Nationale* (Syracuse, N.Y.: Syracuse University Press, 1967).
    [21]Sidney Dorros, *Teaching as a Profession* (Columbus, O.: Charles E. Merrill Publishing Co., 1968), pp. 95–96; Carl F. Kaestle, *The Evolution of an Urban School System* (Cambridge, Mass.: Harvard University Press, 1973).

Whatever the causes, the concentration upon the state and national levels in representing teachers is now compromised. Teachers everywhere are more disposed to local and militant organizational activity, and the NEA has been led into considerable local activity. Also, ever-larger school systems mean more bureaucracy and less informality in personnel relations, and teachers look to local groups to deal with these difficulties. In contrast, the issues of raising standards and federal lobbying, for which the national association stands, often appear less compelling.

In the largest school districts the NEA faces the competition of teacher unions.[22] Unionism is strongest in America's cities, and union-organizing efforts in teaching have more support where both teachers and the public are generally pro-union. Eighty percent of the teachers represented by the American Federation of Teachers are employed in seven large cities. Unions are comfortable with the structure of bargaining "locals" and had an advantage over the National Education Association in this regard. Moreover, many big-city teachers believed that the NEA still possessed its historical rural and small-town, white, Protestant bias; they accordingly identified more readily with the urban "sophistication" of the trade-union movement.

Because bureaucratic annoyances are most pronounced in city school systems, their teachers accepted the AFT principle that improvements must be won over the opposition of both board members and school administrators. Union membership is ordinarily limited to teachers (under a local-option ruling), while the NEA position is that teachers and administrators belong to a single, united profession.

Finally, teacher unionism has been aided by the financial and tactical support of organized labor—which is anxious to extend the union movement into white-collar employment. Should the proportion of men in teaching increase, the union's role would predictably grow still larger. In any case, union appearance as a serious competitor to the NEA has already provided new language to describe the contemporary organizational behavior in the teaching profession: "mobilization," "militancy," "teacher participation," "conflict."

The number of issues over which teachers' groups may negotiate extends from the loftiest abstractions of "academic freedom" to the mundane but worthy freedom of a duty-free lunch period. In the remainder of this chapter, three matters will be discussed for their abiding importance to professionalism. These are the issues of *recruiting, rewarding,* and *retaining* teachers for America's schools. None is solely a matter for resolving by noble rhetoric or by the steely resolve of confrontation politics, for each is deeply embedded in the society's structure and in the school culture.

[22]Michael H. Moskow, *Teachers and Unions* (Philadelphia: University of Pennsylvania, 1966); Alan Rosenthal, *Pedagogues and Power* (Syracuse, N.Y.: Syracuse University Press, 1969); Theodore Zaner, "Teacher Militancy: A Case Study," *Teachers College Record,* 70 (January 1969):321–30; Frederick M. Wirt and Michael W. Kirst, *The Political Web of American Schools* (Boston: Little, Brown, 1972), pp. 50–53.

RECRUITING FOR TEACHING

Even in so large a group as American teachers, social scientists claim to see a degree of homogeneity that permits cautious generalization. Among those actually teaching, their roles prompt a degree of alikeness—from one teacher to another and from one generation of teachers to the next.[23] Among those preparing to teach, there is a measure of anticipatory similarity, probably most shaped by the power of a common image of "teacher," which leads to considerable self-selection of those who see themselves conforming to that model.

Choosing Teaching

The majority of college students make occupational choices while in college. Public school teaching is exceptional, however, in the larger percentages making earlier choices and in the greater persistence during the preparation period—in contrast to college teaching, which is usually a choice made late.[24] One investigation of beginning teachers found that slightly over half chose teaching before their freshman college year; figure 12 details these findings.

A consequence of early choice is the greater opportunity to select a college known for its commitment to teacher education. A small study of advanced education students at Illinois Teachers College showed a larger percentage having made precollegiate decisions to teach: more than 63 percent decided before college, and 25 percent decided by grade six.[25] (Compare these figures with Ward Mason's data.) Conversely, those coming to teaching from another unit of a university make late choices: 20 percent decided in the last two college years, and 49 percent decided after college graduation.[26] Consistently more women than men teachers make early decisions, for the following reasons:

Images help shape occupational choices. The fact that librarianship, college teaching, and research lack clear public images is one probable cause of their high proportions of late deciders. Business has a strong image, but one which has (at times) repelled career decisions by many college students—according to various polls. Teaching has both a clear and a favorable image.[27] Its image

[23]Seymour B. Sarason, *The Culture of the School and the Problem of Change* (Boston: Allyn & Bacon, Inc., 1971), esp. chap. 10.

[24]Kenneth E. Eble, *Professors as Teachers* (San Francisco: Jossey-Bass, Inc., 1972), pp. 91–108.

[25]Richard W. Saxe, "Motivation for Teaching," *Teachers College Record*, 70 (January 1969):314.

[26]Ward S. Mason, *The Beginning Teacher: Status and Career Orientations* (Washington, D.C.: U.S. Government Printing Office, 1961), p. 98. Cf. R. K. Kelsall and Helen M. Kelsall, *The School Teacher in England and the United States: The Findings of Empirical Research* (London: Pergamon Press, 1969).

[27]Donald D. O'Dowd and David Beardslee, "The Student Image of the School-teacher," *Phi Delta Kappan*, 42 (March 1961):250–54.

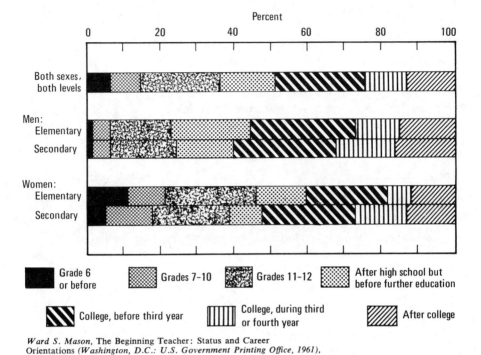

Ward S. Mason, The Beginning Teacher: Status and Career
Orientations *(Washington, D.C.: U.S. Government Printing Office, 1961),*
p. 96. Reprinted by permission.

FIGURE 12 Educational level at which beginning teachers had decided to enter teaching, by sex and teaching level: 1956–57

is both less glamorous and skill-oriented than those of the scientist, physician, or lawyer, and more expressive of warm and personalized giving. While the popular image is sufficiently clear to induce early career commitments, the fact that more teachers are women means that girl students have more sex-linked models, and more grounds for making readier decisions. Conversely, the fact that most college teachers are male means that more male college students possess models than do female collegians; having a college teacher with whom one identifies is one of the more crucial factors in choosing an academic career.

Worldwide studies of teacher recruitment show that former teachers and parents influence choices. There is a noteworthy occupational inheritance in education, as in medicine. Fifteen percent of Mason's sample came from families where one or both parents were educators. Again, more women than men teachers had mothers who were teachers.

Women teachers make earlier decisions because of a restricted range of career opportunities. Relatively few fields have been open to women with the perquisites that teaching offers—and that women, for social and cultural reasons, find highly attractive.

One important consideration for most people is the cost of advanced training. Internalized cultural expectations about the different "needs" of men and
women for advanced schooling and career training help to shape career decisions. The relatively shorter and more generalized preparation for teaching,
when compared to other professions, supports early decisions for women and
a greater degree of deferred choice for men teachers. (On the other hand, a
reason for many late deciders in social work and librarianship is the absence
of formal requirements.)

"Discouragement of the unacademic and encouragement of the bookish
seem to be part of the general impact of the public schools."[28] Girls typically
perform better in schools and have better images of schools as places in which
to be and to work.

We give considerable attention to early decisions to teach, because early
choice appears related to the strength of the commitment to teaching—the
other important variables being indifference to salary and having family approval.[29] Unable directly to affect the latter two, the organized profession
could enhance opportunities to make an early commitment to teaching—as
in better Future Teachers of America programs in the high schools.

Demographic Characteristics of Teaching

Demography concerns itself with the statistical study of certain population
characteristics and their distribution. Comparative demographic data tell us
important things about the sociology of teaching.

Age   The combination of educational expansion (drawing more younger
teachers into the schools) and larger families and general prosperity (reducing the persistence of older, married women in teaching) dropped the median
age of teachers to 36 in 1966.[30] But the probable trend is in the other direction; indeed, by 1968 the figure had risen to age 39. The base comparison
is with women in the total labor force, where the median age has risen by
two years per decade: from age 36 in 1940 to age 42 in 1970. The median
age of beginning teachers is now 24 years, and with advancing educational
requirements and the probable greater future employment of older women,
the upward trend seems inevitable. Should the profession better succeed in
retaining teachers, age averages would further increase.

Age is important on several counts. In the past, the extreme youthfulness
of the teaching body belied its claims of professionalism; even in the pro-

---

[28]Eble, *Professors as Teachers*, p. 94.

[29]Harry Levin, T. L. Hilton, and Gloria Leiderman, "Studies in Teacher Behavior,"
Journal of Experimental Education, 26 (September 1957):81–91.

[30]"Characteristics of Teachers: 1956, 1961, 1966," *NEA Research Bulletin,* 45
(October 1967):87; "Facts on American Education," *NEA Research Bulletin,* 48 (May
1970):35; "The American Public School Teacher, 1970–71," *NEA Research Bulletin,*
50 (March 1972):3–7.

fessed "country of the young," the public's representatives were unwilling to confer decision-making power on so youthful a group. Age also may be related to other behavior. Younger teachers seem more disposed to union activity, especially in the expansive, organizing phase of a local's development. Age may correlate with responsiveness to educational innovation.

Residence   When the United States was a largely rural nation, teachers had predominantly rural origins. How long this rural bias persisted was shown by Florence Greenhoe's celebrated 1939 study of public school teachers. Data on teachers in nonpublic schools show that those teaching in secular independent and in Protestant church schools still come preponderantly from rural and small-town America; Catholic and Jewish schools recruit their teachers from Catholic and Jewish populations, which are dominantly urban.[31] Davis's study of thirty-four thousand June graduates of the college class of 1961 reported public education careers underchosen by big-city residents.[32] (The terms *over-* and *underchosen* are used in a statistical, not a normative sense.) He reasons that this is caused by the poor reputation of big-city public schools; the greater visibility (image-making power) of teaching in small towns; and the fact that small-town students are more likely to attend the types of colleges that offer teacher training. Today's teachers appear as urban-oriented as the American mainstream. Moreover, NEA poll data (already cited) report that big-city teachers express as high job-satisfaction as do other teachers, move less, and are more likely to feel a part of their communities. If the alleged conservatism of the teaching profession is real, it is probably no longer attributable to the "provincial" experiences of teachers themselves.

Religion   Historians conclude that public schools were secularized relatively easily because Protestant churchmen supposed that the schools' caretakers represented a "Protestant establishment" that would perpetuate the old doctrinal teachings under the guise of moral instruction. Studies of teachers and school administrators made when the American population was intensely heterogeneous in race, religion, and ethnicity disclose that up to 90 percent were WASP, with the evangelical Protestant churches heavily represented.[33]

The most recent available data indicate that Protestants still overchoose public school teaching, while today's "typical" Catholic college graduate

[31]Florence Greenhoe, *Community Contacts and Participation of Teachers* (Washington, D.C.: American Council on Public Affairs, 1941); also reported in *School and Society*, 50 (October 14, 1939):510–12, and *Elementary School Journal*, 40 (March 1940):497–506; Otto F. Kraushaar, *American Nonpublic Schools* (Baltimore: The Johns Hopkins University Press, 1972), p. 111.

[32]James A. Davis, *Undergraduate Career Decisions* (Chicago: Aldine Publishing Co., 1965).

[33]Lotus D. Coffman, *The Social Composition of the Teaching Population* (New York: Teachers College, 1911); Frederick Haigh Bair, *The Social Understandings of the Superintendent of Schools* (New York: Teachers College, 1934); Jesse H. Newlon, *Educational Administration as Social Policy* (New York: Charles Scribner's Sons, 1934).

opts for the law or large corporations and the Jewish graduate for the arts or a university career. The Jewish case does not show a low regard for public education; indeed, Jewish groups have been outspoken supporters of public schools. In the Catholic case, however, there is a competing school system, as well as traditions of distrust of public schools once believed to be anti-Catholic. Recent data show that 36 percent of all Protestant college graduates choose teaching, while only 25 percent of Catholics do so—a difference largely caused by Catholic women underchoosing elementary teaching careers.[34]

Race   The 1950 census reported that 7 percent of America's teachers were nonwhite. The civil rights movement's concern with the teaching problems met by minority students and the pressures to improve college opportunities for nonwhite youth increased that figure to 11 percent in 1970–71.[35] Were it not for the Southeast (where black teachers were 24 percent of the total—compared to 3.5 percent in the West and Midwest, and 5.4 percent in the Northeast), the statistical underrepresentation of minorities in teaching would appear greater.[36] The progress made depended upon black college graduates overchoosing teaching careers. The statistical situation now appears unstable. Mason's data on beginning teachers (5.5 percent nonwhite) may portend at least a short-term end to the greater participation of minorities in the subcollegiate levels of the teaching profession. But, where 80 percent of black college graduates once entered teaching, the estimate for the class of 1971 was 46 percent choosing teaching. The future racial balance of the teaching profession will certainly be affected significantly by the relative attractiveness of teaching if other career opportunities open wider for America's minorities.

Social Class   The popular radical complaint that schools are "hopelessly middle-class" is true of the social origins of American teachers only

[34]Andrew M. Greeley, *Religion and Career: A Study of College Graduates* (New York: Sheed & Ward, 1963), p. 80; Christopher Jencks and David Riesman, *The Academic Revolution* (Garden City, N.Y.: Doubleday & Co., Inc., 1968), pp. 365–66.

[35]"Public School Teachers, by Race, 1967–1968," *NEA Research Bulletin*, 46 (October 1968):73; "The American Public School Teacher, 1970–71," *NEA Research Bulletin*, 50 (March 1972):6; Mason, *The Beginning Teacher*, p. 18; *Time* (May 24, 1971):50; Davis, *Undergraduate Career Decisions*, pp. 13, 79–97. From 1951 to 1967, the Fund for the Advancement of Education financed a program in 24 black colleges in 14 states to encourage blacks to enter teaching: Woodring, *Investment in Innovation*, p. 157.

Minority faculties, where found, still cluster in minority schools. Thus, Allen Graubard found black teachers (11 percent of the total of teachers in all alternative schools) "concentrated almost completely in the relatively small number of black community schools and street academies": "The Free School Movement," *Harvard Educational Review*, 42 (August 1972):359. Similarly, black school superintendents appear only when the percentage of black students approaches or becomes a majority. Blacks were 64 percent of Detroit's public school enrollment in 1970, 40 percent of its teachers, and 10 percent of its school principals: Martin A. Larson, *When Parochial Schools Close* (Washington, D.C.: Robert B. Luce, Inc., 1972), pp. 138, 139.

[36]The *New York Times* reported in June 1973, however, that school desegregation in the 17 southern and border states caused 6,000 black teachers and principals to be fired and other thousands to be demoted.

if the middle class is very broadly defined. A better statement is by W. W. Charters: "The teaching occupation draws heavily from the middle ranges of the American social structure: the lowest and highest classes are under-represented. . . ." The typical nineteenth-century public school teacher had a farming father; Coffman, as late as 1911, found 52 percent coming from farm families. Later studies reported the fathers of 18 to 36 percent of American teachers in the blue-collar occupations, the remainder in the lower part of the middle class: in clerical work, trade, small businesses, the semi-professions. Hence, unlike the majority of nurses, most public school teachers now come from white-collar families—but not so often as do social scientists, attorneys, or physicians. When one looks at nonpublic school faculties, one finds a pronounced social-class bifurcation, according to school sponsorship. Church-related schools—whether Catholic, Protestant, or Jewish—recruit heavily from families of below-average income; independent, secular schools draw more than half their teachers from upper-income groups.[37]

Social-class factors show other complexities: career fields, from the first college year to graduation, become less socially diverse; shifts of majors tend toward greater social homogeneity. Among teachers, variations exist according to place, teaching level, and even subject field. Thus, while Mason found little social-class difference when comparing the paternal occupations of beginning elementary teachers with those of secondary teachers, he noted prominent regional and urban-rural variations. Teaching, moreover, has been a field of upward social mobility for more men than for women teachers. Put differently, males come less often from white-collar or professional families than do female teachers (38 percent compared to 51 percent, in Mason's study). Among the occupations open to women (i.e., where their participation is more than token), teaching has had the highest status, and the genteel and respectable qualities associated with "keeping school" made it acceptable employment for daughters of the middle class.[38] Their brothers, however, favored business careers or the more prestigious professions. More teachers should come from the lower class as opportunities for higher education expand. Indeed, *if* the recent rhetoric of middle-class alienation from college-going and from occupational pursuits (and the deferment of college) is played out in reality, children from blue-collar homes (including minorities) will become more prominent in all the professions.

[37]W. W. Charters, Jr., "The Social Background of Teaching," in *Handbook of Research on Teaching,* ed. N. L. Gage (Chicago: Rand McNally & Co., 1963), p. 721; Mason, *The Beginning Teacher,* pp. 11–13; Kelsall and Kelsall, *The School Teacher in England and the United States,* pp. 4–7; Kraushaar, *American Nonpublic Schools,* pp. 109–11.

[38]In a 1947 National Opinion Research Center occupational prestige survey teaching ranked thirty-fifth among 90 occupations; a 1963 repeat of the study found no change. *Among the occupations largely populated by women, however, teaching ranked first:* NORC, "Jobs and Occupations: A Popular Evaluation," in *Class, Status, and Power,* ed. R. Bendix and S. M. Lipset (New York: The Free Press, 1953), pp. 411–26.

Marital Status   Today the average teacher, male or female, is or has been married.[39] Even among Mason's sample of *beginning* teachers, 64 percent of the men and 45 percent of the women were, or had been, married. It is well to remember how recent is the phenomenon of the married woman teacher; in 1931 this group was under 20 percent of all teachers. Teachers are affected by general trends affecting women in the labor force. In 1890 among all married women probably less than 5 percent worked outside the home; by 1960 this proportion was about one-third. In 1970 nearly 60 percent of all employed women were married. Cultural norms against married women teachers have been overturned in the process. Marriage was once sufficient cause for dismissal. In 1890 the New York City regulation read: "Should a female teacher marry her place shall thereupon become vacant."[40] During the Depression years, schools commonly fired married women to provide jobs for men.

Marital status in the profession is important on several grounds. There is the matter of changing the image of the notorious old-maid school-teacher —a change that can affect recruiting. One common means of occupational advancement in America is moving; married women typically have lesser recourse to this than do married men or single teachers. Another avenue of advancement is promotion, movement upwards; single women, with uninterrupted careers, appear to gain proportionately more of such rewards in teaching. Conversely, the group most committed to teaching, to remaining in the same school, appears to be once-married women teachers (widowed, divorced, or separated)—a situation observed in other fields. Such factors are matters of personal concern to individuals planning careers, of institutional interest to those who hire, and of some professional interest to the whole group.

Sex   No characteristic of the American teaching force is as important as the numerical dominance of women. In 1970 women were 67 percent of all public school teachers.[41] Despite small increases of male teachers during the 1960s, the trend of the past one hundred forty years has been to make

[39]In 1970, 86 percent of men teachers and 77 percent of women teachers were or had been married: "Facts on American Education," *NEA Research Bulletin,* 49 (May 1971):47.

[40]"Women as Teachers," *Educational Review,* 2 (November 1891):361. A contract form, dated 1923, and reprinted widely from *The Idaho Educator,* lists as the first of 14 conditions of employment that the teacher agrees "1. Not to get married. This contract becomes null and void immediately if the teacher marries." Furthermore, "Not to keep company with men"; "Not to loiter downtown in ice cream parlors"; "Not to leave town at any time without the permission of the Board of Trustees"; "Not to ride in a carriage or automobile with any man except her brother or father"; and "Not to use face powder, mascara, or paint the lips."

[41]From data in "Public School Statistics, 1970–71 and 1969–70," *NEA Research Bulletin,* 49 (March 1971):30. See also Mason, *The Beginning Teacher,* pp. 4–10; U.S. Bureau of the Census, *Historical Statistics of the United States, Colonial Times to 1957* (Washington, D.C.: U.S. Government Printing Office, 1960), p. 208; Moskow, *Teachers and Unions,* pp. 60–61; "Professional Women in Public Schools, 1970–71," *NEA Research Bulletin,* 49 (October 1971):67–68.

teaching (below the college level) into a woman's profession. To reverse this trend of feminine dominance of teaching in the lower schools would require exempting teaching from the trend of more sex differentiation in the larger occupational structure: there are pronounced tendencies toward greater sex-linking in all technical and professional jobs. Moreover, as an occupational field expands, women replace men at lower-level positions while the upper, administrative reaches are filled by men—a pattern by which occupational status for women declines.[42] Teaching has shown both of these developments, as have librarianship and social work. At the college and university level, women were 20 percent of the faculty in 1900, 30 percent in the 1930s, and 20 percent again in 1960. In this male field women professors are accordingly concentrated in the lower ranks of faculty and in low-ranking institutions. The National Education Association was 54 years old before it elected (in 1911) its first woman president: Ella Flagg Young, a professor and former Chicago school superintendent.

The teaching profession comes to depend upon women when the educational system is expanding sharply and when sufficient men are somehow unavailable. Thus, the percentage of women teachers has recently grown abroad —with universalization and the decimation of manpower by war and economic development.[43] In America, the replacement of male teachers by women began under comparable circumstances. During the public school campaigns many men had left the older states to move westward or were engaged in extending the railroads or in industrial expansion. On the frontiers they worked in farming, mining, and establishing permanent settlements. If the demands created for schoolmasters were to be met, it was by employing the only surplus of manpower: womanpower. Young, unmarried women— anxious to supplement parental income, lacking other jobs suitable for one with some education and middle-class aspirations, and perhaps frustrated in their desire to marry by the temporary absence of sufficient young men—

[42]From 1950 to 1960, medical and dental technicians who were women increased from 56 percent to 62 percent, while women in science and engineering declined from 18 percent to 12 percent, and in mathematics from 38 percent to 26 percent. The proportions of women in the standard professions have declined overall since 1900: Alice S. Rossi, "Barriers to the Career Choice of Engineering, Medicine, or Science Among American Women," in *Women and the Scientific Professions,* ed. J. A. Mattfield and C. G. Van Aken (Cambridge, Mass.: Massachusetts Institute of Technology Press, 1965), pp. 57–61; Dean F. Knudsen, "The Declining Status of Women," in *The Other Half: Roads to Women's Equality,* ed. Cynthia F. Epstein and William J. Goode (Englewood Cliffs, N.J.: Prentice-Hall, Inc., 1971), pp. 98–109.

Nations with equal employment policies restrict women's opportunities for top positions. In the Soviet Union women comprise almost half of all Soviet workers and 53 percent of all professionals; their proportion of the higher echelon positions in the various professional, technical, and managerial fields is 1 percent to 15 percent: Nicholas DeWitt, *Education and Professional Employment in the U.S.S.R.* (Washington, D.C.: National Science Foundation, 1961), p. 529.

[43]Women now constitute 60 percent of Austria's elementary teachers and 75 percent and 40 percent respectively of British elementary and secondary teachers: Philip H. Coombs, *The World Educational Crisis* (New York: Oxford University Press, 1968), pp. 44, 196.

turned temporarily to keeping school.[44] From 1845 to 1865 the percentage of males among teachers dropped from 61 percent to 14 percent—a decline exaggerated by the Civil War. Female teachers outnumbered males two to one by 1892, and the number of men in a growing profession actually declined in many years—especially from 1898 to 1915, when the subprofession of school administration, in which men became predominant, was being formed.

It had once been the common practice in rural areas to hire a female to teach the summer school for the younger children and a male for the winter school—when the bigger boys completed their farm chores and returned to challenge the teacher's mastery. As graded schools slowly replaced the one-room schoolhouse, arguments favoring males as better disciplinarians became less telling. Females could ordinarily control a single grade, and the district might hire one male as head teacher, to assist and supervise several female teachers. The rhetoric of qualifications changed from the ability to "whale the big boys" to the recital of the "female virtues" of patience, culture, and moral rectitude. The argument was clinched by the fact that women could be hired for much lower pay.

Today men slightly outnumber women in high school faculties. Male percentages are also relatively larger among the under-40 group of American teachers;[45] Mason found the proportion of males in his sample of beginning teachers to be 10 percent higher than the national average of all teachers. Yet this need not portend more equal sex-ratios in the future. The woman teacher's work cycle means that many women age 25 to 40 have left teaching only *temporarily,* to bear and raise children. Moreover, male teachers exhibit a greater tendency to leave the classroom permanently, either for a different career in education or for other work. These sex-related characteristics are important. Women's rights groups are concerned that women have been urged to remain at home rearing their families. That there are factors in teaching which do not reward men sufficiently for more of them to remain teachers is also significant.

REWARDING TEACHERS

"Let teachers receive a salary from the state such as a good man shall desire but a wicked man disdain"; this advice of Juan Luis Vives—Spanish humanist

[44]Citing 1865 census data for Massachusetts, Katz observes that among the three fields of prominent employment for women—domestics, factory operatives, and teaching—only teaching was neither arduous, manual, nor filled with those of lower-class (largely immigrant Irish) status: Michael B. Katz, *The Irony of Early School Reform* (Cambridge, Mass.: Harvard University Press, 1968), p. 91. For a brief survey of women's movement into American employment, see Gerda Lerner, *The Woman in American History* (Reading, Mass.: Addison-Wesley Publishing Co., 1971), pp. 39–53; and Robert W. Smuts, *Women and Work in America* (New York: Schocken Books, Inc., 1971).

[45]Edman's worldwide survey found that 26 percent of elementary school teachers in the West and 39 percent in the East are males; among under-40 teachers, the male figures were much higher: 59 percent and 73 percent respectively: Edman, *A Self-Image of Primary School Teachers,* p. 42.

and educational theorist—sought to balance the low extrinsic rewards of teaching by the high moral qualities desirable in teachers of the young.[46] Nevertheless, the fact that more attention was paid to the requirements and responsibilities of teaching than to adequate remuneration for its duties has been the complaint of countless generations of teachers. This section will examine, in turn, the multiple dimensions of an occupational reward system: wage payment, job security, and promotion. The intrinsic rewards associated with job-satisfaction will be discussed in the conclusion of this chapter.

The Salary Issue

To examine payment for teaching services as a social-policy question (and not as a moral matter or a subject for professional exhortation) requires dispassionate attention to the various causes of a prevailing wage structure and to its consequences or correlates.

Probable Causes of Subprofessional-Scale Salaries in Teaching

Instructional salaries are the largest item in the operating budgets of schools and colleges. Nevertheless, teachers ordinarily earn less than those of comparable education, and often less than those of lower job status. The explanation lies in economic and personnel facts, including the following:

The nonprofit, noncommercial institutions that distribute professional services include most schools and colleges, churches, hospitals, libraries, government, and foundations. These provide services below their cost. Therefore, they seldom match salaries paid by profit-making enterprises. Each one is likely to lose employees in times of full employment, but their salaries may become competitive during economic depressions—as industrial wages drop, work hours are cut, and overtime is eliminated. In 1939, for example, the average big-city high school teacher earned 18 percent more than the average chemical engineer in industry; in 1959 the engineer earned 65 percent more than the teacher. While the dollar earnings of American public school teachers annually increased by an average of 3 percent or more from 1890 to the present—ordinarily increasing ahead of inflation—teachers' expectations of commanding professional wages were frustrated. In the mid-1960s their average income was lower than that of all professional employees except social workers, clergymen, dieticians, and librarians. And teachers in nonpublic schools annually earn $500 to $2,000 less than their public school counterparts.[47]

---

[46]Quoted in Foster Watson, ed., *Vives: On Education; A Translation of "De Tradendis Disciplinis"* (Cambridge: Cambridge University Press, 1913), p. 56.

[47]Joseph A. Kershaw and Roland N. McKean, *Teacher Shortages and Salary Schedules* (New York: McGraw-Hill Book Co., 1962), p. 70; Charles S. Benson, *The Economics of Public Education* (Boston: Houghton Mifflin Co., 1961), p. 398; Moskow, *Teachers and Unions*, pp. 59–91; Coombs, *The World Educational Crisis*, p. 44; Kraushaar, *American Nonpublic Schools*, p. 160.

Salary-setting powers in teaching are dispersed among hundreds of employing districts and institutions that are run by laymen and supported by restricted resources. While competition for teachers can drive up wages in occasional communities that are both education-conscious and affluent, the average economic standing of teachers will be little affected. State minimum-salary legislation is easily made obsolete by economic changes and operates principally to protect teachers' economic positions in low-paying districts.

Women have lesser earning power than men and are concentrated at the low end of the earning scale. In 1970, among full-time workers in all occupations, the median income of women was 58.2 percent of male earnings; in 1968, women employed full time were three times more likely than men to be earning under $5,000 per year. At one time sex differences in teachers' salaries were ubiquitous. When female teachers averaged $15 to $20 per month, men commanded $22 to $30; when Susan B. Anthony took charge of a school near Hardscrabble, New York, around 1840, she was paid $2.50 weekly, replacing a man paid $10 per week.[48] As late as 1930, 40 percent of America's school districts routinely paid male teachers higher salaries; by 1953 that figure was only 7 percent. Men also earned more because of their concentration in the better-paying secondary schools.[49] The profession's success in establishing the "single-salary schedule"—more intended to raise elementary school status than concerned with sex equality—has virtually ended formal sex differences in teaching salaries. Under its provisions all district teachers with equal preparation and experience earn identical wages —regardless of sex, teaching level, or teaching field. While it is a highly desirable social policy that men and women should be paid equally for equal work, the general economy does not practice this principle. Accordingly, predominance of women in a field reduces its average wages, affecting its practitioners of both sexes. Conversely, the most financially rewarding professions are those whose members are 80 percent or more men: accounting, dentistry, pharmacy, medicine, engineering, science, and law.

The market mechanisms of supply and demand do not fully operate in teaching. The equal-pay principle means that teaching salaries will be no higher than the school district is willing or able to pay all teachers. Should a district agree to pay more to attract and hold teachers in a shortage area

[48]Elizabeth Koontz, *The Best Kept Secret of the Past 5,000 Years: Women Are Ready for Leadership in Education* (Bloomington, Ind.: Phi Delta Kappa Educational Foundation, 1972), p. 19. Sex differences also have applied to administrative salaries. A 1905 NEA survey of nearly 500 city school districts found male elementary school principals averaging $1,542 annually, their female counterparts earning $970.

[49]In 1915 the ratio of high school to elementary school salary averaged 1.58:1; by 1938 it was 1.20:1—the remaining difference largely the result of high school teachers having more college credits and/or experience, and of the fact that, where school districts are not unified, high school districts tend toward higher salaries than do elementary districts. In the nonpublic schools, Kraushaar reports, elementary school teachers and women teachers are consistently the poorest paid; one device is to pay a woman less under a tuition-free arrangement for her children: *American Nonpublic Schools*, p. 160.

(e.g., elementary school teaching in the 1950s or industrial arts teachers in the 1970s), it cannot do so unless the wage increase is applied to all.

A means of upgrading professional salaries and status is by the use of lower-paid assistants. Thus nursing has markedly upgraded its economic position by employing aides, orderlies, technicians, and grades of nurses below the registered nurse in levels of education, responsibility, and remuneration. Teaching has seen much less of this development to date.

Some theorists cite the fact that teachers are salaried as a cause of their lesser earnings. Yet many professionals have long worked within organizations, including university professors and those once within the church. As long ago as 1870, salaried professionals already outnumbered those who were self-employed. Hence, the fact that most educators are not "free" (fee-charging) professionals does not, by itself, seem crucial.

The Consequences of the Wage Structure

The term *consequences* is used here, but caution is warranted—since two things that go together, e.g., low pay and high turnover, may be correlates, and not in a cause-and-effect relationship, if some other factor is "causing" both.

Job-dissatisfaction studies consistently cite salary as a prominent grievance. That it is not more often a problem that teachers list as their greatest grievance stems partly from the fact that those to whom high salary has high saliency seldom enter teaching and the probability that those most economically disaffected try to leave the profession early.[50]

Men, especially younger men, are most prone to leave teaching posts for economic reasons. Some remain in education, accepting better-paid administrative positions, others contribute to high turnover within a school or district, or leave education altogether. The sex difference in reasons given for teacher turnover is illustrated by an NEA study of teachers who transferred: higher salary was the reason given by 40 percent of the men and only 12 percent of the women. Some of the greater occupational mobility of men derives from their relative greater freedom to move. But more important is the greater weight given to economic factors in all male career decisions. While 5 percent of beginning women teachers projected salary and standard of living as a reason for their eventually leaving teaching, 50 percent of the men so answered. While teaching pays women well, compared to their earning potential in other available fields, it rewards men comparatively poorly.[51] Economic

---

[50]"Are Teachers Happy?" *NEA Research Bulletin,* 46 (May 1968):40–41; "Teacher Mobility and Loss," *NEA Research Bulletin,* 46 (December 1968):118–26.

[51]In 1970–71, the average beginning salary for teachers was 26 percent below that for *men* entering private industry; the discrepancy was less when comparing teachers with *women* college graduates entering the fields of home economics, general business, finance: *NEA Research Bulletin,* 49 (March 1971):29; 49 (October 1971):75–79; 50 (March 1972):8.

analysis alone suggests that, while teaching salaries are sufficiently high to attract very able women, they are not attractive to many equally able men.

Competition for teachers, drawn on salary lines, has affected mobility between states. During the shortage years, higher-paying states such as Alabama and Florida drew teachers away from lower-paying states such as Georgia. A survey of teachers leaving Kentucky gave insufficient salary as the principal cause of departure.[52] The differences in ability to pay that create other inequalities between school districts (discussed in chapter 2) also affect teacher recruitment and retention.[53]

Salary negotiations consume the most bargaining time and arouse the greatest conflict between school boards and teacher organizations.[54] One can now only speculate to which educational issues the organized profession would turn its efforts, should teaching's economic position be sufficiently bettered.

Representatives of public employees frequently note the high incidence of "moonlighting"—or the holding of multiple jobs—as a consequence of economic marginality. The 1963 figure for male teachers below the college level holding multiple jobs was 18.7 percent—a figure higher than was reported in any other occupation. While nearly one male teacher in five held a second job, only 2 percent of women teachers did so.[55] When vacation-time employment is added, the male figure jumps to 60 percent. Large numbers of teachers seek extra compensation for coaching and supervising extracurricular activities —a device frequently employed by administrators to retain teachers whose services they would most miss and to increase the earnings of many male teachers.[56] Considering that the average reported teaching week is 47 hours, and that the summer vacation is counted as one attraction into teaching, multiple job-holding appears dysfunctional to professionalization and job-satisfaction.

Approaches to a Wage "Solution"

Beyond laboring continually to upgrade the relative salary level of all teachers, certain selective proposals have also been offered to increase the

[52]*Teacher Turnover Study, 1966* (Frankfort: Kentucky Department of Education, 1966).

[53]K. George Pedersen, "Economic and Sociological Correlates of Teacher Turnover" (Paper read at the annual meeting of the American Educational Research Association, Minneapolis, March 1970).

[54]Marilyn Gittell and T. Edwards Hollander, *Six Urban School Districts: A Comparative Study of Institutional Response* (New York: Frederick A. Praeger, 1968), p. 93; Moskow, *Teachers and Unions*, p. 219.

[55]Forrest A. Bogan and Harvey R. Hamel, "Multiple Jobholders in May 1963," *Monthly Labor Review*, 87 (March 1964):254; "Characteristics of Public-School Teachers, 1956, 1961, 1966," *NEA Research Bulletin*, 45 (October 1967):88.

[56]One of the complaints voiced in "What Makes Teachers Burn?" *NEA Journal*, 50 (May 1966):13–15.

recruiting power of teaching, especially for males; to lessen the turnover rate; and to increase careerism and leadership by retaining more of the ambitious individuals now finding inadequate possibilities in the schools. The following four approaches are offered as "solutions."

First, the available scarce resources for improving teachers' salaries can be employed selectively. James B. Conant argues that, rather than improve beginning salaries, the big jump in earnings should come when a teacher moves from probationary to tenure status. A further modification would be to adjust the size of increases according to the profile of attrition in any given district; thus, as incentive to remain, the largest salary increases could be placed at the level where teacher dropouts have been proportionately greatest. Another variant is the proposal that temporary or transient teachers (somehow defined) be so classified and paid, with career teachers a distinctively used and better-rewarded group.

Second, the system of faculty ranks used in higher education is another approach to differential reward. It is flexible enough to vary salaries by reflecting differences in performance, changes in supply and demand, and the unequalness of academic fields in their competition with noneducational employment. The principal opposition to this approach is the interpretation of democracy as "sameness of treatment" that is so strong in the public school tradition.[57]

Third, team teaching is a way of differentiating salary according to talent and responsibility. The team leader would be compensated for the additional duties involved. Indeed, some of the vigorous proponents of this system of organizing teaching duties saw it less as a way of improving instruction than as an opportunity for leadership and ambition to find outlets in teaching.

Finally, some 10 percent of America's school districts experiment with merit pay. This system pays bonuses to teachers judged above average in teaching effectiveness. Its aims are to recognize outstanding competence and to stimulate all teachers to try for improvement—as a system of uniform and invariable salary increments does not do. The teaching profession opposes merit-pay plans, as it opposes all differential salary systems that go beyond extra pay for extra duties or for having more in-service training or university course credits.

Security of Employment

What Lortie calls "ancillary rewards" include, in teaching, such conditions of employment as the hours and seasons of the school calendar and the system of tenure that provides most teachers a measure of job security. It is a characteristic of ancillary rewards, however, that while they often function to attract individuals to an occupation, they cease to operate as rewards or

[57]An opponent of rank—himself a professor (of education)—is Arthur E. Lean. See his *And Merely Teach* (Carbondale: Southern Illinois University Press, 1968), pp. 36–38.

inducements to remain because they become taken for granted.[58] In two senses, however, job security in education should not be taken for granted. First, its history in teaching, at all levels, is a very brief one. Second, the tenure system has come under sharp attack.

The campaign to certify teachers and the movement to purify all public employment through civil service principles promoted teacher-tenure legislation in America. Both were concerned with protecting individuals and their duties from political meddling and from capricious officials. It was necessary to design procedures to certify competence, make regular a promotion system, and establish rules whereby orderly dismissals for incompetence or unprofessional conduct could be instituted with appeal provisions. The varied rules and regulations that once covered teacher employment were a patchwork drawn from custom, precedent, and law. The drive toward uniform practices began when the District of Columbia acted in 1906, and New Jersey passed the first state tenure law in 1909;[59] 38 states had passed tenure laws by mid-century. In some cases the courts have extended tenure rights to school administrators, and state and county education personnel are frequently covered by civil service status. In various states tenure operates only if adopted at local option; in others it is mandatory only in school districts above a certain size (as in Colorado), or only in listed cities or counties (as in Connecticut, Florida, and Georgia). In all states without laws that confer permanent status upon teachers who have satisfied a stated probationary period of service (commonly three years), there is some other protection by continuing contract laws that specify that teachers must be given advance notice if their contracts are not to be automatically renewed, or laws requiring annual or long-term contracts. In both cases—unlike the situation of teachers with tenure—formal statements of reasons for nonrenewal and rights to an appeal hearing are not ordinarily guaranteed.

The most comprehensive tenure law does not insure a job. Often a district must eliminate positions because of reduced enrollments. The courts have also upheld school boards' powers to terminate contracts by ending a service or program—e.g., music or athletics. Nor do tenure laws protect a teacher against reduction of salary or reassignment among institutions, unless a court rules such action is not a reasonable measure.[60]

[58]Lortie, in *The Semi-Professions,* ed. Etzioni, p. 31.

[59]Cecil W. Scott, *Indefinite Teacher Tenure* (New York: Teachers College, 1934); Newton Edwards, *The Courts and the Public Schools* (Chicago: University of Chicago Press, 1933); Committee on Tenure, *The Effect of Tenure Upon Professional Growth* (Washington, D.C.: National Education Association, 1940); Committee on Tenure and Academic Freedom, *Teacher Tenure Manual* (Washington, D.C.: National Education Association, 1950); William R. Hazard, *Education and the Law: Cases and Materials on Public Schools* (New York: The Free Press, 1971), pp. 277–89.

[60]In a 1928 case, a tenured teacher who subsequently had married refused to resign and was punitively reassigned to teach an elementary school class in a tubercular hospital and sanitorium. The teacher sued and the board's action was voided by the court: *Dutart* v. *Woodward* (1929), 99 *District Court of Appeals of the State of California Reports,* 736, 279, p. 493.

Most job-security legislation authorizes dismissal only for the causes specified in the laws. In teaching these may include professional incompetence,
mental or physical unfitness for service, conviction of a felony, moral turpi-
tude, insubordination, and chronic disregard of state or district rules. A lack
of descriptive detail and the provision in some laws that dismissal may come
for "good and just cause" leave considerable discretion to school boards and
administrators. Because charges must be proven, however, many officials
become timid about pressing charges and pursuing dismissal. Hence, the
tenure system has not ended all abuses: it sometimes fails to protect the
innocent and the competent, while shielding the guilty and the incompetent.

The arguments favoring job security are several and mostly obvious. Some
workers also view job security as partial compensation for inadequate salaries.
The stability of the teaching force would be even less if normal turnover were
compounded by irregular employment practices. Contracts, therefore, protect
both teachers and the programs of students. Hardest, perhaps, for educators
to articulate to laymen is tenure as the protection of academic freedom. At
least since the thirteenth century, when the faculties of the University of Paris
were struggling to establish the university as an independent third force—
apart from both church and state—educational institutions have labored to
protect the cause of learning by protecting their members. While higher education has been most animated by the academic freedom issue, it is a concern
of all who would teach.

Education cannot be even nominally independent if teachers fear for their
jobs on account of what they teach or who they are. Yet the sensitivity of
schools and colleges as social instrumentalities generates recurring tensions.
Cold-war anxieties have threatened tenure protections with loyalty oaths and
exaggerated interpretations of "just cause," provoking dismissals of teachers,
librarians, social workers—and many in private employment as well. Attacks
upon security of employment have recently been phrased as a ferreting-out of
bias or incompetence rather than of "disloyalty." These scrutinies of tenure
have several sources: government officials speaking for public opinion out-
raged by campus disruptions; critics of the "education establishment"; minority-group spokesmen who see entrenched teachers as obstacles to ending
discrimination and school failure; proponents of radical educational change;
and even cost-conscious groups. As with the other chapters of the book of
education, the story of teacher protection is in the continuous process of
writing.

Promotion in Teaching

It has been said, in a well-turned phrase, that *men* seek "affluence and
influence."[61] Within a field, the normal means of securing both is through

---

[61]Delbert K. Clear and Roger C. Seager, "The Legitimacy of Administrative Influence
as Perceived by Selected Groups" (Paper read at the annual meeting of the American
Educational Research Association, Minneapolis, March 1970), p. 1.

promotion to positions of greater reward, responsibility, and authority. The situation in education is anomalous, however.[62] On the one hand, there is the well-trod promotion route to supervisor, principal, or school superintendent; the fact that almost all such positions are staffed by former teachers means that education has no such "caste line" as exists in medicine, where the nurse can never become a physician by promotion. On the other hand, in education the opportunities for such promotions are numerically small for men, and tiny for women teachers. Moreover, they are not promotions within teaching, but *out of teaching*.

Promotion opportunities, within teaching, are limited by the very flat status structure of the typical school. There is virtually no formal hierarchical ordering within the daily work world of teachers, except perhaps for the department heads found in some high schools. (In 1970 male teachers were 69 percent of all department heads in high schools and 97 percent in colleges.) Teaching is unique in that the most inexperienced and the most seasoned practitioners, and the very worst and the very best, ordinarily perform the same range of functions for the same number of clients.[63] Below the college level, there is no ladder of faculty ranks that is both a promotion system and an opportunity for allocating tasks somewhat differently without ending the teaching function. (Full professors are more likely to teach graduate students, for example, and to serve on important campus-wide governance and policy committees.) The equalitarianism in the public school ethos that opposes salary differentiation also opposes task differentiation in teaching. What has functioned in its stead is an ordinarily informal but rigidly adhered to seniority system. This rewards those who "got there first"—since seniority is considered a "fair" reason for making discriminations in this society. The prizes are, perhaps, a choice of classrooms or of free periods and the right of prior consultation on various decisions within the administrator's purview.

Teachers' responses to this pattern of social structuring are, again, highly related to sex. In one survey 51 percent of beginning male teachers, but only 9 percent of the women, reported intentions of seeking advancement through administrative posts in education.[64] The greater career drive of men, their more continuous work experience, and their stronger tendency to seek additional training help to explain their dominance of such positions; women, on the other hand, reflect the pervasive cultural attitude that for a woman to

---

[62]See Lortie and the Simpsons, in *The Semi-Professions,* ed. Etzioni, pp. 1–53, 196–265.

[63]Henry David, ed., *Education and Manpower* (New York: Columbia University Press, 1960), pp. 13–14; T. M. Stinnett, ed., *The Teacher Dropout* (Itasca, Ill.: Peacock Publishers, Inc., 1970). Cf. Cooper, ed., *Differentiated Staffing.*

[64]Mason, *The Beginning Teacher,* p. 103. This recalls the many "generations" of school officials who preferred women teachers because they were judged more tractable, uncomplaining, and noncompetitive: "They are less intent and scheming for future honors or emoluments [than are men]" (1841); "They are more willing to comply with established regulations and less likely to ride headstrong" (1878): quoted in David Tyack, "From Village School to Urban System: A Political and Social History" (United States Office of Education Project, No. 0–0809, September 1972, manuscript), p. 43.

show ambition is "unwomanly."[65] While women were over 88 percent of all elementary school teachers in 1968, only 22 percent of elementary school principals were women, down sharply from 55 percent in 1928, 41 percent in 1948, and 38 percent in 1958. While almost half of all secondary school teachers were women in 1968, women were principals in only 9 percent of the junior high schools and 4 percent of senior high schools.[66] Cultural attitudes also work upon and against women. These include the beliefs of many, men and women, that women should not be placed in authority over men, and that women are unsuited for the political infighting required of administrators who must deal with school board members and other officials who are predominantly male.[67] Hence, in 1970, men were 99.4 percent of all superintendents.

If the more competitive values of men operated among elementary and secondary school teachers—as they do among college and university faculty —it is readily conceivable that rank and other promotional systems would emerge, increasing the complexity of the occupational structures of teaching in America.

RETAINING TEACHERS

The characteristics of American teachers depend not only on those recruited, but also on those who stay in the classrooms. At present a small cadre of experienced teachers has a disproportionate influence upon the sociology of teaching and the particular "culture" of any given school, because the bulk of "man-years" of teaching is provided by a very small percentage of those trained for the classroom.[68] In addition, people are paid both for performance

[65]"The problem is that 'career' is in itself a masculine concept (i.e., designed for males in our society). When we say 'career' it connotes a demanding, rigorous, preordained life pattern, to whose goals everything else is ruthlessly subordinated. . . . Thus when a man asks a woman if she wants a career, it is intimidating. . . . Naturally, she shudders a bit and shuffles back to the broom closet": Philip E. Slater, *The Pursuit of Loneliness: American Culture at the Breaking Point* (Boston: Beacon Press, Inc., 1970), p. 72.

[66]Cynthia F. Epstein, *Woman's Place: Options and Limits in Professional Careers* (Berkeley: University of California Press, 1971), p. 10; Koontz, *The Best Kept Secret*, p. 44; Women's Bureau, U.S. Department of Labor, *Handbook of Women Workers* (Washington, D.C.: U.S. Government Printing Office, 1962), p. 19; "Professional Women in Public Schools," *NEA Research Bulletin*, 49 (October 1971):67–68.

[67]Under 10 percent of school trustees are women; more than 50 percent of all boards have no women members: Patricia C. Sexton, *The American School: A Sociological Analysis* (Englewood Cliffs, N.J.: Prentice-Hall, Inc., 1967), p. 29.

Women seeking administrative posts are hampered by their lack of graduate degrees. In the 1969–70 academic year, women earned 3,980 Ph.D. degrees; men 25,892. A contributing factor may be that the family supports a daughter's good grades and school successes as "an end in itself," not as encouragement toward a demanding profession and advanced schooling: Carole Lopate, *Women in Medicine* (Baltimore: The Johns Hopkins University Press, 1968), p. 38.

[68]A ten-year follow-up study of one thousand graduates of the University of Illinois teacher-training program found that 50 percent of the man-years of teaching was done by 12 percent of the graduates: W. W. Charters, Jr., "Survival in the Teaching Profession," *Journal of Teacher Education*, 7 (September 1956):253–55.

and for *potential*; teachers are suspect on the second count. Many school boards (especially their businessmen members) feel justified in making smaller investments in those who are known, as a group, to promise only short-term service.

A Historical Problem in America

American educational history amply records the *amateurism* in teaching that results from high turnover.[69] New England's typical teachers, depended upon to advance the common-school crusade, seldom taught two terms in succession. An 1857 survey of Wisconsin's teachers found the lifetime "career" in teaching averaged 18 months. One-third of Illinois's schoolrooms in 1880 had a change of teachers during a single school year. In the first decade of this century, the NEA reported that 80 percent of most states' one-room rural schools opened each year with a new teacher; at that time such schools educated the majority of schoolchildren. A manual for beginning teachers, published in 1908, reluctantly admitted such transiency:

> Many of you do not expect to follow teaching all your lives (it would be better if more of our schools were taught by those who expect to make teaching their life work), but while you do teach, try to act and feel as though you were certain to be a teacher all your life. Do not debase yourself by doing any half-hearted work.[70]

The high rate of movement in and out of teaching was not unexpected in the eighteenth and nineteenth centuries. There was much occupational mobility in a sparsely settled land of varied opportunities and an expanding economy, with a high regard for the generalist jack-of-all-trades and a low tolerance for exclusive privileges to practice a trade. It was quite acceptable to try your hand at a thing, and countless individuals moved through a succession of "careers": business, law, the ministry, politics, and farming.

Schoolkeeping was particularly easy to drift into and out of, requiring none of the capital of a business or farm and little education above the ordinary; it was accessible because of steady demand as school enrollments grew and turnover constantly vacated teaching posts. Such eventually prominent politicians as John Adams, James Garfield, and Robert M. LaFollette, and such literary figures as Ralph Waldo Emerson, Henry David Thoreau, and Walt Whitman were "dropouts" from teaching. But most of the defectors were obscure young women, driven out of the classroom by the determination

---

[69]David Tyack, ed., *Turning Points in American Educational History* (Waltham, Mass.: Blaisdell Publishing Co., 1967), pp. 156–62; Willard S. Elsbree, *The American Teacher;* Kate Wofford, *An History of the Status and Training of Elementary Rural Teachers, 1860–1930* (Pittsburgh: Siviter Press, 1935); Jorgenson, *The Founding of Public Education in Wisconsin.*

[70]Dinsmore, *Teaching a District School,* pp. 4–5.

of the bigger students (who had made "running out the teacher" into a tradition in rural schools) or drawn out by marriage.

Teacher Turnover: A Spreading Problem

At the time of North America's colonization by Europeans, the older countries also experienced low commitments to teaching. Too many teachers were schoolmasters who "meant to leave it as soon as they could find more lucrative employment," in the words of one prominent seventeenth-century educator.[71] The European experience, however, was *not* to build schools rapidly, in advance of creating a teaching profession. Having less-universal educational systems restricted teaching opportunities and created a more stable profession, especially at the secondary level. Now, however, there are worldwide reports of rising "loss rates" among teachers. Educational expansion, general manpower shortages, and the turning to larger numbers of women teachers are factors. So-called planned states experience similar difficulties. A report from Poland shows that half of all teacher-trainees fail to complete the program, half of the remainder leave teaching for other jobs, and the average stay in a given teaching post is three years.[72] And everywhere in the world rural schools struggle with their teachers' desires to move to the metropolis.

THE CONTEMPORARY PICTURE IN THE UNITED STATES

The social conditions supporting high general occupational transiency no longer pertain in the prestige professions. Moreover, the average annual separation rate for all manufacturing employees is only 4 percent. In teaching it has averaged between 13 percent and 17 percent in recent years.[73] (This separation rate reflects those lost to teaching—8 to 11 percent annually— plus those who transfer.) Thus, teaching stands in sharp relief, resembling such other high-turnover fields as social work and librarianship.

The bulk of those who create turnover are the younger teachers.[74] Teacher persistence is concentrated in the older age group and in the large cities, where the median of years of experience is 13, compared to 5.5 years in smaller districts. Attrition, however, occurs first among those 40 percent who

[71]Comenius, quoted in Kenneth Charlton, "The Teaching Profession in Sixteenth- and Seventeenth-Century England," in *History and Education,* ed. Paul Nash (New York: Random House, Inc., 1970), p. 48.

[72]Gusta Singer, *Teacher Education in a Communist State: Poland, 1956–1961* (New York: Bookman Associates, Inc., 1965).

[73]Moskow, *Teachers and Unions,* p. 63; *The Semi-Professions,* ed. Etzioni, pp. 220–21; National Education Association, *The Status of the American Public School Teacher* (Washington, D.C.: NEA, 1957); *NEA Research Bulletin,* 50 (March 1972):3; Pederson, *Correlates of Turnover.*

[74]Among beginning teachers, Mason found a 33 percent separation rate and a 16 percent loss rate—compared to the 17 percent and 10 percent respectively reported among all teachers in 1957–58: *The Beginning Teacher,* p. 100.

complete state certification requirements but do not teach—evidence that many prepare themselves to teach as an "insurance policy" or fall-back position, should the need arise. Thereafter, another 20 to 30 percent leave teaching after one or two years, and only 12 to 15 percent achieve a decade or more of continuous teaching experience.

Rapid school and college expansion drove the profession's experience level lower. A comparison of teachers in 1956 and 1966 showed a decline in the median years of teaching experience from 13.1 years to 8.0 years. The separation rate of women teachers is higher than that of men, yet the median years of experience of women teachers (10 years) was higher than that of men (6.5 years). This discrepancy demonstrates that experience rates are highly influenced by women teachers who leave the profession and later return.

Some 3 percent of any year's total number of teachers are persons just returned to teaching. Except for those coming from military service, men are seldom among the returnees.[75] A much-cited study of career aspirations in 1957 indicated that 15 percent of women teachers planned to remain continuously in teaching to retirement, but 58 percent said they hoped to return to teaching when their domestic plans permitted.[76] As yet, no significant change has reversed this female pattern of *contingent commitments* to a teaching career.

Because patterns of high teacher turnover did not hold during the job-scarce Depression years of the 1930s, some observers expect the prolonged period of projected teacher surplus to strengthen teaching's holding power. Lengthened periods of preparation for teaching should provoke a similar reaction, by discouraging recruits with the weakest commitments to teaching, and by encouraging retention because of the greater personal "investment" (of time and money) made in preparing for the profession. There is some evidence to support these presumptions. Census data show that, among women, the more education one possesses, the more likely one is to be employed. Studies of persistence rates of women in various fields show commitment positively related to extensive vocational training, higher status and responsibility, and occupational success. Pederson reports higher attrition among Michigan teachers with minimal levels of preparation, and higher retention rates among most groups having graduate degrees. And among a sample of all beginning teachers with a bachelor's degree or more, Mason found deeper career commitments among those with more education.

The Case for Retention: Career Professionalism

Continued high transiency and turnover commit teaching to a degree of amateurism contrary to the definition of an autonomous profession. Questions of status and power aside, other reasons support efforts to retain more teachers

[75]*NEA Research Bulletin,* 50 (March 1972):4.

[76]W. S. Mason, R. J. Dressel, and R. K. Bain, *The Beginning Teacher* (Washington, D.C.: U.S. Government Printing Office, 1958).

for continuous service. One is the wastefulness of high transiency. Most of the demand for additional teachers has come from two sources: expanding enrollments, which increase the total number of teachers, and replacement of those who voluntarily leave teaching. The replacement requirement has recently been some four times greater than the expansion need.[77] As population trends reduce the first demand, even more of the recruiting and training function will focus upon needs caused by turnover.

The public costs of training teachers for brief careers and for locating, hiring, and initiating large proportions of new teachers are considerable. These costs include high expenditures of staff time and energy in schools and school districts. Moreover, selection and orientation tend to be less careful when transiency is assumed. It is often difficult to establish worthwhile professional upgrading in an unstable staff, especially the kinds of school-based, ongoing curricular projects that require extended planning, coordination, and cooperation. America's experimenting with staffing to improve learning could not imitate Norway's, for example, in keeping a class with a single teacher for three to nine years; while this would be a relatively simple plan to inaugurate, teacher turnover (compounded by the high geographic mobility of Americans generally) would defeat it.

Exponents of educational change might argue that innovation cannot proceed *without* high turnover, since experience gives teachers time to become socialized to the system and accommodated to the status quo. Some contend that tenured teachers are less interested in new programs and approaches than are those with little training or experience. In addition to the fact that high turnover historically has not provoked innovation, consider these four related arguments:

First, the fact that turnover is highest among young teachers—and the probability that turnover operates somewhat selectively to reduce the proportion of innovative, risk-taking personalities—almost guarantees that the corps of experienced teachers will be both older and less experimental. Put differently, those disposed toward educational innovation *cannot* exercise influence unless they are retained in teaching.

Second, while quantity of work output is stable throughout one's lifetime, the quality of creative work is strongly related to age. The most creative years—generally those between ages 28 and 38—are precisely those where women (the bulk of public school teachers) are pressured by social conventions to remain at home.[78] While domestic duties and child rearing may profit as outlets for creativity, it appears probable that the creativity level of teaching suffers accordingly.

Third, it is unfair and unrealistic to expect *perpetual beginners* to initiate and sustain the burden of professional development. It would be better if

[77]Maxine G. Stewart, "A New Look at Manpower Needs in Teaching," *Occupational Outlook Quarterly,* 8 (March 1964):11.

[78]Rossi, "Barriers to the Career Choice," in *Women and the Scientific Professions,* ed. Mattfield and Van Aken, p. 103.

the most creative and innovative teachers were retained and given the seniority and recognition that would allow their efforts to gain exposure and influence outside their own classrooms, to affect teaching generally.

Finally, brief careers militate against the consumption of research on teaching, and against *systematic* efforts to improve education. They also limit the pool of potential leaders. Many teachers have complained of dominance by school administrators. While traditional cultural deference of women (most teachers) to male authority (most administrators) is one factor, another is the negative effects of turnover on developing leaders among teachers. While a high quality of teaching is often provided by the short-term teacher, it tends to be confined in its influence and interest to the single class-room. The editors of the education supplement of *Saturday Review* were thwarted in their original plans to publish many articles by elementary and secondary school teachers; teachers submitted few articles, and those received lacked a perspective of sufficient breadth.[79] The career professionalism that contributes so much writing on higher education by faculty is much less evident in the rest of American teaching. Consequently, the articulation of teachers' concerns is very much left to others.

Job Satisfaction

Many studies of morale and job satisfaction show women in all occupations more happy in their work than are men. This seems paradoxical, given the concentration of women in lower-paying and subordinate positions. (One-third of all women college graduates enter teaching, and one-third of women high school graduates take clerical jobs.) What is more important than these "objective" discriminations, however, is the psychocultural fact that men face the world of work with more identification, commitment, expectation, and ego-involvement. With higher psychic engagement, men have had more opportunities to suffer feelings of disappointment and dissatisfaction in the meeting of their life-goals through their occupations. The "contingent com-mitment" that many (probably most) women have brought to their occupa-tional roles places lesser demands upon the job for the satisfaction of their needs and ambitions.

Social-class factors apparently also differentiate the more- and less-satisfied. Thus, Zeigler attributes the moderate conservatism of female teachers both to their essential satisfaction with their place in society (primarily middle-class) and with their work; male teachers, being more likely to have sought upward mobility through teaching, consequently feel somewhat thwarted. The fact that among beginning teachers, Mason found nonwhite teachers to be more satisfied further suggests that perceptions of improving one's social position can be powerful factors in influencing job satisfaction.

Elementary school teachers report themselves more content than their

---

[79]Woodring, *Investment in Innovation,* p. 184.

counterparts in secondary schools, a difference that holds even when teachers of the same sex are compared. The former are more likely than the latter to say they would again choose teaching, and to have sanguine attitudes toward their institutions, subordinates, peers, and superiors.[80] One explanation offered is that elementary teaching principally recruits those who are attracted to children, and that the elementary school context and pedagogical culture adequately fits these predispositions. Conversely, those entering secondary school teaching, if interested most in young people, have lesser opportunity to know them well; if interested most in subject matter, they often feel frustrated by the difficulties in arousing a like interest in many of their students. They may have skills that do bring higher wages outside of teaching, and hence they experience more economic dissatisfaction. They find adolescents both harder to teach and harder to like than they imagined. Finally, they are pushed toward frustration by the lack of consensus about the purposes and approaches of secondary education. The fact that junior high school teachers were those most responsive to union organizers, as shown by a study of New York City, suggests the factors within this school level are responsible for militant dissatisfaction; these include the controversial and marginal qualities of these schools, the nature of their curricula, the unusual problems of early adolescence, and the bureaucratic consequences of larger schools.[81]

Low job satisfaction need not drive teachers from the profession; the fact that well-satisfied and gratified women leave teaching so readily testifies to the imperfect relationship of satisfaction to retention. More positively, *dis*satisfaction *can* be exploited—to improve the conditions for education and further professionalization by making teaching more attractive for lifetime careers. The remainder of this chapter will discuss, first, the relationship of teacher characteristics, especially sex, to the organization of teachers in order to influence policies affecting their work, and second, the issue of collegiality.

Participation for Collective Action

There is impressive evidence that dissatisfaction among teachers promotes militant organization. Union membership is strongest among those groups expressing the least satisfaction: male teachers and secondary school teachers. The fact that younger teachers are also more disposed toward unions probably reflects their lesser socialization and lesser susceptibility to the long-articulated thesis that unionism is "unprofessional."

[80]See the discussion of factors in high and low satisfaction in Mason, *The Beginning Teacher,* pp. 81–94, and the analysis in Zeigler, *The Political Life of American Teachers,* pp.19–21, 25. For a sampling of expressions of dissatisfaction among older male teachers, see Dan C. Lortie, *How Teachers Make a Difference* (Washington, D.C.: U.S. Government Printing Office, 1971), p. 59.

[81]The union also had more members in "special service schools," which enroll disadvantaged pupils: Rosenthal, *Pedagogues and Power,* pp. 35–40.

Among all teachers, women are less likely to join unions or to favor their activities. The reasons include these:

1. Women historically have a low level of participation in the labor movement. Where about one in four males in the labor force belonged to a union, for women the proportion was one in seven.

2. Unions are associated prominently with wage issues, but wage grievances are not pressing to many women teachers. In one survey, 89 percent of married women teachers reported having husbands in the labor force (compared to 55 percent of male teachers with employed wives); given the greater earning power of men, such women are better situated economically than are their male counterparts.[82] Indeed, on the basis of family income, teachers are typically above average in most communities.

3. Women and elementary school teachers have been the membership strength of organizations affiliated with the National Education Association. Loyalty and greater faith in the organization for personal protection make them more difficult to divert to a rival organization.[83]

4. The activities of teacher organizations have been historically less visible and controversial than are union activities. These traits better fit the society's expectations of, and for, women.

5. The explicit involvement of teachers' unions in political campaigns runs against the greater preference of women teachers to limit organizational activities to "purely educational" matters.

By whatever organizational form, women are more ambiguous than are men about raising professional standards. The reason seems to be their contingent commitment to almost any occupation.[84] Since they would be personally most injured by requirements for additional preservice and in-service training, and by the demands on time and energy of greater self-government, campaigns to effect such ends have often met indifference. Male teachers, however, in addition to their greater careerism, are more prone to action because they are *supposed* to espouse autonomy, are more likely to see conflict in the present workings of the educational system, and are generally more cynical about accepted strategies to deal with their needs.

The change in virtually all teachers' organizations toward greater activism is one response to pressures for which the profession has been unprepared:

[82]Taking together all public school teachers, the teaching salary was a second income for 48 percent in 1960 and 54 percent in 1971: Moskow, *Teachers and Unions,* p. 62; *NEA Research Bulletin,* 50 (March 1972):6.

[83]Among Zeigler's sample of teachers, 41 percent of the males and 14 percent of the females said that the professional association ignored the plight of a teacher under attack for dealing with controversial issues; 6 percent of the males and 17 percent of the females believed that the association actually defended teachers: *The Political Life of American Teachers,* p. 73. See also "Do Teacher Characteristics Affect Opinion?" *NEA Research Bulletin,* 47 (December 1969):117–21.

[84]Lieberman, *Education as a Profession,* p. 253.

© *1969 United Feature Syndicate, Inc.*

the civil rights movement, calls for community power, organized student unrest, the attrition of confidence in public education. Such pressures—along with the probability that, with teacher surplus, teachers will lose some of the relative gains made during the years of undersupply—promise that a posture of militant activism will grow, even among college faculty.[85] Such a prediction rests on ample evidence in the history of the labor movement. Outside challenges combine with internal unrest to raise basic questions about the relationships of teachers to one another, and to other educational professionals. Accordingly, discussions of collegiality in public school teaching now appear more propitious.

Teachers as Colleagues

For almost a century the leaders of American teachers have been school administrators. But assertions of teacher hegemony are now challenging that alliance with administrators.[86] Several factors appear responsible for this change:

The effort of the National Education Association and its state and local affiliates to include everyone on the professional staff in membership *itself* invites discord. As participation becomes more inclusive, heterogeneity grows, and internal conflict becomes inevitable—especially with those pressures experienced by American schools and teachers in the last quarter-century.

Teachers' unions demand that classroom teachers gain a greater voice in policy making. Union bylaws often exclude administrative membership. As negotiations expand beyond salary issues and grievance procedures—to class

[85]Harold G. Regier, *Too Many Teachers?* (Bloomington, Ind.: Phi Delta Kappa Educational Foundation, 1972), p. 27.

[86]A review of studies in the 1960s of teacher dissatisfaction concluded that "considerable empathy" still existed among teachers and administrators, with teachers' grievances expressed primarily against their boards of education; dissatisfaction with system-wide factors was highly correlated, however, with negative attitudes toward the school principal: *NEA Research Bulletin,* 46 (May 1968):41. By 1971 a majority of teachers believed that administrators should be represented by a separate bargaining unit from that which spoke for teachers: *NEA Research Bulletin,* 49 (October 1971):77. Cf. Dave Findley, "The Secondary Principal: Evaluation and Supervision," and Roald Campbell, "The Changing Role of the Superintendent," both in *Contemporary Education,* 39 (May 1968):276–77, 249–54; George B. Redfern, "Negotiation Changes Principal-Teacher Relationships," *National Elementary Principal,* 48 (April 1968):20–25.

size, scheduling, assignments, transfer plans, seniority, and disciplinary policies —the conflict of interest between teachers and administrators will be heightened.

Unless the social backgrounds of school administrators broaden to keep pace with that of an increasingly *less* homogeneous teaching force, differences arising from social class, ethnicity, and race will compound the different perspectives arising from position and function.

Although male teachers express administrative ambitions far more frequently than do women (51 percent to 9 percent respectively in Mason's study), men do not trust administrators to the extent women report. The probable contributing factors include a general cynicism, a blue-collar distrust of paternalistic management, and the clash of male aspirations with the incumbency of those already in authority—a kind of "status envy." The greater movement of men into teaching, or of male teachers into organizational activity, promises additional future conflict with administrators.

Innovations in personnel policies governing school administrators may weaken further their position relative to teachers, and place new strains on their one-time solidarity. The recent experience of Detroit is a case in point: administrative appointments were no longer to be considered permanent. Some administrators are now being appointed who lack teaching backgrounds.

Administrative dominance was once supported both by sex (being male) and by additional education. The longer and more specialized preparation of teachers and the increasing preoccupation of administrators with non-instructional matters undermine administrative authority as based on superior knowledge.

The great social change of the past century affecting organizations includes the attempted substitution of routinized management for a dependence upon charismatic leadership—what Bowles calls the replacement of decision-making *skills* by decision-making *rules*.[87] The result, called bureaucracy, does not fully describe educational organizations. First, schools and colleges have a flatter shape than the classic pyramidal structure or quasi-military chain of command; when we consider a system of schools or a statewide system of colleges, the analogy fits better. Second, the division of labor based on specialization is imperfect in teaching, especially in the lower schools. Third, the tasks of educating are more ambiguous, the results less well defined, the decision making that deals with myriad daily contingencies more fragmented than bureaucratic theory allows. An informal give-and-take still characterizes the adult workings of the typical school culture. Yet, with increases in size and centralization, elements and specters of bureaucratization alienate some

---

[87]For a case study see "The Rexograph Machine," in Estelle Fuchs, *Teachers Talk* (Garden City, N.Y.: Doubleday & Co., Inc., 1969). Cf. Ronald G. Corwin, *Militant Professionalism* (New York: Appleton-Century-Crofts, Inc., 1970), esp. pp. 105–71; Robert Dreeben, "The School as a Workplace," in *Second Handbook of Research on Teaching,* ed. Travers, pp. 450–73; Samuel Bowles, *Planning Educational Systems for Economic Growth* (Cambridge, Mass.: Harvard University Press, 1969), p. 55.

teachers from administration. The impersonality in human relations—intended to eliminate capricious and subjective management of prebureaucratic organizations—is especially repugnant to the highly personalistic traditions and dispositions of education; depersonalization is even more objectionable than are such "efficiency measures" as installing time clocks to check the arrivals and departures of the faculty. The fact that as much as 10 percent of public school staff in a large urban system is composed of highly paid nonteaching, full-time supervisors and administrators is another irritant.

The more highly professionalized teachers are, the more they will seek control of educational decisions through consultation with their colleagues—in opposition to management by nonteachers and others who are "nonexperts." While teaching in the elementary and secondary schools has indeed been marked by belief in communication, persuasion, agreement, and cooperative planning, *collegiality* has not yet assumed the scope and power found in higher education.[88]

It is possible to say that the average American college or university, on its good and its bad sides, has been shaped by its faculty.[89] It is true that, in many colleges, some colleagues are "more equal than others"—in serving on more of the important committees, rotating the chairmanships among a clique, and "having the President's ear"; such oligarchical government conceals, however, a more inclusive exercise of faculty authority than is found anywhere else in American teaching. Public school faculties seldom set institutional policy on the requirements of a major, the introduction of new programs, the conditions of graduation, the selection of materials; in most colleges and universities, the professoriate possesses de facto authority in these matters, if not the final word in all cases. Even more important for collegiality is that professors recruit their own colleagues and decide on their promotions and retention—subject to a confirmation by administrators and trustees that ranges from perfunctory (in most high-status institutions) to vigilant (in places where faculty professionalization is incomplete).

There are several obvious barriers to extending collegiality to the whole of teaching. There is the admission by teachers that they do not know their associates' teaching. Since the linear construction of elementary and secondary school buildings is no more isolating than that of colleges, one difference lies in the paucity of opportunities teachers have to work together—as on the faculty committees so common in higher education. Another factor is the

[88]Citing a 1967 NEA survey of payment for extra activities, Lortie notes that school officials more frequently reward teachers for taking university or in-service instruction than for such "peer activities" as committee work, supervising student teachers, or holding office in professional organizations. "Does this reward system perpetuate a subordinate, passive intellectual stance for teachers contrasted to horizontal collegial interchanges and personal responsibility?" In Travers, ed., *Second Handbook of Research on Teaching*, p. 488.

[89]This contention is most fully developed in Jencks and Riesman, *The Academic Revolution*.

greater transiency and turnover in the public schools; while professors are also peripatetic, they move among institutions—remaining known in the profession and in their scholarly societies.

Opportunities to teach with another person would multiply the opportunities to build collegial knowledge. Yet team-teaching is more talked of (and opposed) than practiced.[90] An unwillingness of teachers to be placed in the position of judging one another persists. Despite the fact that teachers *do* rate each other informally, merit-pay plans repeatedly arouse denials of the ability to know who are the good teachers and unwillingness to participate in evaluating another teacher.

The factor of sex once again appears implicated. Among teachers, most women do not make of their occupational associates a reference group. Rather, their strong attachments and self-images have revolved around their family roles and the esteem of their students.[91] Should more men enter and remain in teaching, and should male values more influence the school culture, a more authentic collegial relationship among teachers would appear. Regardless, some American teachers have already begun to be swept up by the movements for self-determination that have agitated other sectors of American society.

Underlying this discussion of collegiality is the expectation that a more genuine participation will enhance job satisfaction, retention in the profession, and opportunities to learn while one teaches. There is the hope that the parochial outlook of many teachers will erode, and that the dedication to instruction that many teachers lavish upon a single classroom will be extended to joining in the improvement of teaching generally. There is the concern that teachers have a commensurate share—with administrators and representatives of the public interest—in the creation and maintenance of the structures within which they work.[92] The articulation of the *unique* concerns of teachers has not adequately informed this society's reflections on education. Without such articulation it is unlikely that the balance, of which Hutchins writes, could be achieved: that teachers would teach responsibly and that the

[90]Some reasons are suggested in Woodring, *Investment in Innovation,* p. 150. Cf. James A. Anderson, *Bureaucracy in Education* (Baltimore: The Johns Hopkins University Press, 1968), pp. 151–52.

[91]Simpson and Simpson, in *The Semi-Professions,* ed. Etzioni, pp. 199–200. Most data show that the percentage of women teachers with children has remained the same (about 52 percent) over the decade 1960 to 1970—without indicating family size trends or age distributions of such children. Observation and discussions with many teachers impressionistically suggest that real change may already have taken place in the balance of family life with career interests. The presence on the faculty of married women teachers with preschool children at home seems much more common than even a decade ago.

[92]Opportunities are restricted when "existing vehicles for discussion and planning within the school (faculty meetings, teacher-principal contacts, teacher-supervisor contacts, etc.) *are based on the principle of avoidance of controversy"*: Sarason, *The Culture of the School and the Problem of Change,* p. 71n (italics added).

public would restrain itself in the exercise of its legal rights.[93] There is the further proposition that teachers who experience a sense of personal dignity and collegial respect are a more progressive force than are those frustrated in meeting, within the school, these basic human and social needs.

The last word in this chapter, and in *The Shape of American Education,* goes to that enduring critic of its characteristics and of the culture that sustains the schools. Jacques Barzun writes well and truly that

> . . . tomorrow's problem will not be to get teachers, but to recognize the good ones and not discourage them before they have done their stint. In an age of big words and little work, any liberal profession takes some sticking to, not only in order to succeed, but in order to keep faith with oneself. Teaching is such a profession.[94]

[93]Robert M. Hutchins, *The Conflict in Education in a Democratic Society* (New York: Harper & Row, Publishers, 1953), p. 12.
[94]Barzun, *Teacher in America,* p. 16.

Benveniste, G., 88n
Bereday, G. Z. F., 80n, 124n, 127n
Bereiter, C., 157n
Berg, I., 162, 162n
Berke, J. S., 41n, 42n
Bernard, J., 98n
Bernstein, M., 121n
Bestor, A., 129, 129n, 148-49, 156, 158
Bettelheim, B., 127n
Biddle, B. J., 174n
Bienstock, H., 158n
Bingham, C., 133, 133n
Birch Society, John, 28
Bjork, R. M., 80n
Black Americans: attitudes of, 11, 113-14; in college, 56, 56n, 57n, 128n; cultural awareness of, 25-26, 88, 91, 92; educational issues and, 88, 89, 96, 96n; as educators, 213, 213n; geographic mobility of, 10, 43, 45, 67, 77; in nonpublic schools, 70, 70n; on school boards, 27; segregated schools for, 93-94; social data on, 94, 96, 103, 118-19, 122
Blanshard, B., 156n
Blaschke, C., 73n
Blassingame, J. W., 163n
Blaustein, A. P., 11n
Blocher, D. H., 183n
Blue-collar Americans, 27, 120n
Blum, Father V., 74
Board of education, local: election of, 12, 20, 24; history of, 27, 39; membership of, 20, 21, 22, 23, 70; mentioned, 5, 35, 145; powers of, 14, 191, 223, 224; relation to professionals, 32, 205, 205n, 207, 208, 221, 234n; as state officers, 14
Bock, J. C., 3n
Bode, B., 188
Bogan, F. A., 221n
Bond, H. M., 94n
Boone, D., 133
Bord, N., 23n
Boroff, D., 53, 53n, 55
Borrowman, M. L., 180n, 193n
Bowers, C. A., 7n
Bowles, S., 88n, 235n
Brain, G. B., 44n
Brazil, 80
Breasted, M., 28n
Bremer, J., 163n
Bronfenbrenner, U., 5n
Brooks, V. W., 97
Broudy, H. S., 165n, 174n
Brown v. *Topeka Board of Education* (1954), 12
Brubacher, J. S., 35n
Bryson, L., 128, 128n
Bucchioni, E., 89n, 112n
Buetow, H. A., 71n
Bullock, H. A., 94
"Bundy Report," 72

Bureaucracy: school as, 142, 184, 208, 232, 235-36; in society, 138, 146, 163
Burma, 3
Bush, D., 150, 150n, 156, 156n
Busing, 9, 11, 13, 38, 47n

California: Baldwin Park, 16; Berkeley, 46; Beverly Hills, 16; higher education in, 18, 48n, 57, 62, 103, 109, 113n, 126; Los Angeles, 44, 50, 122; Oakland, 46; Orange County, 29; Richmond, 42n, 197n; San Bernardino, 50; San Diego, 50; San Francisco, 126n, 171; San Francisco State College, 113n; school finance in, 16-17, 47; state officers of, 120, 146, 146n; teachers in, 51, 166-67; tests in, 53; Univ. of, 39, 55, 146
Callahan, J., 44n
Campbell, R. F., 11n, 234n
Canada, 1, 3, 66
Caplow, T., 111n, 178n, 179
Carlson, R. O., 32n
Carlyle, T., 179
Carnegie: Commission on Higher Education, xin, 167n; Corp., 61
Carnoy, M., 161n
Carr-Saunders, A., 203
Carter, J. G., 13
Carver, G. W., 162n
Catholic Americans: and discrimination, 68, 92; and public schools, 3, 23; as teachers, 212, 213, 214
Catholic Church, Roman, 9, 29
Catholic institutions: aid for, 32; enrollments in, 66, 69, 69n; of higher education, 34-35, 55, 56; teachers in, 52, 70; for women, 59, 61. *See also* Nonpublic schools
Caudill, W., 123, 123n
Cave, W. M., 5n
Cervantes, L. F., 113n
Chall, J., 37n
Chapman, J. J., 75
Charles, D. C., 178n
Charlton, K., 228n
Charnofsky, S., 121n
Charters, W. W., Jr., 176n, 214, 214n, 226n
Cheyney, A. B., 115n
Chicago, Univ. of, 140. *See also* Illinois
China, 80, 170
Chinese: -Americans, 92; in Malasia, 3n
Christian Reformed Church, schools of, 69n
Citizens for Educational Freedom, 29
Civic assoc., 23, 30
Civilian Conservation Corps, 64
Civil Rights Act (1964), 9, 11n, 65
Civil War, 133, 217
Clapp, H., 150, 150n
Clark, B. R., 54n, 59n, 153, 153n
Clark, J. M., 6n, 207n
Clark, K., 94, 122, 123
Classics, 157, 158, 193

Class size: and aid formulas, 16; of graduating class, 8*n*; and innovation, 68; mentioned, 70, 166; and school costs, 44, 47*n*, 49, 173*n*; teachers' views of, 173; variance in, 49-50
Clear, D. K., 224*n*
Clifford, G. J., 196*n*
Clincy, E., 73*n*
Cochran v. Louisiana State Board of Education (1930), 13
Coffman, L. D., 212*n*, 214
Cohen, A. A., 156*n*
Cohen, D. K., 42*n*, 90*n*
Cohen, S., 91*n*
Cold War, 145, 145*n*, 224
Cole, K. C., 32*n*, 69*n*
Coleman, J. S. (political scientist), 79*n*
Coleman, J. S. (sociologist): on adolescence, 96*n*, 154; data of, 114, 118, 118*n*, 175; on equality, 76*n*; mentioned, 174*n*, 175*n*; on social change, 142
"Coleman Report," 51, 119, 122, 122*n*, 128, 197
Coles, R., 115, 115*n*
College and univ. admissions: and high school course, 115*n*, 147-48; history of, 36, 134; standards of, 36, 67-68, 113, 127, 127*n*, 151; in world, 80
College Entrance Examination Board, 37, 59, 101
Colleges. *See* Community colleges; Higher education; Students
Colonialism, 3
Colorado, 62, 223; Aspen, 73; Denver, 43; Pueblo, 50
Comenius, 228*n*
Commager, H. S., x, x*n*, 85*n*, 132*n*
Committee on School Mathematics, Univ. of Illinois, 148
Community colleges: characteristics of, 54, 59, 153; choosing, 102, 103, 103*n*, 107; expansion of, 128*n*, 166; faculty of, 176; mentioned, 17; role of, 59, 113
Community control. *See* Alternative schools; Decentralization; Local control
Compensatory education, 17, 120, 197
Compulsory schooling, 3, 13, 33, 39*n*, 86, 88, 90, 127
Conant, J. B., 8*n*, 85*n*, 173, 222
Connecticut, 48, 131, 223; New Haven, 120; New London, 183
Consolidated schools: costs of, 47*n*; mentioned, 17, 189; resistance to, 7, 8, 9, 10
Coombs, P. H., 79*n*, 107*n*, 216*n*, 218*n*
Coons, J. E., 42*n*
Cooper, J. A., 225*n*
Cordasco, F., 45*n*, 89*n*, 112*n*
Cornell Univ., 55, 62
Corwin, R. G., 173*n*, 182*n*, 235*n*
Council for Basic Education, 28-29
Council of State Governments, 57*n*

Council of State School Officers, 61
Counseling, 126. *See also* Tracking
Counts, G., 21, 139
County government, 19-20, 205, 207
Courts, role of in education: and desegregation, 11, 12, 74; mentioned, 9; powers of, 15, 223, 223*n*; and school finance, 41. *See also* Desegregation, school; State judiciary; U. S. Supreme Court
Craft, M., 86*n*, 116*n*
Crain, R. L., 23*n*
Cralle, R. E., 130*n*
Craver, S., 9*n*
Cremin, L. A., 84*n*, 136*n*, 137*n*
"Crestwood Heights," 45
Crossland, F. E., 56*n*, 88*n*, 103*n*, 128*n*
Cultural pluralism, 40, 115, 163
Curriculum: in civics, 26; definition of, 139; history of, 129, 130-36 *passim*, 136*n*, 140, 188, 189; innovation, 27, 68-69, 73; pressures on, 18, 32, 63, 64, 76, 85, 132-36 *passim*, 140, 141, 147-48, 150, 151, 153, 167, 206; professionals and, 31, 130; professors and, 146, 148; public and, 144, 151; state mandated, 39

Dabney, C., 94*n*
Damerell, R., 23*n*
Daniel, J., 183*n*
Daughters of the American Revolution, 29
David, J., 112*n*
David, O. D., 102*n*
Davis, J. A., 123*n*, 168*n*, 212, 212*n*, 213*n*
Dearing, B., 189*n*
Decentralization: abroad, 4, 5; American ideal of, 8, 10; campaigns for, 8, 9, 10, 40, 72, 74, 160; and inequality, 40; mentioned, 5, 101, 219. *See also* Local control
Deerfield Academy, 132
Delaware: school finance in, 47, 47*n*; Seaford, 35*n*; State College, 63*n*
Dennis, L., 134, 156*n*
Depression: education and, 39, 64; teachers and, 166, 215, 229
Deschooling society, 140, 160, 162, 163
Desegregation, school, 9, 11, 12, 13, 16, 38, 46, 72, 74, 122, 126, 160, 213*n*
DeVos, G., 123, 123*n*
Dewey, J., 28, 139, 140, 140*n*, 141*n*, 143, 188
DeWitt, N., 216*n*
Dietz, G., 150*n*
Dinsmore, J. W., 181*n*, 205*n*, 227*n*
Discipline, school: by aides, 201; in history, 139; as issue, 32, 146, 147, 198, 217; time spent on, 38, 175
Domhoff, G. W., 22*n*, 68*n*, 125*n*
Donahue, J. W., 175*n*
Dorros, S., 183*n*, 207*n*
Dowan, E., 112*n*
Dowling, F., 177*n*

Friedenberg, E. Z., 90*n*, 153
Friedman, Milton, 74
Friedman, Murray, 120*n*
Fuchs, E., 89*n*, 109*n*, 198*n*, 235*n*
Fullan, M., 107*n*
Future Teachers of America, 211

Gage, N. L., 174*n*, 176*n*, 180, 183*n*, 185*n*
Galbraith, J. K., 187
Gans, H., 88*n*
Gardner, J., xi*n*, 77*n*, 142, 142*n*
Garfield, J. A., 227
Gary, L. R., 32*n*, 69*n*
Gatewood, W. B., 184*n*
Gauss, J., 182*n*
Gelhorn, W., 55*n*
Gender: and curriculum, 97-98; economic discrimination and, 88, 96, 98, 171*n*, 178, 179, 210, 214, 214*n*, 216, 216*n*, 219, 219*n*, 220*n*, 226, 226*n*; and ethnicity, 100; and school achievement, 96, 98, 99, 100, 111, 112; and school boards, 21, 226, 226*n*; and school culture, 36, 237. *See also* Higher education, faculty in; Women teachers
General Learning Corporation, 37
Georgia: Atlanta, 22; dropouts in, 53; governor of, 93-94; State Teachers Association, 183*n*; teacher welfare in, 221, 223; Univ. of, 57
German-Americans, 3, 23, 77
Germany, 2, 55, 66, 84
Getzels, J. W., 183*n*, 185
Giacquinta, J., 121*n*
"G.I. Bill of Rights," 64, 99, 166
Gifted students, 127, 178
Gilb, C., 204*n*
Ginzberg, E., 77, 77*n*, 118, 119*n*
Gittel, M., 24*n*, 26*n*, 126*n*, 221*n*
Glazer, N., 88*n*, 123*n*
Goettel, R. J., 41*n*
Goffman, E., 78, 78*n*
Golds, J., 71*n*
Goldstein, M. N., 10*n*, 24*n*, 86*n*
Goode, W. J., 216*n*
Goodlad, J. I., 148*n*
Goodman, P., 88, 88*n*, 153
Gould, Sir R., 204*n*
Gouldner, A., 38, 38*n*
Grades, school, 113, 128, 151
Grambs, J. D., 112*n*
Grant, G., 119*n*
Graubard, A., 73*n*, 161*n*
Great Britain. *See* England
Greece, ancient, 177, 182*n*
Greek-Americans, 77, 92
Greeley, A. M., 71*n*, 213*n*
Green, T. F., 156*n*
Greene, M. F., 115*n*
Greenhoe, F., 212, 212*n*
Greenwalt, R. K., 55*n*

Greer, M., 182*n*
Gresivold, A. W., 157*n*
Gross, N., 21*n*, 30
Gross, R., 73*n*
Gustafson, T. J., 18*n*

Hamel, H. R., 221*n*
Hampton Institute, 56
Handicapped children: out of school, 39, 39*n*; provisions for, 42-43, 51
Handlin, O., 92*n*
Hansen, W. L., 109*n*
Harlan, L., 94*n*
Harmin, M., 136*n*
Hauser, P. M., 166*n*
Harvard Univ., 54, 55, 57, 107, 127*n*, 150
Havighurst, R. J., 89*n*, 109*n*, 201*n*
Hawaii, 46, 47, 52
Hawkes, A., 102*n*
Hazard, W. R., 7*n*, 11*n*, 223*n*
Head Start program, 51, 120, 143*n*, 167*n*
Heath, R. W., 175*n*
Heilbrun, A. B., 112*n*
Heist, P., 59*n*
Hentoff, M., 153*n*
Hentoff, N., 153*n*
Heredity, and intelligence, 92, 118*n*
Hernandez, W. J., 89*n*
Hess, R. D., 133*n*
Hicks, L. D., 24*n*
Higher education: coordinating boards for, 14; finance of by states, 15, 48*n*; mentioned, 100, 101, 103, 103*n*; tax exemptions for, 43; trustee authority in, 10, 31; trustee backgrounds in, 22, 22*n*, 23
Higher education, abroad: in Europe, 54, 61; in India, 4; in Malaysia, 3*n*; in USSR, 5
Higher education, American: collegiate tradition in, 54-55, 56, 65; elitism in, 54, 67, 150; history of, 34-35, 62-63, 111, 111*n*, 132, 134-35; imitation in, 34, 35, 39, 55, 57, 70; institutional changes in, 54, 57, 61; popularization of, 134; vocationalism in, 54, 158
Higher education, enrollments: contractions of, 162, 170; expansions of, x, 54, 59, 63, 79, 80, 82, 92, 98, 99, 147-48, 214
Higher education, faculty in: characteristics of, 176; expansions of, 166, 169-70; and gender, 96, 98, 98*n*, 210, 216; mentioned, 155, 187, 198; preparation of, 189-90, 201, 206, 209; prestige of, 177; as professionals, 31, 220, 231, 234, 236-38; roles of, 165, 175
Higher education, institutions of: availability of, 103-9; for blacks, 103, 103*n*; costs in, 101-3, 107-8; diversity of, 55, 56, 57-61, 128; numbers of, 54, 55; postgraduate programs in, 100, 195; public, 1, 7, 15, 18

Higher education, students in: achievement of, 52-53, 59, 59n; completion rates of, 57, 59, 170; and ethnicity, 89, 213; motivations of, 134, 151n, 154, 155; social backgrounds of, 40, 46, 116n, 127n; subcultures of, 53, 59, 134
Higher Education Act (1972), 11
Highet, G., 181, 181n, 186, 188n
High schools. *See* Secondary education
Hilton, T. L., 211n
History of education. *See* Curriculum; Higher education; Immigrants; Progressive education; Secondary education; Teaching, history of
Hofstadter, R., 132n
Holland, J. L., 112n, 183n
Hollander, T. E., 26n, 221n
Hollins College, 57
Holt, J., 153
Hook, S., 129, 129n, 158
Hooper, B., 133n
Hostetler, J. R., 69n
Howard Univ., 56
Howe, F., 115n
Howe, H., 45n
Hoy, W. K., 197n, 198n
Hu, C. T., 80n
Hubbell, G. A., 139
Hubert, D., 120n
Huggett, A. J., 206n
Hughes, E. C., 31
Hunter, F., 22, 22n, 28, 28n
Huntington, G. E., 69n
Husin, T., 128n
Hutchins, R. M., 139, 150, 156, 157, 157n, 158, 237-38, 238n

Iannacone, L., 19n
Idaho, 47, 194
Idealism, 185, 185n, 198, 202
Illich, I., 79n, 140, 162, 162n
Illinois: Chicago, 23, 43, 50, 67, 69, 120, 126n, 128, 163, 216; Evanston, 50; New Trier, 23, 45; studies in, 103n, 206n, 227; Teachers College, 185n, 209; Univ. of, 226n
Illiteracy: functional, 88; in USA, 53, 83, 83n, 187; in world, 4, 80
Immigrants: attitudes toward, 29, 40, 91-92; economic history of, 79, 94, 101, 217n; educational history of, 3, 32, 90-92, 116, 133, 145; mentioned, 83, 83n. *See also* Ethnicity
India, 3, 4, 66, 79, 80
Indiana: Gary, 93n; Indianapolis, 50-51; Muncie, 181n; shared time in, 71; teachers in, 52, 187
Indonesia, 3
Inservice education, 196, 207, 222, 233
Integration. *See* Desegregation, school
Interest groups. *See* Politics of education

Iowa: Dubuque, 50, 70; legislature of, 14; Univ. of, 57; Univ. of Northern, 154n
Irish-Americans, 77, 88-89, 91, 217n
Italian-Americans, 77, 89, 92
Itzkoff, S. W., 163n
Iversen, R. W., 25, 25n

Jacklin, C. N., 98n
Jackson, P. W., 183n, 185, 192n, 199n
Jacksonianism, 75-76
Jacobson, L., 122n
Japan, 2-3, 4, 79, 123
Japanese-Americans, 123
Jefferson, T., 7, 91, 133, 138, 173
Jencks, C., 34, 35, 35n, 56n, 73n, 74n, 76n, 87n, 98n, 99n, 102, 109n, 111n, 116n, 128n, 163n, 199n, 213n, 236n
Jensen, A., 78, 118n
Jewish Americans, 23, 91, 92, 123, 123n, 212, 213, 214
Jewish institutions, 34-35, 52, 69
Job Corps, 167, 167n
Job satisfaction: enhancing, 203, 237; studies of, 162, 185n, 231, 234n; among teachers, 185, 212, 220, 221, 231-32
Johns Hopkins University, 55
Johnson, C., 132n
Johnson, H. S., 89n
Johnson, L. B., 11, 65
Jonçich, G., 138n
Jorgenson, L. P., 187n, 227n
Joseph, S. M., 112n
Jouvenel, B. De, 156, 156n

Kaestle, C. F., 91n, 207n
Kahl, J., 112, 112n
Kallen, H., 40
Kane, M. B., 162n
Kansas: school bonds in, 44; State Teachers College, 194; Topeka, 93
Karier, C. J., 129n
Katz, I., 89n
Katz, M., 86n, 90n, 91n, 116, 217n
Kauffman, J., 134n, 156n
Kaye, C., 112n
Keifer, M., 132n
Keith-Spiegel, P., 92n, 113n
Kelly, J. A., 42n
Kelsall, H. M., 183n, 209n, 214n
Kelsall, R. K., 183n, 209n, 214n
Keniston, K., 59n
Kennedy, J. F., 65
Kentucky, 48, 221
Keppel, F., 47n, 122n
Kershaw, J. A., 167n, 218n
Kett, J. F., 182n
Kettering Foundation, 160
Kindergarten, 24, 51, 70, 91n, 120, 138, 169
Kirk, R., 29
Kirp, D. L., 74n

Occupational structure: changes in, 77, 162, 169, 170; in past, 90n, 227, 228; race bias in, 94, 213; of schools, 225-26; in Third World, 80. *See also* Gender; Job satisfaction

O'Dowd, D. D., 209n

Office of Economc Opportunity, 73

Ohio, 46; Akron, Univ. of, 154n; Cincinnati, Univ. of, 15; Cleveland, 46, 90, 120, 126n; Columbus, 43; Shaker Heights, 46

Oklahoma, 17, 52, 171

O'Neill, W., 146n

Open classroom, 138, 140

Oregon, 13, 24, 33, 51

Orfield, G., 11n

Oriental Americans, 77, 92, 100, 122, 123

O'Shea, D., 9n

Osterman, P., 73n

Ozmon, H., 9n

Pacific Northwest, 50, 167

Page, D., 193

Panos, R., 116n

Parents and Teachers Assoc., National Congress of, 28, 145

Parker, D. H., 153n

Parkinson, M., 127n

Patterson, G. R., 96n

Peace Corps, 167, 167n, 198

Pedagogy, 191-94, 197n

Pederson, K. G., 221n, 228n, 229

Peirce, C., 180

Pennsylvania, 32n, 45, 66, 71, 171; Lower Merion, 50; Philadelphia, 27, 45n, 50, 67, 120, 126n, 163; Philadelphia Academy, 177; Pittsburgh, 69

Performance contracting, 73, 191

Perkinson, H. J., 39n, 91n

Per-pupil spending: in black colleges, 56; in nonpublic schools, 70; and state income, 48; variations in, 16, 45, 46, 47-49

Philippines, 3, 79

Phillips Andover Academy, 68n

Phillips Exeter Academy, 67

Pierce v. *Society of Sisters* (1925), 13

"*Plainville USA*," 7

Plato, 75, 150

Poland, 228

Politics of education: and community style, 26n; electoral mechanisms of, 22-23, 23n, 24, 28, 31, 41, 44, 51, 162; historical perspective on, 25, 27, 76, 206; and interest groups, 17-18, 22, 26, 28, 30, 31n, 32, 36, 204-5, 206; issues in, 14, 109, 121; lay power in, 84-85, 90, 148, 191, 206, 219, 238; party role in, 5, 6, 25, 223; school board, 21, 22

Population trends, 77, 79, 98, 166, 168, 170, 230. *See also* Americans, mobility of

Porter, A., 80n

Portuguese immigration, 101

Poverty, 76; educational correlates of, 41, 68, 190; and school finance, 47, 51, 65; urban, 43, 123n

Powell, A. C., 65

Previn, L. A., 57n, 110n

Princeton Univ., 57, 68n, 127n

Pro-America, 29

Professions, traits of, 182, 183, 187, 196, 202, 203, 205-6, 229

Professional education of teachers, 5, 62, 178, 182, 204, 205, 229, 235; characteristics of, 16, 187-95, 211; criticisms of, 149; enrollments in, 168n, 170, 171; institutions for, 54, 57, 59, 147, 184, 209n, 212; and pupil achievement, 175; in world, 187, 194

Professionalization, 221, 232; of education, 32, 34, 35, 148-49, 179, 207, 211-12; as movement, 190, 200, 203, 204, 205, 206

Professional organizations, 35; history of, 36, 207-8; posture of teachers', 6, 173, 201n, 208, 233-34; purposes of, 32, 35, 204, 206-8, 232; and school officials, 18, 236n; sexism of, 207; and teachers' attitudes toward, 206, 233, 233n

Progressive education: criticisms of, 139, 144-50; reach of, 146, 147; traits of, 136-43, 146, 149-50

Progressivism, political, 39

Project to Improve College Teaching, 190

Property taxation: as basis of school support, 10, 16, 21, 41; depression of base of, 43; exemptions to, 43, 43n, 66; limits on, 9; as local concern, 8; taxpayer associations and, 29-30

Proprietary schools, x, 54n, 176n

Protestant: colleges, 34-35, 56; culture, 132, 157; schools, 52, 69, 69n, 212; teachers, 212, 213, 214

Public opinion: on curriculum issues, 133n, 144-45, 153n; on educators, 31, 173, 183; on student disruptions, 224; on tests, 160; on vacations, 151

Public schools, American: as American "religion," 34, 131; assimilation function of, 33, 40, 74, 77, 91-92, 121n, 133, 145, 162-63; civic purposes of, 26, 132-33, 133n, 146, 146n, 178; defined, 1, 2; enrollments in, 82, 144, 166, 223, 227; history of, 82, 83-86, 90-92, 132-45; as monopoly, 33, 66, 71, 162; questioning of, 155, 159-62, 170, 234; sociability aim of, 76-78; and social reform, 7, 86, 86n, 139. *See also* Education; Local control

Puerto Ricans in America, 45n; educational status of, 88, 109n; as immigrants, 77, 92; in New York, 67, 89, 112, 128n

Pupil achievement, 42, 128; and ethnicity, 112, 114, 115, 160; in history, 90-91; pre-

Sex education, 17, 18, 23, 28, 145, 145n
Sex-role socialization, 210, 211, 225-26, 230, 231, 233
Sexton, P. C., xn, 96n, 226n
Shannon, T. A., 41n
Sharp, L. M., 97
Shaw, B., 177
Shils, E. B., 21n
Silberman, C., 138, 138n, 140, 145, 145n, 173
Siljeström, P. A., 82n, 86
Simon, K., 107n
Simon, S. B., 136n
Simpson, I., 225n, 237n
Simpson, R., 225n, 237n
Singer, G., 228n
Sizer, T. R., 163n
Skinner, B. F., 157
Skorov, G., 80n
Slater, P. E., 226n
Slavic Americans, 77
Smith, B., 9n, 72n
Smith, P., 27n
Smith, T., 90n
Smith-Hughes Act (1917), 63-64
Smuts, R. W., 217n
Sobel, H. W., 161n
Social class, 26, 91; abroad, 4, 125, 127, 127n; and college-going, 61, 109, 109n, 110, 111, 111n, 127n, 147-48; education and preserving, 2, 91, 94, 124-26, 127; of family and school participation, 86, 86n, 98, 99-100, 102-3, 126; of family and school success, 89, 116n, 118-19, 120, 120n, 122, 175; and school attended, 38, 39, 68, 68n; and school personnel, 197n, 201n. See also Social mobility; Teachers
Social mobility, 93, 128; aspirations for, 80, 122, 154; belief in, 75, 76, 77, 77n; through teaching, 154n, 178, 214, 231
Society of Associated Teachers, 207
Socrates, 182n
Sophists, 177
South: congressional vote of, 65; higher education in, 56, 59; nonpublic schools in, 67; school governance in, 16, 19, 20; segregated institutions in, 48-49, 62-63; status of blacks in, 114, 213, 213n
South Carolina, 53
South Dakota, 47
Southern Univ. A & M College, 63n
Soviet Union, 167, 184, 216n; higher education in, 101, 191n; school control in, 4-5; schools of, 42, 143
Spain, 34
Special education, 17, 18, 42, 43. See also Handicapped children
Specialization: in education, 189, 205, 235; occupational, 143, 200-201
Spelman College, 56
Spencer, H., 135

Spiegel, D., 92n, 113n
Spring, J., 162
Sputnik, 64, 129, 167, 189
Stalnaker, R. C., 112n
Standardization, 1, 34-40, 136. See also Local control
State government: and federal programs, 18-19, 62, 63-64; and higher education, 57, 58; and nonpublic schools, 14, 36, 67; powers of in education, 7, 8, 9, 10, 13, 16, 17, 85, 120, 120n, 132, 135, 136, 149, 204, 204n; and school finance, 15-17, 24, 41, 47, 47n, 109, 170; structures of for education, 13-18 passim, 132, 196, 205; and teachers, 51, 162, 166, 191, 205, 229. See also Licenses, teaching
State judiciary, 14-15, 16-17, 41n, 85
Stephens, J. M., 185, 185n, 186
Sternberg, C., 183n
Stewart, M. G., 230n
Stiles, L. J., 184n
Stinchcombe, A. L., 96n, 154n
Stinnett, T. M., 206n, 225n
Strikes, teacher, 6, 26, 168, 171-73
Stuart v. *School District No. 1 of the Village of Kalamazoo* (1874), 14, 85
Student aid, 40, 62, 64, 93, 99, 99n, 100-103 passim
Students: characteristics of, 52-53, 99, 232; in decision making, 72, 74, 163; mobility of, 34, 38-39; preferences of, 10, 40, 50, 56, 153, 154, 183; subcultures of, 153-55; unrest of, 14, 35n, 39, 64, 81, 146, 224, 234. See also Pupil achievement; Social class; Teachers
Suburbs: and cities, 10, 30, 45; class size in, 50; and college-going, 46, 46n, 52; movement to, 8, 9, 38, 45, 46, 126; property values of, 41, 41n, 42n; teachers' salaries in, 42n, 51
Superintendent of schools. See Administrators, school
Swarthmore College, 55
Sweden, 127n
Swerdloff, P. M., 154n
Swint, H. L., 94n
Switzerland, 1

Takei, Y., 3n
Talladega College, 56
Tanzania, 80
Tappen, H. A., 187
Taylor, C. C., 4n
Teacher: authority, 31, 141, 146, 174-75; contracts, 215n, 223, 224; mobility, 34, 37-38, 38n, 212, 215, 220, 221, 228; morale, 119; selection, 10, 31, 72
Teacher Corps, 63, 167
Teacher turnover, 211, 222; concern with, 197, 229-31, 237; in Europe, 228; facts of, 184n, 226-31